The Human Calling

DAOFENG HE

The Human Calling

Three Thousand Years of Eastern
and Western Philosophical History

NASHVILLE

NEW YORK • LONDON • MELBOURNE • VANCOUVER

The Human Calling

Three Thousand Years of Eastern and Western Philosophical History

Published in New York, New York, by Morgan James Publishing. Morgan James is a trademark of Morgan James, LLC. www.MorganJamesPublishing.com

Proudly distributed by Ingram Publisher Services.

A **FREE** ebook edition is available for you or a friend with the purchase of this print book.

[   ]

CLEARLY SIGN YOUR NAME ABOVE

Instructions to claim your free ebook edition:
1. Visit MorganJamesBOGO.com
2. Sign your name CLEARLY in the space above
3. Complete the form and submit a photo of this entire page
4. You or your friend can download the ebook to your preferred device

ISBN 9781631956911 paperback
ISBN 9781631956928 ebook
Library of Congress Control Number:
2021941318

Cover Design by:
Megan Dillon
megan@creativeninjadesigns.com

Interior Design by:
Christopher Kirk
www.GFSstudio.com

Morgan James is a proud partner of Habitat for Humanity Peninsula and Greater Williamsburg. Partners in building since 2006.

Get involved today! Visit MorganJamesPublishing.com/giving-back

Table of Contents

About the Author

B orn in 1956 in Yunnan, a rural province in southwest China, Daofeng He holds a Master's degree in economics from Fudan University in Shanghai and is an adjunct professor at Peking University Law School.

Foreword

Lin Qiu

Reading Mr. He Daofeng's masterpiece, *The Human Calling*, was like watching the curtains rise on a dramatic play. At first, I saw a seeker with a bundle on his back, taking his first steps on the long road of life, through many trials and tribulations, searching and seeking through many sacred texts and asking for the way, walking from village to village, from city to city, knocking on door after door, on an epic search for the truth. This hero on the stage could be Mr. He himself, or myself, or any of the millions of atheists from Red China.

I have not known Mr. He Daofeng long, but as our friendship deepened, our conversation ranged widely, from Hebrew, Greek, Roman, and Chinese philosophy and religion, and gradually moved to the deeper level of discussing our personal faith. I admire Mr. He's seriousness and dedication to the ultimate truth, and I appreciate his commitment to the practice of truth even more. Now his book, *The Human Calling*, has landed on my desk. I am honored to be asked to write him an introduction. I accepted the task because, between the lines of the book, what I saw was a struggling soul, hungry and thirsty for the truth, searching for his ultimate spiritual home. I saw the tireless efforts of a man to fulfill the needs of his soul, despite living in a thoroughly materialistic and atheistic society, Red China.

For a whole generation of people educated in Red China, Mr. He's experiences, and his journey in seeking the truth, are quite typical. A series of revolutionary movements, especially the Cultural Revolution, destroyed China's thousand-year-old Confucian culture because it was seen as a counter-revolutionary; all symbols of Western culture, even a musical instrument like the piano, were destroyed. Traditional Chinese culture was replaced by that heresy of Western culture—Marxism. But this heresy cannot truly answer the fundamental questions of life, namely, what makes us human and how we should live. Marx believed that the capitalists, i.e. those who possess capital, are by nature "greedy and selfish" and therefore out to exploit the "proletariat," and so he prescribed the violent overthrow of the bourgeoisie by the proletariat to seize the means of production. But aren't those who control "public capital" through violent revolution also "selfish and greedy?" And aren't the ones who hold both the state apparatus and public capital even worse? The great experiments of "socialism" in the Soviet Union in the 20th century and China today are the most powerful examples of the self-contradictory utopia prescribed by Marxism.

As one of Mr. He's peers, I understand very well the motivation behind his relentless search for human calling. I have witnessed terrible things, like "counter-revolutionaries" being beaten up and neighbors jailed for accidentally breaking statues of the leader.

In the late 1970s, China's new leader Deng Xiaoping, pursuing a philosophy of pragmatism, began to implement a series of reforms focused on economic development, "reforming internally and opening up externally." China, which had closed itself off, opened a window to the world. In the reopened universities, young people did everything possible to breathe the air of foreign knowledge and culture, approaching this knowledge with great hunger. It was then that I began my exploration of comparative cultural studies, when the first graduate school in China to study Western and Chinese culture comparatively opened.

My experience teaching the university students who were involved in the pro-democracy movement and eventual tragedy at Tiananmen Square in 1989 led me to question Marxism profoundly and, eventually, to leave China for the United States. However, in my new home, I found myself rootless and adrift. I could not speak English, so I could no longer work as a teacher, a job I loved, which also meant I lost my source of livelihood. I was caught in a bind where I had nothing, nothing but the freedom to think; I had gained the sky, but lost the earth. The values taught to me in Red China—"success equals value"— almost killed me. I could not accept that I was no longer successful, and my loss of "human ability" made me lose sight of the value of my own life. I tried to escape by attempting suicide, until I found my way to God and the spiritual home of Christ in my heart.

When I read Mr. He Daofeng's book *The Human Calling*, I felt it had a strong resonance with my own life, because all of us Chinese from that generation had shared the common experience of being "spiritual prisoners." I believe that Western readers, too, would be able to follow Mr. He's thinking and see in this book the struggle of a former atheist and his painstaking search for truth.

First, as a high achiever who had participated in the drafting of China's reform policies, as a successful entrepreneur, and as a reformer of government-run charities, he experienced the height of human achievement thanks to his "human ability." He experienced the fierce conflict between lofty ideals

xvi | The Human Calling

and the reality of society, the confusion in the process of achieving personal goals in life, and the ups and downs in the process of realizing the ideal of social reform.

Secondly, with endless questions about society and life, he began to reflect and search for over a decade, moving through questions of "human ability" to "human capability" and then, finally, to "human calling." He searched relentlessly for his spiritual home in the history, philosophy, and theology of mankind through the millennia, both in the past and in the present.

Thirdly, these painstaking searches and arduous explorations finally led him to experience the great joy of enlightenment, clarity, and insight. Jesus said, "I am the light of the world; he who follows me will not walk in darkness, but will have the light of life." (John 8:12), and again, "Ask, and it will be given to you; seek, and you will find; knock, and the door will be opened to you." (Luke 11:9) Reading *The Human Calling* and following Brother Daofeng's journey towards the truth, I found that Jesus was searching for Daofeng while Daofeng was searching for Him, and eventually the light of the Holy Spirit shone on his hungry and thirsty heart that longed for righteousness, making him understand that Jesus was the very light of life he was looking for. I think Brother Daofeng and I prayed and searched for the same truth. We knocked on the same door, and the same One opened the door for us. Although our paths were different, we were both deeply drawn to this same God and turned to Him.

It was in this way that I, a spiritual wanderer, was found by Jesus one August morning in 1991 at an evangelistic camp on the north side of Oahu, Hawaii, and finally returned to my spiritual home. At that time I had just survived a car accident of my own devising. I had reached the point where I could no longer see any meaning in living, and, not daring to face Death's cold face again, I was living in darkness. My body was alive, but my soul was dead. It was at this time that a hymn brought tears to my eyes, melting my hard heart. This hymn put an extremely simple but powerful message in my heart through the melody of the music, which said, "From that deepest ocean to that highest mountain, all things tell me that God is love!" It was Love that destroyed the hardened shell of a lifelong atheist.

Next, from the speaker's sermon, I heard another spiritual message, that pricked my conscience, "In the dead of night, ask yourself, do you admit that you are a sinner? Are you willing to start over?" I had to face up to the debaucheries I had committed in certain bars, to my emotional abuse of my wife, and I found that I could no longer escape the sin and evil I had committed in my life. The mask of the noble, lonely, decent, moral teacher that I had seen myself as for decades collapsed, and I had to admit that I was a man of no virtue, no ability, and that I was full of sin. I had no choice but to admit that I was powerless to save myself and that I needed to be saved. I opened the door to Jesus, and he told me he was "the way, the truth and the life." He was the God Yahweh that had been incarnated in the flesh, the Creator God Himself.

In 2005, I heeded a special, divine call when I came across the Bethel Series Panoramic Bible Course written by Mr. Harley Swiggum. I have been committed to the sacred calling of spreading this word for 16 years, and have traveled as a Bible teacher to many of the poor and remote areas of China that happened to overlap with many areas where Mr. He Daofeng's poverty alleviation efforts were based, and have equipped over 1,000 pastors with the Panoramic Bible Course, despite all the difficulties and crises we encountered.

One of the most inspiring quotes from the series is:

I hear the dim sounds of trumpets calling me to live in the highlands. At intervals I have heard the flutter of angel's wings, and I struggle with a vague consciousness that I am a stranger in a foreign land who has lost my way. My soul, if I have a soul, goads me to go back to the garden from which I came, but I have no memory of a garden. Is there a path and a person who will lead me there? Is life meant to be more than a struggle for bread? Is it not an accident which begins and ends in pain, a crazy quilt splashed with chaotic color but with neither order nor design? Shall it not end in nothing but the grave? Who am I? What am I meant to be?

In poetic language, this passage asks the questions of the ages. It is precisely the answer to these questions that Mr. He Daofeng has been searching for throughout the six decades of his life. This is recorded in detail in his book, *The Human Calling*. I believe that his readers, too, will be able to find their way to answer these questions with his book.

I was attracted to *The Human Calling* because it offered me a new way of thinking about the problem of alienation. The great Christian theologian and philosopher Augustine, for example, used the term "alienation" to express the relationship between God and man. Augustine saw the incarnation of the Son as God's renunciation of His sacred and untouchable glory and the taking on of the true nature of man. For man, it is through faith in God that man can bridge the gap and become one with God. Augustine used the concept of "alienation" to express the relationship between man and God in transposition (conversion). We know that later thinkers such as Rousseau, Hegel, and Marx all used the original meaning of "alienation" to express their ideas. I would like to go back to the original meaning of "alienation" to understand the beginning of Mr. He Daofeng's journey.

From his years of observation and practice, Mr. He discovered that the conflict between "human ability" and "human calling" was the greatest problem facing human beings today. "Human ability" is necessary for the survival and development of human beings, but the result of its constant reinforcement by human beings is a lack of humanity, morality, order, and rules. For example, in order to enhance the survival of individuals, people need to organize in groups. The development of human communities does greatly enhance the individual's ability to survive to a degree, but the opposite is also true: the stronger the requirements of human communities, the weaker the individuality of each person. The relationship between human survival and the group is then transposed (alienated). Mr. He's unique perspective of examining this form of alienation, and the relationship between "human ability" and "human calling" as a lens to look at the problems of today's society makes Mr. He Daofeng's thinking very relevant in this era of globalization.

Another important reason why I was drawn to *The Human Calling* was because of the depth of the inquiry of the book towards the question of "vocation," which refers to the strong inner motivation to behave a certain way under the inspiration of divine faith. No reflection on the "human calling" can be complete without a search for the biological origin of human beings.

For a serious seeker, this search must lead to a comprehensive study of what makes a human being human, and must consider human dignity, equality, meaning, purpose, free will, moral sense, creativity, intellect, ethical reasoning, aesthetic ability, the ability and need to love and be loved, and other characteristics that distinguish humans from the animal kingdom. The search for the "human calling" or "vocation" must lead to a rethinking of Marxist humanism, materialist evolution, Social Darwinism, atheism, the cult of science, and absolute humanism.

In today's Eastern and Western societies, whether it is Eastern civilization based on Confucianism, Buddhism, Taoism and Hinduism, or Western civilization based on the Abrahamic religions, the practice of denying that human beings are God's creation is rampant, and the denial of man's relationship with God confuses man's reasoning about himself, so that the law of the jungle applies to interpersonal relationships, and causes man to be out of harmony with nature. Water without a source will dry up, and a tree without roots will waste away. If human beings do not return to their original source, they will not be human.

Thanks to Mr. He Daofeng's clear and profound articulation on "human calling," his work has the ability to set our thoughts straight. His book could help us clarify our thinking on the origin of "human ability," chaos and disorder, the abandonment of absolute morality and the spread of pluralism. He helps readers trace the lineage of human thought from the ancient past to the present, and lays a strong foundation for those who follow. As a seeker of the Way, Brother Daofeng has left his mark on the path in his search for absolute truth. As a practitioner of his faith, he has traveled for years to many corners of China and the world for his ideals of transforming society and promoting change.

I, too, have taken up my own burden and taken this road, traveling from town to town for sixteen years in response to the divine call to bless others. Through our common pursuit, we have found our common spiritual home, and we share the same faith, and together, we walk this heavenly path. How blessed we are to be on it!

As I slowly close Mr. He Daofeng's *The Human Calling*, the curtains, too, draw to a close on my imaginary play. The play ends with the seeker finally finding the truth in his heart, but the burden he carries, filled with so many questions, is still so big. On the way to find truth, he found his home, but also revealed another road to an equally long journey. The road is long, but I am not afraid to walk it, to walk the way of the truth!

Preface

As someone who grew up in an atheistic society, I had a long, winding and difficult road to faith.

I was born in the spring of 1956 in a poor mountain village in the southwest of China. It was a small village in the middle of the mountains, 30 kilometers from the county, 300 kilometers from the provincial capital, and 3,000 kilometers from Beijing.

When I was three years old, I lived through the infamous "Great Leap Forward" launched by Mao Zedong, and my mother and I were forced to go up to the mountains as part of the country's drive to make industrial amounts of steel, as part of an effort for China to "catch up with Britain and surpass the United States." Trees were cut down and food rotted because no one harvested it, thus ushering in the "Great Famine" and the era of People's Commune Canteens. Therefore, the first and deepest memories of my childhood are of the long hours of daylight during which I suffered from hunger, the horrible rotting corpses of outsiders who died of starvation beyond the village limits whose remains went uncollected, and the big tree stumps the trees left all over the mountains after being cut down.

The people who survived the famine were still half-starved, and it became very common to eat wild vegetation and leaves. In 1962, I started attending a rural elementary school, and my life gradually improved as Chairman Mao Zedong faded from political prominence and Chairman Liu Shaoqi started to run a more pragmatic and sensible regime.

However, in the fall of 1966, when I was in the fifth grade, the Cultural Revolution launched by Mao Zedong suddenly broke out. I watched curiously as gang after gang of high school students from Beijing and Shanghai started wearing green uniforms and red five-pointed star hats, singing patriotic red songs and shouting slogans, running amok, painting slogans and pasting big-character posters denouncing and persecuting people all over the streets.

The phenomenon of denouncing and struggling against authority figures confused and horrified me. This included everyone from the State Chairman Liu Shaoqi, to the local cadres, to the grassroots leaders, and I knew that these elders, who were being beaten, were good people. Next, they were paraded through the streets and humiliated, and schools were completely suspended for the sake of Revolution.

For the next three years, I witnessed mass "struggle sessions" in front of hundreds of people with thorns, sticks, and gun barrels being used as weapons to beat the so-called "class enemies" to a bloody pulp, and saw the horror and bloodshed of people being killed and then beheaded and gutted. As a teenager, fear and doubt were the most apt descriptors for my mindset at the time. So I fell in love with reading, because the world in books was orderly and beautiful and gave me an escape from the violence and chaos of reality.

In 1969, I returned to middle school, where the junior and senior high school years were shortened from six to four years by the Revolution, and I avoided the Revolution by studying day and night with great hunger and thirst for knowledge.

Although my grades were the best in the school, when I graduated from high school in 1973 I was required to go back to my hometown to participate in revolutionary activities. The universities was partially closed and only those earnest revolutionaries who handed in blank papers during the exams were allowed to study a syllabus consisting of "Mao's theory of continuing revolution." So, denied the chance to attend university, I returned to my hometown and worked as a youth production leader and village teacher.

In September 1976, after Mao's death and Deng Xiaoping's ascendancy, I heard that the college entrance examinations would resume in November 1977. I took the examinations in December, enabling me to enter university. In an academic career that ranged from an undergraduate to a Master's degree, from philosophy to economics, and from Yunnan to Shanghai, I spent seven years of my life finally slaking the thirst for knowledge that had made me addicted to acquiring knowledge.

In 1984, I was selected by Research Center for Rural Development (RCRD), the most famous rural reform think tank in China at that time, because of an article I had published. As a result, I would get to participate in China's rural reform research and draft reform documents and become a disciple of Mr. Du Runsheng, the "father of China's rural reform," which was no small feat. I believed that China could follow the model of both economic and political reform that successful modernizing countries in East Asia had taken, so as to complete the transformation of China into a modern state.

The Tiananmen Square incident in 1989 crushed my dreams of systemic reform. Deng Xiaoping refused to reform the political system, refused to reconcile with the peaceful protestors, and set the precedent of using the military to suppress the peaceful protest movement of unarmed students. I was disciplined for sympathizing with the students. Disappointed, I quit the government and went into business as a private entrepreneur. So I tried to find a way to save my country and myself through industry.

In 1999, when my businesses were first starting to bear fruit, China successfully negotiated its accession to the WTO. Under the condition that state-owned enterprises would be drastically reduced in number to achieve a full market economy, China was allowed to become a member of the WTO, and calls for the reform of non-profit social organizations, for international integration, and even political reform, resurfaced. At that time, my hope for reforming China into a modern country, which had nearly sputtered out, was revived.

I accepted an invitation from the State Council's Poverty Alleviation Office to become the CEO of the China Foundation for Poverty Alleviation, a government-organized NGO or GONGO, but I insisted on keeping to the status of a volunteer only and worked to reform it into a fully independent civil society organization. The subsequent seventeen years of perseverance in this field convinced me that the awakening of civic consciousness through economic marketization and social marketization reforms might pave the way for future political reforms in China to allow a free market in politics as well and enable China to follow the path taken by other modernizing East Asian countries.

Under my leadership, the CFPA became the most influential NGO in China, increasing annual fundraising revenue by 40 times, and founded CFPA Microfinance (CD Finance), which has also grown into the most influential social enterprise in China by providing loans and training services to 500,000 rural women. I was also involved in promoting a network to increase transparency in the philanthropic sector as the second chairman of the Foundation Center Network for the Philanthropic Sector. As a result, I received the Global Philanthropy Alliance's Alga Award in 2014, which is given to only one recipient each year.

However, the Chinese government has not fulfilled the commitments it made when it ascended to the WTO. This can be seen in the post-2009 growth of state-owned enterprises instead of their decline, and their monstrous ballooning after 2012, so that today, state-owned enterprises dominate almost every sector. As a result, the fields in which the international community may invest on a level playing field have shrunk significantly. Criticism that intellectual property and technological knowhow has been exchanged for access to the Chinese market in epidemic proportions has also been leveled as a result.

Internally, state owned enterprises and their relentless rent-seeking behavior have revealed unprecedented corruption. The collusion going on between capital controlled by top Chinese political families and the capital from Wall Street has expanded grotesquely, creating billionaires at a dizzying pace and scale throughout Wall Street on a level of an enormous scam.

Narrow-minded nationalism and arrogant globalism emerged simultaneously and out of the blue, making everyone both arrogant and manic in their greed. All sorts of unprecedented business and capital scams continue to bamboozle the people, and social, moral, and ethical standards are in serious decline.

However, instead of encouraging market competition and the development of social organizations to restrain the social disorder caused by this abnormal expansion of public power, the government continued down the path of expanding its power and squashing freedom of speech for both individuals and social organizations. As a result, the state and the legal system have become tools for seeking profits, and the outlook for socially-conscious enterprises and ethical social governance has deteriorated dramatically. As a result, people are losing their sense of security and dignity.

Once again, I was disillusioned in my pursuit of my ideals in life, in the ideas of social reform and political change. I was also subjected to many personal injustices. I had a feeling that a storm was coming. Unwilling to fight and waste my life where I could do no more good, I quickly spent two years selling all my private companies, resigning from my position as Executive Chairman of the China Foundation for Poverty Alleviation, and retiring to Maryland at the end of 2015 in order to dedicate my time to pondering the meaning of life and to answer the millennia-old questions that have always plagued me.

Since then, I have spent almost four wonderful years in my cozy study in the woods of Bethesda, Maryland, where reading, thinking, and writing are the chief activities during the day, an ideal arrangement for me at this stage of my life.

Meanwhile, although the world has been caught up in the utopian ideal of "diverse and inclusive globalization," although new technologies are changing how humans live every day, most people are just blindly worshipping human abilities and achievements. However, their pride and worship of human beings is no different from the worship of fire by primitive people. In the face of atomized individualism, every person living today faces the threats of being turned into a passive being, of being turned into a cog in a machine, or of being reduced to the bestial, every day. At the same time, endless desires, pressure, violence, and insecurity loom like dark clouds in the sky. Where should one go? What kind of life is really worth living? Is there any other option for human life aside from the modern grind of forced busyness, manipulation by online advertisements, and hatred and violence generated and directed by those who form public opinion? Can we find a way to make human life return to its former graceful and dignified pace, make it encourage inquiring, independent thinking, peaceful communication, mutual respect and philosophical exchange, and connection to the divine source of "the human calling?" These are the questions that I set out to answer.

In asking and answering these questions, I pondered the differences between the philosophies of the First Axial Age in the East and the West. Why did monotheism and the belief in a personal God appear in Jewish history? Why was Christ born and sacrificed on the cross 2000 years ago, and why was a systematic Christian faith defended by two major integrations with the revered philosophical thinking of ancient Greece? Why did charitable and philanthropic organizations develop in Christian civilizations? What was the significance of philosophy found in Christian scripture, the Renaissance and the Reformation for the development of modernity? What are the connections and conflicts between science and Christianity? How did the civilization we call "modern" emerge, and what are the roots of the world's current problems? Why did China, like Japan, go through a historical break in its transition to a modern state, in which the government and people were both prideful and arrogant, thus making them enemies of universal modern civilization? I have read a lot of historical documents on these questions, and I have sorted them out and analyzed them. Combined with my life practice and experience living in both the East and West for sixty years, I have tried to locate these arguments along the spatial and temporal axis of human history.

I discovered a deep thread of logic in the evolution of human civilization: that the thinking about the visible world as opposed to the invisible world split Eastern and Western philosophies into two completely different branches of thought from the very beginning and formed two completely different belief systems. No matter how much one tries to seek common ground in the course of subsequent history, one cannot eliminate these fundamental differences. Today's scholars' attempts to confuse and smooth out the superficial layers in the context of globalization and pluralism are not fulfilling the utopian conception of globalization that humanity expects and are creating an unprecedented crisis in our beliefs as the human race.

What is even more amazing is that in the process of reading, thinking, discerning, and writing, my own beliefs crossed the gulf of atheism from my mother culture, Confucianism and Taoism, and further crossed the gulf between polytheism and monotheism bridged by Buddha under the eternal light of Brahman. The divine light of the one and only personal God of our universe shone through the fog of the institutions, thoughts, and words created by finite man and pierced through my spirit.

This light exposed how foolish I had been trying to reason about the invisible world based on purely materialist Eastern worldviews, to the absurdity of my past search for the absolute truth of God in the relativity of Eastern sages' philosophies. It also cut through the mire of muddled Eastern thinking about the material world which obscured and neglected the spiritual world. My new faith shattered my unreasonable expectation to find absolute truth in the Eastern sages who preached that morality was relative. It also cut off the path to the materialistic gods of the new, moneyed East.

I cried tears of joy and, with great passion as well as full rationality, embraced the true faith I had been searching for for decades. Although I have not yet performed the formal rituals of conversion, I have been completely converted in my soul and have helped a dozen people who were struggling between atheism and faith in God to clear the final doubts on their way to faith. Furthermore, all the injustice, resentment, aggression, hatred, and pride that had accumulated in my heart over the decades of my life disappeared in a flash and melted into the infinite and unchanging grace of God's love and forgiveness.

I now fully realize that I am a sinner, and that Christ is the true Savior, and that there is no other savior than him. All man-made gods are finite things and cannot save us. If they call themselves saviors, they are hypocrites and chief deceivers. Without God, man would still have to resort to making his own gods, whilst bumbling about in the dark like blind men. When one is at a low point of life or when one is weak, one participates in placing others in the place of God, whereas when one is successful or powerful, one's pride and forgetfulness leads one to set oneself up as a god. Such a life, deprived of the divine illumination of God regarding our human calling, without a logically consistent and firm direction, is always spent in either slavery or servitude. So how is it possible to have true "equal rights" alongside one's fellow men, let alone find the path to equality and justice?

How can one truly understand the spirit of love and forgiveness based on God's divine justice?

This book is therefore an account of the long and difficult journey a Chinese atheist took to find God.

The book is divided into 13 chapters. Chapters 1 and 2 are about the human perspective. They show how the conflicting and intertwined histories of human ability and "human calling" defined the history of civilizations in both the East and West. Man in his societies achieved amazing things in terms of human ability through the two tools of writing and organization, enabling him to create community. However, the fragility and vulnerability of the individual means that the search for the "human calling" happened at the same time in the areas of human relationship and spirituality. Without this, the individual would be objectified and lose their unique meaning of life.

Chapters 3 and 4 compare the ancient Greek philosophy of the West and the pre-Qin philosophy of the East on the question of "human calling" and find that Western civilization began from the pursuit of the "invisible" truth and through inductive reasoning discovered that God represents the highest order of truth. This laid the foundation for the natural sciences, social sciences, and Christianity. Eastern civilization and philosophy, on the other hand, started by only recognizing "visible" matter only, emphasizing the public order of society and the role of the individual, which led to the triumph of top-down authoritarian legalism and systems.

Chapter 5 compares the history of suffering in Jewish history, which highlights the dichotomy between God and the universe and man, emphasizes God's creation of man and his election of Israel to become an example of "human calling," and establishes God's covenantal law with man and man's sacred covenant relationship to God.

Chapters 6, 7, and 8 trace the path taken by ancient Rome from a republic to an imperial power and how it made use of ancient Greek ideals and philosophy, which led to an alliance of more than fifty nation-states to introduce a political system with a representative body involved in creating law for that society, such that Roman law is still the basis for modern law today.

The prosperity of the Roman Empire paved the way for the Messianic coming of Jesus, the Son of God, and the divine revelation of the true "human calling" in human history through the birth, crucifixion, resurrection, the transformation of the disciples into apostles, and the birth of the new covenant of love and forgiveness between God and man. The first fusion of ancient Greek philosophy with the Gospel of Christ and the history of the spread of the Gospel, in turn, gave birth to charities and philanthropic organizations.

Chapter 9 takes us back to the Vedic philosophy of Eastern India, which contemplated dharma and the reincarnation of an impersonal god, Brahman, and the one triune god, to answer the various questions of "human calling": Why did Buddha create his Four Noble Truths and Eightfold Path? Why was Buddha expelled from his homeland when he was a compassionate and exemplary person? And, where is Buddha's ultimate nirvana?

Chapter 10 returns to the Eastern Chinese Empire, where the Confucian and Legalist alliances, through political machinations and discourse, defeated the Taoists and gained a monopoly over the creation of man-made gods from the time of Emperor Wu of the Han Dynasty. After five hundred years of failure in creating gods that would be worshipped by that civilization, Buddhism saw a resurgence and became the ruling philosophy of the Tang Dynasty, answering questions of "human calling" during a golden age of China. After the chaos of the late Tang Dynasty and the Ten Kingdoms of the Five Dynasties, Confucianism made a comeback and spread through the civil service system of the Song Dynasty, leading to the joint creation of gods. From then on, Taoism was exiled, Buddhism was secularized, and Chinese and Eastern civilization was stereotyped as Confucian. Materialism ruled the day.

Chapters 11 and 12 discuss the second great axial age of mankind in the absence of the West-dominated East, the spread of the Christian faith, and the second integration of Greek philosophy and Christian apologetics. They touch on how natural theology and scholasticism led to the rise of universities and scientific associations, how the Renaissance and Reformation promoted a new era of reconciliation between human and divine reason, and how this led to the rise of the three major market systems which are the pinnacle of the reconciliation of human ability and "human calling."

Chapter 13 reveals the great dilemma facing man in today's world, where waves of secularization, the cult of technology, extreme liberalism, and the call for universal welfare are eroding and destroying the rights to equality that are human rights, based on the dignity of Man being God's creation. Without these rights, the cornerstone of modern society's equity and justice would be destroyed. Today, we face a third great axial age in which we consider questions of "human calling," and it foreshadows our dilemma of whether to take a great leap of faith or doom ourselves to face the end of human civilization. Can America keep its place as the torch of modern civilization if it abandons its faith in God?

For those familiar with Christian civilization, you may begin with the chapters on Eastern philosophy and beliefs. Readers familiar with Eastern philosophy may begin with the chapter on the transformation of the Hebrew faith to the Christian faith through the Roman Empire. Readers who are pained by the present may also read the last three chapters that touch on the crisis facing human civilization today, and then return to the previous chapters to find correspondences and resonances in the comparative search between East and West. This book is not an empirical work but an attempt to compare the philosophical history of East and West in order to put together the bigger picture.

I am grateful to Pastor Qiu Lin, who has been working tirelessly in the Chinese countryside for sixteen years as part of the Bethel Series to train pastors, for his foreword to this book. Thank you to Ms. Judy Yi Zhou and her team for their hard work and dedication in translating this book from Chinese to English. Thank you to Mr. David Hancock and the team at Morgan James Publishing for their recognition and careful planning of this book. Thank you to my wife Angela He for her long term encouragement and patience as the first person to listen to this book word by word. Thank you to my beloved son, Stanley He, for his extensive work in coordinating publication, distribution, and marketing. It was your inspiration and concerted effort that made the English version of this book possible. I would like to take this opportunity to say that words alone cannot thank you enough for the help you've given me in the publication of this book. I love you all.

He Daofeng

Bethesda, Maryland, 4th July 2021

CHAPTER 1:

Human: traits, nature and public conflict

SECTION 1: THE VULNERABILITY OF BEING HUMAN

We know through empirical research and written records that humans are neither the first nor the only creatures to have ruled the earth. Before Man, the earth was populated by prehistoric beasts and pre-modern wildlife. And, before those, by bacteria and viruses. Compared to these much stronger animals and pervasive microorganisms, the physical vulnerabilities that come with being human might seem nearly insurmountable and, consequently, our current dominance statistically unlikely.

Human vulnerability extends beyond our lack of natural defenses, such as thick fur, sharp teeth, claws, a faster gait, and superior climbing ability:

we also suffer from low birth rates, long pregnancies, and lengthy infant care requirements. In fact, it takes a single human nearly two decades to go from embryo to independent living. During this process, the probability of injury or even death is high: Life is truly risky for humans.

Of course, we do have certain unique advantages over other species. We walk upright and have large brains. Starting 80,000–100,000 years ago, East African *Homo sapiens* migrate to other parts of the world. As they multiply, they gradually replace Neanderthals. The brain size of an adult *Homo sapiens* begins to range from about 1,250–1,400 cubic centimeters, reaching as high as 2,000 cubic centimeters in some cases—equivalent to four to six times that of anthropoids, the primates with the largest brains. The human head, which accounts for less than 5 percent of body weight, consumes about 20 percent of a human's energy. This advantage not only allows people to walk, run, and climb completely upright, but also to become the type of intelligent animal that takes action based on thinking and reflection, instead of solely relying on conditioned reflexes and instinct.[1] But this advantage is not necessarily enough for individual human beings to overcome their natural impediments in relation to other species.

What was it, then, that enabled us to thrive? Was it God? A God that is external to man, who created and orchestrated humanity and nature according to God's reason and laws? This is the central question that humankind has pondered and debated throughout history. Based on their differing conclusions, people have built wildly diverse cultural communities, national governance, and belief systems.

This book examines these systems of belief and governance from all over the world as evidenced in our written histories. With this in mind, it seeks to illustrate how God intended us to live, and how we can best care for one another in this precarious world.

SECTION 2: THE DILEMMA OF FREE WILL

Because of our physical vulnerabilities, people choose to live in groups. Over time, this has led to many distinct methods of communal life. Of course, living in groups is not a characteristic unique to humans, but for us, our communal lifestyles have been both directly responsible for many of our problems and necessary for our attempts to resolve them. Such a lifestyle has certainly been a factor in humanity's extraordinary collective evolution and creation of civilization.

Social life places individuals into interconnected relationships. From the beginning, this interconnectedness has been like two sides of a coin created by God: completely opposite, yet intrinsically interdependent. On one side, our connectedness makes us more formidable against outside threats, strengthens cooperation among individuals, and boosts an individual's confidence and sense of belonging to the community. These connections enhance people's ability to deal with external reality.

On the flip side of the coin, being in close relation to other people also carries increased individual risks. Though other people may be part of an individual's community, they remain necessarily distinct from him or her. This phenomenon means that the individual cannot but experience other people as "others" and part of the "outside world." While the outside world may treat an individual well, guaranteeing their safety and providing them with opportunities, it could also treat them poorly, even seizing what they own, love, or are. This risk of the other is therefore a shared experience among individuals in a group. Our sense of communal belonging juxtaposed alongside the shared distrust of the other illustrates the two aspects of individuals living in a community: on one side is beauty, on the other, darkness. So it has been from the beginning, and so it will always be. Our attempts to ponder and articulate these problems are one of the main things that separates humans from animals.

People tend to draw upon their spiritual nature in an attempt to resolve these dilemmas. Yet where does humanity's spiritual nature come from? From God's creation? From evolution? From outer space? Humans' spiritual nature and unique behavioral pattern of thought, action, and reflection may be due to physiological factors such as ability to walk upright, brain size, and body chemistry that allow for our brains to consume a higher percentage of energy; or it could be that God created humanity and endowed them with a spiritual nature. This is a lengthy discussion that might not yield any meaningful results—it's easier to simply choose one to believe in.

Temporarily setting aside the origins debate, we can recognize that people think before they act and reflect on their actions, which means they have the ability to learn and innovate. How do we explain our learning ability? Some learning is imitating, repeating, or reproducing. People can emulate the behaviors of others or those of different species and reproduce them. But we can go beyond that as well. Our ability to reflect helps us be more selective in what we learn next. Over time, we optimize our communal behavior patterns and achieve a sense of direction and progress.

How do we define innovative ability? To innovate is to discover, not imitate or emulate; it is to invent, not repeat or reproduce. An innovation is not just something new to an individual person, but it also must be new on a group scale, to people across different groups. Through living in communities, our learning and innovative abilities continue to improve. This constant upgrade of our collective *human ability* is a new mechanism that further widens the fundamental differences between people and animals.

Although many scientific experiments have sought to show that other animals have the ability to learn, thus far the results only prove that these specific individual animals are exhibiting learned behavior, or conditioned reflexive action. The internal organization and division of labor of bees and ants, for example, results from a group conditional reflex that assigns a role for each individual. The individual only takes actions that fall within their assigned role, which is designed to fulfill necessary tasks for the group. Take a drone, which only survives for 90 days in order to carry out its role in a group of bees: once it completes its mating task, it dies, and it does so without the free will or individual thinking about choices that humans enjoy. Animal behavior patterns are fundamentally different from those of humans, and it's impossible for them to obtain the freedoms and abilities to learn and innovate in a sustained way like humans do in communal life.[2]

The individual free will of humans flows from our spirituality. Whether this spirituality came from God's creation of mankind or through societal evolution has always been a subject of theological and philosophical debate. The majority of people in the world believe that God is the original source of human spirituality, and therefore free will. Many others believe the source is evolution, resulting from adaptation to the environment. Both positions are equally difficult to falsify or verify. But the inherent spirituality of our free will is fundamental to our humanity.

Free will is a prerequisite not only for thinking before acting, but also for reflecting after acting. Given our history and culture of communal living, there can be no understanding of true individual freedom that doesn't take into account how each person's actions might impact others. It is conditioned upon the particular ethics and legal order of a given community. Still, individual freedom must also be fundamentally centered around the self. Otherwise, it's no longer an exercise of free will by its subject and becomes nothing more than the enslavement of some people by others—true freedom goes up in smoke and collapses into a rubble of lies.

Therefore, an individual subject that is empowered with free will and a self-oriented free will that is empowered by an individual subject are the two most basic starting points and end goals of all discussions of human issues. But how to foster individual free will while maintaining public order and governance in human communities? That's a puzzle that remains difficult to solve.

SECTION 3: THE ETERNAL CONFLICT BETWEEN HUMAN ABILITY AND HUMAN DUTY

Ever since people entered community living, each bringing their own free will and unique behavior patterns, the group vs. individual paradox has existed. The synergy and conflict between the individual and the group shows the two sides of the coin God created. One advantage of community life is immediately apparent: individuals living in groups are surrounded by others, and so increase their safety and security. When individuals connect through community organizations, they increase their ability to cope with nature and the outside world, and the group's ability to compete with other species for resources improves as well.

Once people see the value of acting together and being in an "organization," their vision for and dependence on the organization increase. Humans have cultivated common habits by living in groups. We share true and imagined stories. We gain a common source of emotions, especially when we must respond to crises caused by outside threats. Experiences like hunting together, handling attacks, and surviving natural disasters enhance a sense of pride in and belonging to a group.

Community organization is only possible because of human passion. Passionate individuals form groups, learn and innovate, study and create, imagine and converse, dance and sing. As our community grows larger, we become more capable. The more able the community is to conquer nature and respond to external attacks, the more fully individual passions can be inspired and mobilized. Such communities are more exciting and garner individual pride.

Communal connection is mankind's first great invention—it allows us to exponentially expand our abilities through group organization.[3] It truly has been one of our most important steps in becoming a competitive species on earth.

But then there's the other side of the coin: the conflict of community life. Even as people collectively feel safer in groups, as individuals, they can feel more insecure. As groups expand, the connections between individuals inevitably loosen. Unfamiliarity between individuals increases. When clashes of free will occur, people take the skills they honed in conflict with external challenges and apply them to internal conflict instead. This sharply increases individuals' insecurity. At the same time, the fight for external resources between communities is often violent. In times of group conflict, each individual's free will is further threatened and sacrificed, as the collective interest of the group prevails. While individuals who join groups may no longer be isolated and helpless, unfortunately, this new crisis emerges.

Yet, the crisis of rising inter-community conflicts does not seem to temper our enthusiasm for communal societies. Instead, it fuels the further expansion of community organizations, because people believe that larger organizations equal greater power. Increasingly large community organizations create the need to constrain the exercise of individual free will in the name of the "greater good." This may be because of real needs of the group as a whole, or because a few leaders of the group want to impose their will on the rest.

This issue is a constant source of debate, even today, in human communities. Because access to key information is not equal among people, the free will of the few may be built on the organized enslavement of the many. This is the darkest aspect of human community life. Sometimes it's necessary, but most of the time it's tragically absurd. Often, the imposition of the leaders' free will over the rest ignites people's fury and distress. They deplore injustice and cry out, they revolt and fight, and they even sacrifice their lives.

How can the opposing dynamics of individual free will and organized oppression in human communities be reconciled? How can human beings maximize individual free will while fully integrating into a group and so winning the competition for survival among earth's species? Community issues have become a historic problem of human group dynamics that all of us must face.

The positive side of human free will includes both subjective freedom and objective freedom, which means that each person is free to imagine, speak, and act, as well as enjoy the result of his own actions. It also means that people can freely associate and compete with one another in their imagination, conversation, and actions. But in order to enjoy this freedom, there are other considerations. The first is whether an individual subject is healthy, conscious, and can basically survive. The second is the time and technological situation in which the person lives, which affect how they can imagine, speak, act, and enjoy the results of their actions. So human freedom immediately comes into tension with another problem, that of *human ability*. That is, to what extent *can* one individual be free during a certain time in human evolution?

If, for example, a person lands on a deserted island like Robinson Crusoe, he will only encounter the natural "outside world." His free will is limited by his technology. For example, he can use branches to build a shelter. He can use sources of fresh water on the island. He can pick wild fruit to eat. He can sharpen wood into a spear for fishing and self-defense. He can make marks on wood every day to record human time. He can draw flying birds or imaginary cities in the sand or on rock walls, and so on. These abilities are the best expression of his free will.[4]

But when he returns to society, he will not only encounter the problem of the natural outside world, but also the one comprised of many "others." Now we must face the inherent problem implied by the negative side of human free will. Is his freedom limited when he returns to society? When an individual exerts their free will, does it hurt or hinder the freedom of others?

First, in physical space when a person possesses an object or occupies a location, others are necessarily excluded from possessing or occupying it. So the exercise of human free will can bring about physical conflicts between people. Second, imagination, speech, and other means of empowering human free will are also exclusive to each individual. Community life gives rise to subjective conflicts over things like personal reputation, or an individual's actions may directly hinder the freedom of others in objective conflicts like theft or looting. Ultimately, people's actions may create subjective conflicts that directly harm or even kill others.

Under all of these problems actually lies a larger, hidden question. In humans' unique social life, how can they create a communal public order with the required constraints? And how should individual duty be in play so that one can imagine and act in ways that preserve one's own freedom while respecting that of others? How can *human duty* and *human ability* work together to create proper attitudes and behaviors and build a dynamic, communal society with respect for both individual free will and public order? Such a society is desirable for all of us who share a spiritual nature.

SECTION 4: THE SACRED ANSWER IN LIFE'S UPS AND DOWNS

Ever since the dawn of mankind, our natural special characteristics and free will have driven us to resolve the opposing fundamental dilemmas of *human ability* and *human duty*. *Human ability* is largely about the freedom and achievements of humans as individual personalities. *Human duty* is largely about the definitions and limits of people as public personalities in groups and creates the boundaries of individual freedom and public spaces. Only by building these common boundaries to regulate the excesses of individual freedom is true freedom possible. And in turn, only with the clearly defined and measured freedom individuals obtain in groups can people construct stable expectations and hopes, which make such a communal life worth living. The process of solving these two conflicting issues defines the history of human civilization, with its criss-crossing history of wins and losses in the competition between species, communities, and individuals vs. communities.

Over the history of human civilization, faith and public welfare, as part of our *human duty*, have created public spaces and regulated individual freedom. Their origins, development, and the future hope they promise are all interwoven into our history of civilization. They are worthy of further thought and exploration.

Anyone's subjective or objective freedom is played out in a specific historical space, limited by the technical means available and common rules for public spaces. It's very hard to imagine transcending this temporally defined freedom. But if everyone's actions were limited by a particular time's technology and rules, human freedom would be static; *human ability* would also be static. Then the fate of mankind would be like other species, limited to natural cycles. But human history is not like this.

Human history is full of individual breakouts and group fluctuations. There are always great pioneers who harness extraordinary thought and action to defy the limits of their time's technology and norms, thereby upgrading freedom and updating its rules. But what is the source of this extraordinary thought and action? Where does it gain legitimacy? How are pioneers from different communities able to think and act ahead of their time and often affect the course of history? More specifically, what is the great driving, directional force deeply rooted within the great pioneers' thoughts and actions, and why is it there?

These questions are fundamentally about how humans should live, and they are for all of us, not just the pioneers. The flow of time seems to go on infinitely, but the time we have on Earth is limited. How do we resolve our sense of displacement in this immensity and lead a life of meaning? How do we make sense of and feel satisfied with the time we are given? As the pioneers searched for answers, they found that it is through empathy, the golden rule of getting along in a community, and unshakable confidence and courage in the face of life's ups and downs. This is how we can firmly, bravely, and sacredly face life.

This search in life, guided by a kind of sacred expectation, to achieve self-discipline, self-motivation, and self-affirmation goes beyond duty and ability both. This is our *human calling*.

Throughout our history, as the size of our communities has expanded, their complexity and the resulting alienation among people have increased. With advancements in technology and changes in the ways people communicate, *human calling* often includes unwritten community law and becomes an enforceable prescription for individual behavior in a community. People who violate such rules are strongly condemned and publicly repressed. This shows the ethical and moral aspect of *human calling*, or *human duty*. It embodies the public enforcement of individual behavior in a community situated in a specific time and place, with the hope that everyone responds to ethical pressure by correcting their behavior to live in harmony with the public. But this kind of public morality of *human duty* cannot inspire the passionate imagination of each individual, so it can't bestow individual motivation and determination.

As strong communities like nation-states have emerged, the self-regulation contained in our *human calling* has also been partially converted into national statutes in order to further restrain individual behavior, forming *human requirement*. *Human requirement* is mandated rules the state places on the individual. Failure to comply with such rules can have serious consequences for people, including loss of personal freedom and one's life. Although throughout history, each society inevitably controls people with ethical, moral, and legal rules, the *human duty* decided by the public and the *human requirement* mandated by the state cannot stand in for the passionate imagination and divine reason that drive us towards self-discipline, self-motivation, and self-affirmation. Nor can they account for the great sages who lead us through the fog of history. They can never completely replace our *human calling*.

Human calling can only be found in people's voluntary public spirit and the spiritual realm of faith. Only there is mankind's inexhaustible spiritual source found. Extraordinary thinkers in human history have helped spur great movements that have tried to define and understand our human calling.

The rest of this book will group the great thoughts that have shaped human history into three major historical stages. The first great human reflection on the source of our human calling is the Axial Age. The second, spanning from the 12th to the 19th centuries, considers whether people can attain complete individual rationality in the orderly world created by God. The third is found in the pan-liberal society of the twentieth century and onward, reflecting on where humanity should go.

Although in our current day, humanity has reached unprecedented peaks in empirical science and material achievements, *human calling* is still an issue. Our technological developments of *human ability* haven't made it any easier to resolve. If anything, modern humanity is trapped in a tougher position. Humanity stands on the edge of a precipice. If we do not turn back to God, this could be our end.

CHAPTER 2:

Question: cracking human ability in nature

SECTION 1: DEFINING HUMANITY

According to the latest archaeological research using quantum technology, Lucy[5], the earliest human to walk upright, appeared in Ethiopia about 3.18 million years ago. From the perspective of brain capacity (that is, thinking ability), Lucy is far behind modern humans. Her brain capacity was roughly 400–500 cubic centimeters, which is much closer to that of other primates. The modern man (*Homo s. sapiens*) generally has a total brain capacity between 900 and 1,450 cubic centimeters. Prehistoric counterparts of the modern man with similar brain capacities have been discovered as far back as 80,000–100,000 years ago.

These counterparts belong to both the *Homo sapiens* species in East Africa and *Homo s. neanderthalensis* in Europe. In fact, according to the "Out of

Africa" hypothesis, almost all modern humans are descendants of the East African *Homo s. sapiens* who emigrated from that region approximately 80,000 years ago. These early ancestors of humans slowly dispersed across the globe, adapting all the while to new external conditions. Cutting-edge genetic testing detects genetic markers among all modern humans that indicate a direct descent from those *Homo sapiens*[6]. The 650,000-year-old remains of the famous *Homo erectus* Peking Man, the 600,000-year-old remains of Yuan-mou Man, and other *Homo erectus* went completely extinct in the prehistoric ages. They have no modern descendants. Even European *Homo s. neanderthalensis*, or Neanderthals, whose material remains are found at a number of archaeological sites, went extinct 30,000 years ago. As such, the progression from prehistoric to modern man is hardly straightforward.

These facts add necessary complexity to Darwin's theory of human evolution as a simplistic linear progression from ape to upright man. After all, though more than 300 million hominid fossils have been documented and studied thus far, not a single one is a half-walking, half-crawling "missing link" between the ape and the modern man. Moreover, none have a brain capacity that falls between *Homo sapiens* and *Homo erectus*.

With evidence like writing and cave paintings, we can piece together the progress of *Homo sapiens*, but we cannot prove apes are our ancestors without this missing link.[7] Based on existing relics and written records of *Homo sapiens'* thinking and understanding regarding themselves and the outside world, what we refer to as humans are a specific Earth-bound species with written records. Man's verifiable and species-specific civilization has experienced three major historical movements: animism, metaphysics, and positivism. Today, we must be careful when attempting to use the positivism of the third movement to confirm the nature of prehistoric civilizations and term it "evidential science."[8] Before human civilization possessed forms of writing, it was hard to depict their reality accurately. From our modern vantage point, we can only piece together prehistoric images and analyze them in comparison to existing primitive tribes. This book attempts to combine philosophical and theological perspectives over the course of human history to build on previous analysis of the evolution of the civilization. By observing history, we'll consider what it can teach us about solving the core problems we face today.

SECTION 2: THE INHERENT DRIVE TO VIOLENCE

Human societal interaction with other species first occurs in hunter-gatherer societies. Gatherer societies forage for their livelihoods in a presumably idyllic lifestyle, much like the Garden of Eden. Since foraging is a relatively peaceful and safe activity where the individual poses little to no threat to outsiders, gatherer societies wouldn't need a centrally organized, authoritative power to define and bolster the group's strength. The need for strength in numbers and power wouldn't even come into consideration for such a peaceful people. Gatherer societies are by nature more egalitarian, and differences between individuals are mostly indistinguishable.

But hunting adds a very different element. Life in a hunter society is characterized by violence and danger. Hunter societies reframe the relationship between humans and the outside world as a competitive blood sport. In order to emerge victorious over the outside world, humans need to work together to hone a superior strength. This means creating offensive and defensive weapons and organizing themselves to function as a group for strength in numbers. Due to their need for strength, hunter societies require members to be loyal to the group. They also need individual members to lead and mobilize the collective, especially those who are warrior-like, brave, and self-sacrificing in favor of the group's greater good. In turn, these individuals' sacrifices are memorialized by the group and inspire others to follow in their path. In this kind of hunter society, many individuals shine, and their free will is fully stimulated and realized.

The violent, dangerous, yet glorified community thus becomes a powerful imaginative force that captures the minds of individuals. It inspires the invention of axes, knives, and hammers made from stones; traps; earthworks; bows and arrows; fire; and other offensive and defensive tools and techniques. The threat of danger both draws out individuals' strength and courage and creates a cohesion within the group. For instance, the act of killing a lion, elephant, or tiger requires the sacrifice of community members and perhaps even leaders. People's love, lust, joy, grief, fear, and anger are fully mobilized in this imagined community as they together process the emotions this violence and victory evoke. Individual and group creativity find expression in communal songs, ceremonies, and dancing. This community where blood sport is both necessary and celebrated motivates individuals to improve their abilities to predict and prevent danger, as well as to plan and organize the group. As some individuals rise in the ranks through skill and free will, differences among individuals become increasingly stark.[9]

It could even be said that communal living in hunter societies fully actualizes humans' free will and *human ability*. Through organizational innovations, their communal life creates and stimulates their imaginative powers, learning ability, and technological innovation. It fosters their ability to predict and plan for changes in the external world outside their communities, and it cultivates their sense of belonging to a community. It awakens their ability to express emotions and literary and artistic creativity. In this sense, hunter societies are the most magnificent expression of individual free will in a community. Organizational innovation during this period creates a safer environment where a sense of belonging and self-confidence can flourish. People not only gain a deeper understanding of their own abilities, but *human ability* as a whole also grows. The maturation of *human ability* happens in four major areas: organization, technological innovation, creative expression, and reflection on the human condition.

The first, organization, has to do with defining specific roles, creating new ways for members to relate to one another, and deciding how to draw upon these members to fill those roles. Establishing an individual's family relationships through the mother's line is a natural choice, since paternity in pre-modern times could be contested. The interpersonal connections required in hunting, especially big-game hunting, provide a different set of specific roles to define, as well as guidelines for selecting participants. Excluding women, the elderly, and children from dangerous hunting activities is one example of an organizational innovation. It involves drawing upon past experiences, modeling possible outcomes, and arriving at specific decisions in the present. The result is roles like hunters, trappers, warriors, and caretakers, and decisions like who will rescue and support potential casualties, how to divide the spoils within the community, and how to reward merit. Through taking part in a community, humans develop the ability to build and use public organizations. While these earliest organizational methods seem simplistic today, they actually contain the essential components of modern organizations. Kinship, a unique human invention, is the functional tissue of the "tribal clan" and the earliest public organization that connects individual free wills[10].

Public organizations promote technological innovation by appealing to individuals' sense of status within the community.[11] That is, technological innovations result from an individual's attempts to imitate, improve, and transform existing technology. Technological innovations are not limited to our modern inventions of internet and machines. Indeed, some of the earliest inventions were knives, bows, fire, and cooking methods. Each invention surprises and benefits the community before being copied and replicated by other communities. While this process occurs, its inventor enjoys the admiration of his community and an elevated social status. Each invention opens up a new imaginary space for individual free will. Each incremental technological advancement plays an important role in the cultivation of *human ability*.

Public organizations also facilitate emotional expression between people. Emotional expression is a manifestation of each individual's free will. Appreciation, anger, sorrow, joy, worry, fear, and love need channels to be expressed.[12] Such displays include paintings of hunts on cave walls. The victory of the hunt is celebrated with a collective bonfire party with dancing and chanting, which leads to the invention of the tambourine, bamboo metronome, and other instruments. Deaths are followed by funerals with collective crying, howling, and sonorous singing. Before a battle and after a win, the leader of a group gives a speech. Such emotional rituals inspire the creativity of many individuals, which resonates among their own communities, spreads to other communities, and are even passed on to the next generations, serving as a testimony to humanity's spiritual nature and free will. The significance of these innovative rituals is that they heighten and mobilize people's emotions more fully. These rituals allow the full enactment of appreciation, anger, sorrow, joy, worry, fear, and love and act as a release valve for people's emotional burdens. This synergy between an individual's free will and the coordination of individuals in public groups in part brought about our innovative development and expansion as humans.

Public organizations stimulate humans to be deep thinkers. We ask questions about our origin,[13] including how we came to be on earth, what this natural environment is like, what our destination is, and why we are here. This large-scale imaginative and narrative ability is exclusive to individuals with free will.

Like the cardinal directions humans use to navigate the physical world, the past, present, and future help humanity orient itself within time and reality. Starting from our present moment as an anchor, we can seek to classify the things we've experienced in relation to the past and the future. First, how was the world we inhabit created? What is it made up of? How will it change in the future? Second, how did we as humans and our communities come to be? Where is it all going? These big questions and their answers crucially justify mankind's existence and current social trappings, as well as shape our individual free will through faith and logic. Our ability to explain the world began with our communal lives, and it gave rise to our myths and legends. This unique skill of contextualizing ourselves provides the foundation for individual imagination as well as communal bonds, making the growth and cultivation of *human ability* possible.

As human organizations become more common and their advances and inventions slowly progress in hunter societies, new ways of life begin to take shape. Specifically, humans begin experimenting with nomadic and agrarian forms of social organization. Since hunter societies are limited by natural resources, population expansion results in severe shortages of hunting resources and restricts human development. Moreover, hunting societies suffer from unpredictable and irregular levels of food supplies, which weakens the stability of community life. The worst periods come during long, cold winters or natural disasters like floods and droughts. In these seasons, people have difficulty finding animals to hunt, so the risk of being attacked and losing fellow community members increases. Human communal life faces unprecedented survival challenges.

SECTION 3: THE CREATION OF THE FAMILY UNIT

As *human ability* encounters these challenges, people use their free will to solve problems, and new technologies like animal domestication, transplanting, and grafting arise. This is the second wave of technological innovation, following that of the hunter-gatherer society. For the purposes of this book, we'll refer to the progression of human civilization in three stages of technological transformation. I prefer not to divide the human civilization into three main stages of the Stone Age, Bronze Age, or Iron Age or into primitive, slave, feudal, and capitalist societies. The former is too figurative and narrow to encompass the variety of historical human experiences, while the latter relies too much on subjective ethics and cannot be used to objectively study history. In the first stage using this breakdown, technologies rely on the use of natural power, such as hunting, farming, and handicrafts. The second stage draws upon petrochemical power and includes industrial manufacturing and internal combustion technologies. The third stage is based on digital and genetic technologies, including genetic engineering, artificial intelligence, and machine learning. The shift from the offensive and defensive technological innovations (to increase manpower and hunt animals) to the agricultural innovations of animal and plant domestication[14] is a revolutionary leap.

The basis of these agricultural technological innovations is a major invention of human organization—family units with men at the center. The family unit is the most effective way to make individuals' self-centered tendencies outward-looking and more public, because it expands the "self" and thereby individual power through group organization. Yet it strictly limits this expanded self through intimate familial bonds. The family unit assigns each person a single sexual partner and establishes familial bonds based on a shared lineage—whether real or imagined. In this way, the family becomes a unit for economic activity and engages each individual in a mini-community that requires the individual to think beyond themselves. This family unit facilitates technological innovations and shapes agrarian societies. Its impact on human civilization is profound and far-reaching.

First, farming technology transforms the bloody, violent competitive relationship between humans and other animal species to one that's more subdued and at least appears to be characterized by peace. Domesticating animals allows people to store food and mitigate the risks of seasonal variation and natural disasters. Cultivating plants from the wild strengthens families' ability to domesticate livestock and enables the human diet to become omnivorous instead of carnivorous. This new way of life leads to revolutionary changes in the way energy is exchanged between humans and the outside world and greatly improves humans' ability to survive relative to other species. It also stimulates individuals' ability to imagine freely and to innovate technologically, which further promotes animal and plant domestication technologies. Thus, agricultural and nomadic civilizations are born. While these two societies differ greatly from the perspective of history, from a technological perspective they stem from much the same source. The lifestyle and cultural differences between the two have historically been exaggerated because of differences in geography.

Second, the development of agricultural technology greatly reduces the need for "strength in numbers," because, unlike in hunting societies, the cultivation of livestock and crops are peaceful by nature. The coordinated large-scale offensive and defensive violence of hunter civilizations eventually seems risky and unstable, so such societies gradually recede from the historical stage as small-scale animal domestication and farming or nomadic life take their place. So also the family as an organizational unit replaces the clan and tribal units that were dominant in hunter societies.

Family-based organization starts with a tight-knit bond between blood relatives. The self is at the core of such blood relationships: *me*, *my* parents, *my* children, *my* brothers and sisters, with non-blood connections following those. Next, the family unit is charged with the heavy responsibility of reproduction. People have a clearer, less ambiguous community orientation from birth than in a tribal organization, as well as more direct social responsibilities to the family members. This is especially true in terms of economic responsibilities, so the family unit quickly becomes a center of economic activity.

At first glance, the invention of the family unit would appear to have suddenly limited the scope of community life. On the contrary, its creation actually inspires technological change based on accumulated experience. For example, pottery is created as a staple in everyday life. Clothing and textiles are made from animal skin, tree bark, coarse fabric. For dwellings, thatched huts are invented to block the wind and impede animal attacks. Natural resources like bark, wood, mud, stone, and grass are all used to build shelters. Because of these technological advancements resulting from life experience, people leave natural caves with limited resources and begin residing on larger pieces of land more conducive to large-scale expansion.

In terms of movement, domesticating animals opens up new imaginative pathways. Cattle, donkeys, and camels serve as transportation. Domesticating horses proves revolutionary, because they greatly enhance the speed at which people move from location to location. The use of fire not only changes people's diets and improves their nutrition and immune system, but it also facilitates the development of the copper industry. The addition of mercury to copper smelting produced bronze, a harder, stronger material. Historians often talk about the "New Stone Age" (pottery) and "Bronze Age" to categorize periods of human civilization. But it's arguable that animal and plant domestication was the most essential technology, while others were merely technical extensions of it.

Third, these technological and organizational inventions improve people's ability to express their emotions. The greatest improvement in this vein was the discovery and creation of writing.[15] From the perspective of historians and archaeologists, the earliest known writing dates back 6,000–7,000 years to the Sumerian cuneiform of Mesopotamia. These words were written on clay tablets. They not only recorded the daily life of the time but also the way people admired and worshiped God through ceremonies and rituals.[16] Ancient Egyptian hieroglyphics, 4,000–5,000 years old, were found on the alluvial plains of Egypt. They detail the construction of the pyramids and worship of the Pharaoh.[17] Oracle bones from the Yin-Shang Dynasty period (3,000–4,000 years ago), excavated in China's Henan Province, mostly record the divination of future good or bad circumstances by priests from the upper class.[18] Ethiopian hieroglyphics, 3,000 years old, record the earliest Hebrew Bible stories. 4,000-year-old Hebrew and Hindi and later ancient Greek and Latin are among the first languages in recorded history used to express ideas in abstract writing composed with an alphabet.[19] However, no text is more than 10,000 years old. Meanwhile, farming and nomadic technologies centered around animal and plant cultivation begin 80,000 years ago. It takes civilizations just as long to cultivate these kinds of livelihoods as it does to innovate the written word.

The invention of writing is arguably humanity's highest accomplishment. It marks the final and most essential break with other species. Not only does it fundamentally change emotional expression and lay the foundation for literary genres ranging from poetry to legal charters, it also enables the achievements of individual free will and introspection to accumulate within communities through literary records. In turn, these lay the foundation for further creative innovation and increase individual freedom of expression. This self-reinforcing mechanism of generating and accumulating human expression through literary means is unique to humans as a species. That knowledge and expressions are accumulated means that each individual doesn't need to start from scratch. Rather, they can assume their studies from where another has left off. In this incremental way, the process of learning, innovation, and reflection is accelerated, and knowledge is quickly gained.

Fourth, the evolution of agricultural societies, including domestication and the reliance on familial units, further cultivates the human interest in explaining their origins and place in the universe. The ability to interpret the universe comes in part from life experience and in part from the human ability to reason and imagine. Based on existing archeological and written records, myths have always been a part of human communal life. Agricultural civilization further develops mankind's mythological imagination.[20] Later, philosophers will describe the cosmology during this long gestation period as animism. The animistic imagination partly comes from people's collective longing for the world's mysteries. Another part comes from the stirrings of their deep anxiety over the finite nature of the human condition and the always inconstant future. Yet another contributing factor is early man's expectation of safety in the face of life's fragility and conflicts. Myths are a solution to this desire, as they endow people with collective courage and the confidence to go on with both their own lives and the communal life. Each society has unique myths exclusively passed down through word of mouth that logically and imaginatively interpret the universe. They're full of passion and strength. They describe expectations for an individual's behavior and contribution to society. As they're passed down, the next generation gains the confidence and courage to perpetuate the group's unique culture and pride. After writing is invented, these myths enter the community record of the history of human civilization and become society's sacred treasures.

We've seen that agricultural and nomadic technology based on animal and plant cultivation reduced the risks that previous hunting societies had faced in terms of seasonal changes and natural disasters. Accordingly, individuals organized themselves into family units. Meanwhile the invention of writing and mythological interpretation replaces the large-scale mobilization of individual connections in hunter civilization. This brings unprecedented passion and strength to communities made up of family units. Humans rapidly multiply in that context as individuals are incorporated into different family-based paradigms.

The first civilization paradigm is that of the agriculture-based civilization. These civilizations require fertile land and access to water, which allow plants to take root and flourish. For example, flood plains of the Tigris-Euphrates in the Middle East, Egypt's Nile, India's Ganges, China's Yellow and Yangtze Rivers, and countless others all become birthplaces of farming civilizations because of the availability of these two resources. They are incubators for solving the problem of *human ability*.

The second paradigm is that of nomadic society. A family can choose to live in a tent on a grassland where they will have access to water, and domesticated cattle and sheep will have stable access to food. Once nearby grass is consumed, they can move to another grassy area.

The third paradigm is that of the craftsmen. These families are part of nomadic and farming groups, but they develop their own special skills like pottery making, copper smelting, metallurgy, carpentry, weaving, cobbling, masonry, ornamental craftsmanship, and construction, which meet the needs of farming and nomadic families. They create increasingly strong divisions of labor and craftsmanship.

The fourth paradigm is that of the merchant family. They live with and move through the various families mentioned above, buying the excess goods of one family in one place and selling them to another family who needed them in another place. They create "fair exchange," "trade agreements," and other ways to relate to others that are completely different than those of a hunter civilization, laying the foundation for complex interpersonal connection and solutions to problems in modern society. Meanwhile, they create behavioral patterns like "storage" and "transportation" to address people's needs in certain places and times, which leads to a new understanding of space and time and plants the seeds of modern society's storage, shipping, transportation, communication, and merchandising industries.

These four paradigms of family organization that begin with the development of farming and nomadic techniques contain tighter individual bonds through ties of blood, and clearer relationships of responsibilities and rights. Because they're easier to organize and stabilize, they successfully replaced the "clan" organizational system and became the new form of privatized human organization. These lifestyles may seem small and idyllic, but within them are infinite solutions to the problem of *human ability*.

SECTION 4: OURSELVES AND THE OTHER, IMPLICIT CONTRACTS, AND THE FORMATION OF COUNTRIES

Unfortunately, this idyllic community life organized around the family unit doesn't last long. New problems emerge. Some individuals infringe upon the rights of others and do violence to them. Violent acts include stealing and seizing other's property, stealing mates, violating bodies, and threatening lives. Humans emerge and survive through violent competition with other species, so it follows that human nature must be full of violent tendencies. But when people commit violence toward their own kind, i.e., other people, tragedy and chaos occur on an immense scale. This is because while attacks from other species are relatively easy to guard against, similar attacks from people are difficult to prevent and accept. Human violence against humans becomes the biggest problem over the course of civilization. Modern archaeology has excavated material evidence of burials and killing relics, demonstrating the violence in human nature and its disastrous consequences for humanity.

These violent tendencies take two forms: between communities and between individuals within communities.[21] Internal violence usually manifests as theft and physical harm. External violence usually manifests as collective looting, mass killing, and mass slavery. This internal and external violence begs the question: how do you define community boundaries? If "family" life is defined as "community life," we would discover that the community of the family is difficult to maintain for a long time. When the external violence faced by families is endless, they can't be expected to maintain a positive outlook on the future in the face of constant trauma. In response, families in agricultural and nomadic civilizations band together to lead violent attacks against other groups of families. In other words, family units eventually transform into the clan and tribe organizational paradigms they had initially replaced. They aim to secure their ability to live, produce, protect their property, and protect their way of life, and thereby reduce the extreme insecurity of individuals. In this new era of agricultural and nomadic community life, public organizations like tribes and countries form. The family unit quickly adapts to play an expanded "individual" role relative to the larger tribal public interest. This establishes the first differentiation between private and public organizations.

The first threat public organizations have to deal with is external violence, something even "modern" civilizations like ours find gruesome and terrifying. A national community can selfishly define another community as enemies and launch a war to kill them. Over the tens of thousands of years of human history, defining others this way and shedding their blood has been the norm. In response to such external threats, community leaders' solutions are almost always those that expand the size and boundaries of their community. They seek to increase the number of their members and enhance group cohesion and appeal in order to achieve the "public" goal of being better able to defend the group against external violence.

Obviously, when the size of a tribal community increases and is able to withstand external violence, its members feel a sense of security. The opposite is also true. Undoubtedly, such a community practice gives members who have an advantage in language and organizational capacities the necessary logical power and opportunity to use it. Harnessing collective imagination, rationalizing statements, and the weight of mythology, they convince community members to expand the size and population of their communities. So the contest of large-scale expansion of the human community begins, in the name of defending against external violence and promoting public security. As a result, humans created the limits of the state and its implication of permanency as the largest public organization able to protect individuals from external violence. Meanwhile, they create the largest public organization, the government, to represent the public interest of the state in managing individuals and resisting external violence. The government thereby becomes a national machine against external violence, run on taxes from individuals.

The second threat to deal with is internal violence. Even in a community with a thousand families, there are still thefts, robberies, slander, trespassing, damages, and violent acts. As a community grows in size, such internal violence becomes more severe. Addressing it usually takes the form of a code of conduct verbally outlined by community leaders and punishment for those who violate it. The earliest contractual rules between individuals living in a community are born. After writing is invented, such contractual rules can be recorded, and they become mankind's earliest written law. In this system, individual free comes under systemic community protection and can be maintained by paying taxes and following the rules of *human requirement*. This reflects both the internal dilemmas of individual free will and the group's public will and their solutions.

SECTION 5: THE DEPTHS OF THE PARADOX OF VIOLENCE

As competition and expansion continue, many community leaders find that a strict system to mitigate the risks of internal violence is needed to match its growth. The expansion of the community, in turn, provides sufficient justification for leaders to convince its members that more discipline is needed. As a result, the remedies against internal and external violence feed into one another, promoting effective and rapid expansion of the community up to its most extreme boundary, the state. The state thus becomes not only the extreme boundary of the community against external violence but also the measure and shape of fixed, orderly community life.

Usually a country's borders are based on geographical barriers like mountains, oceans, rivers, and marshes. Nations also often rely on common language, customs, writing, and culture that the community has developed over time to define its boundaries. Government is created by individuals to represent them, mitigate the risks of internal and external violence, and manage the public interest. Generally speaking, the state as a representation of public will corresponds to and is restrained by individuals. On the other hand, the organizational form of a government corresponds to and is restrained by the organizational form of the family unit with the self at the center. But no matter how much governmental organizations differ from private, family, individual ones, they are still made up of people with self-centered individual free wills. Therefore, it is not only possible to make self-centered, individual interests as a tenet of official office, it is almost unavoidable. This is an embodiment of the paradox of human nature. A family made up of individuals expects to escape violence and improve their security by joining a community united by a state and government. They agree to cede some of their wealth and freedom in paying taxes in exchange for protection from internal and external threats of violence, only to find themselves dreaming a broken dream and trapped in a real paradox.

The history of early civilization shows the roots and rich growth of this idea: the Assyrian Empire and Mesopotamian civilization of 6,000—7,000 years ago; the Ancient Egyptian and Nile civilization of 4,000–5,000 years ago; the Kingdom of Israel and Judaic civilization of 3,000–4,000 years ago; the Greek Empire and city-states of 2,500–3,000 years ago; the Chinese Empire and Chinese civilization of 2,000–4,000 years ago; the Aryan Empire of the Indo-Ganges civilization of 2,500–3,500 years ago; and the Roman Empire and European civilization of 700–2,500 years ago. This long line of civilizations demonstrates that any community that can successfully harness the organizational forms of family, state, and government, require the nuclear family to pay taxes in exchange for state protection from violence, and express these ideas in statutes, can maximize its size through expansion. Such civilizations create agricultural empires never seen before, and greatly explore the deep and long-standing proposition of *human ability*.[22]

The historical picture of 2,500–10,000 years ago, pieced together by evidence uncovered by archaeologists, gives a glimpse of the violent competition that took place during the expansion of communities. Whether offensive or defensive in nature, the tragedy of the bloodshed far exceeds that of animal hunts in hunter civilization. It's shocking and magnificent. But the feelings and emotional expressions such violence inspires are strange. Looking at historical expressions of emotion in writing, there is little expression of sympathy, lament, pain, worry, or anger over the violence against individuals and the destruction of their freedom. Epic poems like the *Epic of Gilgamesh, the Iliad, the Odyssey, the Bhagavad-Gita* revere violent, victorious heroes. Clearly fear of violence coexists with desire for violence in the human heart.[23]

Fear of violence is easy to understand, but where does the desire for violence come from? Evidently, it comes from individual desires to exploit the human need for public safety. This exploitation results in the coercion and enslavement of individuals and their families by public representatives, such as royal families, nobilities, and governments. Whether in the Mesopotamian civilizations; Ancient Egypt; or in the Xia, Shang, and Zhou dynasties of China, the rapid and extreme expansion of these communities is made possible through a minority leader group exploiting the public's desire for security, and the internal coercion and enslavement of civilian families by the king, government, and other public organizations. The early history of agrarian societies is, in the end, a history of violence between communities and a history of forced slavery of individual families by a minority leadership circle in the name of their community's public interest. Language and group organization become creative tools for some individuals to mobilize the community to resist internal and external violence. However, these innovations ultimately become tools for initiating violence.

Humankind's desire to prevent and resolve the issues of both internal and external violence inspires innovations in terms of technology and organization.

As a consequence, population growth and the establishment of civilizations is also accelerated. These innovations provide an effective solution to the problem of *human ability* and allow for people to gradually win the competition against other species. On the other hand, these innovations also greatly undermine the order of the larger society and result in the violent deaths of many.

Death has always been humanity's greatest problem. The death of a family member causes serious emotional distress, insecurity, panic, and fear. Excessive violence, especially killing between and within communities, greatly aggravate people's fear of death. The result is that some people start asking questions about *human calling*. Why can't people escape the dilemma of freedom and violence? Can people get rid of the shadow of both internal and external violence and live freely together in peace? If attempts to end violence continuously create more violence, where is the meaning in that? In a time when it's impossible to live alone and the size of communities is continuously getting bigger, how should we live? How should we think and act? How can we avoid enslaving others and being enslaved by others in our pursuit of freedom? How can we maintain freedom while promoting the public interest? And those deeper questions: where have we come from and where are we going? How are our lives logically consistent with the past and the future?

These questions, and others, led to the beginning of humanity's first great philosophical reflection on *human calling* in the Axial Age, the era between 1,500 B.C. and 500 AD. The pursuit of these questions opened a new chapter in the history of humanity.

CHAPTER 3:

The source: the vast depths of ancient Greek philosophy

hilosophers trace the lineage of universal philosophy back to the ancient Greek city-states that flourished between 1,000 and 500 BC. In that era, people in the great river basins and vast grasslands were struggling with new agricultural and nomadic community life. The ancient Greeks leveraged their unique geographical advantages on the Mediterranean to conduct trade based on sea transportation and mutually beneficial exchange between communities, as opposed to violent domination and conquest. Compared with such methods, commercial civilization requires greater respect for individuality and independence, as well as greater literacy and knowledge of others' languages. The Ancient Greeks probed the questions about *human calling* more than any other commercial civilization. It was an era that prized philosophical thinkers, linguists, and orators.

The philosophers can be divided into pre- and post-Socratic philosophers.[24] Pre-Socratic philosophers lived mainly between 1,000 and 500 BC. They were largely comprised of natural philosophers from the Miletus School, the Pythagorean School, and the Elia School, which focused on the relationship between humans and nature. Post-Socratic philosophers lived mainly between 500 BC and 200 AD. They were mostly humanistic philosophers who explore the public relationship of humans and society. They include the three masters, Socrates, Plato, and Aristotle, and schools of the New Academy, the Cynics, the Epicureans, and the Stoics.

SECTION 1: ANCIENT GREEK MYTHOLOGY: THE PASSIONATE ORIGIN OF HUMAN COMPASSION AND REFLECTION

In terms of philosophical thinking about *human calling* and how we relate to each other, the Hebrews were ahead of the Greeks, having explored this between 1,800–1,500 BC, and had reached firmer conclusions. But Ancient Greece left civilization many logically consistent and deeply philosophical essays as well as unique architecture and sculpture, while the Hebrews only produced the Old Testament, which seems at first glance like mere apocalyptic literature. Since the Old Testament lacks rigorous logic, or questions and answers that provoke debate in philosophical terms, it's often excluded from philosophical discussions. But when it comes to the exploration of *human calling*, the mere number of citations is not the best measure of results. In fact, the philosophical thinking implied in the Hebrew Bible is more ancient and deep than the Ancient Greeks'. To this day, mankind has still been unable to fully comprehend its philosophical questions, reflections, and metaphorical answers to the earliest and deepest philosophical reflections, especially on the similarity between the source of human life and the source of nature, which are hidden deep within the Hebrew Bible.

charged with the public affairs of the Greek communities. The oldest of them was Titan, followed by Rhea, and the youngest was Cronus. Because Uranus was afraid his children would replace him, they were sent to the underworld. Only Cronus was spared, protected by his mother, Gaia. Eventually Cronus defeated his father, Uranus, and castrated him. Without fertility, Uranus lost his power and withdrew from the historical stage. Cronus was able to liberate his siblings from the underworld.

Finally, Cronus and his sister, Rhea, produced the fourth generation of gods: the goddess of fertility Hera, the goddess of agriculture Demeter, the god of the sea Poseidon, the goddess of the hearth Hestia, the god of the underworld Hades, the god of thunder Zeus, and so on. Later, Cronus learned from a prophecy that his children would replace him and his pantheon. So he swallowed his children, one by one, until only the weakest, Zeus, was left. Because Cronus felt pity for him and Rhea protected him, Zeus survived. When Zeus grew up, he defeated Cronus and castrated him, toppling him from power. Zeus rescued his brothers and sisters and replaced Cronus as head of the pantheon.

The fifth generation of gods, fathered by Zeus, are the most well-known gods of Olympus, who ruled in the heyday of the Greek city-state: Apollo, the god of the sun; Ares, the god of war; Aphrodite, the goddess of love; Athena, the goddess of wisdom; Artemis, the goddess of the moon; Hephaestus, the god of creativity; Dionysus, the god of wine; and so on.

The stories of these ancient myths are often beautiful. They became central to the identity of the ancient Greeks. The philosophy of truth, goodness, and beauty originated in ancient Greek mythology, and all their songs, literature, music, dance, sculpture, and architecture were based on it. The ancient Greek gods were not only the embodiments of truth, goodness and beauty—they also all had supernatural powers. They were put in symbolic charge of the public and spiritual order of their respective Greek city-states.

But each god also had their own destiny. Although their powers were super-natural, they could not escape their ultimate fate. As a result, they met tragic ends that also ended their public patronage.[28] The gods gained strength through meeting human spiritual needs. This in turn gave human nations public order, public values, and a common spiritual understanding—a source of confidence and strength. But gods had no way to control their destinies. In trying to do so, they met tragedy in the same way that humans meet death.

The tragic ends of the ancient Greek gods brought out the deepest sympathy and compassion in people. It filled the community with sorrow and love, causing them to reflect on deeper realities. People reconsidered their relationships with others, as well as the concepts of public space and public spirit. They thought about the origin and purpose of their individual lives in relation to others, to life and death, and to everything in the universe. In that sense, ancient Greek tragedy was one of the earliest signs of mankind's first great reflection.

SECTION 2: SEARCH AND DEVOTION—THE PRE-SOCRATIC PHILOSOPHERS

Ancient Greek philosophy is the first treasure trove of human thought. These philosophers asked so many questions, reaching across such depth and breadth—it was unprecedented. Humans have never before asked questions from such extensive and profound angles. For the nearly 2,700 years since, every great philosophical reflection, including those triggered by human catastrophe, has had to look to its roots in ancient Greek philosophical treasures to inform new methods and paths. Even today, we return to that treasure trove for inspiration.

The questions that ancient Greek philosophy sought to answer stem from the unique destiny and challenges faced by mankind. At their core is the question of *human calling*. That is, how can humans resolve the paradox of the fear of and desire for violence and move along the path of development? Because the Greek city-states were relatively less violent communities than others, the task of philosophical reflection could be entrusted to great thinkers with individual free will for deeper thought and discussion. The ancient Greek philosophical forum that resulted was a colorful and dazzling scene.

Pre-Socratic philosophy began with the Milesian School.[29] Their representatives, Thales, Anaximander, Anaximenes, and Heraclitus asked questions about the essence of the world. The world we see is heterogeneous and ever changing. Everything flows. Nothing is permanent. It's impossible to step into the same river twice. So, they reasoned, there must be a more essential world hidden behind the phenomenal world. What, then, is the essence behind everything? Though their answers did not agree—Thales said water, Anaximander said what he called *apeiron*, or the unbounded, Anaximenes said air, and Heraclitus said fire—they shared the goal of uncovering the common essence behind the phenomenal world. This line of questioning opened the door for the exploration of what truly lies behind the material world. The exploration of the relationship between humans and nature is known as natural philosophy; the exploration of the relationships between humans and society is known as humanistic philosophy[30]. Although the Milesian School shouldered the monumental responsibility of exploring *human calling* in the relationship between humans and society, they put all their focus on finding it in natural philosophy. As a result, much philosophical thinking about the relationship between humans and society has its roots in natural philosophy. In doing so, they presented the grand proposition that the truths governing nature and humanity share the same source. This idea formed the beacon for Western natural law, where the inner logic of human public order and that of natural mechanisms share common origins. Humanity can always look back and admire the historic beacon of pre-Socratic Greek philosophy and be amazed and inspired.

After the Milesian School, the Pythagorean School emerged in southern Greece, around 600 BC. They made further progress on the Milesian school's question of the phenomenal world and its essence. They believed that the phenomenal world contains pairs of opposing essences[31]: odd and even, limited and unlimited, the many and the one, male and female, light and dark, good and evil, etc. The unity holding these opposite essences together is God and the soul. The essence behind the phenomenal world, the human body included, is God and the soul. The universe is the self-realization of God, and the body is the self-realization of the soul. From that perspective, we are all outsiders in this world. The soul is a divine existence imprisoned in the body. The soul itself belongs to eternal rationality, but when combined with the body, it takes part in the non-rational domain. Since the soul can reach divinity through the truth, and virtue also first comes through truth, people should pursue virtue and truth to bring their souls toward divinity. The Pythagoreans tried to abstract mathematics from natural phenomena to explain the common origin of humans, nature, and all things in the universe. Starting from the antithesis between the tangible and the abstract in all things, they also tried to deduce the opposition between the objective body and the intangible soul, as well as the opposition between physical human beings and the invisible God. In the end, they concluded that people should pay attention to the invisible, abstract world and regulate their behavior toward *human calling* based on this world.[32]

Between 500–600 BC, after the Pythagorean School, the Eleatic School emerged.[33] Its famous representatives were Xenophanes and his student Parmenides, Parmenides's student Zeno, and Empedocles, Democritus, and Gorgias. Xenophanes and Parmenides insisted on denying the existence of change, arguing that change is an illusion, and that "there is no non-existence outside existence." They believed that the rational world is true existence, with no beginning and no end and that the sensory world is an illusion of change and does not exist. Rationality, however, exists in the world of thought, consistent throughout the past, present, and future, independent of time and space, and without differences. The differences that we think we sense are illusory.

Beyond what sense can perceive, the deeper essential difference lies in the opposition of light and heat versus darkness and cold. In their thought, God uses love to unite the two opposing essences, and this unity is good. Evil originates from ignorance of the rational existence unified by God and a focus on the illusory changes in the sensory world.

Parmenides[34] warned that people should not be bothered by sensory illusions and should instead search for reason on the path of truth and passion on the path of faith. Zeno founded dialectics with famous paradoxes like "the flying arrow is motionless" and "Achilles and the tortoise" to defend his teacher's philosophical premise that "the one" is God's rational world, and "the many" and "change" are illusions of the phenomenal world. Because he believed that tyranny violated the democracy and justice of the Greek city-states and was an illusion of "the many," Zeno tried to abolish it in surrounding island states. He was later arrested for his attempt to overthrow the tyrant Nearchus. Never compromising on or betraying his political ideals and convictions inherited from Parmenides, Zeno was tortured to death by Nearchus. He became the first ancient Greek philosopher to die for his beliefs.[35] His death aroused the indignation of the island's inhabitants, who eventually killed the tyrant.

After the Eleatic School, the Atomist School, known as the originator of materialism,[36] was formed. Anaxagoras insisted on introducing the concept of Mind (*nous*) into his cosmology. He believed that Mind is the origin of all things and the existence outside of all things. Like Zeus, Mind sits on the supreme throne and is the first mover of all things, and everything is allowed to move by themselves according to it. As for motion, he believed what is denser gathers at the center of the vortex to form all things in their order, while whatever is less dense is thrown to the edge of the universe. Anaxagoras was the first Greek philosopher to be tried and exiled for going against the dominant philosophy of the Greek city-states.[37] The crime was "corrupting the youth."

Empedocles then came on the scene with his poetic philosophy about the elements and the gods. He pointed out that the universe is comprised of four elements, namely fire, air, earth, and water. The births and deaths of all things are merely a change in form, and death is just the beginning of another new life. The four elements are immortal and eternal. What foolish humans observe through their senses is merely the elements' continual process of separating and combining to form all things. Empedocles further posited that the universe has two intrinsic motivations. The first, represented by the goddess Aphrodite, is love, friendship, harmony, passion, and joy; and the second, represented by the god of war, Ares, is hatred, strife, chaos, and abhorrence. The four elements, driven by the power of Aphrodite, combine with each other to form an orderly universe, while hatred and strife drive short-sighted humans, resulting in endless war, change, disorder, birth, and death. Spirits in heaven are bound by the laws of the gods, and humans even more so. If a spirit acts unscrupulously, taking pleasure in killing, he must be expelled from the land of bliss and enter a deceased body to undergo untold suffering. People can purify themselves through cycles of life. Whether they do good or bad deeds determines whether they rise or fall in these cycles. They can go from an ordinary person to a physicist, prophet or king, or from a sinner to a beast or vegetable. Only through obedience and proper action could a person be purified, avoid pain and sorrow, and gain the glory of the gods.

Empedocles took pride in his perfect philosophical logic. Legend has it that he, convinced he had fulfilled his mission as a poetic philosopher, quietly took his leave after treating his friends to a solemn feast and sacrifice, and was never heard from again. Another rumor was that out of a desire to become an immortal god, he solemnly jumped into the volcanic crater of Mount Etna. One of his shoes was thrown out to be left for the restless, ever-changing world full of short lives. Empedocles became the second great Greek philosopher who solemnly pondered the *human calling* and dedicated himself to the absolute truths that he uncovered.[38]

Building on the philosophies of Anaxagoras and Empedocles, Democritus invented the concept of "atoms,"[39] which pushed the elemental theory of the universe to the extreme. In Democritus's view, the rational world that the Eleatic School believed in does not exist. What did exist is the unity of opposites between fullness and the void, and between existence and non-existence. To him, the void is not non-existent, and all things in the world are the results of the motion of what he called atoms in the void.

The differences among things in the phenomenal world are caused by differences in the atoms' traits, sequence, or position—in short, the structural differences in the atoms' motion. In that sense, the fine atomic system is the universe's soul and eternity. The principles of atomic motion stipulate that heavy atoms concentrate toward the center, becoming soil, water, and other earthly materials, while lighter atoms move outward, becoming fire, air, ether, and other substances of the void. A rational world beyond atomic matter, then, does not exist. People can only gain knowledge by observing through their senses all things that are made up of atoms. The way to obtain truth is through reasoning like a philosopher, living in happiness without worry or fear. Democritus believed that human happiness was not gained by feasting or getting rich, but by having a peaceful soul—like atomic philosophers pursuing rationality, beautiful language, and the fulfillment of obligations.

Because of his extreme atomism and materialism, Democritus is considered the father of materialistic philosophy, and his nickname was the "laughing philosopher." In contrast, Heraclitus was known as the "weeping philosopher." The founders and followers of the atomistic school concluded that humans should uphold a public spirit characterized by loving others, opposing killing, purifying moral errors, seeking sound reasoning, and performing their duties. Yet they didn't outline a rigorous logical relationship between its materialistic foundations and this conclusion. They did, however, provide a sufficient philosophical basis for the sophists, who prevailed after them in ancient Greece and emphasized personal feelings and immediate gratification.

SECTION 3: HUMAN ARROGANCE AND THE DEATH OF SOCRATES

The Sophists misinterpreted Democritus's atomic materialism in ways that misled the people. Greek philosophy under their guidance began to quickly secularize. A contributing factor was that during 466—406 BC, Sicily expelled its autocratic tyrant and attempted to establish democracy, which promoted the flourishing of civil debate and oratory. Sophists, who charged fees for teaching oratory, flocked to Athens, the Greek political center in the Age of Pericles. There they engaged in market-based political debate. Amid the spread of the misinterpretations of Democritus's atomic material-ism, the sophists replaced the pre-Socratic philosophers' profound thoughts about *human calling* with more pragmatic thoughts. Protagoras and Gor-gias were typical examples of these secular sophists.[40] In their elaboration of Democritus's atomism, they went too far down the path of individualism and pragmatism, arguing that the truth and the rational world do not exist and that only human sensations are real. They considered individual sensa-tions in the phenomenal world to be independent, irrational, and unrelated. Rational existence, then, is imperceptible—or even if it were perceptible, it would be inexpressible and therefore non-existent. In this view, humans alone are the measure of all things in the world, the measure of all that exists and how it exists, and the measure of all that doesn't exist and how it doesn't exist.

In essence, this Sophistic movement only valued physical individuals and discarded humanity's public personality and spiritual rationality. It was pop-ular, not only because it catered to the individualist trend needed for political democracy of that era, but also because it greatly satisfied society's desire for public speeches that featured more shallow logic. But this market-based sophistic teaching severely damaged the tradition of philosophical contemplation in the pre-Socratic era, filling the whole society with superficial opinions based on personal feelings in oratory competitions—which were based on skill with words rather than logical guidelines.

Of course, the feelings of individuals vary from time to time and from place to place, depending on their psychological differences. Over time, these feelings are subordinated to secular calculations of personal interest, especially in an environment like the ancient Greece of the sophists. When this happens, an individual's public personality is lost. Public reason is lost. Public truth and public order are lost. Mankind becomes an animal possessing only individual personality. Among younger Greeks, the spiritual world had collapsed. Honor, devotion, and the spirit of obeying oaths and pursuing truth were all lost. Ancient Greek philosophy's reflections on *human calling* faced unprecedented challenges. It was against this historical backdrop that the great Socrates burst onto the scene.

Socrates' thought acted as a watershed in Ancient Greek philosophy, which is why most present-day discussions of philosophy start with him. Pre-Socratic thinkers were mainly focused on natural philosophy: What is the origin of all things in the universe? What is the phenomenal world made of? Do the laws of the rational world and truths about a supreme being exist, and if so, how? What can humans learn from such inquiries and how should they affect their public personality and behavior? By contrast, post-Socratic philosophers tended to focus on humanistic philosophy (or to combine it with natural philosophy). They mostly discussed whether there is a higher existence, that is, a soul beyond a human's physical body that lives on after their death: Should humans be dominated or stimulated by this higher existence? Is this supreme existence virtuous? How should humans deal with joy and happiness? How should their public personality be reflected in the community? And what logical methods should be used to discuss problems and pursue absolute truths? Socrates' thought is what catalyzed this shift.

The second reason history considers Socrates so pivotal is that he applied his unique way of thinking and questioning to interpret his deep considerations of humanistic philosophy, reflecting this in the way he personally acted and even in how he died. Socrates made his mark as the first great ancient Greek humanistic philosopher.[41]

Socrates started from the prevailing sophistic thinking of his era, but he didn't begin elaborating his own views or universal truths right away. Instead, he traveled around asking the sophists to debate with him. He brought his sacred virtues and skepticism of sophistic thought to bear on his interlocutors, using constant questioning to corner them. He shocked and disturbed the sophists, provoking them to reflect on universal, public issues that stand behind individual, physical lives. People became aware of how absurd the solely pragmatic and individualistic atomism that the sophists preached truly was.

Socratic thought, in contrast, held that behind each individual's behavior and each workers' technical experience, stand universal laws that are external to and above them, such as justice, beauty, and usefulness. These universal laws exist as ideas that precede human action. They guide it and reflect its deeper values. They serve as the reasons for humans to act in the first place and provide a standard of perfection to measure the results of those actions. The guidance of these pre-existing universal ideas and the reflection on behavior they provoke create a community that's more orderly and more worth living in. People are not, as sophists claimed, individualistic animals that act entirely based on their own feelings with no ability to pursue wisdom or truth and reflect on their behavior. On the contrary, Socrates's question-based inductive reasoning proved that every ordinary person has wisdom and virtue and that this wisdom and virtue exist as the universal supreme being above individual feelings. They are the moral pillars that support the natural world and the rational world. So Socrates famously admonished individuals to "know thyself," and to know the relationship between themselves and the supreme being, achieving their full potential through rationality and self-restraint.

Socrates lived a simple, natural, and almost slovenly or unrestrained life, disregarding others' praise or criticism. But underneath lay a deep public purpose and his commitment to the perfect virtue of *human calling*. He sought out debates and deep conversations with people, regardless of their status or wealth. Through systematic questioning, he awakened people to the importance of contemplation. He encouraged them to reflect on the variety, individuality, and non-universality of their personal feelings, so they could see the hidden virtues of justice, beauty, and usefulness behind them. Through promoting the profound significance of these virtues, which transcend the life or death of any individual, he dismantled the trap of the amoral, extreme individualism spread by the sophists.

His way of life gained him widespread approval and many followers. When Euthydemus, who thought of himself as knowing everything and embodying justice, experienced Socrates' relentless questioning, he concluded, "The only way to be a worthy man is to talk to Socrates as much as possible." With some, though, he was less popular. His unique style of questioning and irony embarrassed many self-righteous and high-ranking people, drawing the ire of interlocutors, the attacks of sophists, and the sarcasm of other writers. Socrates, for his part, did not pay them any attention and kept living the way he wanted.

Socrates demonstrated his philosophy and values throughout his life, and even through his death.[42] He showed that he believed in the supreme, eternal, and universal existence beyond physical life. This existence is essentially made up of absolute truth, divine virtues, and the immortal soul, which are independent of individual feelings. Although his lifestyle from the outside seemed unrestrained, Socrates had a deep respect for moral law and social order. He despised behavior that ignored *human calling* in favor of personal interests. That doesn't mean he didn't value individual freedom. On the contrary, he truly appreciated creative artists and philosophers who transcended existing social codes, even if their creations caused shock among society and drew widespread criticism. These artists and philosophers were often judged and tortured for being mavericks in their times, but the next generation saw them as martyrs and heroes who voluntarily broke the laws in pursuit of the supreme being. For them, truly legitimate behavior, or *human calling*, means "voluntarily becoming a criminal,"[43] or more specifically, sacrificing oneself in pursuit of the supreme being. For them, the real sin was challenging existing laws just to make others suffer. Socrates also had unique views on death. Death, in his view, is the doom of the physical body rather than the complete demise of the human being. The deeper existence—the soul—doesn't necessarily perish, so it's not so terrible to die for the sake of human legitimacy or *human calling*.

His own philosophical reflection and understanding of the truth informed the way he handled the ancient Greeks and led to what is known as the "Trial of Socrates." He refused to be exiled and refused to appear in court for his crime of "corrupting the youth." He even refused to settle with the court. Instead, they were forced to debate Socrates. His questions showed the flaws in their argument, but his arrogant attitude angered the jury of 300, and in the end, he was sentenced to death. Socrates seemed perfectly satisfied with the verdict. He chose to submit himself to the law of his city-state and not resist. He rejected any kind of compromise or appeal. Finally, he burned incense and bathed, talked and laughed with his followers. Then he drank a cup of hemlock with complete composure and bid goodbye to the material world, and its people—always scheming and plotting for their own interests. He devoted his life to showing how it was honorable to voluntarily become a criminal in pursuit of supreme truth. He also sacrificed himself for the beauty of the public order in the human community,[44] with this final dispatch on *human calling*: "a life without thinking is not worth living." Socrates became the second ancient Greek philosopher, after Anaxagoras, to be tried and the third ancient Greek philosopher, after Zeno and Empedocles, to die in pursuit of truth. His life and death mark a historical milestone in Greek humanistic philosophy's reflection on *human calling*.

SECTION 4: PLATO'S HUMAN "CAVE" AND THE BEAUTY OF THE DIVINE

Socrates prevented the moral decline of the Greek city-states. He started a boom of ancient Greek humanistic philosophy. The small and large Socratic schools were born. But the most important thing he gave the world was his outstanding disciple Plato. At age 20, Plato was obsessed with poetry. Socrates' philosophical arguments so inspired and shocked him that he burned his beloved poetry and followed Socrates. This lasted for ten years until Socrates was sentenced in 399 BC, and Plato and other followers went in exile to Megara. Plato gained experience through hardship. Dionysius I of Syracuse almost sold him into slavery, but a friend bought his freedom, and he went back to Athens. There he founded the Academy, based on his philosophy. He spent the rest of his life in discussion with his followers, living until the age of 81. He left a great number of dialogical works in which Socrates is the main participant. The breadth of the contents and depth of the expositions in his works form an unprecedented ancient philosophical encyclopedia. Anyone researching any philosophical question ever since must return to Plato's texts.

Plato believed that the sophists exaggerated the usefulness of individual sensory perceptions of the world. He compared individuals in the material world to a group of cave dwellers chained to the wall for all of their lives whose only view of the outside world is through the shadows projected by the fire onto the cave wall. Their senses mistake these shadows for the world itself. If one of the cave dwellers were to break free and see the outside world, he wouldn't believe his eyes and would think it was a mirage. If someone seeing the outside world came back and told the other captives what he saw, they would laugh or even kill him, because those who have been accustomed to the world of darkness and shadows are afraid of the light and afraid of the truth. He concluded, "the conceptual world exists prior to and is a higher existence than the world of sensation."[45] People gain knowledge of these concepts through sensations. On some level, it's almost as if people must recall or be awakened to their existence. The conceptual world not only exists *a priori* but is also universal and ordered. Sensation is not enough to understand the world—humans need to merge it with higher concepts in order to consider, understand, and name it.

But where does this conceptual world come from? Plato's *Timaeus* affirms that the eternal creator of the conceptual world is God. As God is perfectly good and absolutely free, he created the world based on his desires and ideas, turning the world from formlessness to form, chaos to order, emptiness to existence. Creation is the unity of God's conceptual thought and action. The human body is just a tool for sensations. The opinions people form through sensations disappear with the death of a human's body, but not the concepts of God, like justice, beauty, goodness, and eternal existence. When people embrace these ideas, they participate in the mind of God and gain pleasure from the perfect good. God is this Good,[46] the cause of good, the realization of good, and the perfection of good.

In the *Republic,* Plato goes on to argue that the human body as a tool is only able to produce illusions. The soul, however, has three abilities: appetite, passion, and reason. It's only through the soul's ability to reason that humans can attain true knowledge. The goal of life is what Plato calls the Good. In order to reach the Good, people need to engage the three powers of reason to make the most of the soul's abilities: temperance, courage, and wisdom. In order to promote this reason in society, the city-state must promote education so that the public good is learned and known. It must make laws to guide the public good, and so help individuals to achieve the Good. In such a city-state, craftsmen represent temperance, guardians represent courage, and rulers represent wisdom. Education must cultivate temperance through music, courage through athletics, and wisdom through philosophy. Education must also encourage the pursuit of beauty.

Plato's *Symposium* and *Phaedrus* deeply explore the logic of love and beauty. He held that behind erotic love is a deep drive for immortality. It's natural, then, for humans to long for the beauty they see in another body and to join with it to create a child and so perpetuate their life. Fame is another, more effective means of overcoming mortality, and when people realize this, their efforts are even more extraordinary. For philosophers, fame, or reputation, was considered a more beautiful way to pursue immortality, because they tend to find knowledge more beautiful than the body, and the soul even more so. The conception of the soul is more likely to evoke a sense of eternality. That's why philosophers are more enchanted by the soul's beauty than by the body's beauty. With this in mind, Plato encouraged people to recognize their own erotic desire and lift it to an increasingly higher plane—from the pursuit of a beautiful body to the pursuit of a beautiful lifestyle, then to the pursuit of beautiful knowledge, and finally to the pursuit of beauty itself, the divine, pure, ultimate beauty. For him, "only the most beautiful life is worth living."[47]

In the *Phaedrus,* Plato discussed the premise that the soul exists before the body. Logically speaking, the soul dies after the body, but the soul also exists before the body. For Plato, the "pre-existence of the soul" is proven by the fact that education can awaken people's "memories" of knowledge, but primates aren't capable of such awakening. The soul can unite with reason and so participate in God's thoughts. In this way, humans can reach eternal truth, which allows them to acquire virtue and wisdom that can guide individual behavior.

Plato also held that after death, there is an afterlife. Souls must accept God's judgment, which doles out rewards and punishments according to the good or evil of their actions. It's the responsibility, then, of all human beings, rich or poor, to share in the public spirit, take public responsibility, do good rather than evil, and unite their souls with divine reason.[48] Plato introduced the concept of the soul and God as invisible realities, as opposed to the visible, physical human body. In doing so, he revealed the truth behind the phenomenal world, namely, mankind's latent longing to unite his soul with God. He provided some of the earliest and most philosophical insights into *human calling*, all while facing violent challenges.

Future generations have continually explored the profound meanings of Plato's insights. Those who truly understood their profound philosophical significance came 500–800 years later: Christian theologians Paul, Clement, Origin, Tertullian, and Augustine. They were the first to fruitfully integrate Plato's philosophy into Christian theology, which laid a deep theological foundation for its subsequent flourishing.

SECTION 5: THE HIGH PEAK OF ARISTOTLE'S LOGIC

Aristotle began as Plato's student at age 18, and he followed him for nearly two decades until Plato's death. Plato constrained rather pushed him. Aristotle spent eight years tutoring Alexander the Great, who later led Macedonia to conquer Greece. He had a profound impact on Alexander's brief yet glorious life and founded the Lyceum and its library with his patronage. Aristotle comprehensively, systematically, and completely integrated the different schools of Greek philosophy and pushed it to its peak.

Aristotle believed that thinking is driven by human curiosity and that freedom is the unrestricted ability to do such thinking and so gain the power of true knowledge. He inherited Plato's idea that there is a universal hidden behind all particulars. Yet while Plato held that the universal exists independent of the particulars, Aristotle argued that the universal can only exist in individual things and that the two are in mutual opposition and mutual dependence. Regarding the world that we can see, individual objects comprise the most real and visible existence. That's because each object is the product of the combination of what he called matter and form. Matter is an object's potential, or the cause of an object's purpose; form is the shape of the thing or the cause of its form; the reality of things is made up of the combination of the two—their function or the cause of their effectiveness. Everything has a "material cause," a "formal cause," and an "efficient cause."[49]

Aristotle believed that living beings are different from other objects because they have life—that is, the nutrition-fueled process of birth, change, and death. The soul of a living person is his material cause, the body is his form or formal cause, and his existence is his realization or efficient cause. The soul's function is contemplation, and its form is different from the body's form. The body's form is primarily related to the four elements of earth, air, water, and fire, while the soul is most related to a fifth element, the divine Aether. Humans do not become skillful animals because they have hands. Rather it is the soul's wisdom that allows them to manipulate countless tools and objects skillfully with their hands.

The soul, however, is not something that only humans possess. Plants have a vegetative soul, since they ingest other things while maintaining their distinctness from these things, allowing for infinite self-replication. Animals have a sensory soul, since they sense other things while keeping themselves independent from those things, and they also infinitely self-replicate. Humans have a rational soul, since they perceive other things through thinking while existing independently of them, and they seek reason and holiness.[50] The human soul, then, represents a higher existence.

Aristotle further developed these concepts of the soul. He argued that there's a difference between the human soul and wisdom, because there are various levels of universals among individual beings, like "species," "genus," and "class." For instance, the lowest universal, species, is most closely related to the individual being, and vice versa. That means that higher-order existence contains the lower. The realization of lower-order existence creates the potential for the realization of the higher, and all lower-order existence serves as the preparation for the higher. For example, the human soul both incorporates the reproductive power of the vegetative soul through ingestion, and the sensory power of the animal soul in its ability to stay separate from other beings. This is something that humans, animals, and plants have in common. What differentiates human individuals from each other is the rational mind, and the universal behind it is the pursuit of virtue and wisdom.

The supreme universal is God. God is the eternal, inevitable, and absolute realization. "Time" and "essence," embodied in God, both exist before the individual experience of humans.[51] Thinking that reasons from universals to particulars Aristotle called "deduction" or "reasoning"—for instance, reasoning from the first universal, God, all the way down to specific objects. He termed thinking that begins with individual objects and argues toward the universals of species, genus, class, and finally God, as "induction." For Aristotle, mankind's purpose is to contemplate and reflect on the phenomenal world through induction, ultimately realizing that God is eternally perfect and that his soul is the "sacred soul." This is the key to solving the problems of a lack of public spirit and code of conduct. If people can't orient themselves toward God, they will deviate from law and justice and fall among the most wretched animals, full of greed, evil, and cruelty. God's justice, then, is the yardstick of human politics and the basis for the orderly operation of the human political community.

Aristotle spent a great deal of energy discussing his method of pursuing reason, wisdom, and sacredness—which he called *Logos*. He formed a complete academic system of logic based on deductive and inductive reasoning, laying an unshakable methodological foundation for logical discussion and study of both humanistic philosophy and natural philosophy over the following 2,000-plus years. To this very day, our social and natural sciences can't do without Aristotle. His philosophical methodology[52] is guided by three aspects: classification and definition, dialectical logic, and formal logic. His methods for accurate classification and definition open the door for scientific discoveries as well as technological innovations. He was the first to use dialectical logic to analyze the unification of the opposites of matter and form, bringing to light the law of conflict and unification in all things and providing a way to discover the changes caused by these conflicts. This method has had far-reaching and long-lasting significance. Lastly, he based his formal logic on what he called a syllogism, a three-stage method to reach conclusions with a major premise and minor premise. This method is universally applicable for rigorous deductive and inductive reasoning. It has guided the methodology of thought, exploration, and argument over thousands of years in human history. Built on these the foundations, the natural and humanistic philosophies that began in ancient Greece eventually became today's social and natural sciences.

SECTION 6: THE TWILIGHT OF PRACTICAL PHILOSOPHY

In addition to three great masters of Greek philosophy, it's worth taking a look at the major movements in what's known as practical philosophy, and the ways they reflected on *human calling*. These are the Cynics, the Epicureans, the Stoics, and New Platonism. They are called practical philosophers largely because they were unable to match the depth or systematic and methodological rigor of the three masters—Socrates, Plato, and Aristotle. As a result, their philosophical focus was limited to guiding and shaping practical behavior for *human calling.* From the perspective of human history as a whole, they mark a mere footnote to ancient Greek philosophy.

The Cynic school,[53] founded by Socrates' student Antisthenes and carried forward by his student Diogenes, believed that humans' longing for pleasure is the root of evil. Only the soul's wisdom and virtue are worthy of pursuit, and wisdom and virtue must be attained by abandoning evil, which allows people to achieve independence and freedom. Freedom is the denial of pleasure. The less people ask for, the closer they get to the freedom of the gods. As a result, wise people hone their minds and bodies, downplay the importance of pleasure, and remain independent and free. Common phrases among the Cynics were "I would rather lose my mind than enjoy life," and "I would rather die than live a pleasant life."

Wise, virtuous people are always able to find happiness in suffering, and it's by despising worldly pleasure that they gain true happiness. The Cynics also held that society will improve to the degree that humans behave themselves. They advocated that people return to nature, for only the power that rules over nature is divine. People should also treat politics like fire, keeping it at a safe distance. If people are too enthusiastic about politics, the Cynics said, they'll be burnt by it, but if they go too far and completely ignore politics, they'll end up being crushed by tyranny. That's why when Diogenes was asked which city he belonged to, he answered, "I'm a citizen of the world."

The Epicurean school, represented by Pyrrho, Epicurus, and Lucretius,[54] began with skepticism of the mainstream philosophy of ancient Greeks of the time: rationalism. They rejected the existence of universal laws and a deeper rationality and believed instead that life is like a dream where every experience is merely a human feeling. Mental concepts arise from a feeling of familiarity, and these develop into sentences that finally form judgments. The soul is the primary cause of feeling, and the body is the primary cause of the soul. Both the soul and body are made up of atoms, like everything else in the universe, but some atoms are subtler than others. The gods are immortal because they are made up of the subtlest atoms, and their bodies cannot decay.

For the Epicureans, the purpose of life is to escape suffering and acquire pleasure. Pleasure runs throughout life, so it must be sought continuously. When comparing different kinds of pleasure, the Epicureans formed a typical circular argument: The mind's pleasure, which is stronger than the body's pleasure, comes from memories of the past and expectation of the future. Yet these memories and expectations are rooted in the body, so in the end, humans still need to seek bodily pleasure. Epicureans saw idealism as illusory, if not hypocritical. For an Epicurean, "I would rather die than fool myself." Their thinking was clearly in line with Democritus's atomic materialism and the sophist Gorgias' belief that personal feelings come first. The result is an over-emphasis on pleasure in life and annihilation after death.

The Stoics, represented by Zeno and Chrysippus, also started with skepticism about universal reason and the unknowable. They claimed to only emphasize logic and practical philosophy. This created a contradiction in their philosophical premises. One the one hand, they held that the feelings humans experience are the result of both external stimuli and inner perception. This is how ideas form—as humans age and gain more experience, they first develop their mind and then reach their soul and finally the gods. On the other hand, they believed the world is ruled by "pre-existing ideas" and "philosophical reason." Everything in the universe is a product of God—immortal, the origin and destination of all things—and the material with which God works. These materials include the four elements of fire, air, water, and earth. For the Epicureans, reason permeates every corner of the universe. Yet, these pre-existing ideas and philosophical reason are also material. This kind of circular argument is self-contradictory.

The Stoics believed that good and evil have their origin as opposites. They influence people's happiness, but not the realization of immortal forces, namely universal laws and natural laws. People seek good only for the sake of happiness. In childhood, people gain pleasure only by succumbing to human instincts. As they grow up, they begin to reflect rationally and are enlightened as they learn from just and honorable sages. Finally, through trials and tribulations, they are able to distinguish between good and evil and move toward goodness, justice, bravery, and moderation. The Stoics recognized the reality that bad people achieve what they want while good people experience adversity, but they held that only the latter deserve true wisdom, freedom and happiness. Good people, then, even in adversity, poverty, rags and deep misery, should reject temptation and injustice and seek the ideals of truth and wisdom. By doing so, they will gain peace through their virtues in the end.

The Stoics enjoyed widespread influence, including over the Roman Emperor Marcus Aurelius, who wrote the famous *Meditations*. Horace therefore called the Stoics the "ragged kings."[55] But during the tyranny of the Roman Empire, when free thought was constrained and most of the population was miserable and pessimistic, the Stoics gradually declined, and many of them committed suicide. The Stoics left the world stage on a tragic and solemn note, making way for the agnosticism and skepticism of the philosophers of Neoplatonism.

Representatives of Neoplatonism include Plutarch, Cicero, and Plotinus.[56] While Neoplatonism is a complicated subject, Plotinus, who inaugurated the school in light of the three great masters, will be the focus here, as his thought is most related to the topic of *human calling*. Plotinus was committed to refuting the materialism of the Epicureans and the Stoics through analysis. He argued that materialism could not convincingly account for the subject of knowledge or explain thought and ideas, and that the mind, knowledge, and soul are certainly immaterial.

Plotinus described a series of existences with the metaphor of a ladder. The highest existence is the "One," followed by "heart," "soul," (including the "world soul," "intermediate soul," and "elementary soul") and the "material world." This ladder progresses both upward and downward. The essence of the highest existence, the One, overflows to create the lower existences. Humans are souls trapped in physical bodies, a result of a kind of "corruption," in which the soul is often misled by other material sensations. Plotinus said we should, through striving for knowledge and virtue, free our soul from its bodily shackles and climb the ladder until reaching the heart, joining with the divine One, and finally receiving knowledge and virtue.

The last philosophical school worth mentioning is the Gnosticism[57] that appeared in the twilight of ancient Greek philosophy. It resembled Neoplatonism to a large extent and also explained existence through the metaphor of a ladder, like Plotinus. On its highest rung is the supreme God of Light, followed by the semi-divine intermediate world, below which are elementary forms of existence. Lower beings mistakenly created the material world, opening the door for the darkness of corruption to imprison humanity's semi-divine souls in the flesh of the material world. People need the guidance of Gnostic teachers to build their knowledge and improve their morality. Diet and sexual abstinence are necessary to help the soul break free from the body, enter the spiritual world of the afterlife, and approach the supreme God of Light.

SECTION 7: THE BREADTH OF THE ANCIENT GREEK PHILOSOPHICAL FEAST

From the perspective of *human calling*, it's clear that the great reflections of ancient Greek philosophers were indeed brilliant, rich, deep, and broad. These philosophers expanded the boundaries of thought, exploring the issue of *human calling* from three dimensions. The first dimension was the relationship between humans and nature, that is, the relationship between humans and all other things. The second dimension was the relationship between humans and society, that is, the public relationship between an individual and other individuals. The third dimension was whether these two kinds of relationships, between humans and nature and humans and society, have a common source or destination.

They asked questions like, is there is a common creator, founder, or master? What space-time dimension do people exist in before life and after death? Why do people exist? Why must people die? Why do people need freedom and break laws for the sake of freedom? Why do people pursue both individual freedom and public reason? After all, *human calling* is about how people explain the world they are in, how they explain the way they think, and how they manage this world. It's about how they self-regulate, self-motivate, and self-reinforce their behavior.

The first dimension of questioning led ancient Greek philosophers to ask many questions and attempt to answer them. First, what are all things made of? Ancient Greek philosophers' attempts at answers included: water, fire, air, earth, Aether, numbers, tiny and indivisible atoms, and so on.

Next, how do all things exist? What is the truth behind all things? Ancient Greek philosophers offered answers like: all things exist in forms that can be sensed by humans; all things exist as the combination of matter and form, possessing a material cause that humans can't feel but can think about; and only existence that's invisible truly exists. In other words, the truth of all things can be felt; the truth of all things cannot be felt but can be thought of; or the truth of all things is found in the inner soul or spirit.

Ancient Greek philosophers also asked: Is there an order that encompasses all things? Is this order beautiful? They offered these conclusions: all things exist in ever-changing chaos, and this disorder and impermanence causes suffering; all things are generated by human feelings and used by humans, so only particulars exist and there is no universality or order; and all things are divided between a visible, phenomenal world that's ever-changing, differentiated, and chaotic, and an invisible rational world that's stable, orderly, and regular, and demonstrates a supreme beauty.

Finally, they posed the question of what relationship people have with the natural world that encompasses all things. Can people find *human calling* in their relationship with this natural world? Ancient Greek philosophers' attempts at answers include that people, though part of the natural universe, are different from other things because they possess advanced souls and minds. People can think and reason. As reason is rooted in the order of the world and existed before the material world, people should seek an ordered, lawful, beautiful, and rational life.

The second dimension of reflection led to many questions and answers. For instance, are people particular or universal? Do they share universal reason? Do good, reason, and virtue truly exist? What is the meaning and purpose of life? Should people deal with life through their feelings or thoughts? What do the public rationality of state and community imply? What is the relationship between the common rationality and order of these entities? How should people interact with others? Should a human society be orderly? What is the relationship between the order of the natural world and the order of the human society? Should people seek reason and virtue? Ancient Greek philosophers gave free reign to their ability to imagine, argue, and reason, producing a wealth of texts that reach a variety of conclusions.

Some held that only individuals and human feeling exist, and there is no universal reason or public reason; but the majority believed that individual feelings are superficial, and that behind them exist a deep, universal commonality—mankind's universal reason and virtue. This commonality produces order and makes human life worth living and its beauty worth pursuing. They said that people should transcend the fog of the phenomenal world and through the power of thought discover and gain insight into the public rationality behind this world. Humans, they said, should seek virtue, be good to others, carry out public responsibilities, maintain the public order and public spirit of the community or state, and realize the beauty of public virtue and order.

The third dimension of inquiry touched on the ultimate issues of life and death. Ancient Greek philosophers believed that the natural world that's free of human beings, and the world that is the community of human individuals, are connected through a common origin. At the same time, they are both heading toward a common future. The two worlds are only temporarily in different physical forms. By defining time in this way, people created a uniquely human dualistic world. The phenomenal world can be perceived by humans, while the spiritual world, existing before life and after death, only the soul can grasp. Such definitions also led to the conception of the physical and spiritual dimensions of life in the present time.

Most ancient Greek philosophers, whether or not they were supporters of atomism (which came to be known as the origin of materialism, or Platonism, which came to be known as the beginning of idealism) believed in the ladder of existence. Lower-order existences, like feeling and experience, serve as a basis for the higher ones, like concepts, soul, heart, and God. As the higher-order existences all contain the lower ones, so all things have the tendency to approach the highest, eternal God. Atoms are nothing more than the material used by Eros to make humans. Meanwhile, some philosophers held that God created humanity and all things, which is why the natural order and human reason exist. Although the physical body must die, the soul is immortal and reincarnates. God rewards and punishes people for their good and evil actions and determines whether their soul rises or falls as it reincarnates. These discussions about life and the afterlife laid a solid foundation for the theology that came afterward, especially for the notion of natural law that humans and nature are subject to common laws and rules created by God.

Based on the above three dimensions of philosophical discussions, the ancient Greeks brought up a fourth discussion: methodologies for philosophical research, evidence, debate, and argumentation. These include the definition of a concept or idea; the classification method of species, genus, class, and higher and lower orders; calculation and expressions of mathematics and physics; the three-stage formal logical method of inductive and deductive reasoning; dialectics of the unity of opposites; and many more. These methods have had, up to the present day, an extraordinary and profound impact on both the unleashing and regulation of individual imaginations and on the collective accumulation of their results. They've especially influenced the ability of individuals to question, analyze, debate, and reach consensus in relationship with humans and society.

CHAPTER 4:

Joining the conversation: China's philosophical awakening: Pre-Qin Philosophers

SECTION 1: THE ZHOU DYNASTY *FENGJIAN* FEUDAL SYSTEM: THE DECLINE OF MONARCHY AND THE RISE OF VASSAL STATES

China's first philosophical awakening to address the question of *human calling* began between 500 and 600 BC with the backdrop of a weakening empire. After 400 years of dominance, the ruling Zhou Dynasty was in decline. The Zhou Dynasty had a storied history going back to 1047 BC, when the leader of the vassal state of Zhou, Wu of Zhou, raised an alliance to overthrow the ruthless and dissolute final emperor of the Shang Dynasty.

The rebel leader Wu found popular legitimacy in a profound philosophical concept proposed by his father, the late King Wen of Zhou who ruled the vassal state of Zhou under the Shang emperor[58]: the Mandate of Heaven. The Mandate of Heaven is the idea that Heaven gives an emperor the right to rule the world. The emperor, in turn, gives that power to the ministers and princes, who govern the people. For his part, the emperor must cultivate a government that cares for the people and maintains order so citizens can enjoy prosperity. If an emperor doesn't obey the will of heaven—and is cruel instead of benevolent, causing chaos and suffering for the people—the mandate is considered rescinded. In this case, it's only right for new leaders to rise and overthrow the emperor, reasserting the will of both the people and Heaven.

This was a major departure from the 500-year-old political philosophy of the Shang Dynasty, which maintained that while the power of the emperor comes from Heaven, the people must worship and sacrifice for him. The Zhou Dynasty thus introduced the first political philosophy in the world that asserted that Heaven endowed people with certain rights that need to be respected, and if not, they had the additional right to rise up and replace their ruler.[59] Wu clung to this philosophy when he finally defeated the last, tyrannical emperor of the Shang Dynasty and established the Zhou Dynasty, with himself as the new emperor.

This marked a change in social organization. Emperor Wu of Zhou's younger brother, the Duke of Zhou, developed a system of rituals and music, transforming the old Shang practices into a complex ceremonial order that regulated hierarchy and established an incredibly detailed code of conduct. This form of behavioral ethics and spiritual guidance placed people in their roles in the hierarchy. For example, a person's status was determined by the amount of land they earned through valor in combat against the Shang, for which they might have been awarded a manor and a rank.

This political philosophy enabled the Zhou to create a civilized order with internal and external peace that endured for 400 years, the first half of the Zhou

Dynasty, also known as the Western Zhou (1045–771 BC). These centuries of Zhou rule were the peak of feudalism in China. While today many people label all Chinese history before the twentieth century as "feudalism," this isn't accurate; the feudal phase was far in our ancient past.

China was the earliest nation to adopt the granting of land as a military incentive. There are fundamental differences between the Zhou Dynasty's *Fengjian* feudal system and the feudalism of Western Europe and Japan that came about 2,000 years later. First, the granting of land was not based on an explicit social contract, so after monarchs divided the land, they no longer maintained ownership by statute. This meant the vassals of the monarch were not legally obligated to remain loyal, like they were in Europe. Also, the power of the state to tax and draw military power from the land implicitly transferred to the vassals. Over time the unspoken obligations of loyalty were swept away, because there were no contracts and because the vassal believed the land to be a deserved reward instead of a gift forever dependent on the goodwill of the emperor. Meanwhile, the implicit transfer of tax revenue and military power to the vassals led to the slow decline of the emperor. This *Fengjian* feudal system of imbalanced power and obligations soon turned vassals and emperors within the empire into political rivals. This, in turn, incentivized the emperor's close officials and relatives to become vassals.

In that sense, the Zhou practiced *Fengjian* rather than feudalism. This system slowly destroyed the Zhou empire through constant division into smaller vassal states. Their relationship was based on a zero-sum game of weakness and strength. All that remained was the weak moral and ethical bond expressed through shared customs of ritual and music. Political power was permanently lost to the vassals. The Emperor of Zhou was emperor in name only, the one with the highest rank within the ritual system and the only one with the exclusive right to perform the most sacred ritual of sacrificing to Heaven. Once all the land had been divided, there were more than

300 vassal states, and the emperor of the Zhou became nothing more than a ceremonial figure.[60]

Meanwhile, the vassals inherited a culture of violence and luxury from the emperor of Zhou. They were cruel and extravagant, killing and conquering each other with the aim of ruling the whole empire. This led to the collapse of the ritual system that had allowed for 300 years of prosperity.

The turning point occurred in 771 BC, when Emperor You of Zhou, the 12th Zhou Emperor, was attacked from the northwest by Quanrong nomads, an ethnic group that resided on the fringes of the empire. Emperor You, the last emperor of Western Zhou, was killed. This marked the beginning of 500 years of decline of the Chinese *Fengjian* system. China entered the Spring and Autumn and Warring States period, where vassal states fought in the absence of centralizing imperial power. This period is also known as the Eastern Zhou (770–256 BC), the second half of the dynasty. The collapse of the social order and the battles for control of the land in the Eastern Zhou were two major triggers for China's first great philosophical awakening. This was when China joined in humanity's quest for *human calling*.

SECTION 2: CONFUCIUS AND MENCIUS: LOOKING TO THE PAST FOR ORDER

Confucius was born in 551 BC in the vassal state of Lu during the turbulent Eastern Zhou Dynasty. His philosophy sought to address the suffering and pain caused by violent confrontation between the various states as they vied for dominance. He looked back to the beautiful ritual order of the earlier Western Zhou Dynasty and hoped to reestablish it. Confucius's philosophy, unlike his Greek contemporaries, Pythagoras and Elias, was based on solving a practical problem, rather than on metaphysical abstractions arrived at in solemn philosophical halls. Confucius held King Wen of Zhou's political philosophy on the Mandate of Heaven in the highest regard. He considered the mandate and the respect for Heaven and love for one's people it required of the monarch to be perfect. The Duke of Zhou, the chief administrator of the Zhou Dynasty, used this idea as the basis of his ritual system. For this reason, Confucius maintained that his followers didn't need to reinvent the wheel, simply restore the Zhou rites and start regulating their own behavior accordingly and behaving in a "restrained and courteous" way would be enough.

What, then, is the core of the Zhou rites? It is the "honorable and orderly" relationship between people.[61] Specifically, this means the relationships between the ruler and subject, father and child, husband and wife, and older brother and younger brother. From top to bottom, the hierarchy is one of respect shown to the ruler, father, husband, and older brother by the subject, child, wife, and younger brother. This order is built then around the two core organizations of the country and the family.

In the ancient China of the Zhou Dynasty, the subject must obey the ruler in the same way a child must be loyal and subordinate to the father. Similarly, the wife must obey and be loyal to the husband, and the younger brother must obey and be loyal to the older brother. These interpersonal relationships form a benevolent order that is the core of the ritual system. Rituals encompass a set of behavioral and etiquette norms that are comparable between each individual's role as a member of a family and the role of a government official in the state. These were codified in *The Book of Rites*, a manual of psychological and behavioral prescriptions for each person's role in society. For everyone in society, *The Book of Rites* assigns etiquette, attitude, clothing, sitting posture, standing posture, walking posture, housing, rites for birth, marriage, death, divorce, grieving, and the prescribed words for celebrations and ceremonies of important events. With thousands of stipulations, the book prescribes a detailed and complex way of life. A specific piece of music was prescribed for each celebration or sacrifice an individual may perform, based on his role in the social hierarchy. Performing these rituals cultivated and reinforced society's psychological expectations for each person.

So how could individuals find meaning in life, while still practicing self-control and reverence for ritual and following complex and tedious protocols? Confucius neither asked nor answered this question. But he seemed to intuit the tension and advocated education as a solution. Who should educate? Confucians. Who are Confucians? People like Confucius. So Confucius gave himself and his followers a unique social role: to look after the world and community and lead by example. The group was dedicated to convincing the kings of the vassal states to restore the beautiful ritual order of the Zhou Dynasty.

Confucius led his disciples for two decades, journeying from state to state to promote his "Confucian" theory and dogmatic order to persuade the kings to put his ideas into practice and teach the people to return to the beautiful society of the early Zhou as he imagined it. But he failed miserably. Ideals are beautiful. But reality is cruel and complicated. Frustrated, Confucius returned home and organized his philosophy into writing. He critiqued the range of extravagant, immoral behavior of the kings of the various vassal states. His legacy to the world is *The Four Books and the Five Classics*. In 479 BC, he departed what for him was an absurd, disappointing world at the age of 72. Perhaps he was worshiped as a sage just because he failed all his life.[62]

One may wonder how one could become a good Confucian. Confucius answered this best with his example and his works, *The Analects*, *Great Learning*, *Doctrine of the Mean*, *Book of Rites* and *Book of Documents*. They explain the eights steps of self-cultivation: investigation, dedication to learning, orienting the heart, sincere speech, proper conduct, ordering the family, governing the nation, and seeking a peaceful world. With this foundation, people could correct their conduct. Proper conduct followed the golden rule of "do unto others as you would have done to you." A person could manage their family by this rule, and even apply that experience to ruling the country, finally realizing an ideal world and political order. An ideal Confucian was neither humble nor overbearing, was ambitious, had good manners and a knowledge of music, and was ready at any time to be called on by the court to practice politics, yet without ever betraying their principles. Confucius laid out their self-cultivation by the decade in *The Analects*, referring to his own path: "At fifteen, I had my mind bent on learning. At thirty, I stood firm. At forty, I had no doubts. At fifty, I knew the decrees of Heaven. At sixty, my ear was an obedient organ for the reception of truth. At seventy, I could follow what my heart desired, without transgressing what was right."[63] Such a person would be a role model for rulers and subjects alike, teaching them to return to the benevolent order that brought about peace and prosperity.

Mencius was Confucius' disciple who further elaborated on and disseminated his master's philosophy. He was widely recognized as Confucius's most outstanding student, but he was born 180 years after Confucius in 372 BC. Mencius resurrected Confucianism, which had fallen into obscurity. His discourse enriched and perfected Confucian doctrine. He dedicated his life to once again calling on the various vassal states to implement the social order Confucius advocated. Thus Confucian philosophy became "the way of Confucius and Mencius."

Mencius's greatest contribution to Confucian philosophy was the idea of "benevolent government and love of the people."[64] In discussing the premise of the king's supremacy, he argued against blind loyalty. He thought the people should be considered heavy and the ruler light. As long as the king values the interests of the people and treats them benevolently, this legitimates his mandate, because Heaven's voice comes from the voice of the people, and Heaven's will comes from the will of the people. He inferred that the essence of benevolent government is "loving the people like his own children." If the king doesn't love the people, he isn't practicing benevolent government. The ministers under him have the right to reproach him and persuade him to become benevolent. If repeated attempts are unsuccessful, they can overthrow him and replace him with a wise, virtuous king with a caring heart. Overthrowing such a monarch is not unethical regicide, but an ordained execution in line with Heaven's will. As weak and unpersuasive as this logic is, such argument is still striking.

Mencius also developed Confucius's views on education. According to Mencius, those who work with their minds govern, while those who work with their hands are governed. The purpose of education is to teach laborers their role in relation to others. These interpersonal relationships at the core of Confucian ethics are set by heaven and brought about by gentleman Confucian scholars who live by the eight steps of self-cultivation. They are the ones to support the ritual order. In their altruistic dedication to persuading kings to adopt Confucian principles, they should not hesitate to sacrifice their lives to provide the right guidance. Their noble character and canniness would make them role models for the people.[65]

Mencius firmly opposed the Yang Zhu School, which advocated the philosophy of every man for himself, whatever the cost. He also disagreed with Mozi's theory that there was constant divine guidance to human actions. Mozi posited that lust and emotion hindered mankind from conforming with Heaven's will. Mohists sought to cultivate a heart of universal love and act on Heaven's behalf to implement rewards and punishments, in order to uphold order and justice.

Mencius believed human nature is inherently good and compassionate, but that the world is fragmented, ever-changing, chaotic, complicated, and unpredictable. There is no fixed abstraction of Goodness for mankind to follow—rather performing specific daily behaviors is the way to find it. Following one's heart, responding to specific situations, cultivating character, and developing rituals based on simple actions can prevent humans from devolving into self-interest and can instead promote the ideal personality of the altruistic Confucian.

This ideal personality is rooted in the speech and practice of sages like King Wen of Zhou, the Duke of Zhou, Confucius, and Mencius. They are the models of Confucian praxis, extraordinary embodiments of the ritual order, regardless of their social roles as king, minister, or civilian. Without them, society would have lost its moral compass.

Mencius said that the essence of kingship is to protect the people, and only those who protect the people are kings. To do this, it was necessary to control the people's property, and only when the people felt that property was fairly administered, could they have peace of mind. A ruler needed to fully understand the saying, "Heaven's time is not as important as favorable geography, and favorable geography is not as important as human harmony." In domestic affairs, a government should love the people diligently, temperately and modestly, and place them first; in foreign affairs, a government should respect the Zhou rites, seek harmony with other states, and thereby restore the ritual order of the Zhou Dynasty. Mencius also proposed an ideal social unit of a "Jingtian system," in which households in groups of eight enclose common land and cultivate it together to pay taxes to the state.

Mencius was the earliest to raise the persistent conundrum of how to regulate the behavior of kings, but his arguments contained major inconsistencies. In his view, all who labor to make difficult decisions, including kings, could be unethical and inhumane. They required oversight from others so they may be corrected or even replaced; yet, most of those who could hold them accountable as the "people's eyes and ears" were laborers, who work with their hands. They were relegated to an inferior role as defined by Confucian philosophy. So how could they channel the power of oversight to correct the king? Did this mean that Mencius advocated killing the king through insurrection? He acknowledged neither the selfishness of man, nor the Mohist position that the loving and peaceful Heaven's will existed above the king, so how could he explain the king's failure to be virtuous and benevolent? If even the king could fail as such, how could the Confucian maintain his virtuous character and become society's benchmark for morality? If people have no self-interest, why do they only have a sense of equilibrium when they can measure their output? These contradictions were largely responsible for the logical incoherence and hypocrisy of Confucianism, which gained increasing influence in political discourse over the next two millennia.

Mencius' life journey largely followed the example of Confucius. He spent two decades living the courageous life of the traveling sage, exerting all of his mental and physical effort to persuade regimes to turn from their extravagant and arrogant "way of tyrants" and to instead follow "the way of kings."[66] His call to action was beautiful but had little effect on his contemporaries. Just like his master, Confucius, who was wounded by his run-in with reality, Mencius grew disillusioned in his 60s. After he exhausted his desire to travel around persuading princes and kings to adopt the characteristics of his ideal king, leaving later generations with countless classic dialogues of rejection and persistence and unending tales of reasoning and wisdom, he disappeared from public life and returned to his hometown to write a book. His seven chapters of *Mencius* enriched and developed the doctrine of Confucius and formed "the Way of Confucius and Mencius." In 289 BC, at the age of 83, he grudgingly left behind a chaotic world that defied his Confucian political ideals.

Confucius and Mencius's theory was not one based on systematic philosophical discussion and debate. Most of it consists of summaries and commentaries on life practices. It's full of aphorisms and beautiful language, food for thought and rumination. Their ritual prescriptions number in the thousands and are detailed and cumbersome enough to give modern people a splitting headache. At the time these were solemn, ceremonial, purposeful acts to bring order to a chaotic society. Their understanding of ritual was beautiful and mysterious, arousing hope and resonating in the spirit. The question of why people needed this particular interpersonal order, as opposed to a different one, was never raised and so never explored. As a result, competing philosophers Laozi and Zhuangzi saw Confucianism as lacking reason and logic and without practical value.

Xunzi, who lived between 298—238 BC, was a key figure in developing Confucius and Mencius's practical philosophical system. He made his greatest contribution to Confucian philosophy by discussing human nature and turning the fragmented, backward-looking Confucian philosophy into a rational logical system. This allowed Confucianism to influence future generations. It became not only a religious, ritual practice but a system worthy of discussion in the annals of philosophy. Although he was never recognized by the mainstream Confucian culture of imperial power, he laid the theoretical foundation for the continued practice of Confucian philosophy.

Xunzi disagreed with Mencius's core belief that human nature is inherently good. He believed human beings are born evil and are often petty, and the good are merely faking it.[67] Goodness is not an inevitable seed nature plants in people. On the contrary, people must fight for position and survival, which inevitably hurts others, so human nature is evil. Because human nature is evil, it can't be trusted, and therefore the ritual order is needed to regulate and enlighten it. Xunzi saw ritual as more than just customary rules and superstitious religious practices—it was the embodiment of the principle that people are the foundation of benevolent government. The ritual at the core of benevolent government was like a carving knife that shaped evil human nature into a well-mannered and benevolent one. If ritual lost its benevolent core, it became a blunt axe, only able to chop the wood of human nature into something uglier. A ruler with benevolent government at his core, then, must be oriented towards his people and enrich them in order to be in line with the way and righteousness. The essence of the ritual order was to make distinctions between people in society, and distinctions mean inequality. But in a hierarchy based on benevolent government, each person heeds ritual distinctions in order to enrich the life of the community.

Based on the philosophical premise that human nature is evil, Xunzi believed that the social order recommended by Confucius and Mencius (ruler-minister, father-child, husband-wife, older brother-younger brother), couldn't be considered absolute. He believed it should be adjusted in certain cases. Although loyalty to one's ruler is essential and loyalty to one's father is "filial piety," a person should never exercise "blind loyalty" or "foolish piety." The way and righteousness should weigh heavily in analysis and consideration. If the way and righteousness behind loyalty and filial piety are violated, that loyalty and filial piety should be abandoned in favor of righteousness and the way. Therefore, "following the way not the ruler, following righteousness not the father, is the humane path."

Xunzi's discussion of relationships that transcend blood and his loyal duty to "the way" and "righteousness"[68] solidified the Confucian foundation of "benevolence and compassion" and "respect and humility." Confucius and Mencius's expectations for fulfilling *human duty* in that era regarding loyalty and piety were based on the way and righteousness. Xunzi was the only Confucian scholar of his time who touched upon unseen universals and absolute truths, and his deep-rooted and logically consistent exposition greatly enhanced the theoretical depth of Confucianism. He rooted its hierarchical doctrine, which relied on historical, redundant rituals, in the philosophical premise that human nature is evil.

He made Confucianism a philosophy worthy of discussion in the classroom. Of course, his focus was still on a set of ethical and practical practices, a kind of guide for human behavior in daily life. This guide was in line with the *human duty* that was imposed from the outside by the public and still lacked a divine source of sanctity and authority.

SECTION 3: LAOZI AND ZHUANGZI: DAOISM AND THE BEAUTY OF MORALITY

There is no known date for Laozi's birth, because after giving the *Daodejing* to Yinxi at the northwestern border, he disappeared from the pages of history. We know that while he was working in the Zhou Dynasty archives, he met and spoke with Confucius, who was visiting Luoyi (now Luoyang), the capital of Zhou.

Apart from the above, there are no records of his writings or life. In that sense he was the archetypal elusive sage. Laozi's philosophy is mostly contained in the *Daodejing*, which gives us a gateway to understanding the chaotic, disordered world of the Spring and Autumn Period and the fall of the Eastern Zhou Dynasty. The *Daodejing* is the world's shortest and most profound philosophical treatise. It stands at just 5,000 words, divided into 81 chapters. The first 37 explain *dao*, "the way." The latter 44 explain *de*, "virtue." Together *dao* and *de* mean "morality," so it could be called "the book of morality" or "the book of morals."[69] It is the most apt and direct response to the first philosophical awakening on the question of *human calling*.

Laozi believed that everything we can see, perceive, and name is merely on the surface of the world of phenomena, or sensory world. None of it is the true reality, which is hidden, but even less knowable is the *dao* within, that governs change in the phenomenal world. This deeper *dao* is unspeakably mysterious. Most people cannot understand it. Only sages can imagine, understand, and follow it. Because this *dao* is the ultimate ruling force of the phenomenal world, nothingness and chaos are born from it. All things in heaven and earth are in turn born from nothingness and chaos. *Dao* is the source of all. Everything that is born and grows must die. After death it returns to *dao*, so *dao* is also the end of all things. Although all things are born and die, *dao* is eternal. It neither increase or decreases, neither lives nor dies.

Though we can't see *dao* itself, we can try to understand it through observing the law of the unity of opposites in the world of phenomena. The essence of this law is that everything that can be named consists of two opposing forces that correspond to and transform one another—life and death, beauty and ugliness, good and evil, difficulty and ease, weakness and strength, tall and short, many and one, movement and stillness, illusion and reality, presence and absence. If it weren't for the connection between life and death, we would understand neither. Life and death transform each other. Plants die in winter but contain the seeds of spring that flourish and die themselves. Other related concepts are united and transformed. The force that causes this change is the *dao* hidden under both opposites. Heaven and earth give birth to all things, not because they are kind and not because of their own purpose, but because of the underlying *dao*.

Precisely because heaven and earth don't have their own purpose and only follow *dao,* it is everlasting. *Dao* sounds illusory to most, or even empty. But in fact, it is everywhere, in the beginning, at the end—all the world's things come from *dao*. But at the same time, *dao* is not far from the perceptible world of phenomena. The opposite is true: it fills heaven and earth, initiating the flow of all things, as the cause of all change, the source of all the world's motion. As a result, we can know it and follow it through feeling and deep reflection.

Laozi believed sages were moral examples, because they do not have their own independent morality or virtue. Their morality is to follow *dao*[70]—to align themselves with it and certainly not be tempted by the material, phenomenal world. Nothing in the phenomenal world is anything like the deep, peaceful, and empty *dao*. Creatures in that world compete to flourish. People have bodies, so they have a sensitive sensory system able to feel the energy and deep attraction of all things, and they think this is what they must seek in life. This causes all kinds of desires and self-interest, struggles and fights, which bring about chaos in society and waste along the way. This is a mistake, according to Laozi. Material things are not worth spending one's life to gain, because even strong things break. Even thriving things die, fragrant things confuse, beautiful things harm, and precious treasures motivate greed and crime. Only *dao* is worth seeking, because it can bring a peaceful, self-sufficient life, natural, long-lasting happiness, and wisdom.

Because of his views, Laozi's idea of morality is completely unlike Confucius's, as well as the definition of morality today. Both versions of morality consist of ethical norms or *human duty* prescribing how human beings ought to treat others in society. Laozi's morality, on the other hand, was about how people should recognize the *dao* beneath the surface of societal machinations and align one's virtue with it, his version of *human calling*. Laozi's virtue of following the way in alignment with *human calling* included his vision of an ordered society that is one with Heaven. While yearning for this beautiful order, people follow the laws of the earth, the earth follows the laws of heaven, heaven follows the laws of *dao*, and *dao* follows the laws of nature.

How, then, does one pursue virtue according to Laozi? First, one must contemplate the *dao*, understand the *dao*, then thoroughly follow and obey the *dao*. By revering the *dao* and ignoring human desires, a person can understand and obey the *dao* and become brave and fearless. When obeying the *dao*, one must consider others before oneself. This allows them to be "behind the body and yet before the body, and outside the body yet present in the body." Obeying the *dao* means not overvaluing power, but rather seeing it as a sacred tool that should not be sought lightly, or it will lead to disaster. Obeying the *dao* means shunning militancy and violence, seeing military force as an ominous weapon, which brings remorse to even the victor when used. It means indifference to ambition, a calm heart, rejecting insatiable greed, and putting service first—that's the true *dao*. Obeying the *dao* means practicing a kind of "non-action" in quiet indifference that is, in fact, "considered action" that complies with the inner logic of the *dao* and allows life to unfold. Obeying the *dao* is to show weakness instead of strength. It's to learn from water, which bears its oppression and humiliation with endurance. It means letting morality flow and unite with the *dao* to become a flexible force that changes the world.[71] Obeying the *dao* means deep, careful thinking. Great knowledge looks foolish, and great discernment may appear slow. Great wisdom looks awkward and is deliberately insignificant. It means to avoid flowery, clever rhetoric. It means regulation and discipline. This is what allows one to truly grasp the logic of the *dao* and form a perfect moral order.

Laozi believed that those who manage the country must acquire the sage's ability to grasp the *dao*. First, they must let go of their own heart and instead take on the people's heart as their own; next they must obey the *dao*, preferably governing through non-action and avoiding reckless rule. Furthermore, they must be magnanimous and tolerant, humble and obedient, submissive to Heaven. Finally they must cultivate their own virtue, modeling Heaven: "I act not, and the people self-cultivate; I am silent, and the people are upright; I meddle not, and the people are rich; I desire not, and the people are content."

Laozi warned rulers to govern their states without deception, without smoke and mirrors, and without violence; to use the *dao*, the proper *dao*, is "to govern the country, rarely using its soldiers, and taking nothing from the world." Otherwise, as the saying goes, "when earth follows the *dao*, horses give manure; when the world ignores the *dao*, horses are used for war." In other words, if the ruler loses the way, horses used for farming will become war horses and be used to overthrow him. Because of this, government officials should study the philosophies of the great sages, use virtue to nurture the world of things born from *dao*, set an example for all people, and encourage them to live simply and plainly, purely and honestly, in a harmonious order in a world at peace. This is the "Way of the Sovereign," or the "Sacred Way"[72] that Laozi advocated.

Laozi believed that Confucius and the Confucians' rules and regulations lacked logical wisdom and had no practical use. Only because the great *dao* was abandoned did they speak of "benevolent righteousness;" only because families were in conflict did they speak of "filial piety;" only because the ruler lost the *dao* did they speak of "loyal ministers." What use did the Zhou ceremonies and rituals have? Wasn't the decline of the Zhou Dynasty and the increasing wars among vassal states during the Spring and Autumn Warring States Period proof that the rituals were useless? What would Confucians bringing the old precepts back accomplish? Apart from exhorting them toward the sacred *dao*, Laozi neither asked nor answered how the *dao* could be made available to the rulers in authority, including those who were far from it. Perhaps his invisible *dao* itself, full of divine power, would punish such rulers in the course of time, and perhaps this was the answer of Laozi.

Zhuangzi lived from 369–287 BC, a contemporary to Mencius. He built on the moral philosophy of Laozi, forming the philosophy of Daoism. At the same time, Zhuangzi didn't leave a text as compact as the 5,000-word *Daodejing*. He left behind ten collections of fables, dialogues, and poetry, amounting to over 100,000 words. Whether as literature or as philosophy, they represent one of the crowning achievements of humanity's first great philosophical awakening. His thought was profound, systematic, grand, and elegant. It was written poetically like the work of the ancient Greek Empedocles and had a far-reaching, deep impact on future generations.

Zhuangzi's thought was firmly rooted in Laozi's basic theoretical framework, which he further developed. He believed *dao* exists *a priori*. It exists even before nothingness. It is the source of all things in heaven and earth.[73] It stretches endlessly and eternally into the past and future; it stretches inexhaustibly in all directions of space. *Dao* generates all things and makes all things perish. It is the starting point and destination of all tangible things.

Zhuangzi believed the world of phenomena which we observe exists in an endless cycle of birth and death. So the various opposites, such as large and small, many and few, long and short, far and near, beautiful and ugly, good and evil, cold and hot, rich and poor, are all related. All distinctions are relative and negligible. Mount Tai may be very small. The thinnest hair may be very large. Children who die may have lived a very long life, while Peng Zu, the legendary Daoist saint of longevity, may have died young at 800 years. Beyond large things are larger things. Within small things are still smaller things. It all depends on the position and relationship between the things compared. The legendary giant roc, the *Peng,* spreads its wings 90,000 miles and flies through the clouds between heaven and earth, so how can a mantis among flowers know the heights of heaven and earth? The phoenix roams in the deep blue sky, picking only walnuts to eat and plane trees to rest on walnuts, so how would the lowly, mud-caked pigeon know to shun carrion? Bacteria does not know the phases of the moon; cicadas are ignorant of the changes of the seasons. There is only the *dao* which is common to all, that makes everything one, or puts everything on the same path.[74]

Of course, Zhuangzi's *dao* had richer layers. Apart from transcending time and space and being the origin of all things, the *dao* also hides within the rules and laws that connect and change all things. It drives the continuity and change in the cycle of life and death. It dominates the rhythm of change in the universe. It doesn't distinguish between good and evil, rich and poor — there is no difference between them. It does not conform to anyone's preferences.

In addition, the *dao* also contains the wisdom attained through mastering daily life and work, especially in perfecting a craft. An example is the *dao* of a butcher when he uses his knife to carve. This *dao* allows one to feel most oneself, and also "one with Heaven." Zhuangzi spent many pages explaining the *dao* of human life. Since people are born from *dao* and return to *dao* after death, life is fleeting. The time before and after life is longer. Death is necessary, but death doesn't mean disappearing completely. It means a natural change of form and the beginning of a new life, joining with the *dao* behind all change.

In his philosophy of *dao*, Zhuangzi maintained and expanded Laozi's theories of morality and non-action. Zhuangzi insisted that one can attain virtue and wisdom through following *dao*, observing *dao*, experiencing *dao*, and thus recognizing the inaction of *dao*, which then leads to fully obeying it and becoming a sage who truly understands and practices morality, authenticity, and wisdom.[75]

To attain this morality, a person should first stop overemphasizing the "self" and the habit of thinking about and calculating its interests. This allows for one's "pure self" be revealed and gives it free reign to think for itself. When thought is released from the "self" and allowed free reign, the true self can experience the *dao's* boundlessness in space and eternity in time and feel its majestic power.

Next, a person should treat social distinctions according to the *dao*. It flows with its own internal laws and unites all things without dividing between high and low, good and evil, cheap or expensive. According to Zhuangzi, the Confucian distinctions between people that made up a social hierarchy are the result of Confucius and his followers having a "heart of division," which finds its origin in people's "heart of competition" and "heart of machination." This calculating self-centeredness, that sees one's neighbors as adversaries in conflict over scarcity, makes the human heart as dangerous as rocky terrain. Instead, those who seek the *dao* should ask themselves to let go of competitiveness and political calculation, resist and abandon Confucian rules and hierarchical order, and return to the equality of the natural law of *dao*.[76]

Third, everyone should try to overcome their heart of division. It blocks people from understanding the *dao* and following the *dao's* reason. People should return to nature, go back to basics, let their hearts connect with all things, limit the chaos of the human world, clear their minds and quiet their hearts, so they can gain clarity. In this way, they can understand the *dao* and get closer to the *dao*. Those who get closer to the *dao* this way are "those who have arrived."

Fourth, those who truly understand the *dao* do not just theorize about it. They know the *dao* and the laws of how it flows through all things and are real people. They live in the *dao* and are skilled at using non-action to achieve active goals, but they are never so anxious as to count their chickens before they hatch. They know how to live and die well, know how to both enjoy life and mourn death.

Finally, those who achieve and follow the *dao* the best are "saints" or sages. Their personal virtue and the *dao* are completely aligned, and they reach the realm where "heaven and earth are one."[77] They have access not only to the way by which all things work and are transformed into one another, but also to the *dao* of society, which is the end of human, or false, behavior.

They know "the usefulness of the useless" and thereby know how to protect themselves from misfortune. They understand that the principle of the "the softness of the world" is, ironically, strong, and therefore know how to "use softness to overcome hardness." They know that "nature follows the *dao*" and "the plan of non-action is active," and so know when to advance, and when to retreat. They understand that "entering is loud, not entering is still," that the "dao flows as one." They know that life and death are an illusion, so life is not happy and death is not sad, and that the *dao* of life and death are wild songs.

The *dao* and the *de* of such saints form a perfect whole; Heaven and mankind are united as they walk through the human world and soar through the heavens. Such saints have entered the world of wisdom and have virtuous action instilled in their bodies; they breathe the yin and yang of the heavens, understanding the illusion of all things. They are neither elated nor sorrowful; they do not seek after fame but rise above material things. They celebrate generations past and look forward to the generations of the future. Such saints have already begun their transformation, and may burn without feeling hot, may cross snowy mountains and yet not feel cold, may see the earth shatter but not fear, are admired but not proud, praised and blamed but never feel shame. A saint like this has achieved the pinnacle of the *dao*.

Zhuangzi and Laozi together produced the Daoist reflection on *human calling*. They used a dynamic, dialectical method to arrive at the earliest natural moral philosophy, which explained the relationships between humans and nature and between humans and society. And for Chinese people, especially independent-minded intellectuals, they created an ideal moral character. Their intuitive imagination and the transcendent literary style cast a mystical fog over their naturalistic philosophy that remains today.

This mysticism contrasted sharply with the 2,000 years of centralized, totalitarian, Confucian legal policy that suffocated free intellectual thought. While it caused endless fascination for some, it also maddened generations of intellectual literati who longed for the soul's escape from such an environment, which led to further development of Daoist thought. Later, Zou Yan, Wang Bi, and others wrote commentaries that described the *dao* as the unified operation of "yin and yang." Later still came the metaphysical elaborations of the philosophy by the Seven Sages of the Bamboo Grove, intellectuals of the war-torn Eastern Jin Dynasty (266–420 AD), who avoided court intrigue in a time of conflict. Finally, 600 years later, Zhang Daoling, Ge Hong, and others created the transcendental but formless religion of the "immortal Daoists."

SECTION 4: LEGALISM: FROM HUMAN CALLING TO HUMAN REQUIREMENT

The Legalists were a group of philosophers who lived during the chaotic Spring and Autumn Warring States period. Legalism, or *Fajia,* is a completely pragmatic political philosophy,[78] but its practice requires justification in philosophical theory. The Legalists' understanding was based on deep reflections on the *human calling* of the public figures in society. They did not believe that Confucius and Mencius's ethical practice based on Zhou ritual could restore public order. They thought only laws and constraints could establish public standards, end conflict, ensure obedience, reduce internal and external violence, and establish public order. But this kind of public order involves enforcement of *human requirement*—in essence, depriving people of certain freedoms to punish disobedience. Such punishment must be justified by *human calling*, otherwise it can lead to "bad law."

The Legalists looked for just this sort of philosophical justification from the Yang Zhu and Daoist schools. Sometime between 450–370 BC, Yang Zhu founded his school of philosophy. Yang Zhu and his disciples believed people should be equal. Whether aristocrats or commoners, after death, all likewise turn to bones. There are no differences between them. Similarly, all people see themselves as the "great self" and make that self the central consideration when weighing pros and cons, gains and losses. So people should be "fully faithful" and "scorn objects and revere life." In other words, mankind should maintain his humanity, which is endowed by nature, by scorning other things and seeking a life in accordance with his true nature. Such a person should have "self-interest for all" and neither harm society nor allow society to harm himself. This would create an ideal society with an orderly government. The Yang Zhu school to a certain extent used Legalist premises[79] and is often considered Legalist.

Xunzi's assumption that human nature is evil also formed a basis for Legalist political ideals, though from a different angle.[80] From the Legalist perspective, the Confucian idea that human nature is good was incorrect, so using Zhou rituals to govern people was totally unrealistic. Wasn't it precisely because the Zhou Dynasty's rituals were based on the assumption that human nature is good that the system hit a dead end? Xunzi instead advocated confronting the selfish nature of humans that gives rise to an every-man-for-himself kind of society.

People go to great lengths in order to gain an advantage. When governing, then, it's necessary to take advantage of their tendencies to seek pleasure and avoid pain and to create laws based on them. But "law comes from authority" and "authority comes from the *dao*," so law can create an "unselfish public." The basis of this law is, "one person uses it, it remains without hearing it, the world follows it, not hearing it is not enough." This is the foundation of the rule of law, the way of benign government. Law must establish the public standard and scope of community life; law must end disputes by determining the ownership of property; in order to be effective, law must be effectively broadcast so it is widely known. Fair rewards and punishments must be implemented for those who obey and break the law. This promotes obedience and self-restriction of harmful behavior, which eventually leads to an orderly society.

Built on the foundation laid by Xunzi and Yang Zhu, the Legalists' reflections on the rule of law were a philosophical adaptation that came after the Zhou Dynasty's *Fengjian* feudal system collapsed into chaos. All the major vassal states attempted reform. The most famous reforms were led by Guan Zhong, Li Kui, Wu Qi, and Shang Yang. Of course, the *dao* of Legalism is only a principle and reason behind the decrees issued, not the *dao* that exists in all things and drives all things as explained by Laozi and Zhuangzi.

Guan Zhong (723–645 BC) became an advisor to Duke Huan of Qi, who came to power in 685 BC. Guan Zhong supported the duke and helped him make policy for more than 40 years until his death. His reforms focused on land laws that emphasized agrarian economics and rewarded farming. They tended to call for fairer tax and commerce laws and using government's authority in taxation, commerce, salt and iron monopolies, mintage, interstate trade, and so on to carry out economic policies. These policies emphasized market stabilization, price control, and the protection of low-income people. They also enacted policies to encourage appointment of talented people, as well as reward or punish effective or ineffective governance, respectively.

The result was the successful development of the Qi economy, which made the state wealthy and strong. The Qi government fulfilled its campaign slogan, "respect the king and resist the barbarians," by taking the lead in performing the rituals of vassal states for the Emperor in the Western Zhou Dynasty and repeatedly making political alliances and swearing blood oaths with others to maintain the feudal political order. Meanwhile, the State of Qi used military force against states and barbarians that violated the Zhou rituals to maintain order among them as well.

Guan Zhong's legal system not only made Duke Huan of Qi the true Zhou Emperor of the Warring States period and put the other states in his service, it also built order and prosperity based on rituals and music. Praised as an exemplary study in Chinese political ideology for thousands of years, the State of Qi's Jixia Academy compiled volumes of treatises on governance called *Guanzi*[81]. It's still a must-read for students of ancient Chinese governance and western Sinologists who comment on contemporary Chinese politics. The work is permeated with the ideals of the political order of the entire scholarly class in the sphere of the centralized empire during Chinese agrarian civilization.

Li Kui (455–395 BC) became an advisor to Marquis Wen of the State of Wei in 422 BC. He carried out the "maximizing land strength" and "flat even" policies. The former was the uniform distribution of peasant land to incentivize farming. The latter allowed the state to collect crops during harvests and release them strategically into the market to maintain a healthy price or lower prices to combat famine.

Li Kui also oversaw the development and execution of China's first written legal system, after Zichan, advisor to Zheng Jiangong cast the laws in bronze in 544 BC. [82] The *Canon of Laws* discusses laws about theft, treason, prisoners, arrests, miscellaneous rules, and ownership, taking into account legal provisions, judicial procedures, and sentencing. It is a relatively logical and complete early legal code.

Li Kui selected the Legalist Wu Qi (440–381 BC) to help him rebuild and restore order to the state of Wei, and it quickly became one of the strongest of the warring states. Wu Qi advised Lu Mugong, Wei Wenhou, Wei Wuhou, and Chu Daowang, all warring state rulers. He was a great general during this period and waged over a hundred battles, winning victory in 80 percent of them. He lost so rarely due to his brilliant leadership and left behind the famous *Wuzi,* a book of military strategy[83].

Yet by 386 BC, Wu Qi was the target of court slander and even King of Wei's trust in him was lacking. When this treatment became more than he could bear, he assisted King Dao of Chu with the famous "Wu Qi Reforms."[84] The most important reform was to limit blood inheritance of noble titles to three generations. He gave them sparsely populated lands far from the center of government, forcing them to relocate. This weakened the rights of aristocratic families and consolidated the king's power. His laws streamlined government agencies, cut redundant staff, set officials straight, fought fraud, and improved government efficiency. They also provided incentives for agricultural development, expanded weapon stores, improved the treatment of soldiers, and encouraged good military training.

Wu Qi's reforms made the state richer and the military stronger. Coupled with his outstanding military ability, the reforms quickly yielded fruit. To the south, the State of Chu put down the Baiyue, the various ethnic minorities that opposed them. To the north they annexed the states of Chen and Cai. They constrained the State of Jin and wrested territory from the State of Qin. In 381 BC, they allied with the State of Zhao and defeated the powerful army of the State of Wei as they continued to rise. Unfortunately, that same year, King Dao died. The nobles who had suffered from the reforms took the opportunity to attack. Wu Qi reportedly ran to the king's body and died shouting "Rebellion! Rebellion!" while arrows hit both him and the king's corpse. Wu Qi was the first outstanding thinker, politician, and military strategist to devote himself to legal reforms during the Spring and Autumn and Warring States periods.

Shang Yang (390 BC–338 BC), however, was most celebrated of the Legalist scholars. He responded to a call for advisors by Duke Xiao of Qin and won his favor after speaking with him four times. In 360 BC, he assisted Duke Xiao in promoting the "Shang Yang Reforms," the most profound and systematic reforms in Legalist history.[85] Shang Yang was an extremely pragmatic politician. He deeply believed in the premises that human nature is evil and that humans tend to seek profit and avoid pain. For him the Confucian "way of kings" method of governance was bad for the country and people. He also considered the Daoist "way of the emperor" method of government and moral cultivation to be empty words. Only the Legalist "way of hegemony," based on achieving a wealthy state with a strong military and rule of law, could unify a world in chaos. Only violence could stop violence and establish a new social order. Shang Yang reflected that the *Fengjian* system of the Zhou Dynasty had profound, incurable flaws. He saw Guan Zhong, Li Kui, and Wu Qi's reforms as piecemeal, targeting small problems without taking into account the big picture. He saw Hao Zhao's reforms for King Wei of Qu as unable to address the root of the problem. He believed that sweeping change was needed—that the Zhou Dynasty's political, economic, and social systems were all obsolete, and a completely new order was required. It was his reforms that allowed the Qin to decimate the competition and unite China.

With his wisdom and understanding, Shang Yang enacted 11 interrelated laws: agricultural, military, sentencing, residential, family, land, tax, prefecture and county, weights and measures, custom, and ideological laws. These laws and regulations implemented a political and social order consistent with Shang Yang's core values and logic.

First, it strengthened the kingship and weakened the aristocracy. It stipulated that noble titles and manors were to be reacquired after three generations, unless they were earned again through military valor. The 36 county chiefs of Qin were directly appointed or removed. The rights of manors to tax and raise armies were abolished and instead unified under royal authority. Apart from short-term economic rewards the nobility received from the monarchy, the permanent ownership of manors was in name only, with the aristocrats having no substantive economic or political rights at all. This essentially put an end to the rise of new vassal kings and the fragmentation it entailed.

Second, it created a new national organizational structure more suitable for agricultural civilization and a less hierarchical society, which inspired enthusiasm for entrepreneurial activity among the lower classes. In the Zhou *Fengjian* system, the ideal was for one ninth of fields to be public property, cared for jointly by eight households and taxed by the dynasty. This ideal turned out to be a fantasy with practically no basis in reality, as powerful vassal aristocrats became the only landowners with exclusive taxation and troop-raising powers. Vassal states constantly reaped rewards from struggling against one another, which created an entrenched nobility on the manors. These hereditary aristocratic families had a strong patriarchal family structure, but they largely bred idle children and depended on servants and tenants. The large hereditary nobility had armed forces. These organizational methods, on the one hand, weakened the king's power. On the other, the large number of manors created an economy that was a mix of feudalism and slavery. This put a heavy burden on the lower classes, as slaves had no legal or individual freedom.

Shang Yang's reforms clearly stipulated that after marriage, adults must register as a nuclear family and pay taxes to the king, in addition to property taxes on the land granted to them. This established a yeoman-based economy well-suited to agricultural civilization. Government officials, meanwhile, were completely linked to the Qin king's power and had a clear division of labor, assigned workload, and widespread supervision. This made it all but impossible to spend their time conniving to exploit the people.

The reforms also reduced the number of slaves aristocratic families were allowed to have. When they became free, they received land to cultivate as farmers. This fundamentally created a private socio-economic organization out of each self-farming nuclear family that related to the royal state government organization, namely, the state of Qin. The Zhou Dynasty order's many hierarchical layers, from the emperor to the lords and kings; to the aristocratic clans; to the various tenant, slave and merchant families, were essentially flattened. This was widely welcomed by the lower classes because it gave them equal economic rights to the aristocrats.

Third, Shang Yang's order abolished hereditary nobility and established a system that gave titles and money based on the number of enemies beheaded. This established a national meritocratic political system, and the army became much more effective in combat.

Fourth, it simplified the tax system from a variety of taxes to a single tax on the land granted to and cultivated by nuclear families. In addition, it unified the currency and weights and measures, doubled the taxes on undivided family complexes and patriarchal household clans, including those with many servants and attendants. The power of aristocratic clans and other family complexes was fundamentally weakened. This made single family farmers the most common economic and social unit in the State of Qin. It made taxes more equal, enriched the king's treasury, and made the lower classes more affluent.

Fifth, in order to make sure political reforms were properly implemented and yielded results, Shang Yang enacted strict household registration laws and a collective punishment law that encouraged mutual oversight among the people. Agriculture was encouraged at the expense of commerce. Population was limited and movement was managed. Vigilante justice and fighting among the people were strictly prohibited. Ideological thought was unified, as competing ideas about the Qin reforms were prohibited as well.

Sixth, in order to promote the reforms, Shang Yang, having personally built a strong legal and enforcement team, entrusted enforcement to the people. He elevated the practice of enforcement to a kind of faith, in which "breaking the law means imprisoning the self," a horrible act.

Shang Yang established that rewards and punishments were given or meted out regardless of an individual's social status. He even punished powerful aristocrats as examples, and kept his word. Once, when he promised to reward 50 taels of gold to anyone who would move a piece of wood outside the city gates, he made good on his promise. His consistency solidified the people's trust in the new laws, which led to success in his reforms.

Shang Yang dedicated 22 years of his life to Duke Xiao of Qin's reforms, sharing with him his political and social ideals. He had clear goals, and his system was logical and consistent. He was passionately determined to write and implement his legal system without compromise. The Shang Yang Reforms formed an integral part of the people's lives in the State of Qin. They became ingrained, bringing improved prosperity for ordinary people at the expense of the hereditary aristocracy. Slaves were able to become free citizens. His new system, centered around the king and his power to tax and appoint and remove officials, replaced the political division of the Zhou "*Fengjian*" feudal system.

Moreover, when Shang Yang deployed the Qin military, it was unstoppable. Before combat began, victory was already in hand. The State of Qin after the Shang Yang Reforms was powerful and invincible. It was only a matter of time before it unified the six states. The famous Emperor Qin Shi Huang owed much of his legendary reputation to the successful new political, economic, and social order created by the Shang Yang Reforms. As the legendary author of *The Art of War*, Sunzi, said, "War is nothing more than a contest of economic power."

In 338 BC, Duke Xiao of Qin, Shang Yang's patron, friend, and comrade in arms, fell ill and died. Before he died, both he and Shang Yang were struck by a foreboding of impending tragedy. The duke suggested that he succeed him on the throne, to ensure that his reforms remained and to fend off political doom. Shang Yang was firm in his refusal. He believed that monarchal succession through the king's bloodline was the best, most ethical political practice that would legitimize the regime, although he knew this refusal would mean he and his whole family would pay with their lives. Shang Yang also knew this with certainty: if he took the duke's position (since this took place during the Warring States period, the throne did not legitimize the ruler), his reforms would appear tainted by his personal ambition and be abandoned by future generations. Ultimately, his reforms would fail. So he decided to protect the law, refusing to defer to the duke, and instead standing by his principles.

When the duke died, Gongzi Qian, Gan Long, Du Zhi, and other old nobles who had suffered from the reforms plotted to attack. The duke's son Huiwen had been expelled from court as a boy, in accordance with Shang Yang's reforms, so the hatred of the old aristocracy resonated with him. He arrested Shang Yang for rebellion and punished his whole family, but the two finally reached a compromise in which he was to be executed, but King Huiwen would keep his reforms in place.

Shang Yang was willing to face death in order to protect his reforms, protecting his laws with his life. The towering *Book of Lord Shang* he left became the textbook of Legalist reform and gave form to the Legalist philosophy. It laid the basic political and philosophical framework for more than 2,000 years of China's political and economic system of centralized power and nuclear farming families. The concept of *human calling* during this first great philosophical awakening completely focused on *human requirement* in Shang Yang's Legalism. Because of this, China exchanged the kingly politics of the Zhou Dynasty for the hegemonic politics of the Qin Dynasty.[86]

Han Feizi (281–233 BC) further developed Legalist philosophy by writing a systematic summary. Like Li Si, the philosopher who worked for Qin Shi Huang, the Emperor who unified the six warring states under the State of Qin, he was a disciple of the Confucian Xunzi. Han Feizi wrote the 55-chapter, 100,000-word Legalist text *Han Feizi*. Because Qin Shi Huang approved of his theories, he was a direct competitor to Li Si, so Li Si orchestrated his murder during a visit to the State of Qin. Although the academic community generally overlooks the influence Han Feizi's Confucian teacher had on him, Xunzi's theory that human nature is evil is the foundation of his philosophy.

Han Feizi believed that people were not only selfish but lazy, "hating work, and seeking leisure," and that seeking advantage while avoiding harm is fundamental to human nature.[87] Han Feizi had a negative view of the average person, but he was even more pessimistic about the upper classes. He thought there were five types of people, which he termed the "five pests," that posed the greatest danger to all of society: the wandering Confucian lobbyists, those who sought to spread the rites and rituals, the Mohists who preached peace but carried swords, those who feared war, and the merchants who all stopped at nothing to gain fame and fortune. He also singled out eight types of people in high society—the king's wives, confidants, father, brothers, staff, ambitious ministers, and ambitious vassals—as the least trustworthy. He termed these the "eight traitors," seeing them as pollutants and contaminants that threated the monarchy and the rule of law.

In his extreme pessimism about human nature, Han Feizi built on Guan Zhong, Shen Buhai, Li Kui, Wu Qi, and Shang Yang's laws to create his systematic and hegemonic theory of "Law, Power, and Art." First, Han Feizi believed, there must be Law: "Those who rule must rule according to human emotions, which can be changed through rewards and punishments. Thus through rewards and punishments, prohibitions can be instated, and the people are governed." With regard to the rule of law, he advocated the thoroughness of Shang Yang's reforms, the seriousness of enforcement, and equal treatment under the law.

Second, he didn't think Law was enough without Power. In order to achieve an ideal legal order, a ruler must project power: "the ruler takes the reigns and prohibits something . . . the forceful win the people's support." Han Feizi's idea of Power is really a justification of the ruler's authority. In

Confucius, this authority came from Heaven. Mencius added the importance of a ruler's benevolent governance and a heart full of morality and love for the people. Laozi and Zhuangzi added saintly knowledge and the principle of *dao*. In Han Feizi's view, these were not enough. A ruler must also project Power to achieve the "unity of Power and Law" and govern well.

Third, he believed that given the evil nature of the human heart and the existence of the "five pests" and "eight traitors," the ruler faces many risks in governing and therefore must learn the "Art" of maintaining power. The main difference between Art and Law is that Law is widely visible and understood and must make express prohibitions; Art, on the other hand, comes from the ruler's heart and takes skillful calculation. The best techniques of Art are mysterious, so that the people cannot easily predict them. This makes them fear the ruler. In his view, these three elements of Law, Power, and Art work together to create effective government.

He also advocated that rulers use their Art and Power in accord with the *dao*, doing their best to achieve "non-action" and "non-rash action." But Han Feizi never doubted the ruler's nature. He knew that rulers are human too, and also have an evil nature. If an evil ruler masters Power and Art, that places the world in danger and causes hardship for the people. Han Feizi's theory[88] was written down 1,700 years before Machiavelli's *The Prince* in the West, and it became the manual of choice for many skilled political rulers who were artful but unprincipled.

He opened the floodgates to tyrannical attitudes in Chinese emperors and remained in favor for a long time among rulers and ministers of the political class. Sadly, his theory bears responsibility for thousands of years of darkness, deceit, and depravity in Chinese court politics. Of course if representative Chinese philosophers like Xunzi and Han Feizi could have gone one step forward past fundamentally questioning the emperor's human nature, they would have carried the truth of human evil to its logical end point. Then China may have discovered faith in one God, and the history of Chinese philosophy, or even history as a whole, may have unfolded completely differently. Unfortunately, history allows no ifs.

SECTION 5: THE MOHISTS: HUMANITY'S EARLIEST PUBLIC WELFARE ADVOCATES

Aside from the three main philosophical schools of Confucianism, Daoism, and Legalism, Mohism is the other pre-Qin philosophy of note. The school Mozi (468–376 BC) founded was the first to introduce the idea of public welfare. Of all the philosophical schools in China's first great awakening on *human calling*, his was the most logical and extensive.

Mozi began his search into *human calling* as a Confucian. But Confucianism's tedious, rigid systems for etiquette could not satisfy his restless nature. So he took the Confucian idea of hierarchical respect between Heaven and earth, ruler and subject, father and son and built his own more logical system. He began giving lectures and operating the first public welfare advocacy organization in the world: the Mohist scholars.

Mozi's theory and his spheres of influence can be distilled into three aspects. The first is in his contributions to humanist philosophy: Mozi began with the ethical outline of Confucian benevolent righteousness and came to believe that Heaven had a personal will. Benevolent righteousness is "Heaven's will." This means that Heaven loves all people regardless of whether they are high or low, rich or poor, dull or intelligent. In the eyes of Heaven, everyone is equal.[89]

Likewise, the family and the state are equal in the will of Heaven, and therefore Heaven doesn't allow violence and domination in the world, where the strong bully the weak. Heaven's will demands that there be mutual love for one another within human nature. All people should "love one another and benefit one another." In relationships, reciprocity must prevail to the benefit of oneself and the other. Heaven's will is for *Shangtong*, or sacred equality, which is the basis of love. This sacred equality leads to benevolent righteousness.

Mozi believed that complicated Confucian rules couldn't lead to benevolent righteousness. So what was his basis of sacred equality? First, the ruler's power is granted by Heaven. The ruler must be deeply conversant in Heaven's will. Then, he must apply *Shangxian*, or "worthy veneration," which is the principle of distributing power according to merit. He must appoint the "three publicans:" the ministers, the province and county leaders under the minister, and the township and village leaders. These chosen leaders must maintain their honor by aligning their virtue with the will of Heaven and form a benevolent government, while also promoting mutual love and reciprocity among the people.

Thus, worthy veneration is an important method of implementing sacred equality. For the ruler to establish a benevolent government, it not only requires proper appointments, but also laws that replace and punish those who do not reach the required moral standard. It must be emphasized that Heaven's will of benevolent righteousness cannot eliminate the existence of evil in the human world.[90] Ministers who don't obey their rulers, sons who don't obey their fathers, people who don't love one another, and a lack of reciprocity is still to be expected. The country, family, and individuals dominate the small and weak, the rich the poor. There is still violence and coercion in society.

This social violence and tendency towards tyranny must be constantly combated non-violently.[91] Violent struggle disrupts productivity, destroys society's order, ends innocent life, and brings people endless suffering. Maintaining a peaceful order non-violently means outlawing domination, bullying, and especially, insubordination toward ministers or parents. To this end, Mozi offered three principles for implementing his philosophy.

First, the ruler is the representative of Heaven's will and should maintain the mutual love and non-violence of Heaven's will. He should implement benevolent government by ensuring that people support each other, give the old a sense of security, help the weak, and take the lead in preventing violence. The ruler should use rewards and punishments to stop the violent domination of the strong over the weak, in order to achieve societal peace and order.

Second, if the ruler cannot implement benevolent government, he disobeys Heaven's will and must receive Heaven's condemnation. Mozi believed Heaven had many spirits in the human world who advanced Heaven's will by punishing human violence. Whether committed by a ruler, minister, or commoner, violent action could be punished by spirits—it just might not happen right away.

Third, Mohists were not to be merely armchair theorists. They were an organized group of scholars who acted righteously on behalf of Heaven and were responsible for the enforcing punishment of those who defied the principles of mutual love and non-violence.

The Mohist Scholars, numbered at 300, were more than a strict public welfare organization. These fierce, self-sacrificing scholars who promoted Heaven's will were active in the politics of the Spring and Autumn Warring States periods.[92] They helped some states punish ministers who killed their rulers and sons who killed their fathers. They helped some weaker states defend against attacks from stronger states. They directly urged larger states to consider not attacking smaller states and formed their own offensive and defensive military strategies, which had a large, lasting impact.

Mozi's second field of contribution to humanity was in science and natural philosophy. He was the only philosopher during the Spring and Autumn Warring States periods to make such contributions.[93] He divided the world of humans and nature into the dimensions of space and time. Space was termed "the universe," while time was termed "age." "Universe" was made of the smallest "edge," and time was made of the smallest "beginning." So time and space were limited as "beginning" and "edge" and unlimited as "age" and "the universe." Movement can only occur in the space-time realm of "universe-age."

Mozi wrote that movement manifests as a sequence of differences in time and shifts in space. Movements outside time and space simply do not occur. Movement is caused by the "exertion" of force, and movement stops because of resistance: without resistance, movement continues. Mozi made many scientific contributions, including defining rectangles, squares, decimals, multiplication, leverage, and using pinhole imaging, among many other concepts. The accuracy of his definitions is comparable to that of the ancient Greeks. His advancements in natural philosophy were often applied by Mohists to invent technologies that defended weak countries against the powerful.

Mozi's third contribution was to the methodology of philosophical debate. He was the only Chinese philosopher to concern himself with this subject.[94] He believed speculation must follow a standard method or no consensus could be reached. His basic method was to depict the "trace outline" of the relationships between all things. Conclusions could then be discussed in "group words," using conceptual phrases to create definitions and reasoning phrases to express judgments and trace their source to a "cause." He used an analogous method of "Choosing according to kind; offering according to kind" to make judgments. In order to avoid "similarities seeming like differences, positives seeming like negatives," a criterion is needed for judging what is similar or different, or right and wrong. With a proper standard for what is "positive," it's clear when to consider something a "negative" when it falls short of that standard. The reason Mozi believed speculation must adhere to this logical method is because he saw understanding as requiring three stages: the ability to use conceptual thinking to "consider," the ability to sense and process a foreign object through "connecting," and logical contemplation, or "understanding." Mozi's methodology can't be compared to Aristotle's logic, but his analogical, deductive, and apodictic reasoning is grounded in logical methods and marks an important achievement in Chinese philosophy. Sadly, the pictographic nature of Chinese characters and the cultural monopoly and exclusiveness of Confucians and Legalists hindered the transmission and development of Mozi's thought. It must be said this was a major missed opportunity for those who inherited pre-Qin culture.

SECTION 6: THE BIG SHOWDOWN BETWEEN CHINESE AND ANCIENT GREEK PHILOSOPHY

In comparing Chinese and Greek philosophy during humanity's first great philosophical awakening, it's not hard to see their similarities and differences.

The two groups of philosophers, who never encountered each other, concerned themselves with four areas of inquiry, including how they operate and why: First, the nature of the relationship between humans and nature. Second, the nature of relationships between humans and society. Third, the analogous relationships between humans and society and between humans and nature, which are also homologous in their temporal and spatial dimensions. Fourth, how methodologies of philosophical thinking and discussion can standardize, promote, and improve human thinking and imagination.

These four areas of inquiry offer answers to questions of *human calling*. That is, how a person should recognize the world in which they live and the relationship between them and the universe, the relationship between people and things, and especially the relationships between people. How and why should people think and act in the world? How and why should they follow some guidelines and reject others? How and why should they face their own existence and death, and how and why they should think about and discuss these major issues in life? The reason philosophers from both cultures paid attention to and discussed these interrelated issues is because they're the most fundamental problems human beings have faced since the start of agricultural civilization.

The first problem they both tackled was how to stop or slow down the internal and external violence that arises in human life. This meant asking how to order community and public life to encourage better communities.

Both Ancient Greece and China created organizations representing the interests of society: democratic city states and dynastic feudal states, respectively. Both types of states related in a certain way to private households and allowed for relatively simple tax collection for the public interest. But the two were very different. Ancient Greece was a civilization of city states in the Mediterranean islands. The combination of land and sea, as well as the openness and diversity of their trade patterns with other surrounding community states, gave them a more pronounced commercial DNA and a more obviously contractual basis for dealing with private and public issues.

China, on the other hand, formed an agricultural society around the Yangtze and Yellow River basins and was therefore a relatively closed community. This resulted in a more obvious agricultural DNA when dealing with private and public issues and a more obvious tendency toward conquest and surrender. This could explain their differences in philosophical thinking.

The second problem addressed was how individuals can anticipate their futures while unable to change the public order of community they live in. How could they both conform their life to that public order while also feeling joy, happiness, and meaning in that context? This question involved individual recognition of *human calling* but also certainly touched on a larger societal issue.

Ancient Greece and China also differed in their philosophical inquiries.

First, ancient Greek pre-Socratic philosophers nearly all emphasized the relationship between humans and nature. They sought to divine the nature and form of the world's composition and existence. The public relationships between people and others may be influenced by the relationship between humans and nature. Among Chinese philosophers, only Laozi, Zhuangzi, and Mozi discussed this problem. Laozi and Zhuangzi's discussion of the source of all things, *dao*, was not about deciphering the material structure and function of the natural world or the structure and function of the *dao* behind the phenomenal world. Rather, it was about affirming the supreme status of *dao* and guiding people to understand how they should act in this violent, ever-changing world. Only Mozi discussed natural philosophy like the ancient Greeks. Sadly, his ideas were never taken up by later thinkers.

Second, the relationship between humans and society was raised and addressed to various degrees by most philosophers. Apart from Mozi and the Daoists Laozi and Zhuangzi, no one discussed whether *human calling* had any necessary or inevitable connection with existence beyond the material world. Confucians and Legalists were more concerned with the material. They were not interested in the abstract world beyond sensation. Confucianism was more concerned with common norms of behavior that people must adhere to when relating to others in public—its philosophical equivalent is the ethics of *human duty*. And these conventions and behavioral norms came from looking back to the previous dynasty in a way a baby always look to their mother, thinking she holds all the solutions to current and future problems.

Ancient Greek philosophers, meanwhile, always turned their gaze to the gods. They thought universal, absolute truths were not found in the world of appearances but rather in the abstract world of the gods. This world existed prior to and would exist after life and the cessation of sensation, so truth and power can only be sought from God. Legalist practical philosophy, on the other hand, slipped into the practical politics of the public interest, emphasizing the power of harsh punishments to maintain order. It could be said that it bypassed *human calling* while going straight to *human requirement*, exchanging one form of violence for another, for the government was itself a violent mechanism with the intention of stopping violence.

Only Daoist and Mohist thought discussed the metaphysical issue of *human calling* on the same level as ancient Greeks. They not only tried to answer why mankind needs a public order to coexist peacefully with others, but they also pointed out the path to realizing such an order and further uncovered the deep divine reasons in the invisible world for why mankind should think and act in this way.

Third, regarding the homologous nature of the relationship between humans and society and humans and nature, ancient Greek philosophers expressed relatively obvious dualistic and humanistic polytheistic tendencies. A majority of philosophers believed that behind the material world there is a deeper, rational world. Nevertheless, the core elements that make up this deeper, non-phenomenal world differed. In the Milesian school, they were water, fire, air, or nothingness; in the Pythagorean school they were numbers, spirit, and soul; in the Elia school they were Mind and Eros, while water, fire, air, earth, and atoms were only materials used by them to form all things. Among the Socratics they were universal reason and highest existence; in Platonic thought they were sacred perfection and the eternal creator; in Aristotelian, the wise soul and eternal, unlimited, inevitable universal law of the gods. For the practical Cynics, it was the inner soul's god-facing, wise virtue; for Epicurean hedonism, it was the godly and ordinary atoms composed of tiny atoms; the pre-existing concepts and philosophical reason of the Stoics with their ragged clothes and noble hearts; the sacred one and heart of the Neoplatonists school; the supreme light of God and intermediate soul of the Gnostics; and so on. But regardless of the differences between them, they all had a dualistic view of existence. They all agreed that beyond the physical world of sensory perception there was another world that could only be sensed through reason. Even the atomic theory of the Elia school, which many misread as monistic, was at its heart dualistic, since they believed the atoms that make up the material world are made up of Eros and Mind from another world.

In fact, in this dualistic view, the first element is visible, individual, formal, and fluid. It wants to embody *human ability* and therefore participate in self-centered competition and struggle. Meanwhile the second element is spiritual and represents the "public spirit." It is invisible and constant, a general law. Its core is love, compassion, goodness, and beauty. It wants to embody *human calling* through restraining selfishness, and transcend the first, physical element. It is the common origin of people and things in the physical world. It exists before us and does not disappear when we die. So human souls remain after they die, and join the higher existence of the spiritual world, whether it is "Mind," "Eros," "oneness," or "eternal creator."

This dualistic worldview is the philosophical foundation of Western natural law. Whether it's relationships between people or relationships between all things, all are governed by a homologous law. The search for how and why this homologous law was created eventually led the West to personal faith in God, which laid a solid cornerstone for philosophy. It could even be said that if it weren't for the early exploration of the ancient Greeks, the philosophical foundation of the Christian faith would not exist and would never have been imagined.

As far as dualistic thinking goes, the philosophers of China's first axial age can be divided into two groups. The first is the Daoists and Mohists. On the surface they could be considered dualistic thinkers because the *dao* is different from the material world. To say that "*Dao* creates all things" seems to imply that *dao* exists in a transcendent world while "all things" refers to the physical world. This means that *Dao* is the source of the physical world.

But due to the inherent ambiguity in the ancient Chinese, the saying "Man rules Earth, Earth rules Heaven, Heaven rules Dao" could seem to imply that *dao* is a separate element from material things and the ultimate source of all things. Yet when you go on to read "*dao* rules Nature," following Laozi's logic leads to the collapse of the dualistic worldview, since it seems to express a hierarchy of worlds rather than a dualistic worldview. Humanity follows the laws of the earth, the earth follows the laws of the sky, the sky follows the laws of the *dao*, and the *dao* follows the laws of nature. But isn't nature all things? The world of *dao* follows the law of nature, but don't all natural things partake in the birth and death of the physical? How can the eternal *dao* follow the law of living and dying things? How can *dao* still be the "source" as the creation of all things?

Mozi, on the other hand, didn't refer to the abstract *dao* but rather to Heaven's will. He believed that spirits aid Heaven by meting out rewards and punishments that maintain mutual love and non-violence in the physical world, thus holding a relatively dualistic worldview. But he didn't question or dig further into the common essence behind the relationships between humans and nature or between humans and society. His Heaven's will idea loses its moral and sacred authority. As more spirits aid Heaven, these spirits lose their moral authority and slip into witchcraft and mysticism. Yet, Mozi explored the relationships between time and space in the physical world, movement and resistance in time and space as well as other mathematical relationships like points, lines, surfaces, and leverage. He is the only Chinese philosopher to have studied the relationship between the structure and function of all things in nature.

The most fundamental difference between the worldview of the Chinese dualists, the Daoist and Mohists, and the dualistic worldview of ancient Greek philosophy is that the dualistic worldview of Chinese Daoism and Mohism is naturalistic in nature, in other words, the law behind all things in nature (either the *dao* or the will of Heaven) determines the law of human relationships. Thus, in Chinese philosophy, the hierarchy that places Heaven above earth is echoed in the difference between human beings of high and low status. This thinking could not possibly give rise to the idea that all humans are free and equal. This essential difference has profoundly influenced the diverging development of civilization in East and West.

As for the Chinese monists, at least Confucians and Legalists lived and interacted more directly with the visible, physical world. They believed that

Confucian ritual and laws, constraints, and orders, were just methods of organizing the monistic world. And this physical order's hierarchy was based on their individual opinions. But they were not concerned with and did not recognize another world beyond what they could see and feel. They were not concerned with a meaning or power beyond the individual. They were even less concerned with agonizing over the meaning of life before life or life after death. They were only concerned with the public order of human life in the present. From the perspective of time, an individual life had no origin or future, unless it was placed in the physical context of blood flowing through the body. As a result, atheism and the veneration of ancestors were the logical cultural legacy of this monistic worldview only concerned with the material world.

Fourth, the issue of philosophical methodology was raised in China, but only by Mozi. His analogical reasoning was truly unique. But in terms of the rigor and systematic nature of formal logic, it didn't come close to Aristotle, which is why Aristotelian logic still guides both the social and natural sciences today. Modern natural sciences originated from natural philosophy, and social sciences originated from humanistic philosophy. Aristotle's formal logic contained concept definition, scientific classification, empirical induction, and deductive reasoning, and was systematic and rigorous.

However, in terms of methods of dialectical logic, the Daoist doctrine founded by Laozi was equivalent to contemporaneous ancient Greek's Pythagorean school, not only it its discussion of how all things contain the unity of opposites, but also in its in-depth explanation that what we perceive as change in the material world is caused by opposing forces and the *dao* beneath all things. A wise ruler is called to recognize and follow the *dao* through "non-action," which prevents him from acting recklessly. Individuals are called to recognize and follow this *dao* by seeking what makes them aware, at ease, and at peace. This control and grasp of the dialectical philosophical method is similar to the logic of "have, lack, change" Hegel articulated in the 19th century, 2,300 years later. This mastery and grasp of philosophical dialectics is as mysterious and profound as the *Rig Veda* and *Upanishads* of India, and has long influenced Chinese and Eastern thinking and cultural paradigms.

Ancient Greek philosophy greatly furthered mankind's ability to think and reason about *human calling*. It expanded the spiritual world imagined by humans in its dualistic thinking. This spiritual world was actually a space mankind created for the public spirit. It reached many pinnacles in humanity's history of philosophy that have yet to be surpassed. But it still did not succeed in saving the ancient Greeks from their civilization's tragedy.

When Aristotle's student Alexander the Great used his cavalry, swords, and fiery enthusiasm and natural talent for war, the brilliant culture of Ancient Greece spread far and wide. It swept through India, Central Asia, Asia Minor, Egypt, and North Africa. After victory Alexander the Great was like a Greek god of war in the realms of mortals. But after he had conquered the known world, his heart still longed for something more. There was no spirituality in the deep rationalism of his teacher Aristotle. So he went down along the Nile, through the jungles of Ethiopia and Uganda to mysterious Lake Victoria and asked a priest to tell him his fate and the secret of immortality. His fate was an early death, but his name will be known forever.

The young and vigorous 33-year-old Alexander the Great was like the gods Uranus, Chronos, Zeus, and Dionysus in the Greek tragedies: able to defeat all their peers, but unable to defeat their own destiny. He abandoned his human empire in the mortal realm and left it behind. Subsequently the ancient Greek empire was quickly divided due to an absence of rightful heirs and declined gradually, making room for the Roman Empire and its philosophy of *human calling*, which was completely incomparable to that of the Greeks.

Where, then, can we go to once again find the confidence, passion and diversity of answers that the ancient Greek philosophers brought to the question of *human calling*? How can we avoid the fate of the gods and men of ancient Greek tragedy? What use are the ancient Greek philosophers to mankind's quest for *human calling*? These questions are left to the generations that came after.

Chinese philosophers during the Spring and Autumn and Warring States periods, on the other hand, reached a different pinnacle in Eastern philosophical speculation. Their thought didn't develop in the context of centuries of peace and democracy like that of the ancient Greek commercial city-state civilization. Rather it developed in an agricultural civilization experiencing hundreds of years of turbulence. As a result, it was not as quiet and calm as ancient Greek philosophy. This prevented Chinese philosophers from considering the purely spiritual side of the dualistic world. Instead, they spent more energy in reconstructing the public order of the physical world. Even Daoists and Mohists who deeply considered the dualistic worldview were inevitably dragged into the politicking involved in reconstructing public order in the physical world.

As a result, discussions of *human calling* turned to more real-world discussions of how humans should behave, *human duty*, in Confucianism or how to impose the law, *human requirement,* in Legalism. To Confucians, without training in the thousands of conventions for thought and behavior encoded in the Zhou rites, which constitute *human duty*, a peaceful, ordered society could not be rebuilt. People could not become benevolent without understanding the spirit of ritual and music.

Legalists, on the other hand, thought Confucian rites were useless, instead prescribing laws, constraints, and orders to impose the ruler's authority and regulate people's behaviors through *human requirement*. If violators faced harsh punishment, others would be deterred, and a non-violent order would naturally be restored. Legalist methods were used to build the insignificant State of Qin into a great empire that conquered and ruled all the other states. Confucian methods were used by the Han, which succeeded the Qin after its collapse. A combination of Confucianism and Legalism replaced the way of kings of the Zhou Dynasty, to pave the way for the hegemony of the Han Dynasty. Daoists and Mohists, meanwhile, were continually plagiarized by the Confucian-Legalist literati after the Song Dynasty, becoming phantom echoes in the culture.

In this sense, the Chinese philosophy of the Spring and Autumn and Warring States periods was more practical than that of the ancient Greeks. But over time it lost focus on the issue of *human calling*, whether this was the question of human free will, the hope for goodness and beauty, or questions of human equality. It ignored fundamental questions of human life, such as spiritual freedom and equality, instead concentrating on a combination of *human duty* and *human requirement* in the material world. The spiritual world, which humans could only encounter at divinely appointed times, was missing altogether. But where is the individual, spiritual free will outside of public order? Is there another invisible world that exists beyond and prior to the physical one we perceive? How does a mortal man with no consciousness before birth and after death face his inevitable mortality? Is the overall public order of society really all that matters? Does a public order that demands an eye for an eye and castrates the free will of the individual harbor an even more horrific political violence? These questions were also left for subsequent generations.

CHAPTER 5:

Forging: the reflections of the Hebrew people in purgatory

A discussion of the first great reflection of humanity cannot overlook the contribution of Hebrew civilization. This civilization grew out of Mesopotamian civilization (5,000–6,000 years ago) and ancient Egyptian civilization (3,500–5,000 years ago). It can be traced back to the semi-nomadic Semitic people on the fringes of the Mesopotamian plains and the semi-agricultural, semi-pastoral tribes comprised of native Canaanites, Egyptians, and other immigrants. This developmental period of Hebrew civilization was from the 13th to the 17th century BC,[95] around 3,200–3,600 years ago.

The significance of Hebrew civilization doesn't lie in the materials it produced. In that arena, it can't be compared with that of Mesopotamia, ancient Egypt, ancient Greece, or ancient China—or even that of its contemporaries Asia Minor and Babylonia in Asia. Rather, it is their particular experience of suffering as a small and marginalized people, and how they pondered the issue of *human calling* while facing unending external violence. Amid the collective thinking of countless prophets, striking and rousing appeals, divine prophecies, and other heroic struggles in defense of the community, the Hebrews founded the faith in the one and only, personal God, Jehovah. They advanced the discussion of *human calling*, also taken up by philosophers of ancient Greece and the Spring and Autumn and Warring States periods in China, to a new and unprecedented height in human history.

SECTION 1: THE LAW OF THE COVENANT WITH THE UNIPERSONAL GOD

In discussing the Hebrews' faith in the unipersonal God, there are three very important contexts to consider. First, about 4,000 years ago, the Hebrews were the first to invent linear writing. Along with the cuneiform of the Sumerian civilization and the hieroglyphics of ancient Egypt and China, ancient Hebrew is among the earliest writing systems that can be broken down into discrete parts. This structuring of characters laid the foundation for ideographic and abstract thinking.

Second, the Hebrew people's belief in a unipersonal God grew out of the context of their semi-nomadic tribal roots. While a tribe provides a way for individual members to have their public interests represented, it's rare for them to have written records. The Hebrew community was connected by a "tribal alliance" rather than a state. Even if this tribal alliance could be called a state or government, it wouldn't compare with the concept of a "natural state" as defined by Douglass C. North in his *Violence and Social Orders*.[96] Most natural states as described by North in agricultural, nomadic civilizations are in fact hereditary states or governments based on the violent control over the majority by a few. A more appropriate definition of the Hebrew tribal alliance is a covenant-based natural state or natural government.

Third, when the Hebrew people founded their faith in their unipersonal God, they had experienced massive historical suffering, being enslaved for 300–400 years by the Pharaohs of ancient Egypt. These three contexts are incredibly important to understanding Hebrew civilization's belief that *human calling* and all things have the same origin.

The Hebrew belief in the God Jehovah as the creator of the entire universe originated from God's creation of the first human, Adam. The worship of this unipersonal God was led by Abraham, the ancestor of the Hebrews, who was even willing to sacrifice his son as an offering to God. Abraham's faith then became a collective belief as the Hebrew people followed Moses, a non-Hebrew that God chose to be a prophet, in their Exodus from Egypt, which ended 400 years of slavery under the Pharaoh. Moses followed God's will and rescued the Hebrews from slavery under the Egyptian Pharaoh. The Hebrews, under Moses's leadership, made a covenant with the God Jehovah on Mount Sinai, where they promised to live according to the *human calling* that God expected from mankind. God promised the land of Palestine, or Canaan, to the Hebrew people. They then promised to be faithful to Jehovah, worship him as the one true God in the universe, reject any form of idolatry (including idolatry directed toward Jehovah), refuse to partake in divination or witchcraft, and maintain the virtues of compliance with the public order of the tribal community and love for others.

By the late 13th century BC, as a result of being enslaved in Egypt and escaping, the Hebrew people began to take root in God's "promised land," which was "flowing with milk and honey." The Hebrew faith began to take shape. The philosophical foundation of this faith is that the *human calling* governing the relationship between humans and society, as well as the relationship between humans and all things in nature, both come from the unipersonal God, Jehovah. He is the creator of all things and humanity. They exist in time and space as defined by God, so they should all follow the laws created by God. These invisible laws form the first and most essential source of Western natural law.[97]

Over the following 200 years of relative peace from the late 13th to the late 11th centuries BC, the Hebrew people gradually mixed with local peoples and formed the Israelite tribal alliance composed of 10–12 tribes. These tribes were not only related by Hebrew blood but also by covenant with and belief in Jehovah. The covenant served to address the needs of both joint defense against external violence and the need for a public order to guard against internal violence within the tribes. And faith in God allowed for a spiritual fellowship of common concerns. The organization of the tribal alliance was fairly loose. The connection of common faith in God among members prevented major conflict. There were no major wars beyond small conflicts during the process of taking root in the area, so there was no need to establish a standing army or a government to collect and manage taxes. Trials to address internal violence were mainly carried out by religious teachers in accordance with the Torah. In this environment, the Hebrew faith in Jehovah found long-term cultivation and development. This great reflection on *human calling* gained rich, new insight full of human reason. It answered questions about *human calling* that ancient Greek and Chinese philosophy was unable to answer.[98]

First, Hebrews believed that Jehovah is the only creator of the universe. There are no gods under or around him, so there is no need for division of labor or functions among gods, and no limitations on his rule. The Hebrew God is infinite, omnipotent, and eternal, so he has neither destiny nor experiences tragedy.

Second, Jehovah is the creator of the universe and all things. He created the heavens and the earth, humans, and all things in the universe, so he is beyond the finite world and time perceived by humans. He is infinite not only in space but also in time. Humans can only perceive the physical world using their God-given senses, while the other world is spiritual and can only be understood through the soul's reflection on its relationship with God. This understanding of the universe resolved the issue of the common origin and pre-existence of the dualistic world, namely the physical world and the spiritual world. This was a frequent topic of debate in ancient Greek philosophy. According to the Hebrew understanding, if a person wanted to understand the dualistic world, they must devote their soul to faith in the one God and establish a human-God relationship. This way of thinking also avoided falling into the circular argument of the ancient Chinese philosopher Laozi, who concluded that the laws of nature also govern the relationship between humans and society.

Third, the God that the Hebrews believed in was a personal god. Humans are created in God's image, so humans and God in a sense share the same nature. By virtue of their special creation, humanity has received free will and dignify of life, and all humans are completely equal before their creator. This belief solved the philosophical issue of people's inequality in the material or phenomenal world in spite of their equality in the spiritual world. It also resolved the contradiction that the Chinese philosopher Mozi faced—how an impersonal heaven could possess "heaven's will."

Fourth, Jehovah is not just the national god of the Hebrews like the gods of other nations. He is the only God in the universe, so the Hebrew people did not choose to worship him, rather he chose them as his chosen people. He assigned Moses as a prophet to rescue the Hebrews enslaved by Pharaoh. Hebrew worship of God was a way of paying a debt of gratitude. As to why God chose the Hebrews, was it because they suffered so long? Was it to show God's goodness in saving the weak and punishing the evil? Or to show that the relationship between humanity and God requires trials and tribulations? The answer to this question can neither be proven or falsified.

Fifth, God's choosing of the Hebrew people is conditional rather than unconditional. The conditions are laid out in the Ten Commandments presented by Moses on Mt. Sinai. The relationship between mankind and God in the Hebrew dualistic worldview is established via "covenant"—essentially a credit relationship. Jehovah is not a God that simply has his way; instead, despite his omnipotence, he acts on covenant. The condition of the covenant is that the other party acts in accordance with the *human calling*. This is the best interpretation by human reason of the concept of *human calling*, also discussed by ancient Greek humanistic philosophy. This covenant is not like the legal provisions in the *Code of Hammurabi* of ancient Mesopotamia, nor the "laws, constraints, and orders" in the *Book of Lord Shang* of ancient China. Neither of them establishes a credit relationship between the two parties—only a unilateral declaration by the supreme royal power of a norm of conduct that must be observed by all his subjects. They only stipulate *human requirement*, rather than *human calling*.

Sixth, the terms of the Mt. Sinai covenant are not complicated. For God's part, he saved the Hebrew people from Egyptian slavery, gave them the promised land, and blessed them with freedom and equality; The Hebrew people's part was to worship Jehovah as the one God and to not worship other gods. They were not to make images or sculptures of God or any other gods. They adopted norms of conduct such as not murdering, not stealing, not committing adultery, and not preying on the weak, in order to safeguard the public order concerning human and property rights in community life. This public order is based on fairness and justice in the human community.

SECTION 2: THE ETERNAL RESIDENCE OF GOD'S ARK IN JERUSALEM

Hebrew faith in the one God was forged in suffering and written in tears and blood. Studying this phase of human history, where faith was borne out of a miserable purgatory of trials, requires a strong heart and willpower.

From the 11th century BC onward, the Hebrew tribal alliance was exposed to external violence. Without the organizational structure of a natural state based on a conventional, trained armed force and a corresponding system of taxation, the alliance found itself in a helpless, vulnerable position. Faced with a continuous offensive of violent attacks from Philistines on the southern coast, the tribal alliance quickly disintegrated and shifted to a hereditary monarchy.[99]

The key turning point was the defeat of the Israelites in a battle against the Philistines in 1050 BC. The central city of Shiloh was captured, and the tribal alliance's central temple destroyed. God's Ark of the Covenant was plundered. Amid the disintegration of the old order, a group of prophets represented by Samuel emerged. They responded to God's call and campaigned in the Hebrew community to form a class of judges who still maintained faith in Jehovah, even after the loss of the central temple and the ark. They adjudicated cases in accordance with the Ten Commandments to preserve the Hebrew public order. At the same time, they spoke through music to awaken the passion of the people for God's blessings and to ignite a strong desire to expel the Philistines from Israel.

Around 1030 BC, the great prophet Samuel secretly anointed Saul as King of Israel, who then assumed the heavy responsibility of expelling the Philistines. He was well-received by the people. Saul led the Israelites in victory over the Philistines and completed his historical mission of expelling them from their homeland. Saul became the first leader of the Israeli hereditary monarchy. He was a moody and unstable man, with fickle ideas reflecting the friction between the old and new systems. He also ignored the fact that the Philistines abandoned the ark in the wilderness and thus incurred opposition from the priestly class. Saul persecuted them for encroaching on his personal authority. Moreover, he was deeply jealous of his son-in-law and subordinate David, who was also a close friend of his son Jonathan. Out of fear that David's heroism and charisma were superior to his own, Saul plotted to destroy David, eventually forcing him to flee to the southern wilderness of Judah. Unable to hold his troops together afterwards, Saul was defeated by the Philistines.

Most of his family members were killed, and a large number of Israelites were massacred. Only one of Saul's sons, Ish-bosheth, escaped to east of the Jordan River and was anointed by prophets as the King of Israel in the north. David, meanwhile, was anointed the King of Judah by other prophets in the south. Israel was thus divided into two kingdoms.[100]

David was an extraordinary political leader full of God's blessings. From 1000 to 961 BC, he won several battles against the Philistines and successfully expelled them from the south, while refusing to use force or even trickery against his fellow Israelites in the north. He attempted to achieve peace between the north and south by taking back Michal, his wife and King Saul's daughter, but he was rejected by Ish-bosheth, King of Northern Israel. He rarely killed innocent people, using war only for God's righteousness. David was considerate of his people's well-being, prudent in the use of public tools, and never extravagant. This contrasted starkly with the words and deeds of Saul and Ish-bosheth, so the public wanted God to select David as king. But when Ish-bosheth was finally betrayed and killed by his subordinates, David still acted according to law and beheaded the soldiers who came to offer the head of Ish-bosheth, demonstrating his righteousness and integrity.

After David completely eliminated the threat of Philistine violence to the north and south of Israel, he was anointed King of Israel with God's blessings. By putting down the invasions of Ammon and Edom east of the Jordan River, he expanded Israel's territory southward to the Nile Valley of Egypt, northward across Damascus in Syria to the Euphrates River, and eastward to Ammon and Moab in the Transjordan. With this expansion of territory, a hereditary monarchical state began to take shape, ending the tribal alliance in Israel's political history.[101] David established a new form of natural state for the Hebrews. In his later years, he tried to use taxation to support government spending, which was becoming difficult to cover with only tribute and trade, and to maintain minimal standing armed forces. This is an indication that a political ecology based on monarchy was roughly taking shape. In sum, the Hebrews gained a new national identity in the land of Israel under King David's rule. Soon after, King David decided to make Jerusalem the capital and bring the ark, forgotten in the wilderness for over half a century, to the city. The people celebrated the move. King David became the representative of Israelites, God's chosen people. In this way, the covenant between God and King David recorded in the Prophets was established. God chose Mount Zion in Jerusalem as his eternal residence in the human world. He chose King David and his descendants as the kings of Israel to implement an orderly, theocratic government.[102]

After King David died, his son Solomon took the throne. From 961 to 922 BC, this monarch, with a sober mind and solid ideas, completed the formation of a hereditary monarchical system in terms of internal control, defense, diplomacy, taxation, and labor. He established 12 provinces in place of the 12 tribes, fundamentally ending the political form of the tribal alliance. Meanwhile, he achieved monumental success in commerce, foreign trade, copper smelting, the iron industry, and more. As a result, Israel was able to build the glorious Solomon's Temple and place God's ark within it.[103] Israel in the era of King Solomon appeared to reach its peak of glory and began to realize what God expected of the Israelites.

Prior to the shift to a monarchical "natural state," the covenant between the Israelites and God was very natural. The leader of the tribal alliance did not play any intermediate role between God and the Israelites. However, once God chose Zion as the place for the ark and King David's family as the permanent governing representatives of the state, things changed. All the earthly glory during King David's rule aside, the government of King Solomon burdened the Israelites with more and more direct taxation. He became an intermediary between God and the people of Israel. He functioned like an adopted son of God, which caused significant tension with the traditional philosophy of the Hebrew faith. A new doctrine for kingship was developed. God chose King

David and subsequent kings to represent the power of God over Israel. The king was responsible for seeking justice in the midst of the pain caused by God's discipline. Kings had to constantly accept blame from prophets called by God and keep themselves from deviating from the requirements of their intermediary role between the Israelites and God.[104]

SECTION 3: THE END-OF-DAYS CARNIVAL OF BETRAYAL

After King Solomon's death, the fragile regime began to fall apart. It began with a proposal by the northern Israelite tribes to reduce taxes and military service. After Solomon's son Rehoboam ruthlessly turned down their proposal, the northern tribes announced their secession from Jerusalem. Soon Jeroboam was anointed as King of Northern Israel, and Rehoboam could only hold the territory of Jerusalem and the southern region. Israel split into the northern state of Israel and the southern state of Judah.[105]

Once north and south separated, regional wars became frequent. Jeroboam in particular tried to establish a new state religion as a counterbalance to that Jerusalem, with a distinct tinge of idol worship that triggered fierce internal disputes. For more than half a century in Northern Israel, kings were replaced frequently through violence. Some of them didn't even go through the basic anointing ceremonies and ruled without God's approval or the support of the people. The political system was rotten to the core.

Similarly, as kings of Judah and Israel married Gentile royalty, polytheism and idolatry made its way into Israelite society. The prime example was the reign of the Omri family between 876 and 843 BC, during which Northern Israel had somewhat regained its power and King Ahab married Princess Jezebel. Jezebel flagrantly built a temple for the god Baal in Israel, promoted the worship of Baal, and even persecuted Elijah, Jehovah's prophet. In response to that, Elijah, Elisha and other prophets chanted in honor of Jehovah, awakening a sense of remorse in the Israelites for the breach of God's covenant. These prophets' actions directly led to the fall of the Omri family in 843 BC.[106] The same thing happened in Judah during this period, to the line of King Jehoshaphat. Athaliah, the wife of King Jehoram, had an altar built to Baal. The Israelites' worship of Jehovah was restricted and persecuted. This eventually led to a massive religious rebellion. Athaliah was killed, and the rule of the Jehoshaphat family ended.

From around 811 to 743 BC, Northern Israel and Southern Judah experienced economic and political resurgence, becoming almost as prosperous as the time of David and Solomon, still alive in the Hebrew people's memory. Especially during the rules of Jeroboam II in Northern Israel (786–746 BC) and Uzziah in Judah (783–742 BC), the two countries frequently won their military conquests. The territory of Northern Israel again extended to the Aramaic region north of Damascus and northeastern of Transjordan, borders comparable to the era of Solomon. Southern Judah defeated Ammon in the east and the Philistines in the south, extending its domain to the rivers of Egypt, rivaling the borders of the Solomonic era, and securing smooth overland and seaborne trade between North Africa and Transjordan. This trade boom and the increase in tax revenue brought division of labor, economic development, and urban prosperity to both northern and southern Israel. The nations seemed to be returning to the peak of *human ability* that God had promised.

At the same time, Israelite society became increasingly stratified, with the rich living an extravagant and self-indulgent life. The upper class was completely unaware of their misconduct, levying exorbitant taxes on the citizens of Israel, whose population was less than a million. The lower classes were miserable. Amid such superficial prosperity, people's behavior deviated greatly from their *human calling*. They were arrogant and debauched. They worshipped idols and foreign gods, even gods of fertility, openly violating the covenant with God. Such social chaos induced Israeli prophets

Amos and Hosea to respond to God's call and indignantly prophesy against the spiritual decay underneath the prosperous appearance of that era. They exposed society's morally corrupt words and deeds and treacherous breaches of Israel's covenant with God. They again explained the logic of *human calling* rooted in the singular faith in God, that is, their relationship of "choice, covenant, compliance, and promise" with God.[107] They prophesied that God would severely punish the Israelites for their "arrogance, breach of faith, disregard for justice, moral corruption," and other misconduct. A catastrophe was bound to befall the Israelites.

These prophecies were realized in Israel's gradual political and social corruption. After Jeroboam II's death, Northern Israel experienced frequent violent coups and rapid shifts of power with five kings in just 10 years. Three of them were usurpers without political legitimacy, neither anointed by prophets nor gaining support from the public. The country was plunged into political turmoil and civil war. This coincided with the rise of Assyrian King Tiglath-Pileser III (745—727 BC). His political ambition was to control all Asian countries north of Egypt and to conquer Babylon in the east. With a population fed by the Tigris River and a land several times larger than that of the narrow, arid zone of western Asia, Assyria was a juggernaut. With its capital Nineveh, the world's largest city and the center of a well-developed iron industry, Assyria had overwhelming economic and geopolitical advantages that aided its political ambitions.

Israel, however, was completely unaware of the looming crisis, blinded by the delusion that Jehovah would unconditionally favor them as his people. The upper class continued to indulge themselves in secular pleasures, unbridled lust, paganism, idolatry, and fratricide. The prophet Hosea responded to God's call and went around weeping, wailing, and lamenting in an attempt to awaken the lost Israelites. He proclaimed that the wrathful God would purge Israel's pagan revelry by the hand of Assyria, and that the end of Israel was coming.

Only when the remnant, the remaining people who were truly loyal to Jehovah, regained momentum, would God again show mercy and grant his favor. Only then would he bring Israel out of the wilderness and ashes of disaster, treating its disease of infidelity and restoring the covenant relationship.[108]

From 737–721 BC, the Northern Israel Kings Pekah and Hoshea forced the southern kingdom of Judah to join them in a series of absurd military struggles. These included uniting with the Egyptian monarch to fight Assyria, surrendering to Assyria, and rebelling against Assyria. In the end, Israel's cities were destroyed, many people died, and captives were made slaves. King Hoshea became a prisoner in 724 BC. Only the city of Samaria lasted for two years before being destroyed in 722 BC. In the last battle, nearly 30,000 Israelites became Assyrian slaves. Northern Israel was no more.

SECTION 4: GOD'S LONG WORK OF "REFINING" AND "CHOOSING"

Because Ahaz, King of Judah, refused to join Pekah's anti-Assyrian league, he was temporarily spared. But Ahaz didn't heed prophetic advice either—in this case the prophet Isaiah. Rather, he directly asked Tiglath-Pileser III to aid him against the Northern Israel-Aram alliance. This was courting disaster. The troops of Tiglath-Pileser III swept through Israel from south to north. Judah was not spared and became a vassal state of Assyria. Yet Ahaz still did not repent. He had no passion for faith in Jehovah. He made an altar in the holy city of Jerusalem to the god of Assyria, publicly violating the covenant with God and bringing him dishonor. He also continued in his corrupt and depraved behavior toward the people, levying exorbitant taxes and oppressing them in order to satisfy the court's extravagant "needs" and to pay tribute to Assyria.

The prophets Isaiah and Micah emerged in response to God's call. They excoriated the pagan worship and corruption in Judah and asserted that the fall of Israel was a punishment meted out by Jehovah through the hand of Assyria for the treachery of the king of Israel. This led to the religious reformation initiated by Ahaz's successor, Hezekiah (715–687 BC)[109]. Hezekiah rooted out various pagan idols, abolished pagan altars, removed a bronze snake said to be made by Moses, purified the main temple and the ark, and returned the nation to pure faith in Jehovah. Hezekiah's reformation contributed to the stability and revival of Judah. Jerusalem's population tripled under his rule. But because he twice ignored Isaiah and launched rebellions against Assyria at inopportune times, he invited a disastrous massacre on Jerusalem.

After Hezekiah died, his son Manasseh (687–642 BC) took power and became a submissive vassal of Assyria. He completely abandoned faith in Jehovah, rebuilt the Assyrian altar, and reintroduced idolatry, resulting in the rampant spread of divination and witchcraft. Israel experienced a full-blown crisis of faith, which led to the emergence of the famous prophets Zephaniah, Jeremiah, and Manasseh, who waged a war against the apostates. Their prophecies and calls awakened the Israelites' inner faith, enabling the religious reformation of Josiah, King of Judah (640–609 BC).

Josiah's reformation was similar to Hezekiah's in that he aimed to restore pure faith in the one God[110]. When renovating the temple, King Josiah found the Torah in the wall. He had the prophets read it and had the people take an oath of loyalty to God's covenant. Paganism and idolatry were removed according to the Torah. Circumcision and the Sabbath were kept along with the Passover and other holidays. Josiah's reign coincided with the defeat of the Assyrian Empire at the hands of Babylon and Egypt. Judah was thus granted 20 years of independence, freedom, and renaissance. But tragedy followed. In 609 BC, Egypt's Necho II attempted to cross Judah's borders to fight Babylon. King Josiah tried to block him but unfortunately met a tragic death on the battlefield. Judah once again became a vassal state of Egypt.

In 605 BC, the strong man Nebuchadnezzar ascended to the throne in Babylon and led its rise. At that time, King Jehoiakim of Judah swore allegiance to Nebuchadnezzar, once again becoming a vassal—this time to the Mesopotamian Babylonian Empire. The rebellion of Jehoiakim in 601 BC provoked the Babylonian army to overrun the city in 598 BC. Jerusalem surrendered. The king, queen, ministers, and a large number of subjects were taken captive as the first prisoners of Babylon.[111] Nebuchadnezzar appointed Zedekiah, the uncle of the previous king, to take the throne. Judah's territory had shrunk, along with its population. In 594 BC, a rebellion of Israelites from Judah imprisoned in Babylon was suppressed. In 589 BC, King Zedekiah led a rebellion that lasted for two years until 587 BC, when Jerusalem ran out of supplies and fell after fierce resistance. Nebuchadnezzar ordered the city to be slaughtered and burned. Zedekiah's eyes were cut out and he was taken to Babylon in chains. Of the 250,000 residents of Judah, a little over 10,000 clergy, officers, civil servants, and leading citizens were sent to Babylon, again becoming prisoners of Babylon.[112] These two groups of captured Israelites spent more than half a century under Babylonian subjugation. It wasn't until 539 BC, when the Persians completely defeated Babylon and formed a powerful empire of their own that these stateless Israelites were released. Bringing with them memories of endless suffering from human violence, they returned to Jerusalem, their holy city in ruins.

King Cyrus of the Persian Empire was an unusually enlightened monarch even by today's standards. He overturned the violent rule of the Assyrian and Babylonian Empires and implemented a policy of great tolerance and conciliation toward the small Asian states they had conquered. Each vassal state or province was governed by a satrap, usually selected from influential community members. As long as they recognized the kingship of the Persian Empire and paid tribute—far less than that demanded by Assyria and Babylon—Cyrus allowed and even encouraged them to follow their own culture and beliefs. That meant that the Israelites were allowed to return to Judah. Cyrus also issued a directive to rebuild their temple, and the Persian royal family even contributed money for its reconstruction. This policy was continued by the successive kings, including Darius, who ruled after Cyrus. This political environment was a rare opportunity for the revival of the Hebrew faith.

As the expatriated Israelites returned, they discovered that the newer generations were a far cry from the keepers of the Hebrew faith of more than half a century ago. Eroded by Gentile polytheism as a result of intermarriage, the pure monotheistic belief in Jehovah, like the ruins and rubble of their holy city, was nothing like the treasured memories of the returning exiles. They were heartbroken. But they quickly realized the importance of rebuilding the temple if they intended to rebuild the Hebrew faith. So they embarked on a grand project led by tens of thousands of returning Israelites in response to God's call, beginning in 538 BC.

The project didn't go smoothly, however, not only because of the political fluctuations of the Persian Empire, but more so because of clash of the returning Israelites and local inhabitants over religious and secular issues. It took over 20 years, until 515 BC, for the second temple of Jerusalem to be completed. The remnant, chosen and purified by God, finally had a place to gather and worship, along with new, enduring symbol of their community after all the suffering they'd endured.[113] During this period, two prophets, Haggai and Zechariah, responded to God's call and played a vital role in rekindling the passion of faith in Jewish society, motivating people to eagerly and conscientiously focus on the construction of the second temple.

However, the second temple did not immediately achieve its intended purpose of restoring faith in Jehovah. The main reason was the blurred religious boundaries between the Jews and non-Jews, exacerbated by intermarriage, that had weakened their faith, passion, and resolve. Low community morale diminished the sanctity of the priestly work, which in turn led to community disillusionment. People paid less attention to the Sabbath. They failed to pay tithes, broke the law, and bullied others—without any constraints. Naturally, the result was a general decline of public and personal morality. The restoration of the Israelite faith in God faced a deeper crisis, namely the reestablishment of the Jewish ethnic group.

In 445 BC, God's call to reestablish the chosen and purified remnant was fulfilled by Jewish exiles Nehemiah and Ezra. Nehemiah was the cupbearer of the King of Persia. At his request, the king appointed him satrap of Judah. Upon returning to Jerusalem, he rebuilt the city walls. With a firm and strong faith, Nehemiah disciplined himself to live off his savings and not accept the satrap's salary or own any property. He rebuilt the holy city with the help of volunteers. Concerned with the well-being of the lower classes, Nehemiah convened meetings with greedy merchants and appealed to their consciences and their faith to renounce the sinful practice of taking advantage of the poor by loan-sharking and cheating them out of their assets. He even ordered some of the worst offenders to be arrested. Nehemiah restored the dignity of the priests, personally oversaw the collection of tithes, and put honest people in charge of the accounts. He also closed the city gates to keep merchants from doing business on the Sabbath, in order to maintain the commandment.

But the problem of intermarriage—even tainting priestly families—proved most challenging. This was the most unresolvable issue in Nehemiah's first term (445–433 BC). During his second term, an exiled Jew named Ezra appeared in Jerusalem with an edict from the Persian King and a Torah. The Persian King authorized Ezra to enforce the Torah among the Jews. Ezra's background is hard to verify today. But he built a wooden platform in the square of the holy city and gathered those from Judah's upper classes, especially priests, who had married non-Israelites. Ezra stood on the platform and read the Torah from morning till noon. The people were deeply moved, and some burst into tears. Ezra himself got emotional and cried before Jehovah, confessing the sins of the believers. In the end everyone, deeply conscience-stricken, admitted to having violated the covenant with God. They voluntarily proposed dissolving marriages with their non-Jewish wives and swore to support whatever Ezra proposed. After more than three months, all such marriages were annulled. The Sabbath was observed, and tithing was maintained. This reform and reorganization once again revived the faith of the Jews.[114]

But the purification of God's chosen ones didn't end there. The tug of war between the maintenance of the Jewish faith and the invasion of paganism continued off and on for more than a century amid the restoration of faith promoted by the Persian King Darius' policy of religious tolerance. At the same time, the rise of Greece and its cultural influence began to creep into the daily lives of Jews. A major event occurred in the fourth century BC when Northern Israel initiated the construction of the temple of Samaria to rival the temple of Jerusalem with support from Athens.

In 336 BC, Aristotle's student Alexander, the first genius military commander in human history, took the throne of the kingdom of Macedonia. In just two years' time, this 20-year-old commander unified the Greek city-states with his personal charm and unique wisdom beyond his years. He formed a powerful empire based on ancient Greek religion and philosophy, and in 334 BC began his Asiatic expedition. Wherever Alexander's sword pointed, his unprecedented, overwhelming phalanx pulverized the mighty Persian army. King Darius died in battle. Damascus and the southern Jewish territory quickly fell. As Alexander's troops drove directly south, the Egyptians were so frightened and so exhausted by Persian rule that the garrison opened the city gate to let in Alexander and his army, and they agreed to change the name of their capital to Alexandria. The Samaritans alone staged an ill-advised rebellion against Macedonia, and Alexander subdued and massacred them. Those who survived fled and settled in Shechem. The Israelites in Judah submitted to their fate and surrendered to the Macedonian Empire.[115]

At 33, Alexander was cut down in his prime by illness in Babylon. He had conquered Europe, Central Asia, North Africa, and India, and incorporated them into his Macedonian Empire, but since he had no child to succeed him, it fell into in the hands of three of his subordinates. Judah became a vassal of the dynasties of one such subordinate—Ptolemy. The collapse of the Macedonian Empire proved to be the ideal fertilizer for the Roman Empire. Yet Alexander's conquest, even after the fall of his empire, allowed Greek culture to blossom through colonization in Asia, Africa, and Europe. The Hebrew culture of faith in Jehovah and the ancient Greek culture of polytheism and rational philosophy collided violently.

Between Alexander the Great's death in 323 BC and 176 BC, the reigns of both the Ptolemaic dynasty and Emperor Antiochus of the Seleucid dynasty saw a great increase in the population of Jews, not only in Israel but also in Alexandria of Egypt and other Asian cities. Despite the impact and challenges imposed by Greek polytheism and idolatry during this period, Jews continually returned to their monotheistic faith in Jehovah through the urging of their prophets.

In 175 BC, with the ascension of Antiochus IV Epiphanes (175–163 BC), an even greater challenge of faith and testing from God befell Judah. Antiochus, the last king of the Seleucid dynasty, fixed one eye on the wealth in the temple of Jerusalem, and the other on building his own cult of personality. He did this by taking over the appointment and dismissal of Judah's high priests, inviting a mad scramble among degenerates to bribe him for the position. Then he had the high priest bring idols of Zeus into the temple of Jerusalem, establish an altar to Zeus, and make offerings of pork on it. He even stole and sold holy objects from the temple. He further encouraged deviation from Jewish monotheistic belief by enforcing Hellenistic religious policies, such as abolishing circumcision and the Sabbath, building a Greek-style gymnasium in Jerusalem, forcing the Jews to participate in nude sporting events and attend the feasts in worship of the Greek god Dionysus, and burning the Jewish Torah. In the end, he even tried to make himself a Zeus on earth. Antiochus

IV Epiphanes put the Israelites in Judah through a purgatorial torment that eventually exceeded its limits and led to a rebellion in response to God's call.

In 167 BC, Mattathias and his five sons refused to lead a sacrifice to pagan gods and killed the Greek court officials on the spot. This sparked a revolt for the purification of the temple,[116] which was carried on by Judas Maccabeus, a son of Mattathias, after his death. The uprising, known as the Maccabean Revolt, became a three-year struggle. The Jewish forces won many asymmetrical and miraculous victories. Eventually the Greeks were driven out of Judah. The Olympian gods were completely removed from the second temple, and the corrosive, humiliating Greek polytheism and idolatry was eliminated from Judah. In December of 164 BC, the Jews held a grand and joyful yet sorrowful meeting to celebrate the rededication of the temple and the return of faith in the God Jehovah, as well as the renewal of the covenant between God and his purified Jewish remnant. The celebration of Hanukkah finds its origin in these events.

SECTION 5: FAITH FORGED IN BLOOD AND FIRE

The purpose of dedicating all this space to the history of the Jewish civilization is to understand the historical process and driving forces of the emergence of monotheistic belief in a personal god. History can help us see how the passion of human faith harmonized or clashed with philosophical rationality to create a unique cultural heritage. It clarifies how faith in Jehovah addressed in its own way the great historical quest for *human calling* in the Axial age of humanity's first great philosophical reflection.

While reading the history of human civilization, many people focus on the material achievements of *human ability* in its conquest of nature. This book focuses, instead, on the turbulent memories of people violating *human calling* as they both conquered nature and competed with one another. In order to stop human violence from trampling lives and destroying the beauty of peaceful order, mankind has continually called for individual rationality and a public spirit rooted in the soil of *human calling*.

Revenge is, of course, one way to restore order at a particular moment, but over time it loses its legitimacy because of its self-perpetuating nature: it leads to continuous and greater revenge. Judgment and punishment are certainly a better way of restoring public order. This method is superior, not only because it involves public punishment, but also because of its deeper roots in public rationality, that is, equality between individuals and fairness in judgment. Yet *human calling* is an even better way of preventing violence and maintaining peace and order. Appealing to *human calling* embeds the sense of public rationality into the behavioral duty of individuals. But whether this is done through persuasion, enforcement, or expectation can make a big difference. Persuasion is based on public ethics, which informs the *human duty* of individual actions. Enforcement is based on public legislation and trials, which forms *human requirement*. Expectation is based on public faith, which forms *human calling*.

From 1700 BC to 100 BC, a span of 1,600 years of written history, the disruption of the order of human society by violence was practically a normal occurrence. This was true for no people more than the ancient Hebrews. No other people in human history have been subjected to violence so frequent, so tragic, and so beyond the limits of a human community. The surrounding peoples were either luckier than the Hebrews and more or less avoided such catastrophic violence, or they were swallowed up by a larger national community during the violent onslaught and lost their original cultural identity. The Hebrew nation was a weak ethnic group that occupied a small area with a small population, and they were enslaved and exiled after the destruction of their country multiple times.

But 1,600 years of violence couldn't wipe out the cultural identity of the Jewish nation. Nor could it keep the Old Testament, with their history at its core, from being preserved. On the contrary—the Jewish people have been able to uphold the earliest faith in human history, that is, faith in the unipersonal God, Jehovah. A telling comparison is with that of the unipersonal god Aton in ancient Egypt during the reign of the 18th Pharaoh, Akhenaten (1351–1334 BC). Worship of Aton flourished for only 17 years before being completely annihilated. It could be said that Hebrew civilization is the greatest miracle of the Axial age. Why were the Jews able to bring about this miracle?[117] What does it mean for humanity's first great reflection? It is worth pondering.

The Jewish faith is the true culmination of human imagination during the first great reflection. It confirms that the relationship between humans and nature and the relationship between humans and society have the same origin: the one and only personal God, the creator. Ancient Greek philosophy dealt with this question to varying degrees, and it's implicated by Krishna in ancient Indian philosophy. The ancient Chinese philosophy of Laozi, Zhuangzi, and Mozi addressed it as well by regarding nature as the source of human philosophy. But none of those philosophies could fundamentally solve the problems of why and how the human-nature relationship and the human-society relationship have the same origin. A polytheistic cosmology doesn't have a logical explanation for this single origin. The Jewish faith, however, unwaveringly holds that natural and humanistic philosophies not only have the same origin, but that their origin is the one God Jehovah. Jehovah is the creator outside of humanity, nature, and the universe. Because he created the universe, nature operates within the rules and logic he created for it. He also created humans, who are made in the image of God. This incredible particularity means that God has endowed mankind with the unique free will to explore the rules and logic of nature, and to handle the relationships between individual humans and society. If people follow their *human calling* as guided by God's expectations, they will gain freedom and equality, and the world will be filled with the beautiful and harmonious order that God desires.

But once the people he created gained free will, their individual drives and desires were immediately open to being exploited by evil. With free will, humans may fail to recognize the sacred meaning of God as the source of creation, fail to recognize that they are equal because they are all created by God, and fail to recognize their own limitations as individuals or communities. They may become blind and arrogant; they may harm or even kill others for their own interests; they may promote polytheism, idolatry, or even build their own personality cult and enslave others. God created the beautiful, harmonious world order, and human beings have destroyed it, leaving the world to languish in bloodshed and chaos. God's disappointment and anger with humans is understandable.

In order to save the humans God created, he chose the Hebrews as his people and made a covenant with them, rescuing them from the violent enslavement of the human world and giving them the promised land of Canaan, or Israel. He gave it to them on the condition that they must only worship him as the one God, reject polytheism and idolatry, divination and witchcraft. They must refrain from murdering, stealing, robbing, cheating, and preying on the weak, and follow the other directives laid out in Moses's Ten Commandments. This covenant between people and God became the Torah, launching a grand project for individual Hebrews and their communities to rebuild the *human calling* of God's expectation based on individual free will and achieve a peaceful public order in the real world.

One may wonder why God favored the Hebrews and chose them out of the countless communities to be his people. This is a question only the heavens know. But we can still offer a reasonable answer with a little imagination: maybe it's because the Hebrew people experienced extreme violence and enslavement that aroused God's compassion. Or maybe God was looking for an instance in which violence and slavery was restrained to show his original intention in creating a world where humans and nature share the same origin.

More likely is that God chose the Hebrew people to conduct a test in the human world. The test was whether people could live according to God's expectations—his *human calling*—while both preserving the free will he granted them in creation and disciplining themselves for the sake of others. This is the way he provided for realizing the beauty of order and harmony among humanity as a whole. If this test proved successful, maybe he could extend similar inspiration and demonstration of his expectations to other individuals and communities. After all, this is what God's rescue plan is all about.

However, God's path in implementing this rescue plan was not smooth. Israelites who settled in the land of Canaan spent a relatively peaceful time from the 13th to the 11th century BC worshipping Jehovah as God, which sounds like the idyllic fruits of achieving harmonious order in human society. But with the Philistine offensive on the southern coast in the late 11th century BC, external violence came to the Hebrew community. In order to curb this violence and restore public order, the Israelites responded with urgent internal consolidation and reorganization of the state between the 10th and 9th centuries BC. They replaced their original public order in the form of the tribal alliance with the hereditary monarchy of Saul, David, and Solomon.

This replacement was like a newly minted coin. One side represented the expansion of Israelite territory, the increase of public security, the trade boom and economic development, and the splendor and glory of Solomon's temple. The other side was the emergence of a monarch who came between Jehovah and the faith of individual Israelites, who not only represented God to a certain extent, but also had the right to tax—and in some cases overtax—the Israelites to maintain public order. These circumstances presented a huge risk that the monarch would replace God as the king of Israel in the physical world. To counteract this risk, the prophets developed a new doctrine around Israel's king and its capital Jerusalem, as Solomon's Temple was built and God's ark was moved into it. On the basis of Moses's covenant at Mount Sinai, God went on to choose Mount Zion, or Jerusalem, as the permanent residence of the Ark of the Covenant, and he chose David and his heirs as God's representatives. This enabled the Israelites to seek their God-endowed freedom and equality restrained by the threat of discipline by David and his heirs. For this reason, King David and his heirs had to endure constant criticism by prophets called by God to hold them accountable and prevent them from deviating from their role as intermediaries of God's righteousness. David's Zion covenant, then, formed the second covenant after Moses' at Mount Sinai. The development of this covenant is logically consistent and extremely powerful.

Over the 800 years from the ninth to the first century BC, Israel experienced the north-south division, apostasy, revival, decay, blasphemy, and decay again; the destruction of Northern Israel by the Assyrian Empire, the resulting exile of a large number of Jews to Assyria, the fall of Southern Judah to a vassal of the Assyrians; the invasion of paganism, polytheism, and idolatry; the enslavement of Judah by the Babylonian Empire, the suppression of Judah's joint rebellion with Egypt and the captivity of the leading Israelites; the erosion of paganism and the apostasy of the dynastic family; another suppression of a rebellion by Judah; slaughter in the holy city and the destruction of Solomon's temple; the second captivity of the prisoners of Babylon for over half a century; the destruction of Babylon by the Persian Empire and the Persian policy of religious tolerance; the return of exiled Israelites and the reconstruction of the second temple; Nehemiah's religious reformation and Ezra's reorganization of Judah's society; the return of faith in Jehovah; several invasions of paganism and idolatry; independence of Judah followed by another surrender to Egypt; conquest of Judah by Alexander the Great of the Macedonian Empire; Israel's rebellion and Alexander's suppression, massacre, and destruction of the second temple; Israel's surrender to the Ptolemaic and Seleucid dynasties; the invasion of the worship of Greek gods and Antiochus IV Epiphanes' forceful promotion of polytheism; the Maccabean Revolt in Judah to purify the second temple, the expulsion of Greek colonists, and the completion of the Old Testament.

Over this long historical process, the prophets responding to God's call played the role of upholding faith in the unipersonal God throughout the unification, division, exile, and return of the Israelites. Famous prophets included Samuel, Elijah, Elisha, Amos, Hosea, Zephaniah, Jeremiah, Isaiah, Micah, Ezekiel, Haggai, Zechariah, Daniel, and many more. The prophets devoted themselves to exposing the apostate behavior of kings, high society, and even ordinary people who betrayed faith in Jehovah, mainly through dancing, chanting, lamenting, and writing prophetic books. Such apostate behavior ranged from failure to follow the basic commandments of the Sabbath, Passover and circumcision, to the cardinal sins of divination and witchcraft, worshiping idols and pagan gods, preying on the weak, or even building one's own personality cult.

The prophets never preached nationalism or incited national hatred. Rather, they attributed the violent invasions of powerful outsiders like Assyria and Babylon to the Jews' violation of their covenant with God and their abandonment of faith in him. Such violent invasions were God's punishment for the betrayal of the Israelite kings and people. Nor did the prophets blindly instigate the revolt and rebellion against the sovereign states that ruled over the Jewish people. Rather, most of the time they stood against the kings, opposing blind rebellion and uprising and instead advocating obedience to God's arrangement. There were only a few times when the prophets advocated rebellion and succeeded. Of course, the prophets also predicted that the sovereign states of Assyria, Babylon, Egypt, Persia, and Macedonia would perish, but not because of their sin of invading and ruling Israel and Judah, but because they forcibly promoted worship of gods other than Jehovah, idolatry, divination, and witchcraft, which led to moral and social decay.

Looking back at this history of human suffering, we are struck by the fact that the prophets, for all the trials and tribulations they went through, managed to stay faithful to the faith in Jehovah. Their predictions were almost never wrong, and they never sowed national hatred. Their steadfastness itself is a tremendous miracle in the history of human civilization, not to mention the many, many miracles of prophesies fulfilled. We humans, as finite beings, are unable to disprove that their actions were a response to a calling from the infinite, eternal, and omnipotent God.

However, since God chose the Hebrews to be his people, why did he make them experience hardship that went so far beyond that of any other people? Why did God allow the Jewish people to be ravaged so many times? Why did God send them into exile, leaving millions displaced? Could it be that God didn't love the people he himself chose? Why would they still worship Jehovah as the one personal God? Would God give his people a promise for the future? Likely the Jews asked these questions countless times during their history of suffering, leaving them confused, exhausted, and sorrowful. This may also be the reason so many resorted to polytheism and idolatry. However, the Jewish prophets stood firmly on God's side, supported by the consistent logic of God's answers to these questions: Jehovah's promise to the Hebrew people was not unconditional. They must comply with the covenants, including the covenant of Mount Sinai and the covenant of Mount Zion. The core provisions of these two covenants included the rejection of any god other than the unipersonal God, as well as divination and witchcraft; the protection of the rites of circumcision, the Sabbath, and Passover; and prescribed actions such as refraining from stealing and committing violence against others. The covenants were serious, not casual. Violation was considered sin.

But ever since the time of King Solomon, the Jews of Israel and Judah, from monarchs to princes and civilians, fell into this very sin. This violation incurred God's righteous judgment. Since the Jews had breached the contract, God had to enact punishment by the hand of Assyria, Babylon, Egypt, the Persian Empire, and the Macedonian Empire, and both judge and purify his chosen people until those who could keep the covenant were left, forming the remnant. Only then would God send his son, the Messiah to Israel to rebuild God's kingdom on earth.

Driven by faith in Jehovah, the Jewish people lived up to his expectations. Over countless cycles of purification and choosing, which almost led to the destruction of Israel, prophets continually emerged at the call of God. There were also leaders like King Hezekiah, King Joshua, Satrap Nehemiah, Satrap of the Torah Ezra, and Judas Maccabeus, each of whom arose and echoed the prophets' resounding calls. Amid the chaos of pagan invasion and apostasy, they launched religious reformation, rebuilt the temple, restructured society, and purified the temple, among other things, in a bid to revive faith in Jehovah. The exiled Jews, for their part, were always able to adapt to the various physical, cultural, and political environments of other countries while bearing the heavy memories of the terrible suffering of their people and living out their earthly achievements and glory. Though thousands of miles from their homeland physically, their souls always held on to the ark of the holy city, tenaciously adhering to their belief in the one God, Jehovah.

Since the 15th century BC, the Hebrew people have miraculously kept their belief in this unipersonal God. They wrote the Old Testament after 1,500 years of baptism by blood and fire and after so many devastating trials—experiencing God's choosing followed by the breaking of his covenant. In this sense, the Jews truly deserve the holy and glorious title of "God's chosen and purified people."

From this study of Israel's history, it's evident that *human calling*—and its implications for the public relationship between humans and society—is firmly established on the basis of the covenant between mankind and God. This kind of *human calling* is filled with the passion of enjoying God-given individual free will and also rich in the rationality of living an equal, covenant-keeping life in compliance with God's expectations. If people can live according to God's ideals for *human calling*, society will be filled with passion, vitality, rationality, and harmonious order. According to the natural law that nature and mankind share the same origin through God's creation, shouldn't the natural world also have a "nature's calling" of its own to follow? God didn't give nature free will, but he did provide it with an operational law. Nature must operate according to this inherent law given by God, and so demonstrate the beauty of God's order in it. This beauty reflects his original intention to create order by subduing chaos. When people apply their *human ability* to nature in accordance with their free will, they need both a recognition of God's operational law for nature and a deep understanding of his expectations, or *human calling*.

It's clear that the Hebrew faith in Jehovah offered a brand-new interpretation of the relationship between humans and society and the relationship between humans and nature, in claiming that both originate in God's natural law. That means that all truths about these two relationships also originate from God, the creator who is outside our universe. While our bodies go through life and death on earth in the time defined by God and according to his natural operational law, our souls orient themselves toward holiness by upholding faith in God and following the rationality of his *human calling*. In this way, both aspects of our being are connected to God's absolute truth. This was significant and had far-reaching implications for the first great reflection of mankind, solving the problems of how to elevate *human ability* based on their understanding of the relationship with nature, as well as how to respond to their *human calling* regarding the relationships between humans and society in community life. It transcends human perception and can only be properly understood by faith in God.

CHAPTER 6:

Call: the Roman Pantheon founded by the sword

SECTION 1: THE INFILTRATION AND GERMINATION OF THE PUBLIC ORDER OF THE "ROMAN REPUBLIC"

External violence from Alexander the Great against the Mediterranean coast set off the gradual decline among the three Greek monarchical colonial empires. Propelled by the collision between the tragic stories of its pantheon and its rational philosophical thinking, Greece actually came nearest to establishing faith in one god. While the fruits of Greek philosophy spread through Europe from the cultural centers of Athens and Rome, Egypt's Alexandria became another center, from which Greek philosophy spread to North Africa, Asia, and Europe. For many reasons, the penetration of this philosophical culture was a gradual process. But with the rise of ancient Rome with its republican politics, this historical process was greatly accelerated.

Ancient Romans, in learning from their tutors the Greek philosophers, themselves drew on the rich political philosophy of Greek city-state democracy and gradually formed their own model and paradigm of political governance. The Roman paradigm was an institutional arrangement of the public will as codified in Roman law, based on the free and equal rights of citizens. It put the constraints of *human calling* on individual conduct. It also raised governance through community public will based on Roman citizenship to an unprecedented new level, along with the external expansion of human community size.[118]

Along the way, the Roman Empire went through a transition from republican politics to imperial politics. Roman Republican politics was based on the study of inherited Greek philosophy and its city-state democratic politics. It was the first aristocratic attempt at political governance using the idea of the separation of powers in human history. The senate of the Roman Republic consisted of 300 assembly members that were a mix of patricians and plebeians. This body was balanced by the consuls with their military and administrative powers and the tribune who supervised the consuls on behalf of the plebeians. Together they constituted a republican political system with a balance of political forces.[119] In building this system, the Romans didn't look for the answer to social public order in the *human calling* of individual behavior guided by God's expectations and philosophical rationality. Rather, they resorted to a direct, pragmatic solution of checks and balances on political power, attempting to place people's behavioral duty under legal provision so it would comply with the requirements of public order. This approach appears very similar to the legislation of the citizens of Greek city-states, but very different from systems in other cultures and periods. The Code of Hammurabi and ancient China's laws, rules, and orders such as *the Book of Lord Shang* and "the criminal code engraved on a bronze tripod" from the Spring and Autumn and Warring States Period are prominent examples.

The biggest difference lies in the legislative process. Both Roman and Greek city-state legislation was finalized through voting after debate among representatives of individual citizens in the assembly and the senate. Legislation, then, represented legal authority derived from the rights of those who qualified as citizens. Those rights, in turn, were rooted in a sense of human dignity manifested as freedom and equality and endowed by the rationality of the gods in ancient Greek philosophy. In comparison, ancient Chinese and Egyptian legislation of laws, rules, and orders was granted by the earthly god Pharaoh or the divine right of kings. Ordinary people were obliged to obey the laws issued by kings, with no right to participate in the legislative process.[120] The Roman laws, which embodied the norms of public order among Roman citizens and those individuals living in affiliated countries and provinces, were proclaimed widely and inscribed on bronze tablets, which became known as the Twelve Tables.

The Roman Republic system allowed the members of the senate to debate, argue, and vote on legislation for the public service of Roman citizens under the supervision of the democratic senate, demonstrating its members' character and talent as the nation's aristocratic elite. The consuls were mainly military leaders chosen to represent Rome's warrior spirit. They fought only for external victories for the Roman community, seeking to demonstrate their military leadership and perpetuate an aura of invincibility. The 300-member assembly was made up of plebeians with civil rights and land-owning peasants, who participated in political life by voting, a similar practice to that of Greek city-state democracies. These Romans possessed the most important assets of the time—not only land, but also the highly prized privilege of Roman citizenship, which entitled them to join the assembly and vote in the election of the consuls. As for the senate, it was mainly drawn from Roman aristocrats. These members always answered questions pragmatically—like whether to protect existing lands or acquire new ones through war and whether to protect existing Roman citizenship or acquire this extremely important right—and based their approach on their political goals. For them, political participation was connected to Roman victory and the interests of the Roman people. To this end, they could all enlist to fight for Rome under a political system designed to turn every man into a soldier. The Roman city-state, with its particular geographical environment of northern Italy and the waterways of Mediterranean countries, along with its particular time in history when Greek political civilization was declining and Roman political civilization was rising, provided an ideal environment for this political system to germinate and grow quickly.

SECTION 2: THE COMPLETE INDUSTRIAL CHAIN OF THE ROMAN BRAND

Rome began as a small city-state. Even including the population of the surrounding countryside, it began with only 400,000 people, comparable to the size of the urban population of Athens in Greece. But once a political-machine-like Rome began gaining momentum, it quickly scoured its peripheral area, expanding its territory by sword and shield. Romans didn't have the Greek mind for business or their taste for the arts, even less so the Greeks' passionate imagination about the gods or inner spiritual response to the gods' tragic stories. As a result, they lacked the deep and rational philosophical contemplation of the Greeks. But Romans' love for the sword and land far exceeded that of the Greeks, which explains the long-existing taste for conflict among its people.

In order to acquire new land, all Romans could apply to join a legion and fight for conquest at any time. Many foreigners were also willing to do so to gain Roman citizenship.[121] Generally at that time, in a country with a million people, the number of conscripts available would range from 10,000–100,000, but raising an army was a big expense, so conscription was limited. However, in Rome's case, since the enslavement of defeated soldiers became a universally recognized norm in the spirit of natural law, Romans often considered the countries they fought as a potential source of enslaved labor. As a result, sources for conscripts were never a concern for the Romans. And it turned out that they were right. Conscripts available for Rome often accounted for 15–20 percent of its citizens, more than twice the proportion of other communities. This was key to the expansion of the Roman community.[122] But Rome never called up or supported more troops than needed to win. They always formed an army on an ad hoc basis, and always prioritized combat readiness and their chance of winning.

But where did the army's fighting power come from? First, soldiers only fought for land and Roman citizenship. The former represented their interests, and the latter their interests and glory. Any time land was gained from a defeated country, the senate distributed it according to merit. Half was given to the underprivileged and to soldiers, and the other half was sold, with the proceeds going to Rome's public spending and rewards for the army. The accumulation of military merits allowed non-Roman freeman to gain Roman citizenship. Later, it also allowed slaves to first gain their freedom and then eventually earn Roman citizenship by securing more military honors. This system meant that the morale of the Roman army was constantly boosted by the promise of material benefits and glory.

Second, consuls were professional military leaders, whose interests and glory rested on military victories and conquests. As a result, they were experts in the study of various countries' military methods. In order to win glory and status among the cheering people of the city of Rome, they trained the army strictly, knew their soldiers well, and valued them. They bound their soldiers with military vows, so that if one made a mistake or deserted, lots would be drawn and one tenth of each group would be punished. Soldiers would never kill innocent civilians. That meant that the army was disciplined, sharp, and highly capable.

Third, the management of the military by the public office of the senate was rational and effective. It wasn't originally corrupt—rather it reflected society's democratic attempt to appeal strongly to people's character and talent. The senate sent embedded officers to keep records on and evaluate military merits, so that rewards were always fair. On this basis, the martial spirit of soldiers and generals in pursuit of victory and glory was passed on to the people. The warlike spirit and martial tradition, greatly stimulated and strengthened from the top down, only grew in Roman civil society. This in turn provided the Roman legion with a large pool of potential soldiers whose strength, skills, confidence, and other military abilities were superior to other troops of the era. Alexander was a genius military leader who happened to be Greek, but the political system of the Roman city-state was designed to be an incubator for cultivating military leaders like Alexander.[123]

The Roman Republic founded on a sword-and-shield basis legislated the spirit of natural law and *human requirement* to the extreme. The Roman code, typified by the Twelve Tables, not only provided the greatest possible guarantee for the rights of Roman citizens, but also brought protections for land and property to unprecedented heights for that era. The code even addressed issues of procedural justice like reducing or eliminating the use of torture to extract confessions from Roman citizens. Rome put such procedural justice into legislation and law enforcement like never before.

Many elements of the Roman Republic system set it apart. These included the senate's composition and working mechanism; the design of the posts of magistrates, municipal officials, and tax collectors under the consuls; the highly systematic administration of the government; the procedural supervision of legislation by the plebeian assembly; the tribunes' oversight of the consuls; and the remedial measures after political crises such as by-elections and appointments of dictators by the plebeian assembly. These elements all revealed the basic outline of modern democratic politics. Its bold attempts at political governance and communal public order based on the "natural law of war" and *human requirement* made Rome a powerful republican empire that harmonized individual vitality and public order better than any other agricultural civilization.[124]

But the civilization of the Roman Republic was based entirely on violent conquest for the purpose of territorial expansion. That is, public order within the community was predicated on subjugation by force of those outside the community. In such a republic, everything evolved around the complete industrial chain of external expansion: selecting the target of conquest, violent conquest, and distribution and governance.[125] When choosing a target for conquest, the Roman senate, owing to its members' characters and its method of open debate, played a vital role as a rational, intelligent thinking and decision-making body, so that Rome never used violence blindly. Rather, the senate made calls depending on the conflicts between neighboring city-states and small tribal states, and even on clashes over succession within the small states.

Essentially, Rome used its influence as a great power to carry out diplomatic mediation. But once it intervened, Roman military conquest suddenly became the most legitimate course of action. What followed was internal strife and warfare among the involved parties in the target state, and Rome ultimately won at no cost to itself. If the party that Rome supported was defeated, the Roman legion immediately launched an attack in the name of justice, winning every battle and expanding the influence of the Roman Republic. If they encountered a difficult battle situation that must be fought strategically, the senate would discuss the issue carefully with the consuls before making a final decision. As in the battles of the Macedonian Kingdom and the Punic Wars against Carthage, once the decision was made, the Roman legion's military experts patterned their attack after the Macedonian phalanx, a legacy of Alexander the Great and the naval warfare of both Macedonia and Carthage, and they simulated every countermeasure. By virtue of this spirit of learning and innovation, as well as their brave, tenacious, high-morale army, Rome managed to defeat its strongest enemies, so that the name of the Roman legion became a massive deterrent for aggression in other parts of the world.

But no Roman conquest won was followed by plunder and massacre. In fact, Rome never killed innocent people nor unilaterally executed its edicts. Rather, its leaders would sit down with the losing party like gentlemen, negotiating with them and signing a contract. Post-war issues such as the amount of reparations, how the losing party would be governed after submitting to Roman authority, and the number of prisoners of war to become Roman slaves, were all settled through contractual agreement and became part of Roman law after the victory. All of this was carried out in a civilized way based on principles of equality and contract compliance. And for the Roman legion itself, warriors were rewarded with land and wealth according to their merit during the fighting. Those whose deeds were worthy received corresponding medals and wealth. Slaves who acted honorably became free people, and free people had the ability to attain citizenship and its rights. Therefore, violent conquest led to the growing size of Roman citizenry, while legal, contractual governance of defeated countries added to the influence and glory of the Roman Republic.

It now becomes clear how, through this complete industrial chain of violent expansion and resulting treaties, Rome went from being a small city-state of 1,000 square kilometers in area in 509 BC, to governing over 5 million square kilometers in the Mediterranean coastal region by 44 BC under Julius Caesar. There were more than 750,000 free citizens in Rome, plus an equivalent number of farmers with citizenship and land and their own large slave population working in the fields. A population of more than 60 million non-Roman citizens paid taxes under the Roman Republic's jurisdiction. It truly created a miraculous paradigm of expanding the community while keeping orderly and effective governance for that era of human history. Its influence on human civilization is deep and far-reaching.[126]

SECTION 3: THE FINAL DAYS OF THE ROMAN REPUBLIC

Republic politics, driven by the natural law of war, was key to the rise of Roman civilization, but it inevitably began to show signs of struggle, leading to the transition of Rome from republican to imperial politics. Specifically, the ideal design of checks and balances between the various political forces in the republic were severely constrained by the levels of organization and technology at the time. As the scale of the republic grew immoderately, the organizational capacity of the plebeian assembly got increasingly out of sync. The tribune lost its intended supervisory role, turning into vassals of the consuls. Meanwhile, the annual election of consuls became impractical, and their replacement usually triggered crises. The senate also became more bureaucratic with redundant members. The total number reached 600—and up to 900 in the later years, nearly out of control—which inevitably led to a drop in the quality of members and a decline in the sense of honor. The pursuit of mercenary interests gained the upper hand. People sought to enter the senate only to gain aristocratic status and benefits. The senate descended into an interest group of aristocrats, no longer an elite decision-making body representing the interests of Rome. Corruption and inefficiency were the inevitable, logical end results.

As Rome grew larger in population, it became more dependent on violent conquests to provide these benefits, making the consuls' responsibilities increasingly heavy. In addition, the effective support that they gained from the senate was waning, so the administrative provinces—in effect dependent states—gradually disconnected from the central command center of Rome.

Meanwhile, corruption spread through all dependent states along with the dispatch of governors by the senate. These governors of administrative provinces frequently turned against the consuls, further weakening their power. At the end of the day, this only intensified thirst for seats in the senate that came with considerable power but no accountability. A vicious cycle was set in motion throughout the whole Roman Republic, adding to the suffering of society's lower classes through bureaucratization and inefficiency. Riots and rebellions emerged everywhere, making the jobs of generals and consuls, who were in charge of both conquests and subjugations, even more difficult. Moreover, Rome found itself in a position where it had to support a growing number of idle people. Around 50 BC, about 300,000 people in Rome were living entirely on the dole, because Roman citizens were no longer landlords with slaves working for them. More and more Roman citizens lost their original longing for land and became completely free Roman urbanites, deriving their welfare and property from distributions of foreign tribute and spoils of war.

Under these conditions, the upper echelons of Roman society were caught up in political battles over their interests in the client states. As for regular citizens, Roman life became nothing more than enjoying the convenience provided by public facilities, as well as the pleasure brought by violent gladiatorial combat in the arena, erotic baths, and other entertainment services. As a result of Roman citizens' extravagant lifestyle without industrial support and the lack of an effective system for information sharing and voting for such a large population, the political democracy of Rome began to lack direction and internal logic, and it lost more and more of its original impetus and constraint.

Without effective restraints from the plebeian assembly, Roman politics became a power game between the senate and the consuls. The meaning of the "republic," in the eyes of the senate, was actually a matter of whether or not its members could guarantee their own interests. They feared that the consuls' dictatorship would curtail the interest of the patricians in the senate, so they were eager to veto consul proposals without considering what they meant for the republic. But when a military crisis broke out in a client state, the consuls were the only ones that they could count on. Once the consuls quelled such rebellions, performing outstanding military exploits in the process, the threat of their dictatorial rule again loomed over the interests of the patricians. Senate members responded by doing everything they could to support other military forces to balance and constrain the consuls. In this way, the seeds of a civil war were planted by the senate's political inclinations and the consuls' pursuit of power. The temptation to stay in power and the pressure to avoid being knocked down by proteges of the senate forced the consuls to actively partic- ipate in this bilateral political game. By the last century BC, this game turned into a prisoner's dilemma that Roman Republican politics could not solve. The political struggles in the era of Julius Caesar best illustrate the intrinsic logic of the Roman Republican political model's breakdown in the end.[127]

The slave uprising of 73 BC, led by Spartacus, shows what conflict and rebellion were like under this political system. At its peak, 120,000 people participated. They attacked and captured cities through skillful maneuvers and engaged Roman troops garrisoned in the client states in close combat. The Roman legion, which had been invincible for over 500 years, was defeated. The strength and momentum of the enemy's army stunned the senate and the patricians, keeping them awake at night with anxiety. Finally, the senate decided to send Pompey and Crassus, the two best generals under the consul Sulla, with elite troops to besiege Spartacus. In 71 BC, they finally wiped out their enemies. Six thousand prisoners were executed and hung in the forest for several months as punishment. The two victorious commanders were required by Roman law to disband their army outside of Rome before entering the city. But they knew this would leave them open to being sued by their senate opponents. Some would charge them with every possible crime, while others would try to sow discord between them, hoping to benefit from their fight.

The senate's ridiculous behavior and lack of regard for the interests of the Roman Republic drove Pompey and Crassus to join forces against their shared risk. They refused to disband the army outside the city and sought the senate's consent to make them candidates for consulship before they entered, protecting them from the disaster of being sued by the senate. Bribing senate members and making direct payments to Roman citizens with their spoils of war, Pompey and Crassus were successfully elected as joint consuls in 70 BC. Their election inaugurated the history of oligarchic joint consulship in the Roman Republic. Julius Caesar himself emulated their rise to political prominence and later ascended to the center of the Roman political stage.

After election, Pompey eliminated the threat of pirates for Rome, making way for unimpeded trade in the Mediterranean. He conquered the lands of Asia, quelled civil strife, and established 39 cities, bringing mountains of wealth and glory to Rome. But he was soon snubbed by the senate, his proposals failing to even garner responses. Pompey's next move was to fully align himself with the ambitious, talented rising star of politics, Julius Caesar. With Pompey's support, Caesar was elected as a consul in 59 BC, joining Pompey and Crassus in the oligarchic alliance known as the First Triumvirate.

Caesar dared to oppose the senate and applied his political skills to send proposals rejected by the senate to be approved by the assembly. He activated the political participation of the Roman plebeian assembly, notably pushing through the land reform legislation that was once attempted by the Gracchus brothers in the second century BC. Under the new law, the land would be allocated to the poor, including soldiers, and to families with three or more children. He even pushed for the passing of fiscal bills that encouraged agriculture and commerce. All of these initiatives helped Caesar win deep support among the Roman citizenry.[128] With regard to political strategy, Caesar was one of the few consuls that could harness the senate and assembly. His measures not only helped curb the erosion of the rights of lower classes by the interests of aristocrats, but also took into account the balance of interests between the Roman Republic and its client states. That benefited the long-term stability of Rome. Unfortunately, Caesar's stellar reputation, strong capability, and great mind made the senate nobles envious, bitter, and deeply anxious.

Despite all the troubles that the senate caused him, Caesar happily accepted its appointment as governor of two of the toughest areas of Gaul from 58 to 49 BC. He put all of his energy into the suppression of the Gaul rebellion and the complete subjugation of the Gaulish and Germanic tribes. In order to bypass a likely filibuster by the senate, he privately formed four legions without their consent. After 10 years of fighting, he claimed victory and created a unique management system that balanced the interests of Rome and the provinces of Gaul, achieving long-term stability in Rome's backyard. He also conquered Britain and Germania and expanded and consolidated Rome's territory in Europe, which reached twice the size of Italy. By bringing long-lasting peace and glory to the Republic of Rome, Caesar became a great hero in the minds of the Romans.

But this period also saw the corruption of Rome's democracy reach an unprecedented level. Crassus and Pompey once again joined forces, but they lacked vision and impartiality. They spent money lavishly on re-election, even resorting to assassinations. Along with the corruption of the senate, the whole society became degenerate. As Cicero described it, "the Tiber was full of citizens' corpses; the public sewers were choked with them." After Crassus was trapped and killed by the Parthians, Pompey began dreaming of his dictatorship. The senate, Pompey, and Caesar knew full well that the chaos and disorder created by the freedom of the Roman Republic had reached a despicable level. Society was calling for new peace and order. The days of Roman Republican politics were numbered. While oligarchic politics might not have been the best way out, a monarchal regime was an important option that could not be ignored.

Caesar's term as governor of Gaul was set to expire in March of 49 BC. He returned to Rome with numerous military achievements and an exhausted body after decades of fighting but found himself in a predicament. He couldn't live a secure life as a normal citizen:[129] he wouldn't stand for election as consul until the fall, and during the gap period with his army disbanded, Cato and others in the senate intended to charge him with organizing private legions and other crimes. Even Pompey was preparing to eliminate him. But if he didn't disband the army, he would be breaking the law. Caesar tried every negotiation tactic he could to resolve the dilemma, but the senate rejected each of his proposals that would guarantee his safety, including retaining his consul title and standing as a candidate for consulship in the autumn election. They simply urged him to disband the army. Later Caesar proposed that his and Pompey's army be disbanded at the same time. The senate passed the agreed-upon resolution, but Pompey refused to implement it. The senate let Pompey's refusal go unchallenged. Apparently, their sights were set on Caesar alone—Caesar who had contributed so much and done such a great service to Rome. Eventually, he was forced to declare war on Pompey, the only way to enforce the decision made by the senate.

Their war was the largest civil war in the 500-year history of the Roman Republic. Caesar took only the 13th legion and crossed the Rubicon River to fight Pompey's vast army, leaving the other 10 legions far away in Gaul. Though Caesar's legion was greatly outnumbered, righteousness and justice seemed to take their side. Everywhere the legion arrived, people welcomed them into the city. Meanwhile, Pompey's unpopular army, having lost its morale and fighting power, retreated all the way to the south. Some senate members also followed Pompey's army in retreat out of Rome. Caesar stationed his legion on the outskirts of Rome and entered the city by himself. He came before the frightened senate patricians and declared an amnesty to stabilize the situation. Then he led his army to defeat Pompey's Spanish forces to guarantee Rome's food supply. Step by step, Caesar drove off Pompey's forces all the way to Alexandria, where Pompey was killed by his subordinates. Senator Cato, for his part, continued struggling in Africa until 46 BC, before finally being persuaded by his son to surrender to Caesar. He committed suicide late at night in the city of Utica. Caesar kindly announced forgiveness for those who opposed him, such as Brutus and Cassius, and entrusted them with crucial positions. He also reorganized the personnel in Rome's dependencies. The civil war was ended.

The senate, shaken and overwhelmed by the power of public opinion, duly appointed Caesar as consul for 10 consecutive years and announced that if he still had the support of the Roman citizenry by 44 BC, his term was to be extended as life tenure. After being elected by the assembly as tribune for life and taking a census with qualifications to vet senators, Caesar was able to centralize power to prevent the political turmoil caused by the old system. Meanwhile, he added 16 additional praetors and 39 quaestors that served various functions and improved administrative efficiency. In order to appease the built-up resentment and dissatisfaction among the lower classes and client states, Caesar took a portion of the land and distributed it to veterans, families with three or more children, and poor families, in addition to stipulating that the land was not to be sold for 20 years to prevent the reconsolidation of landholdings. The move helped alleviate poverty, reducing benefit claimants from 320,000 to 150,000. He also expanded the number of senators from 600 to 900. The additional members were mainly industrial and commercial elites, elites from major client states like Gaul, distinguished retired military officers, and even representatives of slaves. At the same time, he granted Roman citizenship to many prominent soldiers, free doctors, and teachers in client states to strengthen their identification with the Roman Republic.

With no intention of being an emperor whatsoever, Caesar rejected the crown three times. He merely wanted to build a better Roman Republic. He showed incredible magnanimity by forgiving all the senate patricians who supported Pompey and Cato in the civil war and entrusting hard-core resisters like Brutus and Cassius with important tasks. Ironically, it was this kindness that ultimately led to his death. Since the riches won by Caesar in Gaul, Britain, and Germania were largely used to strengthen the national treasury, his own private holdings were reduced to the smallest possible amount for a consul. He lived a simple life, devoting all his energies to saving Rome from the corruption and chaos created by Pompey and the senate, restoring its order, vitality, and prosperity.[130] Nonetheless, his moves to engage the elites from the middle and lower classes as well as client states in the senate wounded the pride and self-esteem of the senate patricians. And Caesar couldn't easily appease them through forgiveness and tolerance as he naively believed. A murder was looming, plotted by Brutus and Cassius, under the auspices of preventing Caesar from legally becoming dictator in 44 BC. Against the advice of his family and friends, Caesar accepted Brutus's invitation to participate in a senate meeting on March 15. As he strode into the senate hall armed with forgiveness, mercy, and great hopes for the future of the Roman Republic, Brutus and others were waiting, ready to strike. They stabbed one of the most extraordinary political leaders in human history until he died in a pool of blood.[131]

After Caesar died, people gathered to mourn his passing. Many Jewish citizens even held a three-night vigil for him, chanting funeral hymns that echoed through the night sky. But the mourning turned violent. People demanded that Caesar be avenged and the perpetrators punished. The whole society fell into a serious riot. With the senate members at their wit's end, Caesar's deputy Mark Antony dispatched the army to maintain order. He also demanded to be appointed governor of Southern Gaul. The senate recalled Caesar's 18-year-old adopted son and heir Octavian, who quickly led his army to seek revenge for Caesar. He, along with Mark Antony and Marcus Lepidus, formed the "Second Triumvirate"[132] which ruled Rome for five years. Revenge for Caesar led to renewed civil war in Rome. The triumvirate executed 300 senators implicated in Caesar's murder and killed the famous orator and jurist Cicero. In 42 BC, they defeated Brutus and Cassius, the governors of Macedonia, forcing the two masterminds of Julius Caesar's death to commit suicide. The victors divided the provinces of the republic, with Octavian taking control of the west and Rome, Antony the east and Egypt, and Lepidus Africa. In 31 BC, Mark Antony, deeply in love with the alluring Egyptian ruler Cleopatra, sought to grant his territories to the children he had with her. Octavian used this as valid ground to declare war on Cleopatra in the name of maintaining the legitimacy of the republic's leadership. In 30 BC, he defeated Mark Antony in the magnificent naval battle of Actium. Mark Antony and Cleopatra committed suicide.[133]

With the blessing of Julius Caesar's will and the spirit of justice, Octavian reunited the Roman Republic and developed the political framework known as the Principate, within which he made himself the "Princeps," or the chief of the senate with the highest honor, for life. Octavian's rule was marked by bold vision and a temperate demeanor. He subsidized the republic's expenses with his private property while living a very simple life himself. This selfless act, coupled with his humble, collaborative, and respectful attitude toward the senate won him their respect and that of the military, the public, and even the slaves. So when Octavian offered to relinquish all his political power in 27 BC, the public called for him to be the sole ruler of Rome. The senate not only refused his resignation, but they also gave him the additional honorable title of "Augustus." Augustus ruled for almost half a century, until 14 AD. His creation of the Principate and a system of stepson succession brought a new monarchal order to the Roman Empire. This new phase of imperial expansion and prosperity lasted for 200 years.[134]

SECTION 4: THE DEPRECIATION OF POLYTHEISM AND LIFE'S "COLLECTIVE MEANINGLESSNESS"

Under the new imperial system, Rome relied on violent external expansion to satisfy the needs of its growing citizenry, especially those of the extravagant aristocracy. At a time when a city's population was generally between

10,000–50,000, there were few metropolises with 100,000–300,000 inhabitants. Rome's population was a staggering 1.2–1.5 million. The inputs and outputs required to support such a large population were unthinkable, as transportation was powered by humans and animals. But the Roman Empire did it—by conquests, seizure, and plunder.

By controlling Mediterranean transport and trade, the Roman Empire managed to dominate North Africa, East Africa, Spain, Asia, Asia Minor, and even Mesopotamia. In Europe, it brought Germania and Britain under control through the region of Gaul. At its peak, the empire ruled over more than 10 million square kilometers of territory, greater than the size of the modern United States. It governed a population that reached 120 million and a number of nation-states equivalent to over 50 nations today. Its geographical and cultural diversity was astounding. As far as its technological abilities and agricultural civilization were concerned, the Roman Empire had indeed reached the pinnacle of its time, an unparalleled miracle.[135]

But here's the interesting part. War produced many slaves who were taken back to Rome as laborers in both urban and rural areas; in the meantime, many Roman citizens were sent to the defeated states to ensure their loyalty to Rome. As Rome sought to expand its territory, more slaves had to be released to meet the growing need for soldiers. Some of these slaves-turned-soldiers would be awarded Roman citizenship for their military service, resulting in the demand for more slaves to fill the gap. As a result, the Roman Empire created a unique pattern of population migration and identity transformation, a long, cumulative process over 500–600 years. It became hard to tell who the people of Rome truly were.

The Roman Empire also administered its client states as provinces and adopted an inclusive social policy of respecting local religions and cultures. Even the splendid Parthenon in Rome was built for the worship of the gods of dependent states. Rome became not only the most economically and culturally prosperous city, but also the one with the most gods in the world. People living in Rome were free to choose which god to worship. Never in human history had faith gained such freedom as in the Roman Empire. However, its history proves that excessive freedom is nothing more than a synonym for disorder.[136]

The influx of gods into the empire soon degraded the holiness of the original Roman pantheon as believers became divided and shrunk in number. A similar phenomenon happened to polytheistic faith itself, for several reasons. First, polytheistic faith necessitates division of labor among the gods. Division of labor means attributing various weaknesses to the gods, which renders the concept of God into the likeness of ordinary humans—God is no longer infinite and holy. Second, humans are selective in how, when and where they worship their god or gods, which implies that they have the power to designate God. In other words, God is no longer omnipotent. This selective worship also gives rise to a specific kind of human-god transaction in which humans beg for the god's blessings as a reward for their faith in him, so divine goodness and mercy is lost. Third, when God is no longer omnipotent and entirely good, he descends to the same level as heroes, which inevitably leads to the creation of gods in the human world. Either people make gods out of other individuals in an attempt to enhance their own sense of belonging and overcome their vulnerability, or those who get too egotistical with their power or influence deceive or force others to worship them like gods. In a sense, people who live in a polytheistic environment are similar to those in an atheistic one. In both environments, it's always easy for people to go down the path of making others or themselves gods, which is exactly what happened in Rome. Any consul, general, or senator, not to mention the Princeps of the imperial era, could build temples and create gods for themselves or their family members. Rome's gods were much less revered than the Greek gods of Olympus. Their sacredness was reduced to the lowest level possible.[137]

With gods so devalued, the moral tension that relies on humanity's awe of and faith in God quickly collapses. People only seek the instant gratification brought by material life, without any sense of guilt, regret, or fear of God's condemnation for their wrongdoings toward others. In such a world, people are at the mercy of their desires and only care about materialistic stimulation. In Rome's case, nobles and the rich spent lavishly, living an extremely extravagant and corrupt life. Ordinary Roman citizens, for their part, sought excitement wherever they could. Rome had over 800 public baths—two of them had over a 4,000-person capacity—that provided catering, music, and even sexual services. There were also large open-air concerts featuring 2,000 singers and 3,000 dancers.

Open-air arenas that could accommodate audiences ranging from 7,000–50,000 were found all over the empire. On 77 days a year, various competitive and often gory performances were held: fights involving gladiators or wild animals, war simulations, and more.[138] For example, Emperor Caligula (37–41 AD) had 5,000 animals, including lions, tigers, and elephants, die in the arena in one day. Emperor Nero (54–68 AD) had 400 bears and 300 lions fight to death. Much more tragic were the events where slaves fought lions and tigers for their freedom: either they killed the beasts and were set free, or the beasts tore them apart. The most violent and bloody of all were the war simulations, like those under Emperor Claudius (41–54 AD). He had over 10,000 prisoners of war or convicted men recreate the bloodshed of the Peloponnesian War. The winners gained their freedom.

In order to sustain such indulgent, materialistic lifestyles, the ruling class launched foreign wars year after year, and there was no shortage of civil wars during the late stages of the empire. Corpses were everywhere, and blood flowed in the rivers. Marriage had lost its significance and binding force, and adultery became rampant. Julius Caesar, for example, was involved in sex scandals with many wives of the patricians. In fact, one of the main reasons

Brutus took the lead in assassinating him was to quash rumors that Brutus was his illegitimate child. Roman senators, generals, and even emperors during the imperial period often committed fratricide or incest with siblings. Emperor Nero, who had his mother killed, shouted upon seeing her naked body, "I never knew I had such a beautiful mother." Blood and filth flowed in every capillary of Rome.[139]

It was under such a system that the two distinctive community structures—the Roman Republic and the Roman Empire—were developed to their logical ends. While these structures organized millions of individuals under Roman law, and their systems were praised by posterity, such organization was achieved through Rome's unique use of violence and coercion. The word *Rome* came to represent *human ability* at its peak. But such achievement of organized *human ability* was built upon the coercion and enslavement of millions of individual human beings by the Roman community. It was built on a total denial of individual free will; a wild trampling of human dignity; a savage attack on equality, fairness, and justice among all human beings. There was little good news to be had for anyone living in that era, whether a Roman citizen or a slave. One tragedy followed another, and one death led to another. The Roman legion could appear at any time and bring a wave of bloody violence that would crush countless precious lives.

Even the powerful in Rome led meaningless lives. The great hero Crassus was captured and killed by the Parthians; the consul Pompey who killed Spartacus and tens of thousands of rebelling slaves ended up being killed by his own men; the great and benevolent Julius Caesar was betrayed and murdered; Cato committed suicide by pulling out his own intestines; the other 300 senators who participated in the murder of Julius Caesar were executed by the "Second Triumvirate" of Octavian, Mark Antony, and Marcus Lepidus; the famous senator, jurist, and philosopher Cicero was killed by Mark Antony; Brutus and Cassius committed suicide after being defeated by the Second Triumvirate;

Mark Antony, the leader of the Second Triumvirate, and his lover Cleopatra, were forced to kill themselves.

One day's madness was the prelude to the next day's death; one day's feast was the next day's funeral; one day's obsession with power, wealth, lust, and fame unlocked the next day's misfortune and downfall.[140] Looking through the lens of time as defined by God, it's evident that life in those ages had lost its meaning.

Where was God in the midst of this chaos? Facing the monstrously violent coercion of the organized "community" of the Roman Empire, God mourned and called for a new reflection on *human calling*. Arriving in Galilee and Jerusalem in the Syrian Province of Judea in Rome, Jesus came to humanity's rescue in response to the call of God, his Father. He carried with him new answers to the question of *human calling*. And the Roman Empire, using its military power, prepared a vast land and a large population for Jesus Christ to build a spiritual kingdom based on the common spiritual faith in the *human calling* of God's expectations.

CHAPTER 7:

Rebirth: the philosophical gospel of Christ's death

SECTION 1: JEWISH DOOMSDAY PROPHECY AND MESSIANIC HOPE

After the Maccabean Revolt in Judah, the Hasmonean dynasty founded by the Maccabees maintained independence for nearly a century. But before they could rebuild the Second Temple, Rome's legions that had swept through European, African, and Asian kingdoms and made them its client states found their way into Asia Minor. In 64 BC, led by Pompey, they ended the Greek Seleucid dynasty which had been entrenched in Damascus, Syria, for over 300 years. The Maccabees, however, blindly resisted Rome, resulting in Pompey's leading the Roman legions south to the holy city of Jerusalem. Jerusalem was besieged for three months. Pompey finally attacked from the north on the Sabbath, slitting the throat of the high priest defending the city, massacring over 12,000 people, and ending the reign of the Maccabean king.[141]

After appointing his minister Antipater as the new king and Hyrcanus as the high priest, Pompey, driven by curiosity, strode into the Holy of Holies in the Jewish temple that only high priests could enter once a year. After casting a contemptuous look at the sacred Ark of the Covenant and golden candlesticks, he left the treasures as they were and returned triumphantly to Rome. But his gross blasphemy planted seeds of hatred in the hearts of the Jewish people that would not be forgotten. In 55 BC, Crassus, one of Pompey's key political allies in the triumvirate, his hands still bloody after defeating Spartacus and crucifying more than 6,000 captives in the forest, went to the holy city of Jerusalem. In order to fund war against the powerful Parthians to the northeast, Crassus stole countless temple treasures, including the solid gold beams in the Holy of Holies. His actions poured salt on the wound that Pompey had made, increasing the Jewish people's hatred of the Romans for their violence, greed, and blasphemy. In less than a year, the proud Crassus was trapped and killed by the Parthians—in a sense, karmic retribution was in play.

Meanwhile, King Antipater of Judea, as Judah had become known to the Romans, led 3,000 soldiers to rescue Julius Caesar in Egypt and so gained his trust and support. This enabled Antipater to further consolidate his power over Judea. His younger son Herod came onto the political scene at the age of 15 but provoked outrage because of his cruel slaughter of the Jews. The Maccabean prince Antigonus took the opportunity to lead the Jews in an uprising and returned to Jerusalem, the capital of Judea, with the support of the Parthians. King Herod's brother was killed, while he himself fled Jerusalem.

Herod knew how to take advantage of the Roman Empire's violent nature to protect himself. He raised another army to aid Mark Antony, who was fighting against the Parthians, and was able to rescue him from an enemy ambush. In 38 BC, Antony repaid Herod for his aid by sending 36,000 infantry and cavalry south to help him retake Jerusalem from the Maccabean prince. After a two-week stalemate, the Romans broke into the holy city, savagely looted the sacred temple, and slaughtered the people. The Maccabean prince was beheaded by Mark Antony, and Herod again was crowned king. Of the 71 members of the Jewish assembly, known as the Sanhedrin, 45 were purged by King Herod. A new reign of terror had begun in Judea.[142]

King Herod was Phoenician by bloodline, Greek by culture, Jewish by religion, and a Roman citizen by status. As a result, he was one part international visionary, one part violent and cruel Roman ruler, and one part eloquent Greek speaker. After the defeat of his good friend Antony by Octavian, later known as Augustus, Herod not only stayed out of the fray, but also quickly gained the favor and support of Augustus. He sent his two sons born to the Maccabean princess Mariamne to Rome to be instructed by Augustus himself. Augustus also helped King Herod expand his power over a larger area to include Israel, Jordan, Syria, and Lebanon, thus extending Israel's territory to a point rivaling that of King David's time. King Herod's most brilliant achievement was the demolition of the old temple and the reconstruction of the Second Temple.[143]

He had it redesigned and refurbished in a way that married the style of Solomon's Temple with Greek and Roman architectural and artistic elements. The temple stood on an elevated platform behind three gates, with the first gate located at the level of the 50th stair, and the second and third higher up. It was surrounded on all sides by colonnades that ended in the Royal Stoa, a massive basilica that overlooked the holy city, the Temple Mount, and the Mount of Olives. The temple, contrasting finely with an elevated piazza twice the size of Piazza della Rotonda in Rome, shimmered in the sunrise and sunset along with Antonia Fortress and the Mount of Olives. It was a consummate masterpiece that perfectly combined grand architectural design and the worship of Jehovah. It was regarded as a manmade wonder of the world at the time, attracting millions of pilgrims from all over the world each year. Generally about 70,000 inhabitants lived in the capital of the Herodian kingdom centered around the temple.

King Herod married the Maccabean princess Mariamne in an attempt to gain Jewish favor. Mariamne, however, was still deeply obsessed with the fallen Maccabean dynasty and was intent on plotting rebellions at court. The royal couple's love-hate relationship, mingled with political benefits and conflicts, culminated in Mariamne's being sentenced to death by Herod. He then preserved her body in honey so that he could still see her. The two princes Mariamne bore him returned to Jerusalem after spending many years in Rome receiving education and even instruction from Emperor Augustus himself. Knowing that they believed him to have murdered their mother and desired revenge, Herod had no choice but to disinherit his sons and have them executed as well. The other 12 children King Herod had with other wives also joined the political struggles to try to usurp the throne. All these toxic rivalries and bloody assassinations completely wiped out the ties of kinship. King Herod changed his heirs and will several times until April 3, 4 AD, when he died of a putrefying illness after ruling for 37 years. Each elimination of an heir resulting from the political battles inside the royal Herodian family left countless people implicated and killed, including military personnel, priests, and even the poor. The kingdom of Judea was overwhelmed by violence and bloodshed. In addition to the burden of heavy taxes from both Rome and the ruling Herodian family to build the temple, King Herod's palace, and the Masada palace-fortress, this made the lives of the lower classes unbearably miserable.[144]

Furthermore, Herod himself hailed from a Gentile family. His irreverent, greedy, corrupt, and cruel personality was a continual offense to Jewish faith and morality. At that time, the Pharisaic priests who controlled the Sanhedrin followed the lifestyles of the Roman aristocrats, living in luxurious Greek villas in the suburbs and indulging themselves in material desires. They worshipped many gods, and abandoned their faith in the Jehovah, marking a radical departure from over 1,600 years of the Jewish faith. At the time, doomsday pessimism was prevalent among three groups: the Sadducees, who held fast to the provisions of the Old Testament, the Pharisees, who explained and applied the Old Testament and the Prophets more flexibly to achieve their earthly goals, and the Essenes, who adhered closely to the Scriptures and lived a strictly ascetic life. This pessimism provided fertile ground for the Jewish hope of the Messiah.[145] Their apocalyptic outlook and Messianic expectation was first formed in the great prophet Isaiah's foretelling of his arrival, penned in 700 BC. He prophesied that God would send the Messiah to the human world in 700 years to carry out his rescue plan for humanity. The Essenes believed that Isaiah's prophecy was coming true in their time. They were convinced that the end of the world was approaching, and that Jehovah had sent the Messiah to the human world to save Israel, bringing the Jews new blessings. This messianic hope was a source of spiritual strength that helped the Jews survive unprecedented worldly suffering in this extremely violent, bloody, corrupt, and degenerate society.

While their eschatological hope and the expectation of the Messiah helped the Jews heal from their earthly suffering and trauma, it caused panic and unease among the rulers of Rome and the priests of Judea. Around 1 AD, there were rumors in Jerusalem that the Messiah sent by God had already been born in the Kingdom of Judea. King Herod, even in the throes of the end of his reign, sent troops to search door to door and have all newborn babies killed.

After King Herod died, Emperor Augustus, who was tired of hearing reports about the cruel court fights of the Herodian family over succession, did away with the Kingdom of Judea and re-established the province of Syria. Judea was partitioned into tetrarchies among several of Herod's children. Jerusalem was downgraded and placed under the rule of Herod Archelaus, while Northern Galilee was given to Herod Antipas. Judea became a land with more hierarchies, more complicated administration, and more intense social contradictions than ever before. Apocalyptic and messianic expectations became even more popular. As a result, rebellions constantly arose, led by those who pretended to be the Messiah but were in fact false prophets. But they were all suppressed by the Roman rulers and the Herodian family. Thousands of people were crucified. Both the rulers and the ruled lived in constant fear.

SECTION 2: JESUS'S SACRIFICE AND THE END OF FIGHTING VIOLENCE WITH VIOLENCE

Against this great historical backdrop, Jesus was born in Bethlehem to the carpenter Joseph and his wife, Mary. Rumors of the Messiah's coming continued after Jesus's birth. His parents carefully raised Jesus to adulthood, even traveling far from home to avoid the infanticide that the Herodian family carried out in fear of the Messiah. Still, Joseph and Mary took Jesus with them on many pilgrimages to the temple at Jerusalem. Since he lived as a carpenter in Nazareth in Galilee, Jesus had a deep understanding of the hardships of the lower classes under the reign of the Roman Empire and the ruling family. Meanwhile, Jesus was greatly inspired by the holiness, glory, and salvation of God demonstrated in temple at Jerusalem. He was engrossed in reading the Old Testament and the Torah from a young age, from which he drew his spiritual power. In adolescence, Jesus was fascinated by the prophets' life of faith and preaching—completely uninterested in the arrangements of material life like marriage and having children. He often preached sermons and did good deeds with his cousin, the famous prophet John the Baptist.[146]

Around the age of 30, Jesus gave up secular life entirely and asked John to baptize him in the Jordan River, before embarking on his journey of preaching and doing good deeds. He mainly moved through the area around Lake Galilee in northern Judea and on either side of the Jordan River, healing the sick, calling for kindness toward all humans through his own deeds. John the Baptist, meanwhile, devoted himself to awakening people to repentance by baptizing them. His sermons were directed at the world's immoral sins that violated the covenant with God. John was later arrested and killed by order of the Tetrarch Herod Antipas for his alleged crime of rebuking the ruler of Galilee, and in response to rumors that John was the Messiah. Jesus focused his sermons on eschatology and messianic hope, pointing out the urgency of the coming of the end of the world and God's judgement. Without hesitation, he claimed that he was the Messiah prophesied by the prophet Isaiah: the so-called "Son of Man," or the "Son of God." He demonstrated superhuman courage in responding to the most pressing call of the era.

But unlike the false prophets, Jesus didn't blindly call for the Jewish people to rebel against the tyranny of the rulers in Roman Empire, Judea, and Galilee. Nor did he enumerate their sins in violating their covenant with God or argue that their current suffering was God's way of testing and refining the choice of his people, as John the Baptist and the Jewish prophets had done. They had attempted to awaken the Jews to the sin of abandoning the covenant, urging them to save themselves through redemption and earn the chance to be chosen by God. Jesus's insight and courage in breaking through their traditional theological logic was, again, superhuman.

His way of redemption had no precedent in human history. Knowing humans were incapable of saving themselves, he would instead carry out a surprising rescue plan. Jesus himself would become an offering and sacrifice, bearing the sins of humanity and their failure to keep the covenant. He would triumph over violence—not by revenge, but by dying a sacrificial death and so securing the path of forgiveness for humanity through his love. His resurrection three days later not only ushered in his nonviolent kingdom, but it also proved that God accepted his sacrifice to redeem the people he had created.

In his own way, Jesus shifted the focus to love and forgiveness. He confronted the reality of human beings' vulnerability as mere flesh and blood, yet argued that in spite of this, God's love enables them to stand tall on the ruins of their vulnerability. Jesus believed that by using forgiveness as a weapon, people could triumph over human vulnerability and the devastation of organized human violence. By doing so, we could instead become strong. We could become those who spread and enact God's love; we could become those who God is pleased with and create a non-violent kingdom filled with God's love and forgiveness, existing outside this violent world rife with bloodshed. His great mind and sweeping vision reached the pinnacle of human imagination and capacity—he was truly superhuman.

Yet Jesus's most superhuman quality was his decisive attitude toward death and his obedience to God's revelation in the face of persecution. His way of defeating death was through God's love and forgiveness.[147] Around the age of 33 or 34, in the spring before Passover, Jesus took his 12 disciples south to Jerusalem in response to God's calling, and entered the holy city through the southern gate on a donkey, as prophesied by Isaiah. The road was thick with followers, the streets congested. Many followers put palm leaves, which were highly symbolic for the Jewish people, on the road in front of Jesus. Many of them loudly called Jesus the Messiah, while others shouted questions at him. One can picture Jesus riding comfortably on the back of the donkey with his signature sad eyes and loving smile. He responded to the followers' cheers and the questioners' inquiries with the same enlightening language that was always full of God's love and forgiveness toward humanity. This only added to the exciting and sacred spectacle.

As Jesus led this massive crowd to the Second Temple, his disciples were amazed, as it was the first time they had seen the magnificent temple. Jesus, however, was shocked by the blasphemous trading of goods under the towering arches of the Royal Stoa. In a change from his usual calm, compassionate, and forgiving demeanor, Jesus strode into the colonnade and overturned the trading tables. He harshly questioned and reprimanded the idolatry of money on display in the society of Judea under the Roman Empire that went against their covenant with God. His authority as the Son of God was on fully display. His reprimands were gripping and soul-shaking, striking a chord with the crowds at the scene.

Word quickly spread about Jesus's triumphal entry into the holy city, in response to messianic prophecy and God's calling. The news triggered serious concern and trepidation on the part of Pontius Pilate, the Roman governor of Judea in the Syrian province, as well as Caiaphas, the Jewish Pharisaic high priest. As countless Jews from around the world regularly made pilgrimages to the holy city on Passover, law and order were always a major issue during this time of the year. On top of this, there were the constant rumors that a kingly figure from God had already appeared in Judea and the fact that emerging false prophets always seemed to lead uprisings against the Roman Empire during Passover. Together these factors seemed to make up the exact recipe for a rebellion, adding to Pilate's fear and anxiety, as he was personally stationed in Jerusalem during Passover. Pilate passed his uneasiness on to Caiaphas, the high priest, and had him crush the rebellion in its infancy. Caiaphas managed to get his men to bribe one of Jesus's disciples, Judas, to arrest him, in an attempt to control Jesus. This meant that Jesus, the Son of Man, had to choose between fleeing and death.

Fleeing was of course the easier option. It would immediately allay Pilate and Caiaphas's fear of a Passover rebellion, and Jesus would be able to survive in the wilderness or rural Galilee. It's the most likely decision a person would make at that time if their life was threatened, and it was the first instinct his terrified disciples had after hearing the news. Leading his followers in a rebellion was another option. However, the superhuman Jesus neither fled nor rebelled. Instead, he chose to heed God's call and confront his death, also prophesied by Isaiah.

He told his disciples calmly, passionately, and sadly that he had decided to die as the Son of Man.[148] After washing the feet of his disciples and saying farewell to them during the last supper, all of them except Judas shed tears. They ate the bread that symbolized the flesh of Jesus and drank the wine that symbolized his blood. Jesus went to the Garden of Gethsemane at the foot of the Mount of Olives to pray to God, as Judas knew he would. Throughout the night, he prayed three times under the olive trees. Jesus overcame the fragility of flesh and blood and chose to face death with strength and faith. While in the garden, he was arrested by the high priest and his soldiers with the aid of Judas, who identified Jesus to the men.

Caiaphas the high priest, Pilate the governor, and Antipas the king of Galilee each passed the buck to the other while Jesus was detained and brought to trial. They were all afraid to be the one to make the decision to put Jesus to death and were all afraid of taking responsibility for the Passover rebellion that Jesus could cause. At the same time, they were all curious about how Jesus would respond to the rumors that he was the Messiah. To their surprise, Jesus's answer was blunt: "I am the Son of God. I am the Messiah." When asked what kind of Jewish kingdom he wanted to build, Jesus gave evocative answers: "My kingdom is not of this world." "My temple is not built by human hands." "If it were, my servants would be fighting." When asked if he wanted to oppose the Roman emperor Tiberius Caesar or incite a tax revolt against Caesar, Jesus had given an answer that was extremely inspiring: "Render therefore unto Caesar the things which are Caesar's, and unto God the things that are God's."

According to Roman law, Jesus had not participated in violent rebellion against Rome or incited any violent resistance, so it was difficult to decide on any charges. Finally, the Sanhedrin, led by the high priest Caiaphas, condemned Jesus to death for the blasphemy of claiming to be the Son of God. They planned for Jesus to be executed in the humiliating form of crucifixion. Yet he did not argue, let alone resist, fully obeying God's plan for the Son of Man. His death would become a legendary, historic event that would be passed down through the ages. The decision he made and the way he lived his life completely subverted previous philosophical and religious reflections on *human calling* and put an end to the taken-for-granted revenge model of meeting violence with violence.

The men of Pilate and Caiaphas did all they could to trample the dignity of the Son of Man. They made a crown of thorns and put it on Jesus's head, to humiliate him for claiming to be the Messiah, the Son of God. They also made him carry the cross that would soon crucify him, walking through the streets in broad daylight before the public, from the southern Lion's Gate to the rocky highlands northwest of the holy city. Jesus's thorny crown and his body were beaten with a leather whip along the way. Blood oozed from his body, head to toe. He was ridiculed and abused in every way possible.

Violence in the human world evokes the sinful nature of humans. The same crowd who a few days ago welcomed the entry of Jesus the Messiah into the holy city of Jerusalem, now stood by and watched the bloody, destructive physical and verbal violence and humiliation done to him. Some cheered along, some hooted and heckled, some hid their faces to avoid the gruesome sight. Of course, some were also sympathetic and sad, and some tried to feed Jesus and help him carry the cross. Yet even his disciples had scattered, all except for John, who followed the Son of Man along with Jesus's mother Mary, and Mary Magdalene. Peter, who dared not admit his relationship with Jesus to the Roman official when asked three times, left in shame. There was no sign of the other disciples.

But for Jesus, violence in the human world could only make his extraordinary sacredness stand out even more. Jesus looked at every detail of the bloody drama with compassionate eyes. His body was pushed to the limits, enduring the greatest pain that the evil of violence could inflict on the Son of Man. His spirit endured as well, withstanding the insults and torture inflicted by the evil of violence on the mind of the Son of Man. Faced with this awful human violence, Jesus was as peaceful and compassionate as he'd always been. He committed no hateful or rebellious acts and showed no angry emotions. He didn't even give resentful looks to those who abused him so terribly. Instead, he prayed for them to his Heavenly Father, God: "Father, forgive them, for they do not know what they are doing." His eyes were still full of compassion and hope even when he fell three times, his body unable to bear the weight of the cross. He endured the sting of the thorny crown, the heartache of humiliation, and the sharp, tearing pain of crucifixion. He just prayed to his father for strength: "Heavenly Father! I obey your will! I don't understand, but I believe in you." He responded gratefully to the women who fed him water and to Simon who helped him carry the cross. Then he turned to his grief-stricken mother, Mary, and his disciple John in great gratitude and compassion, and said to his mother: "Woman, behold your son!" and to John, "Behold your mother!" Jesus fulfilled the glorious mission given to him by his heavenly father through his death on the violence-witnessing cross, gratifying the desire of those in power to inflict assaults and insults on him. Heaven and earth wailed, and the mountains and rivers trembled, for human conscience was shattered.

Perhaps no one at that time understood the true meaning of the death of Jesus except for Jesus himself and his heavenly father. Jesus took a new approach to addressing the organizational violence and coercion arising in human communities—namely love, sacrifice, and forgiveness rather than revenge.[149] Yet the significance of his approach can be seen in the transformation of the disciples—who fled in face of violent threat—into apostles after the death of Jesus. Their apostleship, in turn, was based on the miracle of Jesus's resurrection. In his preaching, Saul, a former Pharisee who became Paul the Apostle after the resurrection of Jesus, explained its meaning through his preaching and in his explanatory writings about Christ's death. The newly transformed apostles' evangelism and sacrifice established the Christian faith as a new sect of the Jewish faith, completely different from that of the Sadducees, Pharisees, and Essenes. Christ's death created a new sacred expectation of *human calling* that resulted in a fundamental break with the Jewish faith, bringing faith in the uni-personal God, Jehovah—which the Jews had founded 3,600 years ago and had held for nearly 1,600 years—to a height never seen before or since.

How this faith came to be is all recorded in The New Testament—so there's no need to repeat the account here. Many historians, cultural anthropologists, and even philosophers have gone to great lengths to prove the authenticity of Jesus's resurrection, leaving voluminous writings behind. Yet it seems point-less to spend time on a question that can neither be proven nor disproven. Faith itself leads an individual heart towards the spiritual world. Faith is the imag-ination and conviction of a human who, as a limited being, tries to connect with an infinite other. It's the imagination and conviction of a human who, as a temporal being, tries to connect with the eternal other. And it's the imagination and conviction of a human who, as a flawed and sinful being, tries to connect with the all-good, all-true other.

Through this faith, characterized by adoration and worship, humans can gain the spiritual power to live their life well and guide their own behavior in this crazy world. This kind of faith cannot be substantiated by the empiri-cal research methods of modern science. Modern science itself, which these researchers have long embraced as a guide, even fails to address the funda-mental problem of the origin of the various laws that they study. Do they never wonder, if Newton discovered the law of universal gravitation, who created the law? Einstein developed the theory of general relativity, but who created the law of gravitation as a property of space and time? Schrödinger discovered quantum mechanics, but who created the quantum world?

The faith of the apostles offered a different answer. Although the New Testament records that Jesus's 12 disciples were chosen during his lifetime, Peter was chosen after his death and resurrection, and Matthias was chosen by other apostles to replace the traitor Judas following his suicide. They were all regular people from middle or even lower classes. They were fisherman, farmers, carpenters, and tax collectors. Only Paul was a Roman citizen. They were simple and earnest, with all the limitations, weaknesses, and even sinfulness of human beings, with the monstrous sin of betrayal by Judas Iscariot as an extreme example. They merely loved Jesus's sermons, admired his qualities of compassion, love, and forgiveness, and were willing to follow him. In short, they were simply Jesus's disciples. When Jesus came into conflict with earthly authorities and faced the threat of death, the limitations, weaknesses, and sinfulness of these disciples as human beings were fully exposed. Judas Iscariot sold Jesus out for 30 gold coins, while the other disciples—apart from John, the virgin Mary, and Mary Magdalene, who followed him to the end—were all terrified and fled without a trace.

But after Jesus died, these same disciples who fled gathered again and became his apostles. They went to different parts of the world to fulfill Jesus's mission of preaching the gospel of the Messiah. They became increasingly full of the loving, forgiving compassion of Jesus, gaining a strong, transcendent will to become saints. By the end, they all became just like Jesus.[150] They cherished their God-given lives and handled their worldly encounters in a way that glorified God, all while living through the violent era of the Roman Empire, when people's lust was rampant and their lives were treated like dirt.

Saint James the Great, who evangelized in Judea, was sentenced to death by Herod Antipas in 44 AD. During his trial, James remained calm, fearless, and unruffled. He kept preaching the gospel, bringing awakening even to the person who arrested and persecuted him, prompting him to declare himself a Christian immediately and ask James for forgiveness. James forgave and kissed him. Both of them were beheaded. Saint Thomas went to Persia to preach, where he gained many disciples. Later when he went to India, a local Brahman priest had him shot with an arrow.

Saint Simeon, the second bishop of Jerusalem after James, was crucified for preaching in Egypt. Saint Simon the Zealot, who preached in African villages and in Britain, was also crucified in the end. Saint Bartholomew, who preached in India and translated the Gospel of Mathew into the local language, was eventually persecuted by local idolaters, beaten with sticks, skinned, and beheaded. Saint Andrew, the brother of Saint Peter, preached in Turkey and was eventually crucified in Edessa. Andrew kissed the cross and prayed loudly before being crucified: "Oh, cross, most welcome and longed for! With a willing mind, joyfully and desirously I come to you! Because I'm a follower and a student of the One who once hung on you; Because I have always loved you and sought to embrace you!"

Saint Matthew, the former tax collector, wrote what became known as the Gospel of Matthew. He preached the gospel in Ethiopia and Egypt, winning more and more believers, before King Hircanus had him thrust to death with a spear. Saint Philip, who preached in North Asia, was crucified and then stoned to death in the city of Hierapolis. Saint Jude was also crucified, whose preaching in Armenia and Persia had a massive impact. Saint Matthias was martyred in Jerusalem. He survived stoning but was then beheaded. Saint James the Less, the leader chosen by the apostles after the death of Jesus and the living embodiment of Jesus's righteousness in the world, was thrown from the walls of Jerusalem by the Pharisees. He didn't die, but knelt and prayed for his wicked murderers: "Oh Lord! My God, my Father, I beg you to forgive them, because they don't know the meaning of what they have done."

James the Less was stoned to death. Saint Peter, who preached in Rome, was sentenced to death by crucifixion at the Emperor Nero's order during his religious persecution. But Peter didn't think he was worthy of the same death as his Lord Jesus, so he asked to be nailed upside-down on the cross. Saint Paul made trips through Rome, Greece, and Jerusalem to preach. He was imprisoned several times in spite of being a Roman citizen, but he went on preaching each time he was released. His early letters to the church explaining the Christian faith became the most important theological basis of the New

Testament and were greatly influential. Paul also died in Nero's great persecution, when he framed Christians for arson. As he was a Roman citizen, Paul was not crucified but beheaded. Before he was executed, Paul prayed for the soldiers who were to behead him, prophesying that they would soon be converted to Christianity and baptized at his grave. He was right.

This rich history of martyrdom poses several questions: What was the power that drove these ordinary people, who were frightened into fleeing after Jesus's execution, to reunite in faith, gaining infinite strength, extraordinary wisdom, and the mastery of language needed to spread the gospel? What was the power that prompted them to change from following Jesus as disciples to shouldering the sacred, yet arduous mission of preaching the gospel in a world full of violence as apostles? What was the power that gave them enduring confidence and perseverance to resist the temptation of a degenerate world filled with human lusts, and instead willingly persevere in the ascetic life of preaching? What was the power that kept them responding to the endless violence of their time with the gospel of Jesus's love and forgiveness? What was the power that made them live their lives and face death in such a graceful and calm way?

No historian, cultural anthropologist, or philosopher who relies on the empirical approach of modern science can offer a logical answer—unless they followed through on the empirical method and proved their answer with their own deaths. The empirical approach itself didn't come into existence until 1,200 years later, at the time of Bacon and Descartes. This is 500 years after Thomas Aquinas's natural theology regarding Christian faith in God. How then can this method be used to demonstrate the origin of such a power? The New Testament's record of the resurrection dates back to 2,000 years ago. It provides its own self-consistent logic, and itself reveals the source of power that turned disciples into apostles. Such power can only be gained through the passion of spiritual faith and logical rationality. It shares the same origin with natural rationality and human rationality, that is, the absolute, sole, and true existence of God.

SECTION 3: RENDER UNTO CAESAR WHAT IS CAESAR'S AND UNTO GOD WHAT IS GOD'S

After Jesus died, the Christian faith grew rapidly, while the rulers of the Roman Empire became more and more ruthless and murderous. They persecuted unarmed Christians, who never rebelled in violence, for 300 years. Why was the Roman Empire, which was broad-minded enough to build the Pantheon, unable to embrace the peaceful faith of Jesus Christ, full of his love and forgiveness? Why did their tolerance of other client states' religions transform into repeated, frenzied persecution in the case of Christians?

Jesus Christ's death awakened the unconditional love and forgiveness for others that's hidden deep in humans' hearts and comes from God the Father. Jesus demonstrated this love and forgiveness by his self-sacrifice, thus inspiring the apostles to preach around the world the gospel of dealing with human violence in a non-revengeful way. Their message awakened in people a response to the *human calling* that God expects. That meant that at the very beginning, Christianity had to break with the nationalist Jewish faith, and it declared war against the polytheism, which was actually atheism, of the Roman Empire.

The Roman Empire, in contrast, represented human violence. It advocated violent solutions, which inevitably brought about revenge. And revenge often meant violent resistance against violence. The Roman Empire would continually respond to such resistance by suppressing it with an even more violent approach. In the end, those who won temporary victories through violence got the crown. The "gods" of Roman polytheism were fundamentally the temporary victors of violence. They ranged from the minor gods like Pilate, Caiaphas, and Antipas, to the major ones like Crassus, Brutus, Pompey, Cicero, Antony, Caesar, and the emperors Tiberius, Caligula, Claudius, and Nero—though all of these human "gods" ended up dying violent deaths at the hands of others.

It can even be argued that the violence and polytheism advocated by Rome represented "all evil" on earth at that time. The Christian faith represented the exact opposite. Their victor was Jesus, the Son of God, the only representative of the Almighty. He was the Good and the True, the embodiment of love and forgiveness, who died by the hand of human violence. Jesus Christ and his followers didn't recognize human authorities or perpetrators as gods. They didn't allow the greatest of evil people to make themselves gods by virtue of their power to organize and enslave others. Just the opposite: they called them false gods, evil gods, the sinful source of the destruction of good order in human society. Thus the conflict between Christ and Rome was innate and irreconcilable. It was essentially a collision between God and Caesar, that would last until the day when this earthly world would be as Jesus said before his death, "Render unto Caesar's what is Caesar's; and unto God what is God's."

The massive persecution of Christians began with the Roman emperor Nero, who held power from 54–68 AD.[151] Nero had always been an embodiment of evil in the world. He ascended the throne by poisoning his stepfather, Emperor Claudius, with his mother Agrippina. Nero loved athletics and personally raced chariots in the arena. His debauched behavior knew no moral bottom. At his lover's instigation, he even ordered the murder of his own mother, who had helped him secure the throne. He also killed two wives by his own hands, one of whom he kicked to death while she was pregnant.

At that time, Rome didn't differentiate between Christians and Jews, as the vast majority of early Christians, especially their influential pioneers and leaders, were Jews. Nero was the one who ordered that Christians be treated differently—and persecuted. In 64 AD, a fire broke out in Rome that lasted for seven days, destroying two thirds of the city's buildings and killing thousands of Romans. The conflagration was said to have been started by Nero for fun, who sang the "Sack of Troy" accompanied by the lyre while watching the fire from his garden tower. Afterward, as the senate had the arsonists tracked down, Nero finally felt the seriousness of the situation. He blamed it on Christians, justifying his launch of large-scale persecution. Tremendous amounts of people were slaughtered, with more than 3,500 martyrs in Egypt alone, over 10,000 in Rome, and countless others in Jerusalem, Athens, and elsewhere. The persecutions were shockingly cruel—beheading, crucifixion, and being fed to beasts, to name a few.

Within two years of Nero's forced suicide, three short-lived emperors were instated, deposed, and violently killed by the military. Vespasian, who was crowned in 70 AD, and his eldest son, Titus[152], both achieved great things in governing the Roman empire. Yet prior to that, as commanders designated by the former Emperor Nero, they massacred numerous Jewish people in Judea and Jerusalem in the suppression of the Great Revolt, initiated by the Jews pushing back against the brutal and greedy empire from 65–70 AD. In the midst of the bloody slaughter, tens of thousands refused to surrender and died jumping from the city walls. Hundreds of thousands were killed. The glorious Second Temple, as prophesied by Christ, was completely destroyed, as was the Masada Palace. In the aftermath of the revolt, millions of Jewish refugees began a worldwide exodus. Since the Jewish and Christian faiths were not clearly separated at that time, many innocent Christians were also killed in the suppression. Tens of thousands of Jews and Christians were sold into slavery in the provincial capitals. More than 2,000 were taken to Rome and cruelly tortured to death through crucifixion and being fed to beasts.

Emperor Trajan,[153] reigning from 98–117 AD, was considered a good emperor: simple, upright, and compassionate toward the Roman poor. His political achievements in both domestic and foreign affairs were remarkable, but his persecution of Christians was surprisingly cruel, affecting believers across Europe and beyond. The famous Ignatius of Antioch was martyred in this vast persecution. The renowned Roman scholar Pliny the Younger, who couldn't bear what he saw, wrote to Emperor Trajan, confirming to him that every day several thousand Christians were being killed without having done anything against Roman law. During all of this, Christians met before dawn just to pray to their God and then disperse, never causing trouble, never stealing, never looting, never committing adultery, never lying, and never deceiving.

From 138–161 AD, Emperor Antonius Pius[154] continued the persecution of the Christians, leading to the death of thousands. The famous bishop of Smyrna Polycarp was burned to death during the persecution in 155 AD. Emperor Marcus Aurelius,[155] who reigned from 161—180 AD, earned a reputation as both a warrior and a philosopher in Roman history. In particular, his legacy of the Stoic philosophical masterpiece, *Meditations*, was admired by later politicians. But Aurelius was also a fierce Christian persecutor. During his reign, tens of thousands of Christians were crucified, beheaded, burned to death, or fed to beasts. The persecution was particularly and shockingly cruel in Lyon and Vienne in France. The famous philosopher Justin Martyr and the 90-year-old French archbishop Pothinus were martyred in Aurelius' persecution.

Emperors Decius and Valerian,[156] who ruled successively from 249—260 AD, both launched fierce persecution of Christians. They issued decrees prohibiting Christian gatherings and forced Christian bishops to make sacrifices to pagan gods. Those who disobeyed were executed. The bishops of Jerusalem, Antioch, and Toulouse were all executed. Pope Sixtus II, the archbishop of Rome, and four acolytes were executed for refusing to follow the decree. Cyprian, the bishop of Carthage, was beheaded. The bishop of Tarragona was burned to death. Christians' property was confiscated, and an untold number were otherwise persecuted.

From 284–310 AD, Emperors Diocletian and Maximian[157] took Christian persecution to terrifying heights. They had all the churches and Bibles burned in the empire, detained Christian leaders, and ordered all soldiers and clergy in Rome to sacrifice to pagan gods. Violators were dismissed, imprisoned, and tortured to death. Untold numbers of Christians were crucified, fed to beasts, shot through the heart with arrows, blinded, or executed by other cruel methods. The empire turned into a living hell. Even soldiers took issue with their involvement in the widespread persecutions and responded in violent resistance, killing the persecutors and twice burning the palace of Emperor Diocletian.

The 10 large-scale persecutions of Christians from Emperor Nero to Emperor Diocletian revealed the cruelty and twisted logic of organized human violence. Earlier violence at least aligned with the motivation of revenge in response to violent conquest, which in turn enabled such organized human violence to continue. Anyone waging a violent war must at least seek to justify it to receive sanction from the members of the community and blessing from its gods. But just as Jesus Christ and his followers drastically subverted the traditional revenge model with their acts of love and forgiveness, the Roman Empire continued to inflict its organized violence on Christians, a group who completely abandoned violent revenge and rebellion and even prayed for their butchers. Such human behavior exhibits an exceedingly confused and absurd logic,[158] behind which lurks the arrogance and madness of man-made gods.

Whether it was Augustus, the nearly ideal Roman emperor, or the evil Emperor Nero who killed his stepfather, mother, and wives without blinking an eye; the outrageous Emperor Caligula nicknamed "little soldier's boot," who tried to make all of Rome worship him as a god; or the many Roman commanders, and governors—all were able to enter a pantheon or build their own temples, receiving lavish praise, false hymns, and ridiculous tributes. The actions and words of these man-made gods were full of falseness, vanity, and hypocrisy. With the power in their hands, they became raving mad and full of themselves, thinking they could merely wipe out the people and things they found displeasing, especially the Christian faith that would expose the falsehood and hypocrisy within them. They mistakenly believed that they could use violence to prolong their hollow souls, their false prosperity, and their corrupt lives.

For all the coercion and persecution, Christ and his apostles never gave up their serious attitude toward life, their love and forgiveness for the other in society, and their grace and calmness in the face of death, which was indeed extraordinary and marvelous. In 10 large-scale religious persecutions spanning over nearly 300 years, hundreds of thousands of Christians were martyred. With their only belief in the one God, these Christians followed Christ in showing love for all lives. They lived noble, moral lives, devoting themselves to helping the disadvantaged, elderly, women, children, disabled people, and even patients with infectious diseases. This contrasted sharply with Rome's outrageous practice of arbitrary god-making; its extremely strict hierarchy and the resulting inequality among people; its ruthless abandonment of women, the old, and the sick; and its brutality of depriving people of their lives for entertainment. All of these practices gradually sickened the whole of Roman society. The calmness that Christians showed in the face of bloody Roman oppression, their forgiveness of sin as their fragile flesh was tormented by Roman violence, and the beauty and fearlessness they demonstrated by their non-violent response to death threats shocked the warlike Roman people. Many even felt obligated to rethink the meaning of their lives.[159]

One outstanding example was Ignatius of Antioch, who was martyred during Trajan's persecution. Even on his way to death, Ignatius continued to preach and pray, strengthening the faith of believers in Christ and passing on God's will to them. He also wrote to the Roman church, hoping that they would not try to save themselves from martyrdom. "Let fire and the cross, let the crowds of wild beasts ... come upon me: only let me attain to Jesus Christ ... I am the wheat of God, and let me be ground by the teeth of the wild beasts, that I may be found the pure bread of Christ."

During the fourth persecution launched by Marcus Aurelius, the 80-year-old archbishop of Smyrna, Polycarp, asked for a prayer before being burned to death; he prayed: "O Lord God Almighty, I give you thanks that you count me worthy to be numbered among your martyrs ... I praise you for all these things, I bless you and glorify you." Then he gracefully mounted the execution stake and was burned in its gorgeous arch-shaped flame. When the famous theologian and bishop of Alexandria, Origen, was still a boy, his father was sentenced to be crucified by the Roman Empire. Once Origen found out, he even wanted to join his father in his martyrdom. Since there was some time before the execution, Origen wrote a letter burning with passion to strengthen his father's determination in martyrdom.

Saint Romanus, a former Roman army officer who converted to Christianity, was persecuted to death in 258 AD. He underwent various kinds of grievous torture in Antioch, but still graciously and calmly preached the gospel of Christ. The captain Asclepiades, who oversaw his torture, could do nothing but cut the flesh on his handsome face to hurt and humiliate him. Still, still Romanus only said softly, "I thank thee, O captain, that thou hast opened unto me many mouths, whereby I may preach my Lord and Savior Christ. Look how many wounds I have, so many mouths I have lauding and praising God."

Christians' love for life, their fearlessness in the face of violence, and their embrace of noble death, all derived from their Christian faith, came as an awakening to the Romans. Roman violence had not only incurred boundless death and suffering but also brought catastrophe to those who used their power to perpetrate violence. In just over 50 years in the middle of the third century, power had changed hands 24 times, and hardly any emperor escaped death by murder. The Roman people, witnessing the filth and depravity of their man-made gods in stark contrast with the Christians' nobility and grace, gradually accepted faith in the one God, and the spiritual showering of Christ's love and forgiveness.[160]

Christ's gospel continued to spread throughout the vast empire, gaining more and more believers. The more violent the persecution, the greater the number that followed Christ. At the height of the empire, when the population under its jurisdiction was estimated to be between 60–120 million, believers in

Christ accounted for 15–20 percent, or more than 10 million. Among the new believers were farmers, craftsman, businessmen, soldiers, military officers, and even high-ranking nobles.[161] As Tertullian said, the violence of the Roman Empire was like a cultivating plow, and "the blood of the martyrs was like seeds" that grew into Christ's "spiritual kingdom." As Jesus had responded to Pilate: "My kingdom is not of this world. If it were, my servants would be fighting." It was the blood of Christ, these terrible persecutions, and his count-less followers who sacrificed their lives that cultivated the non-violent model of love and forgiveness. This *human calling*, full of God's sacred expectation and revelation for human public life, prepared the most brilliant and magnifi-cent stage for the arrival of Constantine the Great.

As a matter of fact, many emperors were influenced by the Christian faith to varying degrees, including Claudius, Hadrian, Commodus, Severus Alex-ander, Galerius, and Constantine. Not much has been written on the extent to which they were influenced by the Christian faith, but it's clear that none of these Roman emperors initiated large-scale persecutions. Rather, they all showed a certain amount of tolerance for Christians and a willingness to read the reports and apologetic works written by some Christian theologians.

By the end of the third century and the beginning of the fourth century, the Christian faith had already become ubiquitous in the empire. Many sol-diers, officers, and even those close to the emperor, became devout Christians. Constantine's mother and wife were both Christians. His mother, Helena, was particularly devout and influential. Under these circumstances, it would be impossible for the emperor not to be influenced. At that time, the Roman emperor would choose his co-ruler under the system of Tetrarchy, with one governing the western Roman Empire, and the other the eastern Roman Empire. Diocletian, the ruler of the eastern empire from 284–305 AD, was one of the last emperors to undertake a large-scale and brutal persecution strat-egy to solve the Christian problem he and the empire faced. After Diocletian,

Licinius also adopted a similar strategy. But once Christ's spirit began to affect the army and the palace, Diocletian and Licinius found themselves persecuting not external Christians, but internal Christians. They had no chance of winning. In the end, whether it was due to the influence of his mother and those around him, or due to his political need to win over the crowds, Constantine's choice to side with Christ was not a hotheaded decision or an accidental event. It was God's hand playing the strings of the natural law that he created.

In 310 AD, Diocletian's successor, Emperor Galerius, who had once assisted Diocletian in his persecution of Christians, developed a strange, rotting, stinking disease of the lower body. Rumor had it that it was retribution for persecuting Christians. In 311 AD, he repented to Christ and signed the Edict of Serdica, also known as the Edict of Toleration, with Constantine, the new emperor of western Rome. The edict granted tolerance and freedom for the Christian faith and gave them the right to build new Christian churches. Along with the emperor of the east, Licinius, who later replaced Galerius, Constantine also signed the Edict of Milan, which granted religious freedom to Christians and all others within the empire. But Licinius was foolish and stubborn enough to initiate another Christian persecution in the eastern Rome, killing many officers and soldiers. Constantine undoubtedly took this as a call to represent Christ and declare war on Licinius, which, unsurprisingly, ended with the defeat of Licinius and the reunification of Rome. The western Roman emperor Constantine became Constantine the Great and ruled over the whole Roman Empire.[162] Christ had defeated "Caesar" in the spiritual realm. Finally, what was Caesar's was rendered unto Caesar, and what was God's unto God.

SECTION 4: THE FUSION OF GREEK PHILOSOPHY AND CHRISTIAN FAITH

Over the centuries of persecution and the subsequent development of Christianity throughout the Roman Empire, debates between Christian and Jewish theologians were ongoing. At that time, Alexandria in Egypt was the second largest city in the world by population after Rome. Because of its location as a trade port adjacent to the Mediterranean Sea and well outside the political center of the Roman Empire, Alexandria naturally became a global commercial center with influence similar to that of modern New York. It was also the era's scientific research center. Well-known scientists, astronomers, physicists, engineers, inventors, and physicians lived in Alexandria, including Ptolemy, Euclid, Archimedes, and Galen. Many Greek thinkers also called it home, due to the impact of centuries of Greek colonial history since Alexander's conquest, as even its name reflected, as well as its importance in the era of the Roman Empire. These included the late "practical philosophers" of Epicureanism, Stoicism, Neoplatonism, and Cynicism.

Alexandria also became one of the major locations of exile for the Jewish elite, beginning from the sixth century BC when the First Temple was destroyed, and the Babylonian captivity began. Ever since, whenever the Jewish people suffered, there was an exodus of the upper rungs of society to Egypt. and especially to Alexandria. After 70 AD when the Second Temple was destroyed, a large number of Jews fled there. Naturally, Alexandria became a place for Jews to gather during the Roman Empire's persecutions of Christians. It's estimated that Jews accounted for more than 20 percent of Alexandria's population of 500,000 at its peak.

This historical migration, along with the frequent movement of eminent talents between Athens, Ephesus, Rome, Carthage, and Alexandria, made Alexandria a center for diverse thought. It hosted the most intense collision, the most thorough debate, and the most valuable fusion of the philosophies of Greece, the Jewish Old Testament, and especially of the Christian New Testament. As a result, the essence of Greek culture and the passion of the Christian faith achieved the most effective integration anywhere in the entire Roman Empire. Apart from the sacrifice of the 12 apostles of Christ for preaching the gospel, Paul, Clement, Origen, Irenaeus, Tertullian, Ignatius, Cyprian, Ambrose, Jerome, and Augustine are names that must be mentioned when it comes to contribution to Christian thought. It was these great souls, who believed in Christ and promoted him with their thinking, speech, behavior, and sacrifice, that finally brought Christian philosophy and theology into their fundamental inheritance and necessary separation from the Jewish faith during the apologetic debates of this period. The traditional doctrine of the Jewish faith, as Christianity both inherited and developed it, shaped the Christian creed into a logical, complete, and empirically persuasive system. This enabled the Christian faith to flourish in an unprecedented way throughout the Roman Empire—and later all of Europe, North Africa and Asia—without falling apart as it branched out. The Christian creed laid a solid foundation for its intrinsic *human calling* to be both passionate and rational. This was truly one of the most fascinating miracles in the early rise of the Christian faith.[163]

At the time, the bone of contention between philosophy and theology was whether Jesus was fundamentally a god or a man. If Jesus was a man, then he was merely one of the many prophets in the history of the Jewish people. All of these prophets answered God's calling and exhorted the Jewish people to do good deeds, usually by means of prophetic books and folk chanting. They wandered among the Jewish communities, day in and day out, decade after decade, calling for Jews to maintain their faith in the unipersonal God, Jehovah, and leaving behind their prophetic books to contribute to the history of the Jewish faith. In this sense, the development of Jewish faith was largely the history of the prophets that ran parallel to the history of the Jewish people's suffering, and the Old Testament was simply the sum of the prophetic books through which these prophets revealed this history.

If Jesus were seen as merely a Jewish prophet, then there was nothing unique about him. Jesus's death would lose its revelatory meaning, and so would the sacrifices of the apostles and countless Christians who followed

Jesus's non-violent model of love and forgiveness. There would be no expla-nation for the source of passion and rationality of Jesus's followers in how they dealt with difficult life encounters, nor would it explain how his model was recognized and preserved by all Christians. That left only one option: Jesus must be God. Jesus was the Messiah whose coming was prophesied by the great Isaiah 700 years prior. He was God's presence on earth. The truth of Jesus as God, then, was the endless source of confidence in Christian faith.[164]

But if Jesus is God, new core issues immediately emerge.[165] First, that would mean both Jehovah and Jesus are gods, driving Christianity away from its roots in the monotheistic Jewish faith and toward polytheism: his mother, Mary, would be a god, each of the 12 apostles would be gods, and future out-standing believers would also become gods. Once the road to man-made gods opened, it would be bustling with crowds—the momentum of polytheism is unstoppable. The true end of polytheism with its many gods, is to essentially have no gods. A slip back into the Epicurean abyss where there is no differ-ence between humans, animals, and things would be inevitable. Neither the Jewish nor the Christian faiths could accept this outcome. Second, if only Jehovah and Jesus are gods, and the path to becoming a god for others is cut off, what is the relationship between Jehovah and Jesus? How must the similarities and differences between them be dealt with? In what way should their roles be divided? What would prevent people from choosing their own god, instead of God choosing people, based on their different attitudes toward Jehovah and Jesus?

These issues have been placed before every follower of Christ since the beginning. Without rational arguments or answers, the spirit of Christ's death could easily be misread and produce different sects, finding itself at the mercy of individual free will. Romans, with their warlike culture, their adherence to the *human requirement* dictated by Roman law, their denial of individual free will, and their total rejection of Christianity, were completely unable to participate in this debate. As for the Jewish people, they had created belief in the unipersonal God through their prophecy, literature, and thousands of years of struggle against idolatry. By virtue of its prophets' accurate predictions in response to God's calling and the power and passion of its literature, the Jewish nation was able to sustain their faith in one God. But they were not masters of analysis and debate. It was time for Greek philosophy, with its rational logic, to come onto the scene. As it integrated the passion of the non-violent love and forgiveness model in Christ's death which replaced the revenge against violence model, the great drama of establishing this most fundamental Christian doctrine on the historical stage of apologetics began to unfold, arising from centuries of persecution of Christians by the Roman Empire.

Some of the thinkers involved in the apologetic movement inherited their Christianity by blood from their fathers, such as Alexandria's Clement and Origen, and the Cappadocian Fathers Basil and Gregory. But many more apologists chose to firmly convert to Christianity in the course of this historical debate and became great apologetic apostles and Christian theologians. These included the famous apostle Paul, the well-known martyr Justin, the extremely eloquent Athenagoras of Athens, Tertullian of Carthage in North Africa, and Ignatius of Antioch. In particular, the distinguished theological synthesizer, Augustine of Hippo, had been a Manichean for more than a decade.[166]

All of these prominent apologetic thinkers possessed profound knowledge in Greek philology, rhetoric, and logic and were well-versed in Greek philosophy. But Greek philosophy had completely lost its direction by that time. The practical philosophers, unwilling to live in the shadows of Socrates, Plato, Aristotle, and other philosophical giants yet unable to find a new way forward, became mired in skepticism. Greek philosophy without the guidance of faith fell into pointless debate. It could not be considered as a reliable guide for practical life, especially for the general public. And that meant it couldn't be integrated into the *human calling* that applied to all human communities.

Likewise, faith without the support of rationality could easily devolve into mysticism, as believers lose their ability to rationally analyze their theology, unable to hold firm to faith in God and Christianity.

Against this backdrop, the debate over the core issues in the apologetic movement unfolded. Apologetic thinkers opened up a new path for Greek philosophy amid the collision of passion and reason in Christianity. They found in Greek philosophy the absolute truths that God existed before the creation and will exist after the disappearance of all things and that humans and nature share the same origin. They also established that humans' inner motivation is to discover the order and beauty that lie behind the superficial phenomena of all things. In doing so, they found freedom, equality, and rationality rooted in ancient Greek philosophy. All of these principles were consistent with the *human calling* ignited by the death of Jesus Christ. Now a solid theoretical foundation for the Trinity, the edifice of Christian theological philosophy, was in place.[167]

This foundation was formed by what these thinkers had achieved in the apologist movement and especially by the sacrifice of the early martyred apostles, which allowed Christianity to quickly develop and expand after Constantine issued the Edict of Milan. But the debate over the core doctrine of Christianity had also become increasingly heated. In order to reconcile disputes and unify ideas, the bishops of the eastern and western Roman Empire, at the invitation of Constantine the Great, gathered for the first time in the history of Christianity at the First Council of Nicaea in 325 AD. The council was attended by 318 bishops. Constantine attended and observed the whole council. After much heated debate, the attendees reached a consensus on the Trinity, namely the unity of the Father, the Son, and the Holy Spirit as three persons in one Godhead. The doctrine of the Trinity, also known as the Nicene Creed,[168] affirmed the divinity of the Son Jesus, as "consubstantial with the Father."

Constantine was eventually baptized and converted to Christianity in 337 AD. He passed away soon after. Nearly half a century later, Emperor Theodosius I enacted legislation in 381 AD that declared Christianity the state religion and invited bishops to participate in a second great meeting of Christians, known as the First Council of Constantinople, which brought together 187 bishops from the main dioceses of eastern and western Rome. The council furthered the discussion of the theological theory of the Trinity. After intense debates, the council affirmed the divinity of the Holy Spirit, and the Nicene Creed was revised to perfection. With the establishment of the trinitarian creed, the Christian faith had finally established itself as the logical continuation of the Jewish faith, with just the right amount of cutting and trimming. The faith represented by the New Testament[169] was now finalized. This had several implications for apologetics.

First, apologetic thinkers and persecuted believers must hold on to the belief that the God of the Christian faith is the same unipersonal God, Jehovah, of the Jewish faith. This meant that they had to fight the then prevalent Marcionite extremism. Marcion of Sinope in the Black Sea region believed that the God in the New Testament is not the same God in the Old Testament. The former is a loving God, while the latter is an angry God. Thus he advocated abandoning the Old Testament.

Second, apologetic thinkers and persecuted believers must hold on to the belief that Christ is the Son of God, the Messiah and Savior as prophesied by Isaiah, and that he is therefore God, the incarnation of God. The goal of his presence and sacrifice was for God to save the Israelites and the rest of humanity in another way. Christ and the Holy Spirit, then, are the embodiment of God's new way of saving humanity, that is, through the love and forgiveness model. This was a new plan for salvation that followed the traditional way based on covenant. To this end, Christianity had to fight constantly against the tendency to separate the Jesus of the New Testament from the God of the Old Testament.

Third, apologist thinkers and persecuted believers must hold on to the belief in God's new way of salvation, that is, the offering and sacrifice of the Son of God, Jesus Christ. Through this sacrifice, humanity's behavioral duty is revealed, and people can sense the love of God. Thus, Jesus Christ is "the way." He became human for the sake of salvation. Gnosticism, however, represented by Manichaeism and enjoying widespread popularity at that time, actually left this "way" for the so-called *gnosis*. *Gnosis* meant knowledge or awareness gained through individual experience. Montanism, meanwhile, openly claimed that the Father, the Son, and especially the Holy Spirit manifested through its founder, Montanus, also leading believers away from the way of Jesus Christ. God had lovingly revealed this way to humanity, speaking directly into both the mystical superstition that blindly looked for the way inside the human heart and the abyss of self-made godhood. If Christianity were unable to stop this tendency, it would eventually slip into a mysticism that lacked a source of rationality, opening the way for man-made gods.

Fourth, apologists further debated whether the Son is consubstantial with or different from the Father. If the emphasis was on the Son's consubstantiality with the Father, wouldn't that mean that there were two gods? And if the emphasis was on the differences between them, did that imply that Christ was created like any human being? This proved a very difficult question to resolve. By emphasizing Christ's differences from the Father and claiming that he was a created being, the school represented by Arius, a Libyan priest, developed into the Arian sect. Later the Council of Nicaea used the phrase, "the Son is consubstantial with the Father," as proposed by Eusebius, the Bishop of Caesarea. This phrase later became the Nicene Creed, and the Arian sect's phrasing was declared heresy. Origen and Augustine of Hippo further argued that the Son is "of the same substance with the Father" and "co-eternal with the Father." This doctrine brought Christian apologetics to a systematic and authoritative level.[170]

Fifth, apologists had to reach consensus on the Holy Spirit. They determined that he arises both from the Father and the Son. According to this doctrine, through the way opened up by the Son's self-sacrifice in obedience to the Father's will, God ensures that the Son lives in the hearts of believers to strengthen their faith in God. The Holy Spirit manifests himself in all places where faith is firm, implementing God's new plan for human salvation. Thus the Trinity of the Father, the Son, and the Holy Spirit cannot be separated.[171]

This apologetic debate in the eastern and western Roman Empire was comprehensive and international, culminating in the theories of Augustine of Hippo in North Africa. Augustine not only strengthened the faith of the church in the theology of the Trinity, but he also struggled against a variety of heretical Christian thoughts, especially Pelagianism. He demonstrated more deeply and systematically God's identity as revealed in both the New and Old Testaments, criticizing the theological dualism that was popular at the time. Augustine held that creation and salvation are the work of the same God at different stages of time, and both are the embodiment of God's grace. He further argued for the absoluteness of God and the finitude of humans, and especially the heritability of humans' original sin. He pointed out the impossibility of true freedom for those who leave God and that humans can only be saved through God's pure grace, shown through Jesus Christ and the Holy Spirit.

In Augustine's view, apocalypticism, humanity's degeneration, and original sin have profound historical origins. God did give humans a common ancestor with free will, Adam, but he exercised it improperly, causing humanity to fall into sin. Adam's sin at its core was an attempt to make himself completely free in the space and time created by God, thus alienating himself from God and from his love. It was also an attempt to become as omnipotent as God through this uncovenanted freedom. Adam's sin brought God's punishments of exile and death to humans. In their exile, Adam and his descendants left the immortal God and entered earthly life limited by birth and death, distancing themselves from God's goodness. Before their death, humans could only extend their limited lives through giving birth. That meant that the sin of Adam was easily passed on to humans who were driven by the desire to love themselves and their lust, even further distancing themselves from God's goodness. The entire human race is caught in a tragic cycle full of mutual violence, murder, and ignorance of the value and significance of human life created by God.

In the midst of such a momentous time, God sent his Son, Christ, to awaken humanity through apocalyptic revelation and achieve their salvation through the sacrifice of his life. This was God's new plan, born out of frustration. Christ, consubstantial with his Father, understood his will. He not only obeyed God's will but, through his own death, fully demonstrated God's love and forgiveness toward human sin and corruption. Humanity, marked by so much sin, certainly couldn't save themselves by virtue of their own free will. Only by the grace of God's rescue plan, by the revelation of Christ's love and forgiveness and the work of the Holy Spirit, could people strengthen their faith and attain salvation. If humans relied on their free will, they would only struggle in the mud of sin, sinking deeper and deeper. This was Augustine's doctrine of monergism, which emphasized the irresistible grace of God. It fundamentally transcended the Jewish faith's idea of the cooperation between God and humanity during the covenant era.[172]

Augustine defended his arguments with the power of Greek philosophical logic and his profoundly insightful Platonic philosophy. In his *Confessions*, he revealed both to Christ and the world his sin and his journey of orienting himself toward God, holding almost nothing back. Readers throughout the centuries have been impressed by both his honesty and the sincerity of his faith in God, as well as his pessimism and frustration toward human nature. Augustine's theology, philosophy, and literature became that era's masterful fusion of Jewish faith, Christian faith, and ancient Greek philosophy. He influenced the inner passion and external reason of the Pope-centered churches of both western and eastern Rome over the following millennium. Regardless of the tug-of-war and later divergence of Arianism and Catholic doctrine, and regardless of the arguments between the eastern and western Roman churches over specific doctrines, Augustine's legacy lives on. Even regardless of the great schism between the eastern and western Roman churches triggered by the controversy over his view of human free will as extremely unhelpful to salvation, it's undeniable that Augustine, based on Christ's pessimistic outlook on human nature, had proposed a profound, systematic argument. He held that people could only control themselves, sacrifice themselves, and orient themselves toward Christ's sacredness to be chosen and saved by God's grace. His arguments have always proved a solid rock of *human calling* in the Christian faith amid the rapid development of the churches in the real world. They guided the evolution of Christianity for a thousand years until the emergence of Thomas Aquinas in the thirteenth century.

Augustine's contribution far surpassed his own era. While Descartes (1596—1650 AD), the father of empiricism, who laid the foundation for modern individualism, made his famous statement, "I think, therefore I am," in the 1500s, Augustine had already anticipated the origin of Cartesian philosophy, essentially stating, "I doubt, therefore I am." Accordingly, Augustine argued that the source of secular political power was the Spirit of God that existed prior to the material world. This idea laid the theological foundation for the source of political power in theocratic states. Moreover, his theology was consistent with the natural law that humans and nature share the same origin of God, providing a convincing argument about the ultimate source of individual freedom and equality, and the authoritative and absolute nature of this source.[173]

CHAPTER 8:

Gestation: humanity's spirit of public welfare under the Christian faith

SECTION 1: THE MOTLEY EMPIRE CREATED IN THE WAKE OF CHRIST

The convergence of the reason of Greek philosophy and the love and forgiveness presented by Christ's death created the Christian faith as a revelation of God to humanity. The Christian faith soon spread through much of the enormous territory that had been conquered by the Roman Empire, attracting countless followers, apostles, and martyrs along the way. Organizations gradually formed with bishops and pastors as teachers and churches as communities of faith and fellowship. These communities rapidly developed common doctrinal codes, culminating in a network of Christian religious organizations bound together by a common belief, with the philosophical theory of Christian theology as its foundation. While traditional family structures and national organizations provided a communal physical life essential for basic survival, Christian community added a richer dimension. Individuals had now found a new communal spiritual life connected to Christ and God. Through this union, they could pursue wholeness and meaning in life in a new way.

These changes were part of an unprecedented wave of globalization in human history, enabling the Christian faith to quickly and steadily develop across the Roman Empire territory. The Christian faith broke out of the cultural boundaries of the Jewish faith, which was largely confined to its own ethnic group due to historic persecution. It also further eroded the boundaries of Greek and Roman polytheism. In the spirit of Christ, Roman subjects increasingly found the *human calling* of love and forgiveness between humans and society compelling. It was completely different from any previous philosophical thought or faith-based discovery of *human calling*.

Love and forgiveness were and are by no means simple concepts of human reason or part of customary laws in any given community, which are nothing more than individual statutes of "human norms." They are cold and without passion. They are ordinary and not authoritative in the ways that truly matter. In contrast, the *human calling* inspired by Christianity's love and forgiveness flows directly from God's love toward the human race he created. Love and forgiveness are deeply intertwined in Christ's decision to offer himself as a sacrifice and be crucified while showing compassion and mercy to humanity. God's testing of Christ at Gethsemane and Golgotha and his redemption of humanity model the love God expects humans to show each other. God's creativity, certainty, infinite nature, and omnipotence make him worthy of humanity's faith in converting to Christianity.

In 381 AD Emperor Theodosius I enacted a law making Christianity the Roman state religion. He invited 187 archbishops to hold a second ecumenical council at Constantinople to revise and improve the Nicene Creed and establish the Trinity as the basis of the Christian faith. This signaled that Constantius' attempt to support the Christian heresy of Arianism—and even more so the apostate Emperor Julian's attempt to resurrect paganism, polytheistic faith, and idolatry—had failed, in spite of their efforts to personally set a moral example and live close to the people.

After the dust settled from the turmoil of over half a century, Roman imperial politicians discovered that Judaism, and Trinitarian Christianity, which had grown from the original Jewish faith, had already formed unrivaled spiritual power in the empire. This power extended throughout the empire's economic, societal, and political capillaries, regardless of the number of believers or the particular theoretical system. Roman imperial politics recognized that its continuity and stability now required them to make full use of the societal foundation laid by this great spiritual power. Otherwise, attempts to maintain power would fail, like sowing dragons' teeth and reaping only fleas. Christianity became not only a grass-roots, bottom-up societal change, but also a top-down initiative personally promoted by the emperors. It enabled the Roman Empire, an aristocratic society with a polytheistic faith to transform itself into one based on a unipersonal God.

The Roman Empire's Christianization proved overwhelming and unstoppable. New archeology findings keep revealing not only ruins of Christian churches, other religious sites, and versions of the Bible in all of the Roman Empire's client kingdoms, but also Bible translations and remains of missionary activities in parts of the empire that were considered barbaric or illiterate (such as the Germanic and Parthian tribes and even the barbarian tribes of the Caucasus and Central Africa). These discoveries underscore the profound and extensive influence of Christianity on the Roman Empire and its surrounding areas at the time.

In spite of their top-down support, those in the upper rungs of the empire failed to fully realize the underlying change this would trigger. Namely, the spread of Christianity in the Empire would erode the foundation on which the

Empire was built, as each one's respective worldview came into conflict. This conflict manifested in several ways:

First, the God in the Christian faith represents the only infinite, eternal, and absolute truth. He represents omniscience and omnipotence. By comparison, all humans have limits, which of course includes the emperor. Thus, although the church often cooperated with imperial powers, compromising its righteousness and ritual in the process, the sacredness of God replaced that of the emperor in the end. The ceremonial life of Christianity constantly reinforced this dynamic. The effect was that the concept of the Christian God denied Roman imperial power's right to set up its emperors as human gods in the cultural consciousness. It essentially dispelled the blind superstition of emperor worship, and people began to hold emperors to higher standards self-cultivation and morality.

Second, the way Christianity reinterpreted the Old Testament emphasized that God created everyone with equal dignity of life. It elevated the recognition of women's dignity to an unprecedented height, and even that of slaves could not be ignored. This change in values was at odds with the hierarchy between nobles and civilians in Roman society. And it was in extreme conflict with the Roman slavery system resulting from the natural law of warfare. While the upper levels of society in the Roman Empire kept slaves for multiple, complicated reasons, for believers, the release and redemption of slaves became a sacred calling from God that guided their actions. This tension constantly buffeted and eroded Roman society's traditional views, gradually deconstructing its deepest structures.

Third, the core values of the Christian faith replaced repayment and vengeance in interpersonal relationships with love and forgiveness. As society embraced these values, doubts inevitably spread about the legitimacy of violence, and even about the culture of exchanging kindness as a means of social transaction. People became weary of the model of "an eye for an eye," upon which the glorious history and the martial spirit of Rome had been built. This ideological conflict, over time, gradually weakened the effectiveness of Rome's army. Historically speaking, the Roman Colosseum was a highly symbolic incubator of Rome's culture of violence. At the height of the Roman Empire, such coliseums appeared throughout nearly all of its territory. They featured battles between man and beast and man and man, war simulations, and executions of prisoners by beasts. These and other scaled violent competitive performances consistently kept the young thrilled. On a deeper level, it caused them to hold violence in high regard while devaluing life, cultivating values that enabled Rome's maniacal conquest of the world. As Christianity's popularity grew, these coliseums gradually became grand stages for dance and musical performances, and the cruel gladiatorial spectacles were officially banned after Constantine the Great. Historians frequently blame the decline of the western Roman Empire on barbarian tribes' decreasing loyalty, as their soldiers made up a large proportion of the Roman army. But the deeper cause was how the advancement of Christian civilization deconstructed and dissolved its violent martial spirit. This manifested itself in the weakening of violent tendencies from soldiers to officials, the decline of martial arts culture among civilians, and a shortage of troop sources in the heartland of Rome, which in turn led to the practice of enlisting troops these from the outskirts of the empire. All these factors, like water dripping on stone, wore away the military power of the Roman army.

Fourth, Christianity's anti-violent approach and emphasis on love and forgiveness is built on the foundation of self-sacrifice at the core of its understanding of *human calling*. This *human calling*, by its inspiring nature, planted and spread the seeds of Christ's love throughout the whole society. It also set the lives of individual Christians apart from those characterized by rampant opulence, arrogance, and disregard for the other. This *human calling* created a sacred connection between lives lived in self-sacrifice and the Trinity itself, imparting higher purpose to their lives and elevating their souls. This way of understanding and approaching life rocked the Roman Empire's materialistic, pleasure-seeking, and brutal climate. It chipped away at its foundation of violent governance, gradually replacing it with more legislated politics within the empire and more contractualized external relationships with client kingdoms. This trend can be traced in the course of history between the rules of Constantine the Great and Emperor Justinian.

During these two centuries, there were far fewer bad emperors than in the post-Augustus age. On the contrary, the emperors of this period—whether Constantine, the apostate Julian, Theodosius I, Justin, or Justinian—were all influenced by the Christian faith to some degree. They were all highly disciplined in their self-cultivation and behavior, and even pursued gaining insight into philosophy and Christian theology to a certain extent. They all very much emphasized the revision and systematization of Roman law, evidenced most powerfully by the publication and implementation of the famous Code of Theodosius and Code of Justinian, or Corpus Juris. Their underlying motivation was to revise Roman law and create norms for individual behavior, or *human requirement*, that aligned with the spirit of God's natural law. They aimed to calm social disorder and deal with criticism of state violence from those who joined the Christian faith during its expansion. At the same time, these emperors still emphasized using military force to preserve the glory of Rome and its expanded territory.

However, in that era of cold weapons in which technological gaps were not significant to determine victory, both military organization and management and internal martial spirit and morale were of utmost importance. These two factors were often the two major determinants of a country's combat effectiveness and military success. With the latter largely eroded due to Christianity's spread, the empire lost more battles. And those lost battles were often followed by diplomatic mediation and contracts signed with client kingdoms to maintain short-lived peace. Political orators, such as Demetrius and Libanius, gained popularity through the need to whitewash these diplomatic agreements and preserve the Empire's dignity. They gave impressive speeches at the Senate and were often able to spin defeats against Persians and Germanic tribes in the Danube River region and the resulting diplomatic agreements as glorious victories for the Empire, gaining enthusiastic support of the 6,000 Senate members and the rest of the imperial society. This political opium and the non-violence encouraged by the Christian faith were two complementary catalysts that numbed the empire's awareness of its crisis of imperial rule from top to bottom and created a historic opportunity for the growth of Germanic barbarian tribes in the northeast.[174]

SECTION 2: THE END OF THE GLORIOUS PAST IN THE SHOCK OF DEEP FAITH

The emperors of the western Roman Empire, starting with Theodosius I, hired the Goths as mercenaries. This proved to be a strategic mistake, as it gave the barbarians insider knowledge of Rome and fed their aspiration to invade the empire. These emperors, starting from Honorius II and the subsequent Valentinians I–III to Majorian, were all weak in the face of external forces. Instead of focusing on military strength, they constantly engaged in court fights and cruelly killed loyal officials, indulging in political corruption. The nobles lived extravagant and corrupt lives while the civilians suffered.

By the end of the fifth century AD, the peoples to the north and northeast of the Roman Empire (the Goths, Vandals, Franks, Huns, and especially the Germanic tribal alliance) had learned much from Roman civilization. They developed a martial spirit comparable to Rome's in its heyday, as well as management skills and an understanding of the rule of law. By that time, Rome's agricultural and iron smelting technologies had been used extensively in those areas. The barbarians, inspired by the Gothic leader Alaric, who had set his sights on Rome and captured the city in a bloody spree in 410, defeated one western imperial army after the next. In the following 70 years, they captured Britain, Gaul, Spain, and North African Carthage. They captured and plundered Rome, the brilliant capital that was once the center of civilization, five times, mocking the strategic mistakes of imperial Roman politicians who had long neglected the Germanic barbarian tribes on the northern border and tried to obtain temporary peace through diplomatic mediation. After more than a century, Justinian, the emperor of the eastern Roman Empire, twice recaptured Rome but could not save the western Roman Empire from its dire fate. According to historians' estimates, the barbarians who attacked Western Rome over the period of a hundred years used no more than 120,000 men, while the Roman Empire had a standing army of at least 300,000. The unbelievable and ridiculous victory of the barbarians shows that the empire's problems went beyond its military failures.[175]

Just like that, the brilliant Roman Empire all but came to an end, with the downfall of Rome and the Western Empire. This empire, which was the first in human history to experiment on a large scale with a political system of aristocratic democracy, popular democracy, monarchal unity, and provincial autonomy, now broke up into multiple ethnically bound European nation-states. Only the Eastern Roman Empire was left standing, with Constantinople as its imperial political center. After learning from the lessons of the decline of Western Rome and enacting a series of reforms, the Eastern Roman Empire managed to linger for almost another 1,000 years in the region that connects modern Europe and Asia.

As has been demonstrated, the spread of the Christian understanding of *human calling* was at the root of the empire's military defeat, underneath the surface causes of internal division and attack by Germanic tribes. This calling extended past commonly held values and into actual lifestyle patterns. The stories of Christ, his followers, and the martyred apostles were preached by bishops and priests in every church in every era of the Empire. The ascetic lifestyle choices of these preachers in particular embodied a paradigm for dealing with human desires and encounters and became an expression to the secular world of the universal values of God and Christ. The result was a transformation of society's values as a whole.

But what is worth paying close attention to is that in between the deep cause of religious shock and the superficial cause of the collapse of imperial politics, another contributing factor is evident: the economic restructuring of the costs to maintain the imperial system. A complicated game was played over the allocation of these costs. For any empire that has existed for a long time, it's expensive to maintain military and bureaucratic operations. Solving the problem of cost-sharing and making the machine work is a great challenge for imperial rulers. At its peak, the Roman Empire boasted an area of 6–10 million square kilometers, covering the equivalent of 50 countries in today's Europe, North Africa, and Asia. Its linguistic and cultural span was unprecedented, with a population of over 120 million, accounting for 40 percent of the world's population at the time. Given the information and transportation technology of the time, the management of the imperial political system was unimaginably difficult, as were its maintenance costs.

During the empire's constant territorial expansion, the dynamic windfall generated by large-scale plunder, along with moderate land-based agricultural taxes, could basically cover the costs of maintaining the imperial system. Additionally, urban and commercial prosperity brought about by imperial control of Mediterranean trade and expanding maritime and onshore trade routes brought in more revenue in the form of industrial and commercial taxes and trade tariffs. The Roman Empire's money-making machine in that era seemed to have inexhaustible income sources. As a result, all levels of imperial society were vying to create the most splendid architecture and luxurious lifestyle imaginable. But in 117 AD, after Emperor Trajan extended the territory to the physical limits of imperial reach and control, the windfall generated by violent conquest and plunder suddenly ceased.[176] The Emperors' desire for construction and extravagance, however, continued to rise. As a result, a gap grew between the maintenance costs and income of the imperial system.

After brewing for some time over the rule of several emperors, things worsened rapidly during the period of Emperor Commodus (177–192) until they reached a turning point during the reign of Caracalla (198–217). Amid the effort to close the gap between imperial income and expenditure, Roman imperial politicians worked out the unique Roman economic model of the later period. Emperor Caracalla devised and legislated two methods to address the gap. The first was to extend Roman citizenship to all non-slave males in Roman territory. Performing military service was one of their obligations, and if they refused to do so, they could pay a compensatory tax instead. Additionally, they were required to pay an inheritance tax. The second was to reduce the content of silver in coins printed with an image the emperor's head by 25 percent to pay for the military expenses of the Roman Legion. The first measure not only failed to increase revenue, but also struck a serious blow at to tax revenue as a whole, since the law stated that Roman citizens did not pay income tax. The second measure triggered serious inflation. In payment for his failure, Caracalla, at 29, was murdered by the army on an expedition to the Kingdom of Parthia.

Caracalla's schemes could have been thought of by any emperor. By the end of the third century, the content of silver coins issued by the Roman Emperor dropped below 10 percent. In many parts of Rome, inflation was constantly on the rise. The Roman nobility and free people often responded to inflation with effective measures, such as buying land to preserve value and using slave labor to decrease production costs and increase value added. But the slave supply, which came mainly from captives of defeated states, was greatly reduced once territorial expansion stopped. Add to that Christian civilization's respect for equal human rights and the rising cost of keeping slaves, and suddenly agricultural taxes were not enough to meet the costs of maintaining the empire. As a result, a greater share of taxes was passed on to indirect taxes like urban industrial and commercial taxes and trade tariffs, which was a blow to the Roman Empire's glorious industrial and commercial civilization. This prompted those involved in urban industry and commerce, free people, and nobles to all join a wave of land mergers, which led to the birth of the manor system.[177]

Under this system, the more land the lord owned and the more people he used, the more he could create an internal division of labor, collaboration, and bartering to resist inflation. He could use the devaluing Roman currency less and gain more political power. Meanwhile, free Roman citizens gradually fell from their former glory and lost their privileges, becoming targets of conscription and taxation. Fleeing into a lord's manor proved to be a more reliable refuge than Christian abbeys. These factors promoted the development of the late Roman Empire's, and later Europe's manorial system, also known as feudalism.

The "villa-style" manor, the earliest form of the manorial economy, was a type of agriculture on a scale more suitable to free men, with several dozen slaves on average engaging in agricultural production. This small manor's economic opportunities and citizen protection strategies were limited, however. Larger manors known as latifundiums, with several thousand slaves on average, and the largest "saltus" manors, at tens of thousands of slaves or free people in most cases, were different. Their size made them capable of complex internal division of labor and well-trained security forces. This hereditary territory became a kind of state within a state under the manorial economy, able to evade taxes through privatized taxation, while providing strong political protections to slaves and free people who fled the city. At the time Roman law stipulated that government bureaucrats were not allowed to enter private territories to make arrests. The lord's manager alone could make arrests, a strong evidence of the lord's ability to provide political asylum. Thus, in the Gaul, Italian, Spanish, and even British parts of Western European Rome, saltus manors popped up rapidly.

Under the manorial economy, 80 percent of the Roman Empire's land was held by 5 percent of the population.[178] The stronger the lords became politically, the more tax revenues that were needed to maintain the empire were forced onto free people engaged in urban industry, commerce, and trade. A vicious cycle of free people escaping to lords' manors began. The result was that previously remote country lords became prosperous, while previously commercial areas receded, splendid cities emptied, and bustling avenues swarmed with thieves. Rome, once the world's most glorious capital, saw its population reduced from a peak of 1.5 million to 300,000 in the second half of the fifth century, completely replaced by the "new Rome," Constantinople.

The collapse of the Western Roman imperial political system was followed by a new rise of European and North African nation states. These emerging nation states were integrated or reorganized after hundreds or nearly a thousand years of Roman rule, a fascinating era for historical stories. Although these nation states did their utmost to restore their national consciousness, they could not resist the legacy and influence the Roman Empire left them with.

The first aspect of this legacy was the influence of the Roman political system and rule of law. Roman history went through the difficult transformation from aristocratic democracy to citizen democracy and to monarchal politics. Its political system was nothing like the majority of political systems generally found in agricultural civilizations. Although the natural law of the era's politics finally forced it to take a form that resembled a monarchy, a closer look reveals essential differences between Rome's governance and the authoritarian family-based monarchy that characterizes the world's agricultural civilizations of all eras. The differences were mainly reflected in aspects of politics that were influenced by Greek philosophy.

First, Roman politics inherited Greece's humanistic ideal of respect for individual human rights and property rights in the community. Even though the definition of an individual was limited to those with the rights of Roman citizens, it was the first attempt in human communal politics to focus on individual rights as foundational to the community. Second, Roman politics inherited and promoted ancient Greek rationality toward the human community and the pursuit of norms and practices for public order. These were mainly reflected in the famous "Twelve Tables," "Code of Theodosius," "Code of Justinian," and other systems of legal provisions. They were also reflected in the famous jurist Cicero's *On the Republic*, *About the Orator*, and *On the Laws*, as well as *Institutes* written in the second century by Gaius, another famous jurist. These very provisions and ideas on the rule and practice of law reflected ancient Greek's philosophical rationality towards maintaining the public order of the human community contained in the Roman political civilization.[179] Of course, society didn't reflect on or and recognize this emphasis on rationality until more than 600 years after the fall of the Western Roman Empire. Finally, Roman political civilization experimented successfully with procedures of political authorization and operation. Whether it was the selection of senate members, election of the consuls or the tribune, operation of civilian parliament, the transition to the Principate system, the procedure of crowning or deposing an emperor, or the emperor's formal reporting system to the later senate, the Roman Empire boldly attempted to and respect "procedural justice" in human's political civilization.[180]

Historically, family pedigree or violent war were the only means of becoming emperor, but as Roman imperial politics changed, these two main sources of power became null. Rather, succession happened by selecting a worthy candidate and making him the emperor's "adopted son." The army supported this succession method in the middle and late periods, while the Senate always played a role in making it procedurally legitimate. Some scholars are wrong to simply analogize political shift in the late Roman Empire to military coups in barbaric politics. The experimental results of Roman imperial politics, that is, the respect for individual human rights, the communal democratic order, and the combination of procedural legitimacy and hereditary power still play a significant part in forming political systems and civilizations. They could hardly fail to have a far-reaching and lasting impact on the governance of the various European countries which later emerged from the collapse of the Roman Empire.

The second aspect of Rome's legacy embraced by its nation states was the Christian faith's shaping of *human calling* in terms of individuals' thinking and action. After Christianity became the state religion in Rome, many new Christians were not as devoted or pure as those who faced early persecution. However, *human calling* in Christianity must be achieved by self-sacrifice. It's founded on pessimism toward humanity's inherent goodness found in the doctrine of original sin, leading to gratitude for God's salvation. That in turn leads to the adoption of a non-violent, anti-vengeance approach to evil in the world, one that embraces love and forgiveness. This spirit that both exposed human sin and offered forgiveness was quite appealing in an era when elevating the value of human life was a growing desire. This message was preached by tens of thousands of believers and apostles throughout the Roman Empire, which accounted for nearly 40 percent of the world's population and nearly 30 percent of the nation states. A spiritual organization formed, led by thousands of theological and philosophical authorities, or archbishops and churches. These communities interacted with each other through discussion of doctrine and the how to handle royal power relations and grew into an umbrella network of Christian organizations centered around Rome with nearly invincible social influence. As a result, more than 50 of today's countries, which were nation states under the rule of the Roman Empire, maintained the Christian faith even after breaking away from the Roman Empire. Not only that, but many barbarian tribes from the Caucasus around the Black Sea and Germanic tribes around the northern part of the Danube River converted to the Christian faith after invading the core areas of the Roman Empire.[181]

SECTION 3: PILGRIMS LONGING FOR THEIR OWN SPIRITUAL KINGDOM

The influence of this lasting Roman legacy decided the direction of European civilization's future. On the one hand, its physical national governance headed toward a monarchal regime characterized by nation-state and manorial economy, as well as laws and regulations of *human requirement* both based on and distinctive from Roman law. On the other hand, its spiritual governance moved increasingly toward Christianity, a faith system with churches as its organizational network and both the New Testament and the conclusions of apologetic theologians as its authority. The result was a set of unified religious rituals promoting *human calling* in everyday life. The physical life of human was finally separated from the spiritual life.[182] No matter how gorgeous and brilliant monarchal power was in humanity's public, physical life, it couldn't compare to the sacredness of *human calling* based on God's authority and the spiritual life of Christ's representatives.

On Christmas in 800 AD, Charlemagne, king of the precursor to France, the Frankish Kingdom, was invited to lead an army over the Alps and south into the city of Rome. (This was 44 years after his father, Emperor Pepin, offered to dedicate the land of the Ravenna near Rome to the Roman church.) The Roman Pope Leo III personally presented Charlemagne with the crown of the Holy Roman Empire, asking his army to lead the way in driving invaders and Islamic North African pirates from its coastal cities and protect Christianity in Europe. From that historic moment onward, it became necessary for the secular ruling authority to be granted by the human representative of God's authority, the Pope, in order to increase the legitimacy and authority of the monarchy. Thus, a new and unique mechanism for independence with mutual checks and balances between church and royal powers in Europe was formed in human history.[183]

These theocratic constraints on kingship were the result of the church's long-term struggle with monarchal power and in its undertaking of sacred responsibility. There are several examples in history. The congregation of Bishop Ambrose of Milan opposed the attempt of Emperor Valentinian III's mother, Galla Placidia, to give a Christian church in Milan to the pagans. The congregation held a long-term vigil, sitting quietly in demonstration after singing hymns all night until the Empress gave up. Saint Paulinus wrote to the emperor, asking him to cancel the brutal gladiator spectacles, leading saints to sing hymns until they were finally cancelled. The famous "golden-mouthed" priest, John Chrysostom of the Church of Hagia Sophia, bluntly criticized the royal aristocracy every time he preached. He called out their indifference toward the oppression of poor and their luxurious and lustful lives, until the Empress ordered him to be expelled from the church. Later, the strong appeal of the believers forced the Emperor to reinstate him. The conflict repeated itself once John returned to his position. The list goes on. The church also continued its sacrificial ways in its struggle against imperial power in the secular world. Although the church was no longer persecuted by the regime as it had been before Constantine the Great, its sacrifice was ongoing.

After the fall of the Western Roman Empire, the eastern remnant claimed the name of the Roman Empire for another 900 years, with Constantinople as its capital. Why then did the Christianity of Rome rather than the Christianity of Constantinople become the central authority of the Christian world? Apart from the various specific historical reasons listed by scholars, the most substantial reason was the spiritual influence the Roman church gained from its sufferings and its conformity to Christ's spirit in the midst of these various hardships.

First, the offered lives of early Christian apostles and martyrs laid the foundation of self-sacrifice. The blood of martyrs like Saint Peter, Saint Paul, and Saint Ignatius during the Roman Empire's persecution of the Christian faith continued to fuel the flame and passion of Christ's spirit in human hearts.

Second, the Roman Church, on behalf of the believers in the fallen Western Roman Empire, held to the Christian faith's trinitarian doctrine and kept fighting against any theology that sought to overstate the difference between God and Christ. It strove to maintain the unity of monotheism in articulating God and Christ's plan for salvation, so avoiding the possibility that the Christian faith would fall into polytheism or mysticism. It was this tenacity and persistence that maintained the Christian faith's orthodoxy and reason.

Third, the Roman church showed Christ's loving spirit during the great plagues of Rome, such as the Antonine Plague of 164–169 AD, the Plague of Cyprian of 250–270 AD, the later plague under Maximinus in 320 AD, and so on. As 2,000–5,000 Romans were dying every day, many people fled from their loved ones who had contracted infectious diseases. Only members of Christian organizations insisted on continuing to care for and seek treatment for such patients, which resulted in many Christians losing their lives to infection.

590 years after the Western Roman Empire had fallen, the already weak Rome was once again struck by a great plague. At that time, Gregory, high priest of the Church of Constantinople, was appointed as the Pope. The city was in ruins, nearly deserted. After he heard that he was appointed to replace Pope Pelagius II, who died from the plague, Gregory fled. On his escape route, he heeded Christ's call and returned to Rome to take over the job, uttering his famous saying, "Apart from those who don't want to be bishop, no one is worthy of being bishop."

During his 14-year papacy, Pope Gregory organized and mobilized believers to resume praying, help the sick and aid the poor, and clear trash. Together they called for the Eastern Roman Emperor and other lords and city-states with armed forces to resist the Lombard invasion and negotiate a truce with them. Pope Gregory set his gaze on the territory of Gaul and the other European countries. He coordinated and resolved conflicts between dioceses, kings, and grand dukes with thousands of papal letters. He developed a persuasive language in response to suffering that was filled with Christ's sacred hope, love and forgiveness, even as the Western Roman Empire continued to fall apart.

His interpretation and regulation of the Roman papal power through his moral example and speech laid the foundation for the Roman papal system and authority for a long time to come. His influence was especially evident in the selection of popes, who were secretly chosen by the more influential archbishops of the European parishes. He left for posterity lengthy works of Bible interpretation, including *Commentary on Job* and *Dialogues*, using plain language and resonant metaphors centering on the spread of Christ's gospel. For Gregory, it was not about enjoying the glory of Christ's crown, but engaging Christ's heart to correctly understand God's boundless love and holiness, dealing with life's desires and tragic encounters through the help of the Holy Spirit, and so finding the joy of life led in constant connection with Christ. [184]

Fourth, the Roman popes and bishops, after Christianity became the state religion, continued to offer their lives in sacrifice. Muslims emerging in the seventh century occupied and fully Islamized the southern parts of the Eastern Roman Empire and North Africa. The Mediterranean became a hotbed of organized pirates, with the chieftain governments of North African cities gaining 20 percent of their income from piracy. The coastal cities of Italy were plundered, with Sicily and Sardinia brutally sacked. At that point, Italy had already disintegrated into countless trading city-states and inland lord tribes. The Roman Pope had no armed forces or support from the Eastern Roman Empire. He was also limited in his military actions by the ethos of love and forgiveness, making it impossible to defend against the jihad of the North African Muslims. He had no way to stop pirates from attacking cities along the coast from Spain to Italy's Tyrrhenian Sea, Ionian Sea, and Adriatic Sea. Numerous monasteries and even Saint Peter's Basilica were robbed several times.

In response, Pope Gregory IV recruited Christians in 827 to form an army led by Bonifacio to confront the forces of jihad and won its first victory. In 830, Pope Gregory IV led his troops to guard Rome and fend off invasion. One year later, Muslims captured the city of Palermo in Sicily, and 60,000 people died in the battle for its defense. The Christian archbishop was taken as a slave. Under the Pope's constant efforts and organization, Christians finally broke free from the military implications of their creed of love and forgiveness in 847. Realizing the lack of protection from a unified secular regime, they began to form their own armed forces to counter the Islamic invasion and other external threats. In 848 Pope Leo IV organized Italian city-states to carry out a crusade to defend the Christian world and won the famous Battle of Ostia. He also urgently called on city-states of Amalfi, Pisa, Genoa, and Venice on the Italian coast to organize armed forces against Muslim forces and North African pirates.

In 877 AD, Syracuse in Sicily fell after staying strong for nine months. Islamic jihadists shouted slogans such as "there is no faith outside Allah" and "death to the dogs of Christ." Seventy of the most prominent Christians, including the archbishop, went nobly to their deaths. The island of Sicily fell wholly into the hands of North African Muslims. The Eastern Roman Empire and Christian Europe turned a blind eye, doing nothing to save them. Horror enveloped the Mediterranean, and the portal to the Italian peninsula was wide open. In 918 AD, the Roman Pope John X formed Crusaders and led a drafted Christian army south, recapturing the fortress of Sigiriya in the first battle and then the long-term pirate landing port of Wedleyville. His Crusaders raised a banner of guard over the Christian world, inspiring confidence that a collapsing Christian Europe could still manage to defend the gateway to Rome. Unfortunately, he was murdered in 928 AD.

In 1087 AD, small Italian city-states in Amalfi, Pisa, Genoa, and Venice responded to Pope Victor III's call to build 300 warships for the Crusades. For the first time they went to the North African political center Wanrubi to rescue Christians taken into slavery. After over a month of fighting, they were victorious and forced the defeated to sign terms of surrender, marking the beginning of 200 years of European countries joining the Crusades.

From the eighth century to the tenth century AD, hundreds of thousands of Christians, including many bishops, were taken as slaves to the key Islamic towns of Algiers and Tunisia in North Africa. Even popes sacrificed their lives during this chaos, with 13 popes murdered in only 32 years in the first half of the tenth century. Through the trials of this long tribulation, the Pope and the church put on the crown of Christ's spiritual kingdom.[185]

It's evident that the centrality of Rome and the Pope's authority in Christianity were by no means the result of canonized earthly authority or a plot by the popes. Rather, it was the result of the Roman church and the popes' hundreds of years of adhering to Christ's spirit of offering and sacrificing in the face of extreme external violence. It was Christ's flower watered by the sin and suffering of the human world, and the crown of thorns placed by Christ on the Pope[186]. It was also a trial of Christians' ability to integrate with the royal order after the collapse of secular dominance in the Roman Empire.

Out of such intense hardships, Europe developed the Christian Church as represented by the Pope of Rome and a theocratic political system headed by the kings of European countries. This church and state, independent and mutually constrained, formed a unique public order in human history, which finally came to be after 900 years of turmoil. It aligned not only with the Hebrew monotheism of Christianity's roots, but also with ancient Greek philosophy's axiom that the "spirit is higher than and precedes all things." It incorporated the order of the "rule of law" of the Roman Empire, as well as the emphasis on love and forgiveness modeled in Christ's offering and sacrifice. This system truly fulfilled Christ's statement, "Render unto Caesar's what is Caesar's; and unto God what is God's."

However, as far as spiritual devotion to God, this system wasn't without problems. When the Christian faith became a mainstream religion free from persecution, secular desires and ambitions inevitably threatened to invade the church and Christian organizations, turning some churches into a means to accumulate money and pleasure. Meanwhile, the emperors wielded their secular power to heavily intervene in theocratic matters, often turning the church into a vassal of royal power and appointing corrupt church leaders. As a result, those who sought to follow Christ's way of offering and sacrifice no longer felt a sense of sacredness or religious guidance from the church. Against this background, devout Christians, represented by Saint Jerome (340–420), set off to oppose this shift and follow Christ as part of the monastic movement. One member of this movement was Anthony (251–356). He declined Constantine the Great's invitation to meet him, maintaining his commitment to the eremitic method of controlling one's desires and minimizing the material needs of life. On Colzim Mountain near the Red Sea, he lived a reverent, monastic life until his death at age 105. His harsh denial of his own desires gained the admiration of Christian monks and led the charge among Christian monks to deny their physical needs for hundreds of years.

Pachomius (287–347) did not lay down to sleep for decades due to his commitment to promote cenobitic rather than eremitic monasticism. He devoted himself to the construction of nine monasteries and a convent and first introduced the "rules for cenobitic life."

Saint Jerome, in addition to building monasteries and leading cenobitic monasticism in Jerusalem, Bethlehem, and other places, spent the final 34 years of his life living in a cave. He relinquished all temptations of the material world and wrote many works criticizing the luxury and decadence of princes and nobles in the outside world. He had extremely harsh moral requirements for Christians, even repudiating Origen, the famous theologian archbishop of North Africa. He also wrote beautiful poems in Latin to women of the time, admonishing them to join monasticism and promoting the rise of convents.

Saint Augustine founded the first African monastic group, known as Augustinians. He established the rules, rituals, and precepts of life for the Christian monastery and sought to feel Christ's sacredness and solemnity through self-restraint and painful experiences. Even in his last days at the age of 76 as the Archbishop of Hippo, he was still practicing monasticism while he bore the heavy weight of a declining Western Rome. During the three months of a siege by the Vandals, Augustine persuaded the people to hold on within the city while he urged the Vandals to stop rebelling against Rome and return to Christ. When he felt his days on earth were numbered, he wrote for himself the epitaph that would capture the attention of future generations: "What makes the heart of a Christian heavy? Because he is a pilgrim, and longs for his country."[187]

In addition to the example of sacrifice set by these saints and monks, many secular figures greatly influenced the practice of penance, namely Paulinus (353–431), Melania the Younger (383–439), and Benedict (480–548), who were all born into nobility. They auctioned off ancestral property, donated its proceeds, and fled from their life of riches into the monastic life. Benedict even threw himself naked into thorns to reject his physical desires. They renounced material wealth and status, striving toward a sacred attitude toward life, which influenced many and promoted the Christian monastic movement as a social trend.[188]

SECTION 4: THE BIRTH OF CHARITABLE ORGANIZATIONS

The monastic movement greatly influenced the way the Christian faith spread and the shift toward public charity in European society. This movement provided a way to pursue martyrdom in the absence of persecution. After becoming the state religion, Christian groups could receive financial support to build magnificent churches and could live a solemn yet luxurious life under the shelter of Christ's reputation. The Christian faith's original values of offering and sacrifice and love and forgiveness gradually eroded. Extravagant sins ate away at orthodox Christian churches, and this luxurious life had a numbing effect on its members, making them insensitive to human suffering around them. Christians who participated in the monastic movement distanced themselves from them by rejecting the glitz, and instead painstakingly following Christ's sacred ethos of love and self-sacrifice.

The monastic movement advanced the Christian faith in European cities and towns in two forms. The first was its "community centers," such as churches and chapels in populated areas for Christian worship and communication. The other was its relatively simple monasteries in remote villages or mountainous areas where monks could lead a "cenobitic life," somewhat similar to the Buddhist temples in the East. Around the end of the twelfth and beginning of the thirteenth century, there were about 8,000 monasteries throughout Europe, with more than 600 in Frankish territory alone. Of course, as times changed some of these monasteries became rich and corrupted by continuous donations, which caused Christ's spirit to further diminish. In response, in the late Middle Ages there were reformation groups like the Franciscans and Puritans who aimed to purify the increasingly trendy and corrupted monastic system.

Another arena where the monastic movement's influence was felt was in maintaining Christianity's place in the public sphere. Amid internal pressures on Christians and external pressure on organized Christianity after it became the state religion, the monastic movement constantly prevented the worsening trend of Christianity's bureaucratization. It did this by creating and promoting generous public welfare organizations, keeping its public care activities based on untainted donations and Christ's love, and separated from the functions of government. This was a significant and pioneering development in the history of humanity that deeply influenced the course of human civilization for thousands of years to this day.

The movement's power and influence lay largely in how its Christian organizations differed from state governmental organizations, and how they interacted with the family unit. State political organizations had the upper hand over families from the beginning in terms of political power. Whoever obtained state power had the right to tax the family-based economic unit within the national community, and the family was rewarded by services that protected it from internal and external violence. Between them was a kind of contract. But because of the "one-to-many" nature of this contractual relationship, it could only be implicit rather than explicit.

The one (the state) could impose its will on the many (families), often involving an increasing amount of violence toward individuals and families in the community. Because of this imbalance of power, the fairness of a contract between a state and families within a community had to always rely on periodic re-interpretation and adjustments, as good and bad leaders oversaw prosperity and chaos. Add to that the violent conflicts between communities or states as they expanded which characterized the history of civilizations in this era, and families were often given little recourse or choice. This form of national organization often offered individuals and families an empty choice that they could only passively accept, since they had no way to get out of the contract.

The organizational form of Christianity, meanwhile, was a small societal organization based in a community with common spiritual faith. It was founded on the individual rather than the family, on shared faith rather than interest, and on freedom to enter or exit the community. Its organizational income was based on voluntary, sacred donations, rather than mandatory taxation. Typically, members of the organization put coins in a donation box at each meeting. The use of this revenue was determined by the church's governing body elected by members who knew each other well within the community.

Thus, we see the complementary creation of three organizational forms: the family, the nation and the church organization. The family was a group that integrated the functions of wealth creation, emotional life, consumption, human reproduction, etc. It was generally run by the head of household, namely a patriarch, with the father, or in his absence the eldest son, at its core. As discussed in previous chapters, the family as a basic organizational unit was present in early agricultural civilizations. Later, the tribal natural state or monarchal nation state levied taxes on families via contract or compulsion to maintain order and protect families from violence. The state was an organizational form created by humanity to manage the relationship between the individual and public interest. The widespread appearance of Christian church organizations introduced a third organizational form. Through voluntary donations of money and time as a way to advance one's divine faith, the Christian church helped human individuals build faith in God through embracing pain and suffering. These values created a culture of love and forgiveness rather than violent revenge in the face of life's difficulties. This form became a public organization for the human spirit. Its financial structure—including the source of its income, the communal ownership of its property, and rules prohibiting such property from being used for trade or gifts—were already fully reflected in the *Code of Justinian* of the sixth century.[189] Monastic organizations can be considered a subset of Christian organizations, since there's no fundamental difference in terms of nature and structure, except for a greater emphasis on the individuality of their founders and a more demanding management in their organizational structures and sense of mission.

Christian churches became large-scale charitable organizations and developed numerous professional philanthropic organizations. In so doing, the church became the first and most important medium for the transition of

Europe from theocratic states to modern civil states. It advanced the understanding of *human calling* further than any previous civilization. Ancient Greek philosophy emphasized reason in public order; ancient Rome focused on a public order built on the philosophy of natural law, legal recognition of citizenship, and the results of war; and ancient Hebrew society emphasized a public order based on the covenant between God and humans codified in Moses's Ten Commandments. But none emphasized the sanctity and equality of human life or the importance of righteousness in the relationships between humans and society like the Christian church.

This kind of righteousness means caring for others in alignment with the *human calling* that God expects. While a society with public order is much preferable to a chaotic, disordered society, it doesn't necessarily have a truly good—or righteous—public order. A truly good public order must be based on the common dignity of life God that created, resulting in individuals caring for others in a righteous way. All of this comes from God's goodness to his creation and from his rescue plan for humanity through Christ's offering and sacrifice.

It was this *human calling,* marked by deep reason and passion for the dignity of life, that drove Christians and churches to oppose to the trampling of life under Roman rule. They opposed slavery and the gruesome violence towards slaves in the Roman arena, opposed infanticide, and opposed using living people as funeral and altar sacrifices. It's why they wrote letters to the Emperor and the Senate and organized demonstrations and chanting of classics and hymns all night long, pioneering the "public advocacy for public welfare" in human history that is still ongoing today. Through their unyielding efforts, infanticide and violent competitive performances were abolished by Emperor Valentinian and Emperor Honorius at the end of the fourth century and beginning of the fifth century, respectively.

This same *human calling* drove them to oppose the discrimination against women in the Roman Empire and in all pagan cultures, including polygamy, gruesome vaginal closure surgery, widow burials, veil wearing, and other demeaning practices. They opposed prostitution, while the surrounding society saw it as "easing the rigors of monogamy." They applied the solemnity of God's blessing in the church to bless women with equal rights and dignity in monogamy. Women were free to join the church and, once Pachomius established the first convent for his younger sister, many women joined the ranks of the monastics. The Benedictines also developed many convents that gained popularity. Men's monasteries often became centers of technical training and artisanal training, such as winemaking in agriculture, production technology in industry, and even alchemy in chemistry and astronomical research. Women's monasteries often became charitable institutions that cared for orphans, widows, the old, and the sick, as well as educational centers for language, rhetoric, logic, music, geometry, astronomy, and mathematics, collectively referred to as the Seven Arts. Convents often elected promoters, or sponsors, from their believers. They not only managed the convent but also participated in the religious, political, and society events of the upper class, exerting unique influence. By the twelfth and thirteenth centuries, the development of these convents reached its peak, with more than 500 in the Germanic region alone. This had a significant and far-reaching impact on the development of women's liberation and rights in human history.[190]

It was this *human calling* that also inspired Christians with the spirit of the apostles to launch a number of charitable organizations with the purpose of saving lives. Representative groups were the Trinitarian Order and the Mercedarians, whose purpose was to use peaceful means to rescue Christian slaves imprisoned in Islamic North Africa.

After the collapse of the Western Roman Empire, Italy and Spain fell into various lordly estates and small city-state nations. Coupled with the Christian concept of non-violence deeply rooted in people's minds, and the custom of the North African tribal governments to take a 20 percent cut from the pirate industry, all these factors led to Muslim jihadists and organized pirates from North Africa targeting coastal cities in Italy and Spain from the sixth century to the end of the eleventh century. During the capture of Sardinia, Sicily, and other coastal cities by Muslim pirates, the number of Christians taken and forced to work in North Africa reached one million. This mission of liberating slaves began the Crusades, although this original intention was forgotten by European politicians from the end of the second Crusade onward.

In 1197 the French Christians St. John de Matha and St. Felix of Valois and the English monk John established the Trinitarian Order. In 1199, they successfully bought back 186 ragged and emaciated French Christian captives from Sudan and went to great pains to transport them back to Marseille. Europeans were inspired to donate to the cause. The second time, they bought back 110 Italian Christian captives, who had been subjected to unbearable torture. The Trinitarian Order thus earned support and donations from the Pope and the people from all over Europe, gradually becoming an international non-governmental organization that saved Christian slaves. Apart from rescue actions, the Trinitarian Order built hospitals in key captive settlements in North Africa to help alleviate the ailments of those who were yet to be redeemed. De Matha fought for this cause until 1213 when he died. In his 13 years of rescue operations, he liberated 7,000 captives. Research shows that the organization lasted for 500 years, rescuing a total of 500,000 slaves—a truly amazing feat.

Another famous charitable organization of its kind was the Order of the Blessed Virgin Mary of Mercy, also known as the Mercedarians. It was founded in 1218 by the Spanish Knight Saint Peter Nolasco. Members sold their property to raise funds for rescue operations. When they were underfunded, they pledged themselves as hostages to North African captors to free the captives first, then waited for their companions to raise funds and rescue them. The Mercedarians began their first operation in 1222, buying back 160 emaciated Spanish Christian captives from Algiers. The whole of Barcelona was moved and sent donations to sustain their rescue operations. In six years, a total of 6,000 captives were freed. Nolasco survived 38 years, risking his life countless times until he died in 1256. He followed Christ with his whole life, establishing the Mercedarians even beyond the borders of Europe. This great charitable organization remained in existence until 1779. In its 557-year long history, it recorded 334 rescue operations and brought nearly 100,000 Christian captives to freedom.

These two full-fledged charitable organizations founded by Christians were the epitome of the development of charity under God's call of righteousness in those times. Their spirit and acts of righteousness would put any contemporary charitable organization to shame.[191]

Christianity's understanding of *human calling* also inspired believers and churches to launch the earliest and largest compassionate ministry to the sick in human history. In a culture where the warrior spirit exalted violence and revenge, health and heroism were celebrated, while the sick, old, and weak were neglected or even cast aside by society. Even the famous philosopher Plato believed that abandoning the old, weak, and sick who were not capable of working made for a more robust, powerful society. This is powerful proof that society in this era believed that the strong should prey on the weak. Human compassion was discussed in many cultural contexts, such as the Chinese philosopher Mencius's belief that all mortal humans are inherently compassionate or empathetic, or the Nepali-born Buddha who believed that the essence of Buddhism was *Karuṇā*, or compassion for the lives of other people and even all sentient beings or animals. Christ, on the other hand, gave up his life to carry out God's love for man, in hopes that people would perform acts of love for others, namely their "neighbors," In particular giving medical treatment and caring for the elderly, the weak, the sick and the disabled.[192]

The first orphanage and nursery in history was built by Christians in Rome. Later, at the urging of Saint Basil, Tertullian, Saint Augustine, and others, most churches developed orphanages. Some organizations turned into specialized management agencies for orphans' housing and education, helping them look for adopted parents or sending them to families willing to adopt them into a normal family life.

This was just the beginning of orphan ministry stretching through the centuries to modern day. The famous Holy Spirit Society was one of these charities specializing in helping orphans. By the end of the thirteenth century, the Holy Spirit Society was managing more than 800 orphanages and raising tens of thousands of orphans. A German student of Christianity named George Müller, inspired by his mentor, began to start orphanages and raise orphans in 1836. By the end of his life, he had cared for more than 8,000 orphans. These kind Christian actions were spread around the world by missionaries after the discovery of the New World. One example is the Orphan Train, founded by American pastor Charles Brace in 1853, which sent countless orphans by train to Christian families across the United States. Today's global volunteer community can be traced back to an initial network of Christian organizations who gave their offerings and sacrifices to help the weak.

The earliest nursing homes for the elderly who had no ability to care for themselves were created by Christians in Constantinople during the reign of Justinian. Likewise, the first hospital for the housing and treatment of the spiritually sick was donated by Christians in the second half of the fourth century. The first hospital for leprosy patients was founded in Caesarea by Saint Basil in the second half of the fourth century. Although today, for-profit hospitals have spread around the world and the birthplace of modern medicine is Alexandria, the modern hospital can be traced back to the earliest Christian charity rescue operations. The first two charitable hospitals in history to provide "modern" medical care were founded by Archbishop Saint Basil in Cappadocia and Edessa in 369 and 375 respectively. Afterward, the wealthy widow Fabiola, influenced by Saint Jerome, donated all her property so that two hospitals could be established both in Rome and in the remote villages south of Rome in 390 and 398. Here, helpless dying patients could receive medical treatment or hospice care. Such good deeds gained the praise of Augustine, Archbishop of Hippo, and Pope Gregory I. Concerted efforts and support from these and other church leaders raised Christianity's enthusiasm for donating to hospitals and patient care. Hospitals quickly grew in European countries and were introduced to the Muslim region of Arabia in the eighth century.

By the fourteenth century, a country like the United Kingdom with a population of four million had more than 600 hospitals known as "Houses of God." Institutions for patient care were even more common. In the middle of the sixteenth century, the Benedictines alone had over 37,000 monasteries with attached institutions that specialized in patient care. A large amount of historical evidence shows that, with the development of the New World, the idea of hospitals was brought in by Christians who helped build hospitals through donations in America, from north to south.

Even Chinese hospitals in the modern sense were founded by Christians as they evangelized. Examples include: the Canton Hospital founded in Guangzhou in 1843 by the American Board of Commissioners for Foreign Missions, St. Luke's Hospital founded in Shanghai by the American Episcopal Church in 1866, Tongren Hospital in Beijing founded by the Methodist Episcopal Church from 1886–1899, the Baptist Hospital in Yangzhou founded by the Southern Baptist Convention in 1890, Renji Hospital founded in Shanghai by English Christians in 1844, the Gulou Hospital founded in Nanjing by the Canadian Christian Macklin in 1892, the Franciscan Sacred Heart Hospital founded in Tianjin by Italian Christians in 1922, and the Xiehe Hospital founded in Beijing by Christians of the Rockefeller Foundation in 1921.

In 1859, the Swiss Christian Henry Dunant and four of his friends, after a long period of research on charity, joined with 24 representatives of 16 countries to establish the International Committee of the Red Cross to provide humanitarian aid. Dunant's determined efforts at humanitarian relief left him bankrupt and living on the streets. During the American Civil War, the great female Christian Clara Barton, who was known as "Angel of the Battlefield," founded the American Red Cross.

One could certainly argue that before hospitals took their current commercial form, the *human calling* of the Christian faith as it developed over the course of history illuminated the path for medical treatment, voluntary care, and hospice care. Christian charity inspired the operating and management processes of the hospital as a charitable organization while also building public spaces for humanitarian relief outside the public affairs of government. All of this ultimately came from the love of God for which Christ sacrificed himself. As Saint Augustine of Hippo said, "Without love, there is no righteousness."

Lastly, *human calling* caused early Christian believers to create charitable educational organizations for the growth of human reason and the popularization of knowledge,[193] setting a precedent for expanding individual human intelligence and creativity.

Education began with the catechism in Christian churches in the second century. The great Justin Martyr, before he was killed by Emperor Aurelius in 165 AD in Rome, built catechistic schools around 150 AD in Rome and Ephesus, which became the seeds of formal western education. After the practice and efforts of Clement, Origen, Athanasius, and others, these schools generally allowed boys and girls to be taught together and gradually added courses of rhetoric, logic, mathematics, and so on, apart from the catechism. From the fourth century to the tenth century, church schools were very common. In addition to Christian doctrine, the Seven Liberal Arts were taught. The rhetoric and language taught were that of the Latin or Greek of the era and region. So widespread were such ecclesiastical schools that in the iconic city of the Renaissance, Florence, in the early 14th century, a total of 8,000 to 10,000 boys and girls were reported to be enrolled in liberal arts schools. In that sense, the first large-scale educational school in the history of human civilization was not a public organization supported by a government's public taxes, but rather a charitable organization supported by sacred donations from Christian believers. This was completely different from the privately-owned, commercial, fee-based educational organizations of other countries in the same period.

Much later, Christians developed the area of special education. Devout Christian Charles-Michel de l'Epée developed sign language for the deaf community in Paris in 1775. Laurent Clerc introduced it in the United States, and in 1817 he co-founded the first school to teach sign language in Connecticut. Later, the famous Gallaudet University in Washington, DC, was founded and spread the gospel of Christ throughout the deaf world. In 630, Christians in Jerusalem opened the first asylum for the blind. In 1834 after going through all kinds of hardships, the blind French Christian Louis Braille created the Braille letter system of six embossed dots to bring the gospel to schools for the blind, and human history thereafter featured schools for the blind.

The organizational origins of modern universities that undertake scientific research and higher education date back to Saint Benedict in the early sixth century, who established a sophisticated library collection and management system in the Benedictine monasteries. This system flourished in Europe along with the monasteries. For centuries, the academic preferences and abilities of truth-seekers, as well as the atmosphere of inquiry among the whole academic community, had been well-nurtured and cultivated. As a result, many academic professions, experts, and professors emerged with profound academic insights. At the beginning of the twelfth century, the University of Bologna in Italy, recognized as the first university in history, was formed on the basis of library accumulation, academic research and discussion, and the professorial system in church schools. In the year 1200, the University of Paris formed and gradually grew on the foundation of previous academic innovations. These were the two earliest universities in human history. Additionally, the University of Bologna became the mother of early church universities in Italy, Spain, Scotland, Sweden, and Poland, while the University of Paris did the same for early church universities in Oxford, Cambridge, Portugal, and Germany. The University of Cambridge birthed Harvard University. The majority of well-known universities in the United States, such as those in the Ivy League, were all built with Christian donations. Even the top ten universities in China were no exception.

In this sense, many specialized education organizations and universities of higher education were initially funded by sacred donations of Christians rather than governmental organizations funded by public taxation. The university system of recommendation for deans and professors was created and governed by public welfare organizations like autonomous associations of professors, students, and scientific societies. This happened by means of equitable nomination, instead of the top-down approach of government bureaucracy. A full picture of the philanthropic origins of the educational institutions of universities comes into view. This also explains why schools, even public schools, in developed countries today all adopt the management mechanism of non-profit organizations and this social recommendation system of leaders.[194]

Many historians focus on negative stories of Christian churches during the long course of medieval history, such as corruption, decadence, luxury, hypocrisy, and even promiscuity of some churches or faculty members. But if we look at the greater history of humanity, we can't deny that Christian churches, over the course of their historical development, have stuck to and strengthened their confidence in God's new rescue plan for humanity. They've offered and sacrificed themselves to follow Christ and respond to God's sacred expectation of love and forgiveness as true *human calling*, meeting the needs of vulnerable individuals in a charitable way. Christian believers and churches in general have always focused on charity and care with the equal rights of individuals at the core. In response to God's sacred expectation, they created a new model of public interest relations in human history—the charitable public welfare organization.

In terms of public interest relations, the new charitable public welfare model differs in many ways from the traditional state model. The implicit contract of taxes in exchange for protection discussed earlier can easily hide inequitable negotiations and trades. The public power of the "state machine" can easily lead to authoritarian violence used against the community by a minority of controlling individuals. Anthropological history bears this dynamic out countless times in natural and monarchal states. The charitable public welfare model, however, is based on a sacred faith in God and Christ and a willingness to help others, and on the sacrifice of individuals that ask for nothing in return. By entrusting such offering and sacrifice to those charitable organizations with contract revoking authority and are under strict supervision of the principals, the public's charitable interest is enacted on behalf of the vulnerable without distortion. Such transfer of public interest brings about a new sacred relationship between donors and beneficiaries who are able to share a sense of compassion and move closer to Christ together. It can't be denied that these gospel values are unprecedented in the history of human public interest relations.

CHAPTER 9:

Divergent roads: mysterious Eastern kingdoms

I n order to better understand the two different directions the East and the West took during humanity's first great philosophical awakening, we again focus our historical lens on the East, or more specifically, India. This South Asian country saw a mysterious flourishing of its civilization during the philosophical awakening of the Axial Age.

The northern part of the Indian subcontinent is delineated by the towering Himalayan Mountains, where more than 40 peaks over 7,000 meters are covered in snow year-round. Its center is divided by the 1,100-kilometre-long Vindhya Range that runs from east to west. The southern part of the subcontinent is covered by the Deccan Plateau, which stretches 1,500 kilometers from southwest to northeast. The Indian subcontinent also has a coastline of over 7,000 kilometers on three sides, but due to its other geographical features, the majority of Indian people at that time neither knew it existed or accessed it. Meanwhile, the three major rivers that flowed from the northern Himalayas, namely the Indus River in the west, the Ganges River in the east, and the Brahmaputra river in the center, formed the mysterious cradle of ancient Indian civilization. This was before great age of sea-faring discovery. From here, the land to the farthest east of the ocean were the islands of Indonesia, while to the farthest west of the ocean was Africa. As a result, India's contact with the outside world occurred mainly over the Persian Corridor in the northwest, over land, which connected it to Mediterranean and Eurasian countries. Today's Pakistan and Afghanistan were areas to the north of ancient India.

Its geography meant that India was fated to be a highly mysterious land divided into many tribes and difficult to unify. In its long history before the British Empire claimed it, no monarch ruled all of what we now call India—with the Maurya Dynasty and its famed leader, Ashoka, a notable 150-year exception. The Indian subcontinent has always featured a political ecology in which tribes and kingdoms peacefully coexist on the same land. But what truly amazes is the deep unity that Indian spirituality seems to possess, combining Hinduism's Vedanta philosophy, the rituals of life described in the *Grihya-sutra*, and Buddha's humanistic and compassionate ideals. These became vital sources for Eastern civilization's answers on the value of human life and how we ought to behave.

SECTION 1: THE ARYAN MIGRATION AND THE FORMATION OF THE CASTE SYSTEM

Existing archaeological data confirms that Indian civilization has a long history. Genetically speaking, all humans on earth share a common ancestor in the East African *Homo sapiens* who lived 80,000 years ago. As for India, archeological records of human civilizations in the past 10,000 years are found there, including stone, pottery, bronze and iron tools. One significant event during that period was the migration or invasion of the Aryans, who lived in the area north of the Mesopotamian Plain and south of the Caucasus Mountains, between 3,500 and 4,000 years ago. The Aryans' migration as an alien civilization precipitated a collision with the indigenous civilization of northern India, marked by great physical violence and, in most cases, conquest and assimilation. Records of written Indian Sanskrit, a significant marker of human civilization, appeared in this period, though many of the Vedic histories recorded in Sanskrit were already popular among the native Indians long before the Aryans moved into Punjab.

The Aryans brought a nomadic herding culture with them as they came through the northern Punjab and eventually into the Ganges River basin. During this process they gradually abandoned their nomadic lifestyle in favor of settled agriculture, creating a new civilization that incorporated indigenous Indians. Judging from the descriptions in the *Rigveda*, the "Battle of Ten Kings" that led to the establishment of the earliest monarchy on the Ganges Plain was not a war waged by the Aryans against the indigenous inhabitants. Rather, it was a battle between Sudas, king of the indigenous tribe Bharatas, and an alliance of ten tribal kingdoms on the Aryan settlements. With the support of the Aryans, Sudas won the battle and became the first king of the Ganges Plain to claim divine legitimacy. As the victorious king, the *Rigveda* gave him this legitimacy, and the defeated rulers acknowledged his supreme power as monarch and voluntarily paid tribute to him. The legitimacy of the battle was confirmed by the record and eulogy of the *Rigveda*, which became the earliest natural law of war in the East.[195]

After the Battle of the Ten Kings, the Aryans gradually learned how to survive on the great continent. Since they didn't have a numerical advantage, they tried to dominate the Indian subcontinent through culture. Inspired by their belief in the Supreme Personality of God, they shouldered the extraordinary responsibility of bringing blessings to Indian society by sharing their sacred knowledge of this God.

As part of this responsibility, the Aryans gradually developed a complete theory of caste. According to the *Rigveda,* people were divided into two castes, one that could "regenerate" through certain mysterious rituals and one that could not. These two groups were further divided into different ethnic castes based on divisions of labor and responsibilities within society. The castes that could regenerate were: the Brahmins, small in number but highest in social status, who were in charge of the spiritual life of society, communicating with the supreme God, and disseminating sacred knowledge; the Kshatriyas, a larger group made up of warriors and administrators who were dedicated to defending the country and society; and the Vaishyas, the most populous caste in Indian society that included workers and laborers engaged in business and agriculture to provide necessary food and materials for society. The fourth caste was the Shudras. As a small group, they were servants and slaves of society and of the physical body, with no right to regeneration.

The Indian caste system has been continually criticized as the darkest side of Indian culture, as it contradicted the notion that all people have equal rights. It solidified class differences, preventing movement between different groups in society, which was not conducive to the spread of new ideas or social progress. It's often assumed that the ruling class with political power created the caste system out of a need to consolidate its dominance. But if we look at it through the lens of its historical context in ancient India more than 3,000 years ago, examining the social conditions and historical needs of the subcontinent during that era, we might gain a different viewpoint from that of most historians.

Ancient India covered an area of more than 4 million square kilometers, including the equivalent of today's Pakistan, Bangladesh, and at times a significant portion of Afghanistan. Due to the natural barriers formed by the towering Himalayan peaks in the north and the vast Indian ocean in the south, the probability of violent invasion by external forces was small. Its unique geography also created a warm, rainy, and humid climate, which, coupled with the alluvial plains of the three major rivers, made it relatively easy to obtain food, live a simple and leisurely life, and maintain peaceful and friendly inter-personal relations in an agricultural civilization. Furthermore, the high alti-tudes of the Vindhya Range in the center and the Deccan Plateau in the south created a landscape of fertile plains dotted with rolling hills and vast forests, which, contrasted with the mysterious, lofty, and snowy peaks of the Himala-yas, greatly inspired Indian poetry and philosophical thought.

Such a vast, fertile, diverse, mysterious, and poetic land, with natural abundance and barriers, was a favorable environment for different tribes to live in alliance with one another and get along well together. If it weren't for the invasions of the Aryans, Alexander the Great of Greece, and later Islamic forces, India may, like the African continent, have maintained that same pat-tern of allied tribes.

Still, the Aryans arrived in the land 1,500–1,700 years before Alexander, and both brought with them written language and new ideas. It was those very Aryans, that used their written script to record historical legends of the land, that gave us the Indian epics such as the *Mahabharata* and the *Ramayana*, which are eight times longer than the epics of Homer. They also left us the *Rigveda*, *Yajurveda*, and many other classics of Vedic philosophy, as well as the great philosophical classic, the *Bhagavad Gita*, written more than 2,500 years ago.[196]

None of these works of human wisdom had a specific author like the ancient Greek or ancient Chinese classics. Rather, they were the works of a special class of communicators with divine forces behind them on behalf of society. This class of thinkers and priests of the Brahmin caste were active on the vast subcontinent between 3,800–2,500 years ago. They certainly didn't hold political power, nor were they the wealthy class of the society. Rather, they had extraordinary knowledge, love of thought, and high moral standards for themselves. Hailing from a long lineage of noble Aryan Brahmins families, they never ceased to pursue the ideal methodologies of questioning and answering. They spent much of their lives learning from Brahmin teachers and practicing asceticism in the forest alone. With their rarified thoughts and refined manners, they performed rituals and ceremonies for society and answered questions about life, death, and society. They became indispensable to both regular people and the elite, even to kings.

For Brahmin thinkers, the caste system was thought to be the ideal structure for the division of labor in society and its proper functioning over the long course of history. The number of natural and theocratic states on the Indian subcontinent, even during the height of unification during the Maurya Dynasty, was never fewer than 20. At other times, the subcontinent saw the coexistence of dozens and even hundreds of tribal states connected by alliance. The frictions and wars that did occur among these tribal and theocratic kingdoms were far less serious than those in Europe, Central Asia, East Asia, and North Africa. Peaceful coexistence was the main theme of ancient Indian society.[197] Significantly, the caste system founded by the Brahmins, accompanied by a complete set of ritual ceremonies and a cohesive theological and philosophical system, was widely accepted by the people of each tribal state and became the spiritual paradigm that solidified the tribal alliances in ancient India.

SECTION 2: SEEKING THE MEANING OF LIFE IN THE MYSTERIOUS JUNGLES OF VEDANTA

The *Manusmriti* has an incredibly important place in both Indian and human history, as it is not only the legal code of Indian society from 1200 BC to 500 BC, but also humanity's first written "code of natural law." In the *Manusmriti*, the four *ashramas* (or phases of life) and four *varnas* (or castes) expounds the *dharma*, or higher doctrine, that defines people as individuals and their relationships with one another.[198]

As a starting point, human life has a chronological axis. Its greater history is that of the inner self in which the Brahman dwells, which can be divided into the past life, the present life, and the next life. Such reincarnation of a life happens through "karma." The lesser history is that lived in the realm of the spiritual "inner self" and the physical "private self." In order to follow the *dharma*, the spirit of life in India, one must live according to the four *ashramas*, or phases of life in this world. These four phases are: *Brahmacharya*, the phase of learning the Vedic classics from the Brahman guru, a period that varies depending on caste; *Grihastha*, the phase in which to marry, raise children, and fulfill the responsibilities of the secular world; *Vanaprastha*, the phase of handing over family responsibilities to the next generation after raising them to adulthood, and returning to the forest to contemplate the inner self through asceticism, yoga, and other methods to get closer to Brahma; and finally, *Sannyasa*, the phase of becoming a monk in old age and traveling in search of peace, simplicity, and the spiritual life, finally disappearing into the jungle.

The *Manusmriti* also further developed the four castes, or *varnas*.[199] Without exception, every person is born into one of these castes, in accordance with the *dharma*. However, the caste system at the time was not a discriminatory ethical code defined by the color of one's skin, as it is perceived today. It was a covenant that determined the division of labor, delineating the responsibilities and duties of different members of society. Everyone was born to play a role in the social order as defined by the *Manusmriti*.

The *Manusmriti* does stipulate the Brahmins' superior position in society, specifying that members of this caste be educated for a period of up to 36 years, with nine years as the minimum amount of time it would take to become a Brahmin. A Brahmin's social duty was to communicate with Brahma, the creator-God, and spread sacred knowledge. Their main occupations were philosophers, priests, and teachers. Brahmins pursued a spiritual life, and their material needs were met not through taxes but through donations or their own efforts. The *Manusmriti* holds Brahmins to a high ethical standard, and they are required to have good manners, a noble temperament, profound and extensive knowledge, and devotion to the spiritual life and renunciation of material things, in order to maintain their status of respect in society.

The Kshatriyas were educated for fewer years than the Brahmins, but they were still required to study for a minimum of six years. They were expected to be strong and courageous, always ready to fight and sacrifice for the country and the safety of society. Their income came from taxes paid by the Vaishyas, but taxes usually didn't exceed ten percent of the income of the Vaishyas during peacetime, and during times of war it was not to exceed one-third. The Kshatriyas were to be faithful to their duties, ensuring the safe and orderly management of the country.

The Vaishyas formed the largest group in society and consisted of merchants and farmers. Their duty was to provide food and other material supplies needed for Indian society, and they were obligated to pay taxes. They received fewer years of education than the Kshatriyas but still needed basic education. They were required to work hard, be diligent and responsible, and create material wealth to meet society's needs.

The Shudras, on the other hand, were slaves required to do menial labor. They didn't receive any education and weren't required to fulfill any societal duty besides what their masters told them to do. As a minority group, they were the lowest elements in society. Considered obdurate and lazy, their souls had no right to regenerate.

Each caste was expected to comply with the *Manusmriti*, fulfill its social responsibilities, and avoid committing crimes. If they did commit crimes, Shudras were to face the lightest punishment, while other castes were punished twice as severely as their next lower caste for the same crime. That meant that Brahmins faced the severest punishment, four times more than the Kshatriyas caste. This is because the Brahmins were expected to be the most aware of their social responsibilities and the *Manusmriti,* and they had the deepest understanding of the impact virtuous and sinful behavior had on society. The principle was that greater knowledge of the crime should result in harsher penalties. A king who wrongfully accused and killed innocent people was also subject to a very heavy sentence, and even to execution. Kings were not allowed to be autocrats. Instead, they were required to have a committee of 10–21 noble, virtuous Brahmins to help them make judgments and decisions, to ensure their decisions were rational and righteous.[200]

Why did people need to develop the four *ashramas* and the four *varnas* as a basis of division of labor? Because humans are limited by our "private self" while in the phenomenal world. We're unable to see the flow of time in the larger cycle that passes through past, present, and future lives, let alone the unchanging infinite and absolute beyond it. And that absolute, unchanging infinity is Brahman.

Brahman has three forms, or *Trimurti,* namely Brahma, the creator of everything in the world including humans, Vishnu, the preserver of all things, and Shiva, the destroyer of all things, whose destruction gives rise to the reincarnation of all things. Regardless of how all things in the universe, including humans, go through the cycle of reincarnation, Brahman is unchanging. It is absolute and eternal, forever peaceful, tranquil, and silent. It resides inside the private self in the flow of time, but it is the original inner self, that is, the immortal soul.

The combination and separation of soul and body is a difficult process, which relies mainly on the *karma,* or consequences of an individual's behavior, to achieve reincarnation or transformation. Such transformation could bring happiness or hardship. According to the *dharma,* each individual is responsible for the consequences of reincarnation in the living soul, or inner self. If people desire to approach the absolute, infinite peace and tranquility of the Brahman, they must be released from the cycle of reincarnation. Only

Brahmins, who renounce the material temptations of the world and possess sacred knowledge, can fully understand this, transcending the private self of the material world and approaching the Brahman, and so be able to share and impart this sacred knowledge. They alone can guide the practice of the four *ashramas* through rituals and education, living by their own noble virtues as an example to help people of other castes find the absolute inner self within the private self. In this way, other castes could either reincarnate or get release from the cycle of reincarnation altogether and approach the absolute, everlasting Brahman.[201] This was the philosophy behind the four castes and the system for division of labor.

The noble Brahmins created this unique approach to *human calling* 3,000-2,800 years ago, demonstrating deep philosophical thinking and imagination. Their teachings are scattered in over 200 philosophical *Upanishads,* largely written anonymously, but containing profound insights into the tolerance that characterized ancient India's mysterious order.[202]

The *Bhagavad Gita*[203], written more than 2,500 years ago, takes the form of a dialogue common in philosophical works of the first Axial Age. The first speaker in the dialogue is the Kshatriya General Arjuna, who is leading a great army of soldiers and cavalry in preparation for battle. The other speaker is Krishna, the Supreme Personality of the Godhead, who has turned himself into Arjuna's charioteer in order to dispel doubt from the general's soul. As they move toward the battlefield, General Arjuna presents a series of sophisticated questions about spirituality to Krishna. Both the questions and answers are shocking.

For example, Arjuna asks: "Should I fight when fighting entails killing, and killing so many lives makes me sad?" "It grieves me to kill those men, whose wives and children must be devastated. Why must we win, and can violence not be avoided in winning?" "If the violence in this battle is not a crime, then why is other violent killing a crime?" "What drives people to commit crimes rather than do good deeds?" "What transcends doing good deeds?" "What are Brahman and the inner self?" "How can eternal truth be approached? Is Yoga a method to approach eternal truth?" And so on.

Facing this series of questions, Krishna patiently gives General Arjuna deeply profound answers. Krishna says: The human soul is not the same as the body. The soul is unchangeable. When the body dies, the soul follows the karma of the deceased's previous life and transforms into another life form. Killing the body does not impair and certainly does not destroy the soul. War does not destroy anything, he tells Arjuna, so you don't have to be sentimental. Violent war is necessary to maintain the principles of religion Krishna established, such as justice. If you don't fight, the invaders will violently kill your wife and children, and the principle of religious justice will be lost. And religious principles are superior to political and social principles. It is your sacred duty as a Kshatriya to follow the religious principle of defending your society. As this duty is also formulated by Krishna, if you don't carry out your duty, it implies you are motivated by your private self that is afraid to die, which makes you a criminal. Yet even if you die on the battlefield after fulfilling your duties, as long as you are not motivated by your private self, you have committed no crime. That is the difference between the two kinds of violence. What motivates people to evil are the material desires of the private self, while goodness is focusing only on fulfilling sacred duties without obsessing over the outcome of actions. What transcends doing good deeds is recognizing the soul or the inner self, because that is the universal principle that Krishna has placed in the life of all individuals, that is, Brahman.

He continues: Dear Arjuna, everything is this world was created by me, Krishna. I existed before this world. Therefore, I am the Personality of Godhead above Brahman, and I am the absolute and eternal truth. Approaching the eternal truth is more important than doing good deeds. People can approach me in two ways. One is Samkhya Yoga, that is, reaching me by transcending the motivation of the private self through the path of philosophical thinking; the other is through Active Yoga, that is, reaching me by transcending the motivation of the worship of the private self through Bhakti activities. Dear Arjuna, hurry and let go of the obsession you hold onto; instead, go into battle and fulfill the sacred duty as a Kshatriya.

When he heard this, all of Arjuna's doubts were dispelled. Having gained divine power through the light of Krishna's wisdom, he immediately led the army to the battlefield, winning a great victory and fulfilling his glorious duty as a Kshatriya warrior.

In the *Bhagavad Gita*, the *Upanishads* reach the greatest heights of theology and philosophy. In the context of the violent conflict of war, reveals the universality and immortality of the soul that transcends individual lives. It advances humanity's understanding of the dilemma of life and death, fulfilling our duties, and the greater *human calling*. It also glorifies the pre-existence and absoluteness of Krishna, while affirming the Hindu pantheon, specifically praising Krishna as the Supreme Personality of the Godhead. This is a big step forward from the understanding of Brahman, and just a small step away from a monotheistic God. The *Bhagavad Gita* is certainly a pinnacle in humanity's first philosophical awakening. The diverse and philosophical *Upanishads* mention a wide range of gods, numerous concepts, and profound philosophies.[204] Generally they urge people to penetrate the fog of the phenomenal world, and through practice gain insight into the true, immortal inner self, soul, and Brahman. They advocate overcoming the fear of the death of the physical body and the material world, instead measuring the value of this life by one's degree of enlightenment and the liberation of the soul. Of course, the various Vedanta philosophies and religions of India are so complex that a small step into this field is enough to plunge the student into a sprawling jungle that few can penetrate, much less share its mysteries with outsiders. But in general, the faith of India, based on the Trimurti of Brahman and the caste system, played a vital role in bringing unity to public, spiritual, and cultural life in its vast and diverse ethnic and political ecology. It also maintained and enhanced the understanding and tolerance between tribes and greatly reduced violence between them, preserving peace until the invasion of Alexander the Great, and establishing an extraordinary foundation of belief in the search for the meaning of life.

This near-magical and peaceful land was a fitting setting for the appearance of Buddha, just as the blood and iron of the Roman Empire was an appropriate setting for the appearance of Jesus.[205] The difference is that Jesus had to deal with the unresolvable disputes between humans about contested land, particularly the endless violence, coercion, and bloodshed that resulted from the political machine of the Roman Empire. Buddha had to deal with suffering and the tragic cycle of life, old age, sickness, and death in a relatively peaceful environment, which human beings couldn't resolve individually in their own time and history.

SECTION 3: THE BUDDHA: COMPASSION FOR ALL LIVING THINGS IN A SEA OF SUFFERING

Vedanta philosophy was plagued by the inherent contradictions of the caste system arising from the absolute Brahman, a hierarchy based on inequality from birth. It attempted to correct this inequality by imposing special obligations and punishments for crimes committed by the higher castes. While this was a fine ideal, it was very difficult to put into practice. In actual practice, the high moral demands made on the higher castes were not as reasonable as the *Manusmriti* and other Vedic classics made them seem. The complexity of real life severely eroded the caste system's original ideal, and the division of labor and more stringent sacred obligations that high castes Brahmins and Kshatriyas were bound by. As a result, the caste system became more and more determined by lineage, increasingly discriminatory and unfair, which resulted in greater resistance among the lower castes. This tension accumulated and finally gave rise to a reformation in Indian Vedic religion with the appearance of Buddha. The Jainism of Mahavira was also a response to this tension and occurred around the same time.

In the 6th century BC, Buddha, or Siddhartha Gautama, was born in the home of Śuddhodana, King of Kapilavastu, one of the dozen Indian tribal kingdoms at the time, located in modern-day Lumbini, near India's border with Nepal. Siddhartha, born a noble Brahmin, was not interested in the easy, luxurious palace life his father prepared for him, nor was he interested in inheriting the throne. Instead, he was drawn to the ascetic life of the wise Brahmins who had renounced the secular world and lived in the jungle, contemplating and searching for the value and meaning of life. Siddhartha was filled with deep compassion for all life forms, grieved by the hardships of human life, and deeply disturbed by and fearful of death as a phenomenon of life.[206]

The king had provided a life of perfection for Prince Siddhartha, giving him a beautiful bride who bore him children and keeping him ignorant of the pain and suffering of reality. But Siddhartha still witnessed the difficult stages of birth, aging, sickness, and death during the few experiences he had outside the palace. These experiences made a deep impression on his sensitive heart, and the pain of this cycle of life left him restless, worried, and confused. After struggling with these thoughts and consulting his father, Siddhartha broke ties with his family at the age of 29, escaped from the palace and the mundane reality of daily life, and headed to the jungle. There he began his journey of contemplation, which ultimately led to him becoming a Buddha.

Siddhartha visited many well-known Brahmin teachers, and found nourishment in the *Vedas*, the *Upanishads*, the *Manusmriti*, and other Indian Vedanta texts, but he didn't find the answers he was looking for. He then turned to the Brahmins' difficult practice of approaching the inner self through physical mutilation of the body to bring the soul closer to Brahman and achieve liberation from its attachment to the material world. Siddhartha punished his body to subdue his desires and nearly lost his life, but he still didn't find the answers he was looking for. Finally, he gave up this austere ascetic practice, treated his body with more kindness, and simply meditated like a Yoga master under a Bodhi tree. Seven years after leaving his home and family, Siddhartha attained complete enlightenment and became the Buddha.[207] He embarked on a mission to spread his ideas, preaching for 45 years, until the age of 80, when he liberated himself from the "eternal suffering" of mortal life and attained Nirvana under his tree by the river outside Vaishali.

In understanding Buddha's ideas, we must detach ourselves from the now overgrown Buddhist doctrines and theology and return with a respectful heart to his original way—the true Buddhism. The contours and threads of Buddha's origins in Indian Vedanta philosophy will become more clearly visible, as well as the innovations he introduced, avoiding the trap of confusing the way itself from matters of practice, a trap that plagues the various factions and schools in Buddhism today.

The way to enlightenment that Buddha discovered under the Bodhi tree can be most simply summarized as the "Four Noble Truths" and the "Eightfold Path." The so-called Four Noble Truths, as revealed by Buddha, are *Dukkha*, *Samudaya*, *Nirodha*, and *Magga*. These can be experienced—but not seen— by individuals within historical time as defined by Brahman, and they exist prior to and eternally outside of individual lives.

Buddha spoke of his Four Noble Truths in the context of Indian Vedanta philosophy and the Brahmin faith. Buddha himself was a noble Brahmin. He began his path along the Four Noble Truths through belief in Brahman as the highest existence and Trimurti as its three forms. In other words, Buddha acknowledged that he lived during the era of the Trimurti as defined by Brahman. The embodiment of this Trimurti in human life is that we are in an endless cycle of reincarnation that includes past lives, our present life, and the next life. As to the question of whether this reincarnation is under the jurisdiction of the three personal gods of Brahma representing creation, Vishnu representing guardianship, and Shiva representing destruction, Buddha refused to answer.[208]

Like Jesus, Buddha held one of the most pessimistic views of life among the great religious teachers in the history of humanity. According to Buddha, the life we experience in this world is tragic and defined by suffering.[209] Every stage of life is filled with this tragedy: the suffering of birth, ten months of pregnancy, and the blood and pain of labor; the suffering of aging, as the body withers and one faces the inability to carry out one's desires; the suffering of sickness and disease, struggling between life and death; the suffering of death, the soul's departure from the decaying body, and the deep sorrow of friends and relatives when someone dies. Apart from this, there is also the suffering of desiring something or someone without gaining it.

Life is also defined by impermanence. The rich may be robbed, the beautiful may be ruined, the gifted may be envied, death may result from political or military power, and mutual slaughter and bullying may be prevalent among people. Individual lives are always thrown into phases of misery. The final suffering is the transient and finite nature of life, with a person going through all the necessary struggles to earn wealth, build a business, make a name, and gain power, only to die before they can enjoy the outcome and leave their children with the same endless sufferings. For Buddha, viewing life in this way allows humanity to abandon the superficial, false riches of the material world and face the essence of life's suffering, the essence of death, and the reality that the future holds only more of the same in an endless cycle. Such a view is truly enlightened and profound.

Thirdly, Buddha took the "Law of Karma" or "Law of Cause and Effect" in Indian Vedanta philosophy to the extreme. He was the thinker who most insisted on the causal link between human behavior and its results in human history.[210] In Buddha's view, all the sufferings of human life come from *Samu-*

daya, or the accumulation of good or evil in human behavior. This accumulation isn't limited to the present life but also includes the karma of past and future lives. The law of karma never fails. Therefore, the tragedy of a person's present life is the result of their accumulation of good or evil karma from behaviors over all previous reincarnations. If you are your own cause, and you are your own outcome, there's no need to search for external reasons for your suffering. It is only because of humans' short-sightedness, focusing only on the current world without seeing the boundless and enduring influence of karma, that they fail to understand. Buddha saw people, then, as fundamentally lost, much like Jesus told people, "You are all like lost lambs."

By fully exploring the law of cause and effect, Buddha awakened humanity to the broad and long-lasting consequences of any behavior. This understanding of responsibility results in a sense of duty and righteousness, an embodiment of human's high rationality. His call to introspection sounded loudly in an era when the Brahmins were often looking to the Indian *Upanishads* for absolute truth like the ancient Greeks looked to philosophy, and the lower classes were beginning to worship the Godhead through transactional religion. His teaching that "everyone is the master of their own fate" was like a bell ringing out in the darkness, reverberating through the secular world under Brahma, and awakening the world to the reason for life and goodness. So many people, from the king to Brahmin ascetics, from rich merchants to ordinary people—even his father, former wife, and son—heard Buddha's clarion call and sought enlightenment.

Buddha's spiritual sight penetrated not only the material world but also the past life and the next life, and so the entire cycle of reincarnation. In doing so, he revealed a way to avoid suffering once and for all, which he called "Nirodha" (Nirvana). Nirodha means liberation from the law of karma, allowing life to reach a realm of silent Nirvana, like Brahman, known as the realm of "bliss." Nirvana was thus a concept introduced by the Buddha.[211]

Obviously, Buddha's understanding of reincarnation and liberation were inherited from Indian Vedanta philosophy. Liberation in Vedanta philosophy was a kind of escape or deviation from the law of karma. Yet the question became, if the soul, or inner self, still exists by the time it escapes but isn't part of Brahman, then where does it go? This was a problem that Vedanta philosophy didn't resolve.

Nirvana as revealed by Buddha was obviously not annihilation or "non-existence," nor was it the "existence" of Vedanta philosophy—more or less a limbo when a soul has left one body but not entered the next one, wandering in the Bardo space described in Tibetan Tantra. Buddha's Nirvana was a kind of "existence" that doesn't depend on any time, space, or condition. It's the transcendental bliss of not returning to the causal cycle and not depending on anything in the material world. It's about having great compassion for suffering in the material world governed by the law of karma, and yet being enlightened enough to not participate in reincarnation.[212] This was the desired goal of the present life that Buddha was committed to pursuing and helping others achieve through practice.

Taking all that into account, what methods could be used to endure the complex, varied sufferings of the present life and even of the past and the next life? How could people free themselves from this cycle of suffering and attain the blissful state of Nirvana? Buddha's answer was to prescribe a methodology for his disciples as well as for humanity. This methodology is the famous "Eightfold Path."

The Eightfold Path is the basic principle of individual practice that Buddha recommended for the present life, but its underlying premise is the "Middle Way," which means abandoning any two extremes. One extreme would be severe penance or abuse of the body. Buddha emphasizes that the body should receive basic, fair treatment. This doesn't mean people should love the body and overlook the soul, but being fair to the body should be the basis of spiritual development. The other extreme would be to indulge in the pleasures of the body and vulgar materialism. This would result in losing the ability to think, completely undermining spiritual development.

Having understood the Middle Way as its basic principle, we can trace the Eightfold Path of spiritual practice according to Buddha's teachings. This Eightfold Path consists of eight practices. The first practice is called right view. It's about understanding Buddha's most fundamental insight that everything in the material world is impermanent, according to the Four Noble Truths. Impermanence comes from *pratitya*, or the law of cause and effect. Everything governed by this law exists or ceases to exist depending on other things, which gives rise to their impermanent nature and creates an endless cycle. If people can take an eternal view, turning away from impermanence and the law of cause and effect in the material world, then they can see that the whole material world is emptiness. This knowledge is right view, the most fundamental insight to keep in mind during spiritual practice.[213]

The second is right resolve. Right resolve means maintaining compassion for lives currently incarnated in the material world on the basis of right view. Compassion comes from sympathy toward impermanent lives still governed by the laws of cause and effect in the material world, and so having good thoughts and being willing to help others. But helping others should have boundaries, as one should become too involved that it generates new karma. To practice right view, one should always be on guard against the emergence of ātma-grāha, or the grasping self, which is greed, anger, and infatuation with the material, phenomenal world. If people don't get rid of their attachments, they won't be able to attain a compassionate and *bodhisattva* mind that can move forward in spiritual practice. [214]

The third is right speech. Based on right view and right resolve, right speech means communicating with an honest attitude and sincerity, expounding the truth with attention to logic, enlightening people, and promoting understanding of the material world and the eternal world of Brahman. Right speech requires peace of mind, rejection of extremes, maintaining a compassionate middle way, and avoiding misunderstanding and misdirection. It also means refraining from lies, swearing, and violent language, because this kind of speech represents the evils that arise from material desires.[215] Using false, obscene or violent speech to attain the path would be like barking up the wrong tree, or expecting good fruit from a bad tree. In its emphasis right speech, Buddhism's tendency to rest on words rather than action becomes clear, and reveals a fundamental difference from Christianity's call to act lovingly toward others. This difference has deep implications for how these two faiths organize charity and social justice movements.

The fourth is right action. Right action is based on right view, right resolve, and right speech—proper conduct that improves one's karma. The purpose of spiritual practice is to release the soul from the karmic cycle and enter Nirvana, but this is an ambitious goal. In the meantime, people live every moment of their earthly life under the laws of causality. A person's speech and especially their actions continue to bring about consequences in this life and future lives. If someone doesn't sow the proper karma, they can't expect to reap good results. That's why right action is needed. But what is right action? Right action transcends consequences for an individual's life and is performed through behaving thoughtfully towards others, society, and all living things. If humans can think beyond their individual selves, then they can also be freed from the law of cause and effect. With the consistent practice of right action, the power of good karma manifests, establishing the path to liberation and Nirvana and naturally setting a person on this path.[216] During Buddha's time, people found it difficult to differentiate between right speech and right action, and this became a flashpoint for disputes between factions of Buddhism.

The fifth is right livelihood. If one's spiritual practice leads them as far as right karma in action, it's necessary to go further to attain the proper attitude toward life and behavior. Buddha's Four Noble Truths are based on the premise that human souls may be reincarnated into any sentient life form in the material world based on their karma, not just other humans. This informs Buddhists principles for life and behavior. The most central discipline is not to harm the lives of others, and people must persevere in it even if they are treated unfairly by others. The second core behavioral discipline is to refrain from killing or eating sentient creatures, which people must do even if threatened. Such right livelihood is very difficult to maintain, but failing to maintain it means immediately falling back into the karmic cycle and losing all cultivation of spiritual practice. [217] Right livelihood has since also become a flashpoint of factional disputes and divisions.

The sixth is right effort. If all the previous practices are maintained, the soul will gradually break away from individual karmic cycles and transform into the great soul of all sentient beings. It will accumulate karma that doesn't just arise from selfish individual actions. This is right effort. Since right effort is gathered as a whole,[218] it won't fluctuate randomly—up and down, hot and cold, back and forth.

The seventh is right mindfulness. When a person attains right mindfulness, their soul has essentially entered a state in which right view, right resolve, and right action are coordinated. No matter how complicated the situation is in the world, the soul can steer steadily. Faced with the rise and fall of thoughts, the mind and the body move in accord,[219] not subject to temptations or the karmic cycle.

The eighth is right concentration. Right concentration is the ultimate result of lifelong spiritual practice. Buddha understood the suffering of life, transcended it and, before approaching the end of his life, escaped the karmic cycle of death and life. Buddha freed himself from this supremely powerful karmic law and attained a quiet and peaceful soul. Although he was filled with sympathy and compassion for incarnated beings, Buddha decided not to return to participate in the cycle of reincarnation. Buddha prepared for the end of his life compassionately and peacefully, his soul attaining the transcendental bliss of not having to depend on any time, space or condition for its existence. This is right concentration: being ready to peacefully enter the realm of Nirvana at any time.

Buddha, through his personal experience and 45 years of preaching, reached Nirvana and immortality. He also founded the Buddhist order, passing down many detailed rules for the monastic life, and laying a solid foundation for Buddhism to become a major world religion. Buddha also made the difficult decision to accept women into the Buddhist order, after persistent pleading from Ananda and other disciples. Later historical evidence would show that this decision greatly eased Buddhism's absorption into Hinduism.

Buddha was a wise seeker of truth. He was extremely gentle and extraordinarily broad-minded. He thought carefully and stuck to his middle way. This is one reason he never touched the basic faith framework of Indian Vedanta philosophy. He always kept his iconic smile and silence when asked about Indian Vedanta's Brahman Trimurti.[220] He knew that if he acknowledged the Hindu godhead of the Trimurti, he would promote belief in them that would lead people to fall into the sacrificial methods of worship that were spreading at the time. He was against its transactional religion in which people gave sacrifices in exchange for rewards, and he also opposed all religions that sacrificed sentient beings. He believed it was a kind of superstition. But if he denied the fundamental Brahman of the Trimurti, Buddha feared that he would deny the universal, absolute, and eternal soul beyond the phenomenal world and thereby fall into nihilism. That's why he maintained his famous silence about Indian Vedanta philosophy.

When asked whether the inner self of every living body existed, as claimed by Vedanta philosophy, Buddha again responded with his usual smile and silence.[221] That's is because if he recognized the individual inner self as universal and the basis of change, it would mean agreeing to worship the inner self as the eternal soul. But if he denied the individual inner self, it would mean admitting to materialism and that there was nothing after death. These are two pitfalls that Buddha worked hard to avoid.

Buddha also faced a dilemma regarding the individuality of the soul. If the eternal soul is individual, that's good news for the one-to-one correspondence between one's behavior and justice in the law of karma. Buddha's profound and certain law of karma warned that mankind as a living being need not go outside themselves to seek refuge in other gods and prompted them to turn inward to perform good actions consciously. This is precisely in accordance with Vedanta. Vedanta considers such solid philosophical beliefs as fulfilling *human calling*. But it's bad news for his concept of Nirvana, because if the individual soul still exists under the law of karma and receives its just retribution, where else can it go after rising to become a noble Brahmin? How far was Buddha's ideal of reaching the level of the noble Brahmins—not based on birth but on practice—from the "existence" in Nirvana that is free from painful reincarnation? What more can a noble Brahmin aspire to? What would motivate him to seek liberation and eventually attain Nirvana? All that's left is the great goal of giving up the body to become one with the universal soul or "non-self," that is, to be rid of the desires of the individual soul. But if the goal is for all to become one with this "non-self," the individual soul disappears. And if the soul isn't actually individual, but becomes part of a universal soul that only matters as a whole, then does the law of karma lose its incentive for the individual soul in the present life? Will the law of karma, which is based on the goodness of humanity, be lost as a result? This philosophical dilemma in Buddha's thought led to his disciples splitting into the Mahayana and Theravada schools, which are now irreconcilable.[222]

From a philosophical perspective, it's clear that Buddha tried to break free from the theism of Indian Vedanta philosophy and religion, represented by the

Trimurti, and replace it with enlightenment about the law of karma. He also replaced the four *ashramas* with the monastic practice of enlightenment and preaching. Buddha also tried to turn the increasingly entrenched elite caste of the Brahmins into a status that could be reached through spiritual practice, thus leveling the playing field. He made a way for all people to aspire to be liberated from the tragic cycle of reincarnation and attain Nirvana, which is reminiscent of the primacy of human reason and heroism in ancient Greek philosophy. But Buddha couldn't discard the absolute, infinite, and eternal Brahman of Vedanta, otherwise there would be no place for his conception of Nirvana. This is another dilemma that Buddha faced.

From a larger comparative and metaphysical perspective, Buddha's silence wisely circumvented the dilemmas that his questioners at the time brought before him. It certainly reflected his awareness of both the internal consistency of his own philosophy and its unresolved problems, as well as his divine wisdom in the face of advanced questioning.[223] Buddha's doctrine is often interpreted by his later followers as a kind of science, while some followers still believe that Buddhism is the religion with the greatest affinity to science. This is a gross misunderstanding of the Buddha, science, and faith, and a dead end that pushes the Buddha and his philosophical insights to the edge of plausibility.

That's because of the true nature of technology, science, philosophy, and faith. Technology is based on empirical facts and requires study of the relative truths of functional solutions to problems of *human ability* in the lower-order material world. It depends on repeatable, accumulated technical experience. Science is a discipline that studies relative truths supported by higher-order experience, which can be demonstrated through mathematics and logic. The universal laws it reveals can be verified by repeated tests with relevant techno-logical applications. Philosophy is an unquantifiable hermeneutic that studies inductive, inferential, analytical thoughts supported by higher-order experience in the material world. It studies universal rules and human thoughts, which lie between absolute truth and relative truth and can only be verified by logic and other similar methods. Faith, meanwhile, transcends all the above academic approaches, because it studies absolute truth and ultimate truth. It does not discuss relative truth, but rather absolute truths that are infinite and eternal. For this reason, it cannot be confirmed or falsified, relying on both "passion based on faith" and "reason based on philosophy."

The truth uncovered by the great Buddha is the absolute truth about the eternity of life and satisfies all the elements of "faith's passion and philosophy's reason." Buddha affirmed the need for compassion and care for other people and other living things, as well as the eternity of the soul in the endless cycle of life, thereby helping people in the East overcome the fear of earthly death. He brought them belief in the universal, enduring, and effective connection between people's own karma and fate. He attempted to abandon the worship of the absolute Hindu Trimurti to focus instead on *human calling* both in psychological and behavioral terms, and so strove to incorporate *human calling* into the calculation of karma for the individual soul, encouraging wise, rational "altruism in self-interest."

He also encouraged those who had accumulated sufficient good karma to completely abandon the individual soul and to merge into the mass universal soul, realizing Nirvana and Buddhahood. These reflections still have a profound influence on the Eastern mindset and have long enchanted and captivated people. In this sense, the great Buddha is not a man but a god, or at least a god representing the eternal and absolute. If, however, scholars lower Buddhism to the level of science—to the level of the scientific method adopted by humans in studying the material world's causal relations between low-order phenomena—the "Buddha" they would develop could be trounced by a high school student in a laboratory. A person can't see the Buddha with insight into the eternal and absolute truth in another person's heart, just as they can't see the space-time continuum even if it surrounds them. That would be on a level of absurdity akin to God trying to converse with a cat.

Regarding the question of whether Buddha and his faith are absolutely and eternally universal and pre-existent, Buddha's silence is all we have. His silence demonstrates his inner humility and compassionate wish for all beings to break free from reincarnation and attain Buddhahood in Nirvana. The Buddha's compassionate hope for the world and his compassionate treatment of all living things are certainly compelling, and the reason why many people follow his teachings.

But when it comes to faith, humans still need a representative of absolute truth. We still need a holy example that represents eternity and infinity. We still need an absolutely good, omnipotent being to help us overcome human weakness—to help strengthen our faith when it's disturbed and threatened by the madness of the world and we strive to orient ourselves to the divine and eliminate the evils of human nature. We need a holy example that can create a sacred context for us to approach and hold on to the truth, goodness, and beauty in our hearts. It can enable us to handle our relationships with other people and other living things with a compassionate heart and righteous actions. That way we can look at events in our earthly lives with sympathy, attain liberation from the suffering of reincarnation of our past, present, and future lives, and finally live up to the *human calling* as defined by Buddha. Life in a society without the light of absolute truth is not worth living. Sadly, the great Buddha's absolute truth collapsed because of his compassionate and humble silence. This can be seen in the history of humanity after Buddha attained Nirvana.

SECTION 4: THE WANING OF BUDDHISM AND THE RESURGENCE OF VEDANTA

After Buddha attained Nirvana, his remains, which he saw as his earthly "skin," were cremated in accordance with Vedanta beliefs. His remains, known to his disciples as śarīra, or relics, were kept in towers in various tribal countries based on a peace treaty. The Four Noble Truths, the Eightfold Path, and other teachings Buddha unfolded during his lifetime were gradually recorded as texts. That was how the complicated *Sutras* came into being, based largely on the memory of the disciples who experienced them, complemented by the narrator or recorder's understanding, and recognized by the many assemblies of Buddhists.

Alexander the Great's violent occupation of the Indian subcontinent in 326 BC, its second encounter with an alien civilization, led to the emergence of the most brilliant empire in the history of Indian civilization, the Maurya Dynasty. Buddha's influence on the subcontinent reached its heyday during the reign of Emperor Ashoka of the Maurya Dynasty, when Buddhist temples that housed relics and other remains flourished. Once the Maurya Dynasty had receded into tribal alliances, the Gupta Empire tried to again unify the subcontinent under a single ruling body, but its size was dwarfed by that of the Maurya Dynasty. Its sphere of influence hardly reached the central Vindhya Range and the southern Deccan Plateau. The subsequent rise of the Arab kingdom and the occupation of areas northwest of the Punjab never affected the vast inland jungles and coastal hinterland of the Indian subcontinent, and the unified Indian empire of the Maurya Dynasty was never re-established.

It wasn't until the invasion of the British in the 18th century, bringing the trade rules and colonial codes of modern industrial and commercial civilization, that India became a single nation once again. It gained independence in the 20th century via non-violent, nationalist confrontation led by Mahatma Gandhi to become what is today's modern India. Of course, Muslim Pakistan in the northwest and Bangladesh in the east are also now independent. Over the more than 2,500 years of history from Buddha's attainment of Nirvana to today, the Indian subcontinent maintained peaceful coexistence between multiple tribal groups, with Vedanta and Buddhism as its religious and philosophical basis for approximately 2,000 years.

The faith founded by Buddha prevailed for about 1,000 years on the subcontinent.[224] It peaked during the reign of Emperor Ashoka and then gradually declined. As for external influence, starting from the 1st century AD, the Mahayana branch crossed the mysterious Himalayan mountains in the north and arrived in Tibet and the great inland areas of China. It took root and blossomed in that vast land and migrated to Korea and Japan via China. To this day it still has a deep influence in East Asia on people's values and attitudes toward life. Its Theravada branch, on the other hand, went through Sri Lanka and crossed the vast Indian Ocean before reaching areas like Malaysia, Indonesia, Thailand, Myanmar, Laos, and Vietnam on the eastern shores of the Indian Ocean. It still deeply affects these peoples' attitudes toward life and morality.[225]

As for its internal influence, Buddhism was gradually absorbed and integrated into Vedanta and eventually became part of the revolutionary Vedanta faith known today as Hinduism. Buddha was incorporated into Hinduism as an incarnation of Vishnu, the preserver in the Trimurti of Vedanta philosophical faith. By the 8th century AD, Buddhism had a large number of believers, and yet monasteries ceased to exist in India, lost in the tangled, intricate, deeply rooted branches of the Indian Vedanta.[226] This has deeply shocked and confused later philosophers, theologians, and anthropologists, even causing sadness and regret. Why did the Indian people drive Buddhism, this great spiritual treasure that purified humanity's soul and was created by their countryman Buddha, from the subcontinent?

The answer to this thousand-year-old mystery can only be found in Buddha's compassionate smile and his silence. His silence circumvented any claims to an absolute God that represented the infinite and the eternal, such as the impersonal god Brahman and its three incarnations (Brahma, Vishnu, and Shiva) in Vedanta, and or the personal God in the Christian faith and its Trinity (Father, Son, and Holy Spirit). Instead, he attempted to resolve the problem of life and morality through absolute reason, through teachings like the Four Noble Truths and the Eightfold Path. Buddha's soul certainly qualified as an absolute spirit, but his unnecessary humility, implied by his silence, prevented him from proclaiming himself as the only incarnation of Brahman. Nor did he name Brahman as the only way to redeem the world. If he had, then he could have completely overhauled the Vedanta belief system.

Doing so would have opened up many possibilities for his disciples to integrate and systematize Vedanta and Buddhism. They could have fundamentally absorbed Vedanta's concept of *human calling* in interpersonal relations, as implied in the four *ashramas* and four *varnas*, and replaced them with the new Buddhist faith. If Buddha hadn't humbly suggested that "everyone can become a buddha," or an absolute spirit, then he could have prevented his ambitious disciples from hoping to become one. His subsequent followers could have been freed to devote their energies to the interpretation and protection of Buddhism, the improvement of Buddhist theology, and the simplification of religious ceremonies in observance of the fundamentals. If they had, Buddhism could have completely replaced the creeds of Vedanta.

Buddha's humble silence and his hope that everyone could become a buddha also opened up a huge imaginative space for humanity's sins and left a permanent loophole for his followers. As a result, it was the powerful forces of Brahmin thought within Vedanta that actually incorporated Buddhism, rather than the Buddhism incorporating it. Adherents of Vedanta philosophy did everything possible to incorporate Buddha's Four Noble Truths into the system of Brahman's Trimurti. They absorbed and assimilated his thoughts by highlighting life's sufferings and the retribution for karma in the three-phase reincarnation cycle. They dealt with Buddha's vast influence by transforming him into an incarnation of Vishnu, the guardian deity. They turned his Eightfold Path into a method for monastic spiritual practice, maintaining the four *ashramas* and the theoretical system of the four *varnas* as the basis for interpersonal behavioral duty. Their efforts were not met with any resistance because of Buddha's silence. The assimilation was nearly completed in the eighth century when Vedanta philosophical classics such as the *Upanishads* and the *Bhagavad Gita* were re-annotated by the great master of Indian Vedanta philosophy and the Yoga religion, Shankara. The system of faith that Buddha created was absorbed into Brahman because of his attempt to treat the question of absolute truth with silence.

Buddha's disciples, however, had the same dilemma as any founders of a faith: the journey of advancing spiritually (for them, attaining Buddha's state) was difficult, if not impossible. Typically, they embarked on the important path of annotation, interpretation, and preaching. Because of Buddha's unnecessarily humble silence and his belief that everyone could become a buddha, many disciples were essentially motivated by their own "limited inner self"—and they went so far down the path of interpretation that the *Sutras* kept expanding and thickening. The *Sutras* lacked the clearly marked boundaries of the Bible, as evidenced by fact that the Chinese translation of the *Sutras* is now 74 times its length. In the end, the *Sutras* became an extremely vast and all-embracing system of Buddhist philosophy, theology, and rituals, making it difficult for people to distinguish between true and false teachings.

And as the religion was ritualized, it became impossible to establish the divine authority of Buddha without making him and the truths he discovered absolute, so it became impossible to truly popularize the faith he founded. Yet, if Buddha and the truth he discovered were made absolute, it would violate his own teachings, the negation of deities of personality his silence implied, and the principle that everyone could become a Buddha. This is the profound and unresolvable paradox contained in the silence of Buddha.[227]

History provided two paths for resolving this profound paradox.[228] First, Vedanta Philosophy in Hinduism maintained the relative truth of Buddhist philosophy, declaring Buddha an incarnation of Vishnu and thereby integrating his doctrines. Second, the great spirit of Buddha's concept of Nirvana and the truth he discovered spread far and wide through Northern and Southern Buddhism to countries in East Asia and Southeast Asia, becoming more absolute as they did. Outside his homeland, Buddha was divorced from Vedanta, and became the de facto new god that he least wanted to become in his lifetime, the incarnation of the infinitely powerful, infinitely merciful holy spirit of Krishna. He represented the omnipotent, good, and true god that Easterners sought. Buddha could not avoid being misunderstood and deified, despite trying so hard to avoid this fate through his silence. What Buddha hoped for—that humanity would be able to attain Buddhahood through their own human reason—was in the end not to be, just as Greek philosophy had failed to establish an absolute human reason.

The history of humanity, as evidenced by this period, bears out the fact that people cannot arrive at absolute truth through human reason. Only by worship of the infinite and eternal absolute truth, through divine redemption, can individuals understand absolute truth, reach infinity and eternity, and attain the moral standards that God expects. Only in this way can they make life worthwhile, make society worthwhile, and give hope to society. Only then can the proliferation of man-made gods, in the pursuit of fame and fortune in this world, finally come to an end.

CHAPTER 10:

Division: an overview
of the Chinese Empire

In order to trace Buddhism's influence and the divide between Eastern and Western interpretations of faith, we bring the lens of history back once again to the Chinese Empire during mankind's first great philosophical awakening.

Historians tend to attribute Qin Shi Huang's defeat of the six states in the Spring and Autumn and Warring States periods (Yan, Zhao, Qi, Chu, Han, and Wei) and his unification of China under the great Qin Dynasty to superior military force. However, this is a misunderstanding. In fact, the view that the Chinese Empire was established due to Qin Shi Huang's military conquests is overly superficial. What really led to the defeat of the six states was Legalist strategist Shang Yang and Duke Xiao of Qin Ying Quliang's Shang Yang Reforms, which began in the State of Qin in 360 BC and took 22 years. The great Chinese empire owed its existence to the practical Legalist philosophy behind the Shang Yang Reforms, which guided the strategic organization of the state's economic and political systems.

SECTION 1: THE PHILOSOPHICAL GAP UNDER THE QIN DYNASTY, CHINA'S BLACK EMPIRE

The core of Shang Yang's and Duke Xiao's strategy was:[229] first, to establish an aristocracy whose power came directly from absolute imperial power, rather than the weak political ecology during feudalism. This centralized system of direct imperial command included placing county and prefecture administrative units directly under central imperial authority, so that officials were directly appointed or removed. Since the salaries of these officials were paid directly by the imperial authority, this system replaced the method of paying them through land taxes, which is what had weakened the Zhou Dynasty. Officials at all levels were appointed by the emperor as local administrative managers, military managers, and monitors, each fulfilling their own duties and constraining each other.

Second, all taxes were directly paid to and controlled by the emperor. Manors and estates were divided and given as honorary possessions to families that had won victory in war and displayed honor. All income for administrative bureaucrats could only be legally drawn from salaries directly paid by the emperor.

Third, adult brothers in the vast rural areas were forced to live separately, and large, intergenerational families were collapsed into nuclear families. This made the single nuclear family the solid unit of agricultural production and taxation, maximizing the efficiency of agricultural production and tax revenue.

Fourth, a system of mutual supervision in the rural villages was implemented to establish imperial power there.

Fifth, slaves were liberated, and the number of servants aristocratic families could employ in the city was severely limited. Land was allocated as a reward for merit. This freed up the slave labor force for use on the battlefield or in agriculture and reduced both the extravagance of the upper classes in the cities and the consumption of human resources in the countryside.

Sixth, laws were passed with imperial authority, replacing vengeful, vigilante justice driven by family feuds. Lynching was banned as well. A new political order with imperial power as the supreme authority was established. From the time Duke Xiao gained imperial power, he required vassal lords under the Qin Empire to judge disputes during the day and read reports at night.

Seventh, a military force centered around imperial power was established, and talented military generals were appointed. Military security forces serving the emperor were strengthened, preempting threats to the emperor's safety or the imperial order. These security forces were known for their cruelty, creating a strong deterrent to major sources of such threats, such as the emperor's family members.

By the end of the Zhou Dynasty, its ritual system of connecting to Heaven through sacred ceremonies and music, had declined. Like a "newborn baby" of Chinese theology, it was dumped out with the bathwater of the chaos that marked its later period, caused by its division of royal power among separate princes.

The new Qin political system saw absolutely no need for the Zhou Dynasty's rituals, music, ceremonies, or faith. All that remained was the mechanical management of people. Though there was conflict, the vitality of philosophy was lost. Chinese culture fell into the terror and violence of the way of tyrants and a surreal philosophy based entirely on survival.

Of course, the empire under the Qin Dynasty also fundamentally shed the Zhou Dynasty's fascination with high-minded ceremonies that were exclusively performed by the emperor. These had been performed even as the empire fragmented into smaller and smaller divisions ruled by extravagant and permissive lords as it fell into war and disorder. Now they were largely obsolete.

The new system was an agricultural civilization with centralized imperial power that could manage and control single families. Everything was centered around the maintenance of imperial power, which is what lent it its greatness. The system strengthened nuclear families and agricultural cultivation, advancing population growth and economic development. A national spirit of civil militarism arose through the liberation of slaves and the promise of imperial rewards for violence.

This new Qin Dynasty system of highly bureaucratic control, absolute imperial power, and close-knit, single-family agricultural cultivation was refined over nearly a century and a half. Up until the end of the 3rd century BC, the old ranks of the *Fengjian* aristocrats, civilians, and slaves of the six states of the warring period that it conquered, found it impossible to rival the State of Qin, regardless of what agricultural, military, or economic strength they could muster. It was only a matter of time before the State of Qin defeated them, unifying China. In this way, Qin Shi Huang's great achievement was merely the logical consequence of Shang Yang and Duke Xiao's reforms, as the curtain of history opened over the years 235–221 BC.

The powerful King Ying Zheng of Qin crowned himself the "First Emperor"—the literal meaning of Qin Shi Huang. This title elevated him to a god-like status, surpassing even the five ancient Chinese emperors that preceded him: the Yellow Emperor, Emperor Zhuanxu, Emperor Ku, Emperor Yao, and Emperor Shun. He attempted to claim the highest supremacy to ensure the legitimacy of his family's political rule for generations. But apart from harsh suppression and rigorous regulations that maintained political order, the State of Qin did not provide a political philosophy or theological justification for the unified empire.

Because of this, there was widespread suspicion of the legitimacy of the First Emperor's rule. The Legalist scholars who advised him, such as Li Si, did not offer any more systematic philosophical thinking to justify the unification of the six kingdoms, other than issuing his laws and upholding them with bloody violence. In a country where thinking is forbidden by power, and power is used to violently control the people, the atmosphere that allowed pre-Qin philosophy to flourish at its height vanished. As a result, Qin Shi Huang could only borrow the practical philosopher Zou Yan's extremely metaphysical yin-yang philosophy to comfort the people and indirectly justify the unified Qin Empire's replacement of the Zhou Dynasty. Because the Confucian "way of kings" was scorned by the Legalists in power, many Confucian books were burned during this era, and Confucianism all but disappeared from Chinese thought.

According to Zou Yan's theory, the fundamental element of the universe is *qi*. *Qi* is formed according to the five elements and yin and yang in order to achieve mutual balance. Yin and yang are the opposing forces in all things, and apart from the balance of the two forces uniting in mutual opposition, things would collapse. Within the balance of yin and yang, *qi* exists in the form of five elements, namely wood, fire, earth, metal, and water. These five elements of *qi* mutually form and absorb each other. Mutual formation follows this order: water forms wood, wood forms fire, fire forms earth, earth forms metal, and metal forms water. Similarly, the order of mutual absorption is: metal absorbs wood, wood absorbs earth, earth absorbs water, water absorbs fire, and fire absorbs metal.

This theory didn't rely on any logical reasoning based on empirical observations, but rather on vivid metaphors and analogies. A person could, through observations of nature and the use of imagination, experience the mysterious power of its mystical language. Yin-yang scholars that followed Zou Yan continued to elaborate on his theory of the five elements by applying it to the social sphere, using it to infer the fate of those in society in order to pinpoint any cause of the imbalance of yin-yang or the five elements.

This gave rise to uniquely Chinese professions like yin-yang specialists, fortune tellers, and Feng Shui masters. Some later combined these with King

Wen of Zhou's divination book *The Book of Changes*, or the *I-Ching*. The result was a whole set of increasingly complex, sprawling, mystical theories surrounding the divination of human fate. This attempt to predict fate and crack the problem of destiny had a long-lasting and widespread influence on Chinese people's fatalistic worldview[230].

After the unification of the six states, Zou Yan's disciples tried to match some phenomena seen in the relationship between humans and nature, and all phenomena seen in the relationship between humans and society, with the five elements of yin-yang as a kind of theory of everything. For example: east, spring, green, and the number eight corresponded with wood; south, summer, red, and the number seven corresponded with fire; west, fall, white, and the number nine corresponded with metal; north, winter, black, and the number six corresponded with water; center, yellow, and the number five corresponded with earth.

This theory, half based on imagination and half on analogy, claimed that the Zhou Dynasty was of fire, and the Qin Dynasty was of water, so the reason the Qin Dynasty succeeded the Zhou Dynasty was because water conquers fire. Thus, Qin Shi Huang's government celebrated the beginning of the year with winter in October. The empire's official color, reflected in official clothing, banners, the palace, and chariots, was black. Also, everything the emperor used was in multiples of six. For example, the emperor's chariot had six horses and the country was divided into 36 counties (six squared). In this view, only if the Qin Dynasty followed these rules could it guarantee that the Ying family continued governing the 3.4 million kilometers and 15–20 million people that the empire encompassed. This was the beginning of Chinese mystical philosophical thinking.

This doctrine lacked rigorous observation of the truth behind the world of natural phenomena, as well as insights into the relationships between people. It could neither divine the logical relationships behind the world of phenomena nor give guidance for human behavior. Rather, it gave the logical order of governance put in place by Legalism a fatalistic cloak, encouraging the upper classes of the Qin Empire to use mystical justifications for their arbitrary and increasingly violent behavior. This eventually led to a spiral of violence 15 years later.

After Qin Shi Huang died, the eunuch Zhao Gao conspired with Li Si, the prime minister, in a plot to destroy the eldest prince, Fusu. They planned to make the second eldest, Huhai, emperor, and kill the military commanders and their allies. In order to do this, Zhao Gao brought a deer before Emperor Huhai and said that it was not a deer but a horse. He forced everyone, from the emperor to the court officials, to make a statement either agreeing or disagreeing. Was it a deer or a horse? The architects of the Qin political order, Shang Yang and his successor Li Si, never imagined that the mighty imperial politics of the Qin, based on Legalist philosophy, would be challenged by a test as trivial and embarrassing as this. If a person said the deer was a horse, they could go on living and enjoy riches and luxury; if they said the deer was a deer, they and their whole family would be annihilated by Zhao Gao with the full force of imperial power. Naturally, this spelled the beginning of the end of the Qin Empire.

Chen Sheng and Wu Guang, two Qin army officers, led the great Dazexiang Uprising, lighting the spark that led to the end. Just over two years after the yin-yang mysticism was inaugurated, the Qin Empire disintegrated. Next came the battle between Xiang Yu, the warlord of Western Chu, and Liu Bang, the tax collector of Pei County. Eventually, Liu Bang won, unified China, and established the Han Dynasty. However, the core philosophical void of imperial legitimacy left by Legalism remained a major problem that needed to be remedied.

SECTION 2: THE EMERGENCE OF MONOTHEISM UNDER THE CONFUCIAN-LEGALIST ALLIANCE OF THE HAN DYNASTY

Emperor Liu Bang, during the feast to celebrate his victory, sensed that a large number of military commanders, who had fought battles during the dispute between Chu and Han, supported forced decentralization. He decided it was necessary to strike a new balance between the decentralized vassal system of the Zhou and the centralized imperial system of the Qin.

A hundred and thirty-seven deserving ministers who had aided Liu Bang in his quest to become the Han Emperor needed to receive their allotments. The ministers and imperial Liu family members representing him signed scrolls[231] of wrought iron, contracts outlining the estate grants to the aristocrats and their loyalty to the Liu family's imperial power. Each side was given half of the metal scroll. The minister receiving the estate retained one half, and the other half was held in the ancestral hall of the imperial Liu family, in a manner similar to that of the Israelite ark of the covenant. The matching scrolls were indelible, irrefutable evidence of the covenant and represented its seriousness and sacredness.

But the memory still lingered of hundreds of years of ruthlessness and false loyalty between the Zhou and the feudal lords during the Spring and Autumn and Warring States periods, causing Emperor Liu Bang, despite his supreme power and imperial status, many sleepless nights. The threat of separatist powers seemed to haunt imperial tyrants like an undeniable psychological shadow.

Liu Bang's response was to once again return to the tyrannical law of the jungle. His first recourse was to bolster the Liu family bloodline. He conspired to eradicate the threat to imperial power from Han Xin, Peng Yue, and other officials outside the family, enacting the policy that "non-Lius may not ascend the throne."

Clearly the one who first tore the covenant of the metal scrolls to shreds was Liu Bang, and not the lords who received the estates. As internal struggles within the Liu family became a greater threat to imperial power than any external threat, not even husband and wife could be confident of each other's loyalty. After Liu Bang died, his wife Lü Zhi and her extended family almost completely appropriated the Liu family's status as the core of imperial power. Only after Lü Zhi died in 180 BC did the highest military leader, Commander Zhou Bo, help Emperor Wen of Han restore the Liu family's imperial power. After that, the Liu family retained the Han Dynasty imperial power for nearly 400 years. Finally, a consistent logic of succession was perfected: imperial power was absolute, passed on to the eldest son so that political control could be retained in the way of tyrants. Now a corresponding political philosophy was needed to justify it.

These nearly four centuries of Han Dynasty history may be divided into two periods, each with different explanations for the justification of imperial power.

The first period featured the Huanglao political philosophy adopted by Emperor Wen and Emperor Jing's so-called Wen-Jing Government (180 BC–140 BC).[232] Emperor Wen, Emperor Jing, and Empress Dou were born poor. They were pushed out of court life and exiled to the northwestern territories, so they came to know the hardships of the people. Emperor Wen's mother, Empress Dou, particularly advocated the use of Huanglao governance.

The Huanglao philosophy held that people should follow Laozi's "way of saints" political approach, that is, people should behave in accordance with the law of the external natural world, just as nature follows the seasons. The emperor must cultivate "virtue" to realize the "moral unity" of the way of saints in government: imperial power is the highest representative authorized by the god of nature to manage human society. As such, he must follow the laws of nature, have compassion for the people's suffering, exercise thrift, and avoid extravagance—and as a result reduce taxes, making the people rich. The emperor should use simple precepts and lead by example to advocate honest folk customs.

This approach realized the Daoist principle of ruling: "I act not, and the people self-cultivate; I am silent, and the people are upright; I meddle not, and the people are rich; I desire not, and the people are content." Building on

Liu Bang's simplification of Qin law, Emperor Wen and Emperor Jing further simplified the laws issued by the emperor, choosing not to disturb the people so they would be able to improve themselves and not over-burdening them so they could rest and recuperate.

The Wen-Jing reign was a golden age when Chinese imperial power truly served the needs of the people. It used, rather than abused, imperial power, governing according to the principle of non-action, or the way of saints. It's the political philosophy most worthy of praise in Chinese culture. During nearly half a century of history, Emperor Wen and Emperor Jing built no new palace buildings, not even a pavilion. The skirts of the emperors' wives were patched many times, but much land was reclaimed for the people's cultivation. The population grew from 15 million to over 30 million, and the wealth of the people also increased. The state treasury was full, the world peaceful and prosperous. Emperor Wen and Emperor Jing truly exemplified Laozi's ideal ruler-saints.

The second period was the reign of Emperor Jing's son Emperor Wu of Han. The reign of emperors Wen and Jing was very effective in terms of the Chinese Empire's internal governance, but an ambitious and talented man like Emperor Wu of Han found it limiting. He was eager to expand externally, so the theory of both minimizing taxation and not disturbing the people greatly curbed his thirst for conquest.

Emperor Wu of Han ruled for half a century, stirring up hatred for the Xiongnu and launching several large-scale foreign wars, attacking the Xiongnu in the north, Northern Vietnam in the south, Northern Korea in the east, and sending Zhang Qian as an envoy in the west in order to develop the frontier. Taxes were raised to accomplish this, which burdened the poor. But even this was not enough to sate Emperor Wu of Han's ambitions.

He continued to use the "Discourses on Salt and Iron"[233] that Sang Hong-yang took from Spring and Autumn Warring States era Legalist Guan Zhong, establishing the earliest state-owned enterprise: a salt and iron monopoly that disallowed private ownership of two key resources society was just beginning to need. The power to issue coins was again centralized.

He also established a system to monitor the 13 provincial governors, strengthening imperial power at the expense of lesser rulers and incorporating all royal activities into up-to-date secret surveillance reports made directly to the emperor. This increased power supported Emperor Wu of Han's policy of external expansion and taxation of the people. Thanks to Wei Qing, Huo Qubing, and other famous commanders, the empire's territory during the reign of Emperor Wu of Han expanded by more than 5 million square kilometers. In terms of area, it was comparable to the peak of the Roman Republic, but due to years of foreign wars, the population dropped by over 10 million, nearly reaching the population before the rule of Emperors Wen and Jing. The treasury was empty, people were dying, and the land was desolate.

Emperor Wu of Han's policies of external expansion and internal dominance were in line with the way of tyrants. This set the stage for the revival of Confucianism.

During his reign, Han Emperor Liu Bang consulted the leading Confucian, Shu Suntong, on ritual. As a result, Shu Suntong designed a dramatic spectacle for Liu Bang in line with the traditional ritual system. Liu Bang performed a ceremonial tribute to his ministers with Changle Palace as a backdrop, demonstrating a return to the ritual order. After more than a month of practice, the military and court officials were ordered to wait in the palace before the event began. Liu Bang slowly entered on a chariot designed for the occasion. There was solemn ritual music. The ministers were asked to congratulate Liu Bang on the performance in accordance with their official ranks but were forbidden to look at him, which immediately generated an atmosphere of oppression.

Then, the ceremony started. Officials present were ordered to bow at Liu Bang's feet but not look up at the monarch. Only when the host announced the commencement of the ceremony did the ministers rise and participate. Then the ombudsman entered, and ministers who were not behaving in an orderly way were expelled one by one for the crime of "disrespecting the ceremony," sentenced to flogging, dismissal, and other penalties. Historically, China had been a country where governance was conducted through mutual respect and cooperation. This ended with the Han introduction of their version of Confucian ritual system.

Shu Suntong thus entered the court, becoming Liu Bang's trusted advisor. Confucianism was now divorced from Confucius and Mencius's original objective of encouraging royal self-restraint. Now, the "ritual and music" that was supposed to establish benevolent government and a harmonious social order was appropriated to maintain strong, centralized imperial power.

Emperor Wu of Han's political ambition and tyrannical tendencies meant a return to the violent repression of Qin Shi Huang. The politically ambitious Confucians, who had been out of favor since the rule of emperors Wei and Jing, now finally found their voice again in the Confucian thinker Dong Zhongshu, who adapted Confucianism to the new conditions. Dong Zhongshu learned from Confucius' travels throughout the country to persuade the princes to restore the ritual system of the Zhou Dynasty, teaching them the history of stability due to obedience to the Zhou emperors. He also learned from Mencius's travels to persuade the princes to improve their own self-cultivation in order to become benevolent rulers. To this he added the philosophical thought of Xunzi, who believed that human nature was evil and required ritual constraints. To a considerable extent, he was also influenced by Mozi's idea of "Heaven's will." Finally, he also incorporated the yin-yang doctrine of the Daoist Zou Yan and combined these ideas in a new, syncretistic Confucianism, developing it into a set of rational and legitimate teachings for the dictatorial rule of imperial power.[234]

In this doctrine Dong Zhongshu advocated that heaven, earth, and the people were interrelated and indivisible. "Heaven births it, earth grows it, humans become it, none can be lacking." The will of Heaven, on the one hand, is carried out throughout the universe through the unity of opposites of the two primary forces, yin and yang. Yang represents the sun, light, and masculine qualities, and yin represents the moon, night, and feminine qualities, with the union of yin and yang giving rise to new things. All things possess the natures of the five elements: metal, wood, water, fire, and earth. These five natures are mutually exclusive but can combine to form a dynamic balance. On the other hand, the will of Heaven is carried out on the earth by the Son of Heaven, namely the emperor, and when the people trust him, it allows for earth to prosper and human society to be ordered. Thus the vertical stroke in the character 王 (wang, "king"), which is part of the word 帝王 (diwang, "emperor") is like a vertical path that runs up the horizontal layers of earth to heaven. The will of Heaven is granted by Heaven and responsible for the cultivation of the earth and the people.

As part of this cultivating work, the emperor should establish a seasonal calendar to govern the work of farmers—plowing in summer, harvesting in autumn, and resting in winter—and to guide the people's ritual sacrifices to Heaven to ensure good weather and abundant harvests. The imperial college's Confucianism taught again the necessary ritual and music to manage the people and encourage them to obey the proper order of the universe and human relations: heaven guides earth, earth follows heaven; the ruler guides the subject, the subject follows the ruler; the father guides the sons, the sons follow the father; the husband guides the wife, the wife follows the husband; the older brother guides the younger brother, the younger brother follows the older brother. If they all act out their roles, stay within their places in society and avoid causing trouble, society will be well-ordered, and the world will be peaceful. If the emperor implements this decree strictly, anyone, no matter their position, who goes against court etiquette, daily rituals, or filial piety, must be severely punished.

Dong Zhongshu's brand of absolutist Confucianism, which held centralized imperial power at its heart, was quickly adopted by Emperor Wu of Han. In fact, he decreed that all other schools of thought be abolished, so Confucianism alone reigned.[235] Confucians, no longer sidelined, now advised and trained kings, princes, and even emperors in self-cultivation. The emperor more fully became the embodiment of Heaven's will, being granted absolute authority to manage the land and the people. Top Confucian scholars became inseparable from this absolute authority, developing a whole set of rules of etiquette to ensure the total loyalty of officials at all levels of imperial power and in every social relationship, from relationships within the family to all relations between inferiors and superiors. Every social relation was imbued with ritual, and imperial authority issued decrees and laws to enforce them.

In this way, Confucian scholars went from fulfilling their historical role as instructors, mentors, and religious counselors to princes and kings to essentially becoming royal slaves groveling at the feet of the emperor. Wielding his supreme authority to issue decrees, they transformed themselves into tutors that stood above all others, teaching people how to stand and walk, how to speak to those of a higher status and on different occasions, how to act and think.

Many scholars call the dynamic of this time "internal Legalism and external Confucianism." Perhaps more accurately, it was the Han Dynasty Confucians manipulating what could be called the "Confucian-Legalist alliance." When the Confucian-Legalist alliance made imperial power absolute and the emperor sacred, they completely lost the spirit of both the Confucian and Legalist masters of the Spring and Autumn and Warring States periods. These masters, including Confucius, Mencius, and Xunzi, as well as Guan Zhong, Li Yang, and Shang Yang, were full of ideas on governance. This new Confucianism was completely assimilated by the scheming and silver-tongued "imperial Confucians" like Dong Zhongshu.

Dong Zhongshu, most representative of Confucianism in the Han Dynasty, viewed the emperor as the Son of Heaven, the only incarnation of Heaven's will, and the master of the whole world. Learned Confucians were reduced to mere servants of the emperor, the only god in the human world. Daoists were exiled to the mountains, influencing only folk culture, and disappearing from the upper classes. This view borrowed heavily from Mozi's idea of Heaven's will as an impersonal god, but his core ideas of mutual love and non-violence were completely abandoned and faded from the Chinese mind. Endowing the Emperor with these god-like powers required the mechanism of state violence to suppress dissidents. It also relied on the costly construction of a prestigious, luxurious palace, which people bowed to, and absolute control of information in order to maintain an air of mystique and secrecy.

But even as a human god, the emperor was still a human, after all. All humans are limited, mortal, and fallible, so of course, he was too. Even worse, because he could do whatever he wanted, he could easily act on his sinful nature and tendency toward evil. As a result, emperors were often caught up in cruel or even inhumane political intrigue.

Emperors during the final years of the Western Han Dynasty and even more so the last emperors of the Eastern Han Dynasty acted in ways that were beyond absurd, as court intrigue became increasingly strange and cruel. In particular, a large number of castrated men were brought in to serve the court, in order to protect palace women from being abused. The result was a large faction of eunuchs. They took advantage of this opportunity to get closer to the human god, the emperor, and participated in brutal court intrigues with informational asymmetry, growing ever more strange and perverse.

And since imperial succession was a matter of national importance, anything affecting it, such as the emperor's death or choice of an empress or heir, involved the destinies of everyone at court. The women the emperor married or favored, along with their extended families, were actively or passively involved in court political struggles. Families leveraged the emotional entanglements between the women and the emperor, the legitimacy of his marriages, and his wives' ability or inability to bear sons to battles for his favor and take part in a brutal political game of succession.

Needless to say, the emperor and his court often fell short of the ideal of Confucian behavior.[236] Of the more than 100 human-god emperors throughout the 400 years of the Han Dynasty and the over 400 years of the Three Kingdoms period and the Wei, Jin, and Southern and Northern Dynasties, very few were worthy representatives of Heaven's will. Of the 14 emperors of the Eastern Han Dynasty, only Liu Xiu and his son ascended the throne as adults. The rest were crowned as children. The youngest emperors were only eight and two months old respectively—breastfeeding babies. The powers behind the throne of such emperors were empresses or concubines' extended families, eunuchs, and Confucian scholars.

These court intrigues were unimaginably cruel. The losers were not only arrested and imprisoned, but often executed, with their families facing complete annihilation by imperial order. Execution methods included hanging, beheading, and dismemberment, just to name a few, acting as a harsh deterrent for the lower classes. The winners gained favor and the blessing of the emperor's seal, reaping the rewards of nepotism and showing off their status. Such victories were often short-lived, historically speaking, merely sowing the seeds for the next round of even fiercer contention.

To put the reigns of these "human gods" into historical perspective, from the beginning of Qin Shi Huang's victory in reunifying China under the Qin Dynasty to the end of the Ming Dynasty—over 1,800 years—the average imperial reign was no more than 10 years. Yet they believed they ruled the universe and society's life cycles. In comparison, the emperors of the earlier dynasties, the Xia, Shang, and Zhou, averaged more than 20 years. Clearly the Confucian-Legalist alliance's emphasis on absolute imperial power intensified court battles and cut emperors' average reign in half. This shows the increasing social disorder that resulted from rapidly changing regimes, as well as the emperor's ordinary human limitations: mortality and fallibility. Every time Confucian rituals and ceremonies made the Emperor out to be an absolute god, calling for him to live a thousand years and claiming his infinite majesty, they merely proclaimed the greatest lie known to man.

The sad thing was that these brutal struggles between mortals and their man-man gods couldn't help but suck the rest of society in. The court dramas of most Chinese dynasties reenacted the original spectacle of forcing people to "call a deer a horse," when Zhao Gao set this whole system in motion. All such human-god emperors fell into this pattern, with the exception of the founding emperors of dynasties, such as Liu Bang and Liu Xiu, or a handful of wise emperors like Emperor Liu Che or Emperor Wen and Emperor Jing. These emperors were unusually adept at controlling factions, relying on their own experiences of suffering, and so avoiding being controlled by the eunuchs, extended families, and Confucian scholars. They instead maintained a core of political balance and stability, with no need to resort to methods that openly denied the truth and basic common sense in a show of violent political power.

But these were indeed exceptions. The vast majority made shocking demands, and their intrigues are truly eye-opening. The gist of their contortions of the truth was always to make subordinates take a stand that ran contrary to common sense or reason—to choose sides and conform to the prevailing school of thought. Officials who emerged on the side of the winners were in fact liars promoted for untruthfulness, whereas those who stubbornly adhered to the truth were weeded out. This meant losing their positions, material security, and basic dignity as human beings. The most terrifying punishment was mass murder of families up to the ninth generation, so that errant officials' fathers, grandfathers, great-grandfathers, and great-great grandfathers, all the way to their children, grandchildren, great-grandchildren, and great-great-grandchildren on both sides were killed. Not even women and children were spared.

That meant that every few years, or every decade, society experienced catastrophic trauma from top to bottom, with emperors seen as a terrifying sacred authority. Their names could not be spoken, and their words, deeds, and lifestyle were beyond reproach. To criticize them would be to risk being reported and having your entire family wiped out. Such a society could maintain peace for about 30 years, which historians would be quick to praise as a time of prosperity. But the next round of drama would already be brewing.

The Confucian ideology that made the emperor a "god of the mortal world," along with its etiquette and punishment systems, caused two major problems in the Chinese Empire: first, the emperor's status as a god killed Chinese philosophy's tolerant spirit of looking past human fallibility to divine absolute truth, because obtaining the absolute position of imperial power was accomplished through armed violence. By adopting relative truth as absolute truth, the spirit of imagination and inquiry was completely cast out of the people, and instead, all political thought was dedicated to buttressing imperial power. Great thinkers were rare, and for those who did arise, the best they could hope for was for their thoughts to be herded into the stables of the current surreal philosophy, with the emperor and his favorite ministers as the frame of reference for absolute truth.

Second, the emperor's limitations and absurd behavior were well-known to historians and Confucian bureaucrats, but they tried to cover them up. Exposing the truth to society would be embarrassing and unbearable. It would cause the emperor, Confucian bureaucrats, eunuchs, and the consort families to lose their source of legitimacy and moral authority. Cover-ups, whitewashing, and camouflaging the truth became an ordinary skill of all parties in the power struggle.

Hypocrisy and duplicity became necessary qualities in people to keep this system in operation. However, once they became accustomed to such falsehood, everyone was required to live a double life of saying one thing and believing another. This habitual split of the individual's psyche gradually permeated the atmosphere of the culture, becoming part of society's collective memory and passed on from generation to generation.[237]

By the final year of the Eastern Han, after more than 300 years of domination, the Confucian ritual and punishment system of the Confucian-Legalist alliance pieced together by Dong Zhongshu had made outstanding achievements. The territory of the unified Chinese Empire reached a peak area of 5 million square kilometers, with the population under its jurisdiction exceeding 50 million. According to these two most crucial indicators of an agricultural civilization, the Chinese Empire was indeed an Eastern powerhouse. It reached heights comparable to the most powerful empire in the West, the Roman Empire, which had 6–10 million square kilometers of land and a population exceeding 100 million under its jurisdiction. But structural and soft indicators reveal a stark difference between the two empires.

First, society in the Roman Empire was based on the individual freedom of Roman citizens, and a legal order of rights and duties. The Western approach of Roman law as a foundational structure allowed the philosophical ideas of individual freedom, rights, duties, equality, fairness, and justice emerged as crucial legal and philosophical issues. These vital seeds remained for a long time in Western history, even after the Roman Empire fell, doubtless because it planted them deeply.

On the other hand, the societal foundation of Chinese Empire was the emperor's absolute power and sacred nature. People rejected individual thought and speech in service of absolute obedience to servile rituals and stylized etiquette under imperial power in order to avoid its systematic penalties for violators. As a result, the seeds of absolute imperial power were also planted deeply, and the pursuit of individual freedom and equal rights disappeared into the collective of the "nation," "families," and "clans" of imperial power. The structural logic of such decrees, from start to finish, relied on a strict top-down order. There was no legislative consideration of fairness in regard to individual rights or citizen rights. This is the most fundamental difference between the Roman and Chinese legal approaches.

Second, the Roman Empire, while encompassing comparable land and population to the Chinese empire, was held together as a rather civilized political union of independent countries with more than 50 religious faiths under the same imperial banner. As long as they acknowledged the authority of the Roman Empire, payed taxes, and adhered to its national imperial cult, these countries enjoyed relatively wide freedoms in faith, speech, and culture. In contrast, most of the jurisdiction of the Han Empire was over areas that practiced Han civilization and culture. There were small numbers of other ethnic groups under imperial rule, such as Xiongnu, Diqiang, Xianbei, and other minorities, but they never rivaled the Han. As a result, all these groups followed the precept to worship the power of the emperor as a human god. Ethnic minorities were subsumed, given the choice to "surrender or be conquered"— it's difficult to create unity when smaller states retain spiritual autonomy.

Third, the spiritual worldview of the Roman Empire allowed for a pantheon of more than 50 different gods, incorporating those of countries who surrendered, with the human emperor as one of the gods. But as discussed previously, faith in the one and only God Jehovah, the monotheistic innovation of the Hebrews, called the worship of human gods, or any other gods, idolatry. This led to conflict between the faith of the conquered Jewish people and the faith of the Roman Empire, which was greatly escalated by the death of Jesus. The Roman Empire violently suppressed the monotheism represented by Jesus Christ, so that the blood of Christian martyrs flowed, bringing this faith to the fertile soil of the nearly 50 countries that had surrendered to it. This eventually brought about the Roman Empire's collapse after a thousand years.

Although these surrendered countries returned to their previous status as nation states, a sturdy city of God was established on the vast land won by the Roman Empire's sword and law, resulting in a precious, unified Christian faith. Belief in God as an absolute, limitless, and eternal figure outside the world, yet who created the world and humanity, gave tens of thousands of believers equal and independent personal dignity, individual imagination, and behavioral accountability. Under this belief system, the emperor and kings descended from the human gods of ancient Rome were downgraded to public representatives of secular affairs. They could still possess supreme human authority and enjoy nobility and luxury in life, but they had to accept the constraints and accountability of God's spiritual representative, the church. That notably included constraints of Christ's light and God's expectations on their behavior. This meant that even when their behavior was problematic, it could be explained by their limitations and sinfulness as humans. This ensured the relationship between people to be relatively authentic, direct, and simple.

The spiritual world created by the Han Dynasty Empire, however, was completely held together by the idea of the emperor as a human god. The emperor was the moral exemplar for all men, while the empress was the moral exemplar for all women. Yet the combination of their finite and fallible nature as human beings, their infinitely exaggerated and absolute image generated by their supremacy in order to win public favor, and the cruelty of the power struggles at court, meant that when the skeletons in their closets were revealed, they lost their moral authority and could only rely on propaganda to cover it up. The resulting hypocrisy had a profound and far-reaching impact.

On the other hand, although China's emperors were called the Sons of Heaven, they seemed, at the same time, to have an authority similar to the "divine right of kings." But because the concept of Heaven was an impersonal god that lacked deeper definition, it was easy to confuse it with concepts like nature and the universe. When the emperor's authority is defined as controlling the social order and the order of the universe—a role entrusted to him by Heaven as the Son of Heaven—what is the difference between the Heaven who entrusted him and the Heaven he oversees? "Heaven's" absoluteness and sacredness disappear in this circular argument.

What is left is this Son of Heaven relying on violence to maintain authority. The violent authority of the emperor limited the people's imagination and became the limit of their speech.[238] These limits prevented free thought and the search for absolute truth, because society provided answers to everything and didn't allow them to ask questions. Unrestricted questioning would uncover the limits and relative authority of the emperor. It would also pierce through the flaws and hypocrisy in the laws and decrees issued by the Confucian scholars under the pretended authority of the emperor, as well as the hypocritical motives hidden behind the Confucian order. It would make it impossible to hold the incompatible logical tension arising from the Confucian system of thought that materialized spiritual beliefs and absolutized relative truths.

SECTION 3: THE SUPREMACY OF BUDDHISM DURING THE TANG DYNASTY

Around the end of the Eastern Han, at the end of the second century AD, the Confucian-Legalist alliance lost its dominance over Chinese thought.

Over the 400 years and 30 emperors from the Western to the Eastern Han, the majority of emperors' moral behavior in no way reached the benevolent ruler ideal Confucius and Mencius hoped for, even less so the ideal of the "vessel of Heaven," a human god in charge of the universe and social order according to Dong Zhongshu's reformed Confucian-Legalism. Apart from the tiny minority of emperors like Emperor Wen and Emperor Jing, most emperors were increasingly foolish. They were selfish, prideful, extravagant, moody, and violent, and abused their authority. As a result, the country's tax burden grew excessively, causing undue hardship for the people.

Under the banner of the emperor's divine status, the emerging Confucian-Legalist bureaucratic class, extended royal families, and high-ranking eunuchs purchased large amounts of real estate, forming new aristocratic clans with great economic and political power. They were both government bureaucrats and landlords, accumulating huge amounts of wealth through corruption and rent. They retained large numbers of domestic servants, which gradually evolved into private defense and armed forces. Their lives were extravagant and corrupt, advocating violence with their eyes on earthly power. The emperor's supreme power had a bewitching effect on these powerful aristocrats. They stayed behind the scenes to size up the situation, while waiting for the chance to achieve their political ambition to take the throne.

While natural and man-made disasters forced the vast peasant class from the small landholdings they depended on, the greed of the Confucian-Legalist bureaucracy and other elites continued unabated. They often leveraged their proximity to the emperor's supreme power, using his seemingly arbitrary laws to take advantage of taxes on commodities and conscripted labor.[239] For example, when crops were harvested, no commodity taxes were imposed. When farmers were out of grain during the off season, they contributed to commodity taxes through their labor. Farmers were often coerced into selling their grain for low prices and had to pay taxes too. Meanwhile, the influx of labor during the off season caused it to be devalued. Also, tax burdens caused many farmers to hire help during the busy season. Sometimes the government simply used money to generate labor, and the burden of taxation was passed on to the poor. In the later Eastern Han Dynasty, the vast middle and lower peasant classes were terribly exploited by tyrannical landlords while being squeezed by imperial taxes. And officials at all levels called on their services in the name of the emperor, robbing them of the labor they depended on for survival and burdening them even further.

These conditions increased the tyranny of the strong, widespread disharmony and violence, social disarray, and death, revealing the fragility and meaninglessness of life. During a large famine and widespread starvation, the hungry rose up and attacked from all directions, causing great bloodshed. Four hundred years of imperial rule by the Liu family during the Han Dynasty had reached its end.

What came after was nearly half a century of war between the three kingdoms of Wei, Shu, and Wu (roughly between 220–280 AD). Cao Pi, the descendent of legendary general and final grand chancellor of the Eastern Han, Cao Cao, took over the Kingdom of Han and replaced it with the short-lived State of Wei (220–266 AD). Sima Yi's descendent Sima Zhao then staged a coup and replaced the State of Wei with the State of Jin.

From 291—306 AD, during the "Rebellion of the Eight Kings," members of the final generation of the Sima family of the absurd Jin Dynasty fought and killed each other for the throne and prime ministerial power, bringing immense suffering to society and leading into the century-long "Five Kingdoms Rebellion," the establishment of 16 kingdoms, and the nearly 200-year split between the Northern and Southern Dynasties.[240]

China was not unified again until Yang Jian established the Sui Dynasty in the first half of the seventh century. In the interim, the population experienced more than 400 years of war and violence. The northern region was gradually taken over by ethnic minorities like the Huns, Xianbei, Qiang and other Mongols. The magnificent city of Luoyang with a population of 600,000 was burned to the ground by the Huns. Han rule was also strained in the south, and power quickly changed hands; internal dynastic infighting was intensified by a number of small kingdoms. Clearly, this long, fraught history and frequent imperial turnover proves the failure of the divine emperor figure created by Dong Zhongshu's Confucian-Legalist theories to maintain China's social order, let along the order of the universe. The lies of the Confucian-Legalist ideology were laid bare. The emperors' and empresses' moral authority was completely undermined. Strict laws and edicts were unable to constrain behavior. All that remained were naked power struggles and the law of the jungle. China's thinkers and intellectuals were incredibly disappointed. Their only choice was between joining the senseless fray of political struggle or retreating into the mountains to escape the disorder of society.[241]

Of the thinkers who emerged in this period, Wang Chong, Wang Fu, and Cui Shi are the most notable. They attacked the empty ideas of Confucianism and its burdensome rituals and behavioral prescriptions, saying that Confucian assumptions filled society with lies and superstitions. Confucianism after Dong Zhongshu was criticized for its hypocrisy of corrupting society and plundering the underprivileged on the one hand, while constantly granting amnesty to criminals on the other. These philosophers argued that Confucianism's methods would only encourage more degeneracy and crime, making their sick society even sicker. But apart from critiquing Confucianism, they didn't delve into deeper questions because they didn't dare touch on the core issue of the emperor's absolute power. Hundreds of years of wars made the intellectual class disgusted with the old order and eager to call for new freedoms. But the freedom they called for lacked individual human rights. They argued for freedom and responsibility with logical arguments, but lacked a sacred, authoritative source like a supreme God that affirmed the absolute freedom of the individual and their duty to the public.

Instead, Daoism, which was attentive to and imitative of the way of nature, returned to claim center stage in Chinese thought. The New Daoists now rose to prominence.[242]The famous "Seven Sages of the Bamboo Grove" appeared in the context of waning imperial power in the State of Wei, when Sima was staging his military coup. At this time, all political dissidents were brutally persecuted, creating an atmosphere of terror in which those who toed the line prospered and those who dissented perished. In an attempt to escape court politics, these literary thinkers brought a new interpretation of Daoist philosophy into Chinese history and culture.

The Seven Sages of the Bamboo Grove had no comprehensive theories. Rather, they were a group of educated, middle-class literati. They witnessed violent rebellion against the Confucian principles of loyalty, filial piety, benevolence, and righteousness in the form of a power-grabbing coup. They experienced yet another replay of calling a deer a horse when everyone was forced to agree with Sima Zhao, the emperor. What had become of the ruler-subject relationship? What had become of the sacred authority of the emperor as the Son of Heaven? All they saw was violent abuse of power, collusion, transactional bids for influence, flattery in exchange for protection, and a world where liars were rewarded, and truth-telling was suicidal.

Their response was to lose themselves in drink and poetry, develop an attitude of circumspection, and discuss Daoist metaphysics in order to escape persecution. Even so, Ji Kang, the leader of the Seven Sages, was still accused of rebellion by Sima Zhao due to his refusal to heed official calls to enter his court. For this, Ji Kang was unjustly executed. Even at his execution, Ji Kang refused to plead for himself and died with dignity, only requesting that the song "Guang Ling San," which had resounded through the ages in China, be played as an eternal footnote to his death. It was a poignant symbol expressing the hope the Seven Sages left us in their art, that is, the hope of a new order based on the freedom of human beings as individuals, one that transcended the suppression of human nature that Confucianism was unable to justify. This new order that the Seven Sages had yearned for over a century, became the *Dao* that future generations of Daoists put their hope in. This *Dao* of individual freedom, from then on, represented the ideal social order in the hearts of Chinese intellectuals, and it hasn't faded over thousands of years.[243]

But their metaphysical exploration of the truth could not continue. One reason was that the country had always used organized violence to suppress speech and thought, curbing the Chinese people's freedom to think and question the structures of society, especially through limiting free speech. This greatly hindered the freedom of individuals and their ability to ask questions that led to absolute truths. A second reason was that the form of written Chinese, and in particular the strictures of formal classical Chinese, greatly limited the expression of ideas. It limited logical debate and methods of analysis, such as deductive reasoning, since its strength lay in analogical reasoning and rhetorical flourishes.

These two reasons ensured that the new Daoists' pursuit of truth must both abandon Confucian metaphysical dogma and keep from rising to the absolute spiritual world of abstract metaphysical thought and inquiry. The naturalism of the Daoists had the benefit of alleviating the boundless suffering caused by 400 years of war and natural disasters. But it couldn't explore the meaning of life, because while nature is very rich and figurative, this kind of thinking requires abstraction and rigorous logical reasoning. Instead, the spiritual needs of the Chinese were met by Buddhism, as it traveled from the Indian subcontinent along Central Asian trade routes. This spawned a new absolute, metaphysical truth regarding the individual freedom of humanity, which spoke to the disordered state of China's material society.[244]

These two spiritual streams of Chinese thought and Buddhism first met in the second century AD. The greatest hurdle to mutual understanding between earlier Chinese spirituality and the Buddhist faith was the idea of space-time. Before Buddhism, the Chinese idea of space-time didn't go beyond Heaven and earth. Heaven and earth were concrete concepts, arising from the simple act of looking up and down. Heaven appeared to form a curved dome due to limited human vision. Earth was everything a person could see from a high vantage point, stretching to the horizon where it intersected with the curve of Heaven. No one in China had ever thought that the curve of the dome was the result of the earth being a sphere. Instead, Chinese thinkers long believed that the sky was round and the earth square. China was the kingdom at the center, surrounded by "barbarian" states. One could argue that before Buddhism reached China, Chinese lacked both the concept of the universe and the larger world, having only the concept of "under Heaven," its only conception of space-time. This space was not only the maximum imaginable from an individual perspective, but it was also the most space that a divine human emperor could imaginably control.

This is in contrast with the ancient Greek and Judeo-Christian faith's views of space-time, in which God created the universe from outside the universe, a far more metaphysical concept. Even compared to the concept of space of "Brahma" in the Indian Vedanta Philosophy of Buddhism, it's exceedingly metaphysical yet concrete.

There were two ideas of time according to Chinese thinkers. The first was based on life as a continuation of family inheritance, defined by ancestor worship. The other was based on the period of an emperor's rule. But each of these two times are very limited. And given that an emperor only ruled for an average of ten years, an ordinary person's life may go through several political eras.

The second challenge of the encounter between China's spiritual world and Buddha's faith was their outlook on life. Buddhism, which is rooted in Vedanta Philosophy, is completely pessimistic about life. Life is entangled with desire—it can't break free from the power of causality and falls into a meaningless cycle of reincarnation. This cycle of time is defined by Brahman as eternal time, so suffering is eternal and infinite. Buddha's insight was that people should find a way to wake themselves up from this time cycle, so they can shake off eternal suffering and enter the absolute truth of "Nirvana" that doesn't depend on any external conditions. This abstract thinking was difficult for the Chinese to understand, but Buddhism's appeal was great in those extremely turbulent, painful years for at least five reasons.[245]

First, since humans seemed unable to stop the endless war, famine, hunger, and suffering, people wondered if there was any reason or meaning to the suffering. Buddha taught that this suffering was the result of people's karma, the consequence of behavior, so there was no need to look for an outside reason. Everything had its cause, and all seeds yielded fruit. This couldn't be understood from within finite space and time. In infinite space and time, however, all these finite realities were extensively connected, and there was no need to worry about one's ignorance while confined to a finite space and time. Buddha provided a rationale and source of pain for the world's boundless suffering in his idea of karma, and introduced this new view of space-time, which meant that everyone was largely viewed as equal. To both the suffering elites and lower classes of China at that time, this kind of thinking was truly shocking.

Second, there was so much unfairness and evil in this world. Those who were rich and powerful were also savage and arrogant. The situation of the intellectual and lower classes was abject, and yet no one seemed to care. If no one cared, how could there be justice and order in the world? Clearly, the earlier Chinese expectation of benevolent rulers had been popped like a bubble and was no longer useful. Many emperors were incredibly evil, completely lacking morality or any talent for governing society. So how could continuing like this lead to good governance in Chinese society? Could Chinese people have any hope in the future? According to Buddhism, the mess they saw before them would by necessity result in consequences in the next life. The injustice and evil of people in the present were seeds that would bear fruit. No matter how much power or status someone had, the results of their karma were pre-determined and inevitable.

This pre-determined quality rose above the human sphere of influence and was instead determined by transcendental dharma. This theory was the first introduction of a dualistic world into Chinese philosophy. This dualist philosophy recognized that there was a pre-existing transcendental world beyond the visible, physical world. There was fairness in the human world, as well as righteousness and justice, which were determined and controlled by the invisible transcendental world's righteousness and justice. This theory subdued the sadness and resentment in people's minds regarding the suffering in their current lives. They could believe that good and evil had consequences, which helped them build confidence in the present life, since it gave rationality and meaning to the idea of a future life.

Third, the introduction of Buddhism expanded the Chinese view of time and the afterlife. According to Buddhism, the physical death Chinese people feared most was not the most tragic outcome. The most tragic outcome was when the soul, after death, was forced to retrace its steps in the "six paths" of sentient life, so that suffering became an eternal calamity. This was the first time Chinese philosophy seriously confronted and discussed the death of the visible body.

The Buddhist belief that the human soul does not die had several important implications. It meant that there was a second, invisible world that contained x number of previous "past lives" and x number of "future lives" after death. Humans, then, have only a very limited understanding of life in their current lives, so they must be full of respect and humility toward life. Also, since the soul is eternal, its repeated combinations within different bodies traps it in a restless, directionless wheel of reincarnation. A self-interested effort must be applied for the soul to go from lower levels of the six paths to higher ones. As a result, public good deeds in Chinese Buddhism are not motivated by the interests of others but are, unsurprisingly, self-interested at heart. The most important implication was that since after the soul's body dies it still exists in another transcendental world and can return to combine with other bodies, death is not so terrible or frightening. Could people not, then, adjust their feelings and attitudes to deal with suffering in life, and free their souls from needless pain and tension to find tranquility and happiness apart from the world of phenomena?

Fourth, Buddha's explanation of the endless sorrow inherent in the soul raised the question of what good-hearted individuals living in an evil age could do to change the status quo and bring meaning to life. His answer was "cultivation," "enlightenment," and "becoming a Buddha." So-called cultivation meant righteously adjusting one's heart to Buddha's values and adjusting one's behavior in the phenomenal world accordingly. It meant making one's words and deeds meet the demands and requirements of Buddhism.

So-called enlightenment meant increasing one's understanding of Buddhism through self-cultivation and thereby knowing the soul's immortal quality and its opposition to the phenomenal world in which sentient beings reside. It meant understanding that behavioral karma causes the soul to combine with the sentient body via reincarnation and recognizing the need for Nirvana. To "become a Buddha" was to reach the realm of the Buddha, that is, Nirvana. Nirvana means to break away from the wheel of karma and escape from the eternal, cyclical calamity of reincarnation and enter a state of existence that isn't dependent on any condition. It is a kind of infinite, eternal, absolutely true existence, the far shore of life. When humans accept this thinking, the chaos and pain of the phenomenal world disappear from view. For the Chinese intellectual elite of that era, this set of theories was as refreshing as a tall glass of water and caused a revolution in values.

Fifth, the Buddhist vision of human life was that of an individual, with a discrete, independent, free soul. This didn't necessarily depend on family and social relationships such as ruler-subject, father-son, husband-wife, or older brother-younger brother. This idea broke from Confucian theory, in which the importance of each person's role in society was emphasized to such an extreme degree that the freedom and independence of individuals was all but lost. In Confucian philosophy, the purpose of human life was not the value of that individual life, but rather the benefit the person brought in their role in society, a role prepared for them in advance. All a person had to do was memorize their lines every day. Such a life ruled out new ideas with its rigidity. When the world was harmonious and orderly, people endured these constraints without complaint. Not so under the chaos and abuse of power at the end of the Eastern Han, Wei, Jin, and Northern and Southern dynasties, despite many emperors' professed Confucianism.

Deep down, many felt extreme aversion to this illogical system of rules, which negated individual personalities and freedoms. The New Daoism that emerged as a result of the high degree of philosophical compatibility between Buddhism and Daoism, as well as the Mahayana schools of Buddhism that gradually separated from it and developed over a period of more than 400 years, finally broke the stranglehold of Confucianism. Individual independence received a new lease on life, instead of societal responsibilities. Since individual freedom had been tightly constrained for a long time, these new philosophies exerted a seductive spiritual influence on the Chinese intellectual elite. Chinese thought began to return to the spirit of the Spring and Autumn and Warring States periods.

Buddhism took the freedom and independence of people as individuals, especially when linked to the pursuit of absolute truth, and placed it above traditional family responsibilities. Buddha's own great sacrifice in pursuit of absolute truth is the best example of an individual's independence and freedom transcending traditional family roles. Indian Vedanta Philosophy and Buddhism were not interested in answering questions of societal governance. They didn't see such an earthly answer as worth searching for. If one couldn't answer the question of the meaning and value of each living individual's existence, where it came from and where it was going after death, how could one solve social problems or answer the question of how to govern the people? In Buddhist thinking, not asking the questions of life's ultimate meaning and simply discussing social relations and governance instead was like trying to get blood from a stone. The Buddhist approach was revolutionary. After all, millennia of Chinese philosophy hadn't addressed the meaning of individual existence.

It was these five factors that allowed Buddhism to seed itself into existing Daoist theory, as it was gradually introduced to China from the Indian subcontinent. These seeds germinated, took root, and flowered. In the beginning of the third century, the first translations of Mahayana Buddhist scriptures began. From 200 to 265 AD, an average of 2.5 Buddhist scriptures were translated into Chinese every year, but between 265 and 317AD, that rose to an average of 9.4. By 340 AD two important cities in northern China, Luoyang and Chang'an, had already built 180 Buddhist temples and had more than 4,000 full-time Buddhist monks.

At the same time, great Buddhist translators and preachers like 79-year-old Fotudeng (232–348 AD), who came to live in Luoyang in 310, Dao An (312–385 AD), and Kumārajīva, who came from the Western Regions to Chang'an in 401 AD, appeared in the north. The Nagarjuna school of Buddhism was also introduced, and Buddhism spread in the south of China. Buddhist temples sprung up, Buddhist monks increased in number, and important Buddhist leaders like Huiyuan (334–416 AD), Zhidun (314–366 AD), Zhu Daosheng (365–434 AD) emerged. Of course, the most important patron of Buddhism in the south was the famous Emperor Wu of Liang, who reigned from 502–549 AD. He not only donated large sums of money and land to Buddhist monasteries to support the development of Buddhism, but he was also ordained several times. He would even enter monasteries as a monk before allowing himself to be redeemed by his ministers for large sums as a show of his great faith in Buddhism.[246]

In 581 AD, the Northern and Southern kingdoms were once again reunited in a Chinese empire—the Sui Dynasty, led by Yang Jian of the Northern Zhou. But because of his corruption, his son and successor, Yang Guang, who abused conscript labor to build the Grand Canal and launched three unnecessary wars against Korea, provoked the peasant uprising of 617–618 AD. Once again, chaos and violence broke out, like the chaos after the reunification under the Qin and Han.

After more than 30 years of glorious reign, the Sui Dynasty was replaced by the Tang. The territory the Tang Dynasty controlled was greater than the Han, and so was its population. This degree of economic prosperity was unprecedented in China. The Buddhist and Daoist faiths formally replaced Confucianism as the official imperial faith. They helped the Sui reunite China and also enabled the Tang to prosper for 300 years.

In Buddhism, in accordance with the guidelines adhered to by Huiyuan, monks—such as Xuanzang, immortalized in the Chinese classic "Journey to the West," who personally went to India to collect the scriptures—were exempted from prostrating before the emperor. Secular bureaucrats were required to do so, while the emperor himself had to pay homage to the Buddha upon entering a temple. Wu Zetian, the legendary Tang Dynasty empress, not only gave a great salute to Buddha when master Shenxiu came to the palace to discuss Zen Buddhism, but she also personally greeted his chariot. This was an about-face from the days of regarding emperors as human gods, and represented an official recognition of the existence of a spiritual world beyond the phenomenal world with an absolute, eternal nature. Under this philosophy, the emperor was just an embodiment of Buddha in the material world.[247]

Buddhism flourished in the Tang Dynasty. Buddhist monasteries were built along the country's most famous mountains and rivers. The city centers of great cities like Chang'an and Luoyang were also full of Buddhist temples. During the heights of Tang prosperity during the reigns of Li Shimin and Wu Zetian, there were thousands of Buddhist temples and nearly a million Buddhists. The sound of chanting could be heard everywhere, and Buddhist iconography and art developed like never before. Buddhist concepts, ways of thinking, and spirituality took shape in new ways through Tang poetry. This was the first era in more than 2,000 years since the Qin unification of China in which the human personality could be fully expressed.

In addition to the donations to monasteries by the emperor and other dignitaries, merchants and landlords also donated a great deal of wealth. These donations included land, buildings, and Buddha statues. The poor, during the annual Lantern Festival, Buddha's Birthday, and Ullambana, the three major Buddhist festivals, participated in Buddhist celebrations and donated money for incense. At other times, they "made a wish" at the temple. If the wish was fulfilled, they would return to the temple to donate. Furthermore, the temples sublet lands to tenants, charging rent, and welcomed lay visitors to the temples for a fee. In addition to covering the basic costs of maintaining the monastery, the money was spent on charity, such as disaster relief, adopting orphans, repairing roads and bridges, etc. But overall, the charitable activity of Buddhist temples, in terms of scale, level of organization, and level of standardization, were no match for that of the Christian church.[248]

Of course, the introduction of Buddhism to China and its rapid growth and development involved scriptures. However, they were unlike the Christian Bible, which has a canon that cannot be added to. That Buddha announced with great humility that "anyone can become a buddha," which tempted certain disciples to establish their own idiosyncratic followings, some with selfish motives. There were many self-styled "Buddhas" in different times and regions. This led to a proliferation of bodhisattvas, lohans, and vajrasattvas, and the production of more and thicker sutras, such that the number of Buddhist classics translated into Chinese is equivalent to 74 times the length of the Bible, enough to induce a headache.

But sheer quantity of scriptures doesn't mean more truth. On the contrary, the proliferation of Buddhist scriptures created differences of interpretation among the four major schools of Tiantai, Pure Land, Zen, and Huayan. After the tenth century, further divisions were created with the introduction of

Caodong, Ōbaku, Tibetan, and other major denominations. These sects often emphasized one point and ignored the true core of Buddhism, which caused misleading tensions that were always in flux, preventing the spread and understanding of the true Buddhist faith. An example of a point of contention was whether one should be "self-propelling"—reaching the realm of Nirvana on one's own—or "propelling others," which meant helping the public reach Nirvana. Other controversies included whether the path to Nirvana was a gradual enlightenment or an epiphany, whether Buddhism should be preached openly or retain secrecy, and whether it should be taught with texts or without.

In actual fact, many of these questions are not at the core of the Buddhism. Masters like Xuanzang, who could truly reach the depths of insight into the absolute truth by seeing Buddhism as being opposed to the secular world, were few and far between. The majority of "Buddhist Masters" focused on the minutiae of religious practice, getting further and further from the core ideas of the Buddha. They combined Buddhism with China's tenacious folk religion, providing imperial rituals for the emperor, practical material and healing services for the people when they experienced natural disasters and illness, and hospice and funerary services when they neared death. This meant they received donations from people from all strata of society as the logical compensation for services rendered—a fairly direct transaction with the gods—revealing the mercenary nature of Chinese faith. It was also the inevitable consequence of Chinese cosmology, which only recognized the visible material world once it had absorbed the dualistic world of Buddhism.

With the decline of the Indian Maurya Dynasty (322 and 185 BC) after Ashoka (268–232 BC), the interests of Brahmin nobles and Kshatriya aristocrats wrapped up in Vedanta Philosophy saw a resurgence. Brahmanism rose again. Buddhism was quickly absorbed by Brahmanism on the Indian subcontinent. Buddha became the embodiment of the god Vishnu in Brahmanism. The solemn Buddhist temples Xuanzang saw when he visited India were quickly subsumed into the jungle of Vedanta Philosophy after the eighth century. China, meanwhile, became an emerging center of Buddhism in East Asia. The Buddhism on the Korean Peninsula and Japan was gradually introduced from China between the sixth and eleventh centuries. But in reality, Chinese Buddhism and the fundamental principles taught by Buddha had already faded. All that was left was the shell of Buddha's faith. This was unexpected, and terribly sad.[249]

Why did this happen?

First, the underlying script of Chinese philosophy only recognizes the visible world of phenomena, which seriously limited the abstract understanding of eternity in Buddhism. It also limited abstract understanding of the spatial concepts of "emptiness" and Nirvana, which in turn limited the logical speculation about absolute truth that represents eternity and infinity. These restrictions prompted Chinese Buddhist thinkers and evangelists to find Chinese concepts that were easier to understand to explain Buddhism.

They interpreted the world of visible phenomena with a visible, audible aspect. The "essential" world behind the phenomenal world that could only be understood through abstract thinking was termed the "original face," which in the end encompassed the entire visible aspect from the perspective of eternity. The relative meaninglessness or emptiness of birth and death was interpreted as "nothingness." The Chinese word for nothingness, 无 (wu), is a synonym for non-existing and was used for objects that aren't visible or audible to the subject. The perfection of the spiritual world was described with the very physical phrase "round and full;" spiritual awareness became the highly visual "enlightenment" or physical "breakthrough." A lack of awareness of the truth of Buddhism was translated as "lack of clarity," and understanding the Buddha's ultimate truth, the abstract state of Nirvana, as "passing on." The soul being reincarnated was described in the visual terms "turn of the dharma wheel" or "turn of the world." Karmic causality was explained as "sowing goodness to reap goodness" and could be substituted with giving money to charity. The accumulation of good karma through changing one's behavior took on a more literal sense with the phrase "putting down the knife and becoming a Buddha." The list goes on.

But as Buddhism spread, its dualistic worldview, rooted in Vedanta philosophy, in which humanity and God, matter and spirit, the individual and the public, the other shore and this shore exist in opposition to each other, was molded back into the Chinese monistic worldview by use of linguistic and logical differences.

This process occurred after Buddhism arrived in China, and the secular Chinese culture absorbed and transformed it. In other words, China's mainstream monistic thinking from the Spring and Autumn and Warring States periods transformed Buddhism. In the deeply rooted monistic thinking of the Chinese Confucian-Legalist alliance, the theory of intellectual elites had long only recognized the existence of the visible, audible, tangible, material world. They were highly skeptical toward the existence of an a *priori*, transcendental world outside the one we can sense. In that sense, they remained stubbornly atheist.

However, when living beings encounter death, disaster, bad luck, psychology, the eternal flow of time, the infinite intersection of space and inexplicable chance, the public spirit in individual conflicts, and the will to do good, the monistic materialistic worldview proves unhelpful to human rationality. Because it fails to stimulate the human appetite for good, it therefore can't help people decide what to do or encourage goodness in individuals or the community. These unmet spiritual needs give rise to folk belief in polytheism and animism, or the belief in various gods and spirits.

As discussed earlier, the Confucian-Legalist doctrine of the Dong Zhongshu era introduced the worship of the emperor as a human god. Under this system, people still stuck to the public conventions of "Confucian" relations to address the lack of social good and public-spiritedness. But the biggest problem for Confucian theory was the emperor's fallibility despite being worshipped as divine, which destroyed the credibility of the philosophy in the minds of the intelligentsia. The dogmatism of Confucianism and its legal punishment for deviation from prescribed roles could not resolve the spiritual needs of the general public for something to worship and for a faith that would create a good society.

The people responded by developing various secular folk faiths based on polytheism, worshipping earth gods, childbirth gods, wealth gods, kitchen gods, door gods, and ancestors. This supplemented the rigidity of Confucian dogma and injected spiritual power into the individual's response to God's expectation of *human calling*. These two systems were mutually inconsistent, but for a long time they ran parallel among the Chinese intellectual elite and the general public.

When Confucianism encountered challenges in the Wei, Jin, and Northern and Southern dynasties, the rise of Daoism and the introduction of Buddhist concepts attempted to replace the spiritual void after Confucianism faded. After nearly eight centuries of dissemination, assimilation, and absorption from the second to the tenth century, Buddhism had indeed become the first true systematic religion in China. It possessed the complete elements of religion, namely, the recognition and acknowledgement of an immanent and sovereign God; the recognition of a transcendent and a *priori* other world relative to the finite nature of life in this world; the existence of creeds, precepts, and rituals for believers to follow; a systematic theory of Buddhist beliefs; a generally negotiable and coordinated organizational pattern among sects; and a dynamic system for managing their meetings.

However, when Buddhism was absorbed into the Chinese monistic mindset in the course of its spread in China, Buddha's absoluteness disappeared. He was gradually transformed into a wise teacher, similar to Confucius and Laozi, in the Zen Buddhism favored by the intellectual elite. He was reduced to a teacher of how to deal with human problems such as life and death, sadness and joy, cause and effect, and good and evil. As long as they practiced conscientiously, anyone could become a buddha.

But for the general public, a mentor who has neither infinite nor eternal characteristics couldn't satisfy their spiritual needs, so Buddha was inevitably raised to the status of a god. But he still didn't reach the absolute status of the only god. He was only a high-ranking bodhisattva among the gods and bodhisattvas in Chinese Buddhism. His powers were boundless but not absolute. There were also many similar buddhas, bodhisattvas, arhats, city gods, earth gods, and all kinds of other gods arranged in a hierarchy according to their level of power. People could harness this power, so they chose who to worship and make use of, and they decided to continue worshipping a god only if doing so benefitted them in the material world. If something didn't work, they would abandon the god without a second thought. But as people chose which gods to worship, the absoluteness of the gods was eroded, and Buddha was no exception. This was the trend of Buddha's faith after it transformed into a monistic faith in China.

Second, although the Tang Dynasty emperors mostly supported and tolerated Daoism and Buddhism, they still maintained a strong sense of vigilance and were especially alert to preventing shamans from usurping kings. Their recognition of Daoism, support of Buddhism, and chilliness toward Confucianism was not based on their own spiritual beliefs but on realistic considerations of how to benefit politically from these worldviews.[250]

The Tang emperor's promotion of Daoism was a result of 400 years of Confucianism's failure, and the rising popularity of Daoism for political ends during the Wei, Jin, and Northern and Southern dynasties. The Li family of emperors of the Tang Dynasty respected Daoism mostly because their ancestor Li Dan, who is known as Laozi, was a Daoist. Daoism was like the Mandate of Heaven for the Li family, a way to find historical legitimacy for their imperial status. The Tang emperors supported Buddhism because it had grown in popularity since the time of divided kingdoms in the Northern and Southern dynasties, among both the intellectual elites and the general public. Supporting the development of Buddhism was conducive to gaining political support from these groups.

The reason Tang emperors discouraged Confucianism was because China's intellectual elite, ever since the Wei, Jin, and Northern and Southern dynasties, generally attributed the social suffering from the chaos, war, and disorder of the Eastern Han to Confucianism's worldly dogma. Furthermore, the Confucian idea of the emperor's divine status led to unrealistic demands on his behavior. Thus their attitude helped to cement political stability.

But on the pragmatic side of things, emperors of the Tang Dynasty still practiced the Confucian theory of honoring the emperor as the supreme Son of Heaven and the sacred ritual of sacrificing to Heaven, which was only to be performed by the emperor. The Tang emperors didn't introduce Daoism and Buddhism into the country's primary ceremonial systems. On the contrary, in 738 the Tang Dynasty completed the compilation of the *National Ceremonies*. During major national ceremonies such as "sacrifice day" and "altar day," Dong Zhongshu's norms were maintained. Only when a royal child was born, married, or died, was the ritual aspect of Buddhism introduced in order to fill the void left for the spirit before birth and after death in Confucianism.

This kind of pragmatic approach to religious tolerance, as opposed to choosing a spiritual faith according to one's inclination, is particular to China's cultural tradition of a monistic, material worldview. It marked a crucial difference from contemporaneous European monarchs, whose hearts first belonged to the spiritual world of God and Christ's grace, and then translated that into a dualistic approach to political power and state governance.

In the middle to late Tang Dynasty, the emperor issued a number of national laws restricting the expansion of Buddhist organizations. They forced Buddhism, Daoism, and Confucianism to return to the realm of Chinese monism. Either subjects prostrated themselves at the feet of the human-god emperor and worshipped imperial power, or they had to flee to the wilderness, disappearing out of its reach. Under these ridiculous conditions, supporters of Daoism and Confucianism began to compete with Buddhism and launch campaigns against it. In 845, the "extinguish Buddhism campaign"[251] promoted by Emperor Wuzong was the prelude to the inevitable end of its preeminence.

Third, starting in the middle Tang Dynasty with Xuanzong's permit system, Buddhism and Daoism were placed completely at the mercy of the government. The core of the permit system was that only monks who had obtained a license were legal. Monks without them were guilty of violations, which could lead to their being forced into secular life or sentenced to punishment. And the number of monks who received permits was limited by the government: between 0.1 and 0.8 percent of the population, and never more than 1 percent. This limited number of permits created a discrepancy between supply and demand. In essence, it brought about the problem of the secularization of Buddhism.

What made this more frightening was that a decade into the An-Shi Rebellion, taxation by local military governors intensified. The central government's finances were dire. Emperor Suzong went to great lengths to get himself out of the quagmire of the An-Shi Rebellion and restore centralized control. In order to solve his financial difficulties, he actually followed the advice of the eunuchs and increased in the number of permits at a lower price to generate revenue. From that point until the Tang fell in the early tenth century, over 150 years, emperors used these sorts of "permit fire-sales" to increase government revenue from time to time. This policy measure greatly accelerated the commercialization and secularization of popular Buddhism and Daoism, as well as making it more superstitious.

In order to support the development of Taoism and Buddhism during the late Northern and Southern Dynasties, the Sui Dynasty, and especially the early Tang Dynasty emperors, also periodically passed laws exempting professional monks—monks, nuns, Daoist priests, and Daoist nuns—from taxes due to the imperial court. This policy added secular incentives to adopt Buddhism and Daoism apart from actual belief. These incentives included exceptions from over-bearing Confucian requirements like fulfilling undesirable marriages arranged by parents or staying single for life after a husband's death, as well as avoiding heavy tax burdens and dangerous servitude as farmers and businessmen.

Especially in 780 AD, after Emperor Dezong gave up the originally implemented "equal land system" and "common rent regulation" and implemented instead the two-tier tax system, the appeal of buying a low-priced permit grew for businessmen. Becoming a monk not only exempted one from taxes, it also could increase one's social status. It helped enhance the legitimacy of one's business within a professional culture that discriminated against businessmen. Another more important factor was the paramilitary system that divided the country into 34 "provinces," which Emperor Suzong put in place after the An-Shi Rebellion in order to strengthen the emperor's military authority. This system resulted in more than 750,000 infantry soldiers of various provinces falling under the direct control of the emperor, together with the power of various local fiefdoms to divide the country. Add the demands from a variety of local military governors, and the number of soldiers the Tang Dynasty could raise exceeded what a community of 50 million farmers could afford. This was one of the factors that led to the decline of the Tang Dynasty. Being registered as a monk became the best means of escaping military service and the scourge of war. In this way, the abuse of the permit system came from the demand side, which furthered the secularization process of both Buddhism and Daoism.[252]

The combination of these three factors, that is, China's deeply rooted monistic worldview from the beginning of history, the emperor's political use of and extreme pragmatism toward Buddhism and Daoism, and the permit policies, sowed seeds of the destruction of Buddhism and Daoism's sacredness. It created a long-term, vulgar, market-oriented atmosphere in Buddhism and superstition in Daoism. The core issue behind the market-oriented shift was that permit fire-sales led to more and more monks, with no spiritual faith of their own, becoming monks expressly to seek material gain. This led to the top thinkers, apologists, and evangelists responsible for constructing systematic theology in Buddhism and Daoism experiencing a shrinking number of followers. They also lost access to intellectual debate and exchange in theological discussions with able thinkers.

Instead, doctrine had to adapt to this transactional atmosphere, since many followers were demanding material rather than spiritual benefits. This kept the Buddhist and Daoist faiths from seeing past the pre-existing monistic worldview into a more dualistic one. Faith quickly degenerated into philosophies of life that focus on solving problems in the material world.

Inevitably, by midway through the Tang Dynasty, many people grew up with faith in secularized versions of Buddhism and Daoism. Chinese folklore generated all manner of heavenly deities, hellish punishments in the afterlife, and mythological creatures. Traditional Chinese polytheistic beliefs, Buddhism, and Daoism were mingled together in an inconsistent mix. The result was a largely secular, multi-faith hodgepodge among the lower strata of Chinese society. This hodgepodge was deeply rooted in the rich soil of traditional monistic worldviews and beliefs in ancestor protection. It took deep root in the lower rungs of society and spread through word of mouth over tea and food. Spirits were worshipped in family ancestral homes, and incense was burned in temples with the aim of receiving blessings and aid from multiple gods. Foreign scholars have summarized these practices as "spirit worship."

In a society like China with such a large lower class, most people began their spiritual inquiries with specific real-world problems, rather than spiritual dilemmas, when they attended various ritual activities to worship spirits. It was not clear to them, nor did it matter, what the essence of Buddhism or Daoism was or what their fundamental differences were. All they cared about was the material cost of good fortune during important life events like marriages, funerals, births, illness, and disasters. In response to these material needs, a system of superstition mixed with Buddhism was invented. It involved asking for signs, reading physiognomy, divination, fortune telling, Feng Shui, cures, disaster relief, praying for security, praying to officials, praying for money, and methods for saving dead souls. So grew a complex, mystical system of religious practice among the general public in China.

This complex, mysterious religious system was very hard to trace logically to the Buddhist and Daoist faith of elite society to derive a systematic religious faith from top to bottom. So the Buddhist theology of elite society gradually diverged from the folk faith practices of the common people. In the Buddhism practiced in society, Buddha was depicted as a heavenly god like the Jade Emperor but separate from the all-powerful gods. He had three forms, "past," "present," and "future." He co-existed in a friendly manner with the Jade Emperor (believed to be the King of Heaven) and through agreements with other gods and goddesses like Guanyin, Wenshu (Mañjuśrī), Puxian (Samantabhadra), and Dizang (Kṣitigarbha), helped handle the major good and evil events of the human world. The current emperor, then, was the highest-ranking charge of the Jade Emperor in the human world. After dying, he could rise to heaven and become immortal.

The underworld, on the other hand, had a king, as well as a spirit that recorded the good and bad deeds of individual lives. Records of the existence of everyone in the world were kept with him. Good or evil deeds extended or shortened a person's existence. When a person's time came, Yaksha, a broad class of nature-spirits, were sent to claim their life, and they died. Then in the underworld they were punished or reborn according to their earthly deeds. The details of how each situation was handled are complicated, unwieldly, and contradictory. In the end, belief in the afterlife took the form of the duality of Heaven and Hell, which is easy for those with a monistic view to understand. The governance structure of heaven and earth was depicted as being identical to the Confucian-Legalist bureaucratic structure of the human-god emperors. But the evil, corruption, and hypocrisy of the emperor and bureaucracy was removed. This was a highly idealized government and had the advantage of persuading people to do good for the sake of the "yin virtue" in the afterlife and for the next generation. Its disadvantage was that it opened the door to all kinds of superstitions and scams, thereby increasing superstition among the lower classes.[253]

Daoist believers, on the other hand, were interpreted as skilled, mysterious masters who could cure diseases and extend their lives through alchemy and other spiritual practices. They lived in inaccessible places, among the clouds and misty mountains. They drank the wind, sailed on the wind, and soared in the clouds. Some were rumored to live to 800 or even 1,000 years. They could exorcise demons with spells and bring people back to life. These mysterious Daoist masters had supernatural power over all things. With immortal wind, freedom of form, going and coming without a trace, they were the spiritual exiles of a society that longed for freedom under millennia of Chinese imperial supremacy and Confucian doctrine. These beliefs about Daoist masters were the most extreme and illogical products of the imagination in a monistic worldview. While they did encourage people to desire and seek individual freedom, they also opened the door to a wide variety of quackery and fraud. Out of over 20 Tang emperors, at least five were deceived by these Daoist masters' superstitions and were poisoned to death using longevity pills.[254]

As for the set of beliefs founded by the Buddha, they helped people move toward the divine and search for absolute truth. Laozi's *Daodejing* exhorted people to search for virtue and cultivate the natural way of life hidden behind worldly desires and concepts, yet they too disappeared into a sea of superstitions. This great loss resulted from more than 200 years of chaos in the late Tang Dynasty and the following period of the Five Dynasties and Ten Kingdoms. Yet this affliction prepared the necessary political soil for Confucians to regroup, innovate, and make a comeback in the guise of Neo-Confucianism, i.e., science and psychology, following Dong Zhongshu.

Historians recognize the An-Shi Rebellion as the turning point that heralded the decline of the Tang Dynasty's prosperity. It took place in the middle of the Tang Dynasty during the reign of Emperor Xuanzong, when local military leaders An Lushan and Shi Siming rebelled. On the surface, it was caused by Xuanzong's love for Yang Guifei, a famously beautiful concubine, and neglect of politics, so that the Yang family took political advantage of him. Closer examination reveals that this situation only provided a historical opportunity for An and Shi to seize. The political system of the Tang Dynasty was designed to emphasize the privileges of the Emperor's and generals' families, leading to more and more cliques of powerful families. They represented their own vested interests, consuming more and more of society's resources, increasing the tax burden on the lower classes, and blocking the rise and movement of new social forces. The percentage of tax revenue that the imperial family consumed annually during the reign of Emperor Taizong was well under 8 percent. During the reign of Wu Zetian and Zhongzong, it rose to 15 percent and peaked at well over 15 percent during Emperor Xuanzong's reign. Other powerful families followed their examples, increasing the indulgence and corruption of the entire upper class.

In the early Tang Dynasty, a system called "tenant transfer" took back the land that the elderly were unable to cultivate and regularly redistributed it to the young, ensuring that the social structure of subsistence farming continued to be the mainstay of government revenue. It also effectively promoted population growth and the reclamation of easy-to-cultivate land, basically ensuring that tax revenue could meet the luxurious expenditures of the upper class and the public needs of the state. As the emperor and royal families expanded, the number of political, military, and aristocratic families also rapidly expanded. When easy land reclamation was developed, the Tang population grew from less than 20 million in the early days to 60 million.

The Tang Dynasty's glory was not only in its abundant population and land, but also in the majestic temples and palaces built all over, thanks to agricultural surplus. Later, however, the highly logical tenant transfer system, developed early on and guaranteeing independent farmers' interests and dynastic revenue, came to an end. The growing population could no longer be assigned to reclaimed land, and the original powerful families—and some new ones—continued to benefit from natural and man-made disasters to buy the land that had belonged to independent famers. They then rented it to the original farmers to earn extra income and maintain their extravagant lives. Each local warlord gradually learned to use the army they maintained, the farmers on their land, and other methods to shift their tax burdens downward, and reduce their payments to the national treasury.

The emperor's power gradually eroded in the face of compromises with local warlords, royal relatives, noble clans, and influential eunuchs. It was no longer feasible to take land back from strong families and distribute them to new farmers, so as the proportion of independent farmers fell sharply, the proportion of tenant farmers rose. Taxes that were originally paid to the emperor were increasingly converted into rent flowing into the pockets of royal relatives and aristocrats. Tax revenue sources for the emperor were increasingly drying up. Many emperors didn't understand the logic of what was happening. They only knew administrative methods to increase tax sources. But tax increases by the emperor were exacerbated at every level before finally becoming the burden of tenant farmers. In years of severe droughts and floods in China's particularly monsoon-prone climate, the large group of tenant farmers who had to bear the heavy burden of exploitation had no way to survive, which resulted in many abandoning their land or getting evicted. A new social class rapidly emerged—landless vagrants. As a result, the whole society would eventually lose its safety baseline and become unstable. The An-Shi Rebellion occurred against such a historical backdrop.

After the rebellion, the emperors Suzong and Xianzong of Tang made several attempts to restore the former glory of the empire. However, the 34 military fortification systems based on the lessons learned during the rebellion accelerated the number of soldiers raised by the empire. This in fact further increased the empire's demand for taxes, which in turn expanded the space of possibilities for military conquest and armed rebellion by local warlords.

After the An-Shi Rebellion, Buddhism and Daoism became more secular and superstitious, and the use of such superstition to cheat people out of their money led to the emergence of charlatans and a chaotic spiritual industry. The Tang Dynasty entered the inevitable stage of decline in China's historical cycles, until it finally reached its end, giving way to the Five Dynasties and Ten Kingdoms period of war and chaos and social conflict. This decline led to immense suffering and loss of life—the population fell from more than 60 million people at the height of the Tang Dynasty to about 20 million. By the end of the period of the Five Dynasties and Ten Kingdoms, which saw 200 years of war, the population further declined to about 15 million people. The scene was of utter, haunted desolation.[255]

SECTION 4: CONFUCIANISM'S POLYTHEISTIC TRANSFORMATION AFTER THE SONG DYNASTY AND THE PUZZLE OF CHINESE DECLINE

After the mid-Tang Dynasty, Confucians regrouped. They fought to revive Confucianism and, with it, the hegemonic control of a human-god emperor. To this end, they integrated Buddhism and Daoism into "Song-Ming Confucianism," introducing a new "Confucianized" socio-political paradigm of "imperial gods and divine officials."

Han Yu (768–824 AD) and Liu Zongyuan (773–819 AD) were the two Confucian scholars and court officials who took the lead in reviving Confucianism by launching the Classical Prose Movement.[256] On the surface, this literary movement disparaged the popular "parallel-writing" literature of the time, which required the consideration of textual counterpoint, rhyme and jingles, and instead advocated a return to the ancient prose literary movement of pre-Qin literature, which placed emphasis on meaning and reasoning. However, this was just a thin cover for a tactful and clever attempt to unseat Buddhism and Daoism and re-establish Confucian orthodoxy.

Liu Zongyuan, who lived during the early ninth century under Tang Dynasty Emperor Shunzong, participated in the failed 180-day reform of Wang Shuwen, an attempt by imperial Confucians to replace the system of military management with Confucianism. Han Yu, for his part, was demoted from assistant minister in the criminal department to prefectural governor of Chaozhou in 819, because he opposed Emperor Xianzong's reception of Buddha's bones, recounted in his famous *On Buddha's Bones*. He narrowly avoided execution.

On Buddha's Bones was essentially a public expression of the deep frustration of Confucians, who had been marginalized for 600 years since the Wei, Jin, and Northern and Southern dynasties. Confucian scholars were nostalgic for the post-Dong Zhongshu Han Dynasty, the glory days that they enjoyed as the uniquely powerful assistants to the emperor, the only human god. Under the Tang Dynasty, they faced the rule of military men and governors, as well as the widespread popularity of Buddhism and Daoism among the common people. Confucians could barely contemplate, let alone criticize the faults of the emperor and his military governors. That meant they could only divert their energies to compete against Buddhism on the spiritual field.

In fact, Han Yu did not understand Buddhism at all. In his essay, using the analogical reasoning so typical of Chinese philosophy, he argued that Buddhism came from a barbarian land, not China. He pointed out that the Five Emperors of ancient China, King Wen of Zhou and Emperor Wu of Zhou all lived a long time, at least 90 or even 100 years, and not because they had faith in Buddha. Buddhism began during the reign of Emperor Ming of Han, but he reigned for only 18 years. Emperor Wu of Liang was the most devout Buddhist, but he ruled for just 48 years before being forced to starve to death by the usurping general Hou Jing, and the State of Liang died with him. For Han Yu, this showed that Buddhism shortens lives and brings about disasters. "Wise emperor, why believe in this Buddhism that will bring you a shorter life and ruin your country?" he asked. Moreover, he argued that Buddha's bones were nothing more than bones of the dead—ominous objects. Receiving them and placing them in the palace would be an ill omen. He wrote, "These actions of yours make me feel ashamed. The proper thing to do is to place the bones of the dead in water and fire to protect the living. If some disaster comes, blame it on me."

Naturally, Han Yu's statements enraged Emperor Xianzong, because they subtly manipulated ancient legends of imperial China and drew analogies with the fate of arbitrarily selected Chinese emperors who ruled after Buddhism was introduced in China. His conclusion, that Buddhism brings misfortune to Chinese emperors, lacked logic. His philosophical understanding of Buddhism was superficial. In fact, what he was against was not Buddhism itself, but the superstitious trust placed in theology, rituals, and pilgrimages—incidentally three components in almost all human religions. But were the tedious ceremonies and worship of ancestral spirits and gods in Confucianism less superstitious and absurd than the Buddhist bone ceremony? If not, then why didn't Han Yu condemn Confucian superstition instead of praising it? The only reason left was that Buddhism came from outside China, while Confucianism was homegrown. If being homegrown is what matters, Daoism and Mohism are also homegrown. Why was Confucian theory and etiquette ethical and true or Confucians the only ones that could help the emperor rule the country? Obviously, Han Yu's position was far-fetched and his argument thin. He wasn't after the truth, but political power as a Confucian. The strange thing was that Han Yu became a model for Chinese Confucian intellectuals for a thousand years because of *On Buddha's Bones*. While it lacked logic, it proved very persuasive and became a classic, which is truly incredible.

In the mid-to-late Tang Dynasty, Han Yu and Liu Zongyuan were the standard bearers of Confucian revival. In addition to leading the Eight Masters of the Tang and Song in the Classical Prose Movement, they achieved brilliant works in Song poetry and strategic prose. However, they didn't make any substantial contribution to the revival of Confucianism or go beyond the Han Dynasty's Confucian-Legalist system formed by Dong Zhongshu's mixture of Daoist and Legalist theories.[257]

In 960 AD, after the 200 years of political turmoil and war of the late Tang Dynasty, the last commander of the palace guards of the Later Zhou of the Five Dynasties and Ten Kingdoms Period, Zhao Kuangyin, planned and staged the famous Chen Qiao Mutiny south of the capital in Kaifeng. Zhao's subordinates "forced" him to put on the golden robes of the emperor. After Zhao Kuangyin declined three times, he "reluctantly accepted public opinion" and announced to the world that he was replacing Emperor Gong of the Zhou, becoming Emperor Taizu of the Great Song. The system of military governorships of the late Tang had greatly diminished imperial power. Furthermore, rebel warfare and disputes among the warlords of the Five Dynasties and Ten Kingdoms also highlighted the dangers of increasing the power of military men, especially since the emperor's position came from a military coup – the Chen Qiao Mutiny. Fearing that a military commander would one day use violence to seize power, Emperor Taizu decided to abandon the Tang military system and explore the possibility of a civil servant system in the Song.

So Emperor Taizu put his advisor Zhao Pu's plan into action in the incident known as "defanging the military over wine." The plan was simple, yet moving: at a banquet he gave, Emperor Taizu burst into tears, saying he had spent many sleepless nights in worry since he assumed the position of emperor. He recounted his nightmares that one day, one of the military generals would kill him at a banquet and he would be left to rot in the open air. No matter how much the generals swore eternal loyalty, Emperor Taizu claimed he had no peace of mind, and the generals were forced to ask him what would restore it. Taizu's answer was that they should give up their military power and become local officials, allowing military power to be handled by civil servants. Taizu's frank conversation and vulnerability over wine reduced the generals to tears as they wept together and reached a covenant. As a result, the military generals, on whom Taizu relied to gain power, agreed to give up their arms and their military power and work as local officials. From then on, both civil officials of the court and new generals were appointed as civil servants through the new imperial examination. Emperor Taizu couldn't have predicted that this scheme would have such a significant and far-reaching effect on the political and economic Confucian revival of the Song Dynasty.[258]

Previously, generals were selected through the life-or-death battles in war. Civil servants, on the other hand, were selected through the ability to write essays. This was the talent pipeline for China and much of human history for thousands of years. Warriors focused on courage, officials on stratagems. Emperor Taizu asked the first generation of courageous generals to enter local government. After this generation, everyone was selected through the essays they wrote, whether civil servants at court or military commanders at the border. However, this resulted in talent deficit. To solve it, the Song Dynasty had to expand the scale of the civil and military imperial examinations of the early Tang Dynasty under Empress Zetian and improve their talent selection operations.

The education and imperial examination system reached an unprecedented level of development in the Song Dynasty. Emperor Taizu ruled for 17 years, establishing the basis of the civil servant political system; his brother Emperor Taizong (Zhao Kuangyi) ruled for 21 years and his son Emperor Zhenzong for 25 years, further consolidating the civilian service regime. The Song Dynasty experienced 60 years of peace. The values and cultural habits of this civil service examination system were hard to shake.

The characteristics of this civil servant system were:

First, nearly 100 percent of the top civil servants in the Song Dynasty came through the imperial examination system, compared with less than 10 percent during the Tang Dynasty. It was unthinkable for someone without exam qualifications to hold a civil service job close to the emperor, let alone reach a higher position.

Second, Tang Dynasty military commanders were assessed on their merits alone, regardless of origin. The most important criterion for Song military commanders was passing the examinations and being awarded either the military equivalent wujinshi (censor) or wujuren (martial censor) degrees.

Third, less than 15 percent of the hundreds of thousands of officials in the entire Tang bureaucratic system passed the imperial examinations, while 40 percent of the 1 million officials of the Song bureaucratic system did. Later this number rose to 70 percent. The reality was, if anyone wanted to achieve a high socio-economic status in the Song Dynasty, their only option was to take the imperial examinations.

Fourth, the entire examination process was quickly standardized to direct the flow of talent from the provinces to the palace. *Xiucai* and *Gongsheng* were selected from the qualifying exams of *Xianshi* (county exams) or *Gongshi* (tributary exams), enabling them to take the exam at the township level (*Xiangshi*). *Juren* were selected from *Xiangshi*, and went onto participate in the *Huishi* (municipal exams) or *Shengshi* (provincial exams), which picked

Jinshi (advanced scholars). Of all the *Jinshi*, the top three were selected by a palace test personally attended by the emperor and ranked as *Zhuang Yuan* (top scholar), *Bang Yan* (runner-up), and *Tan Hua* (third place). Succeeding at the exams meant a high rank, a good salary, and family honor. As society was divided into Confucian scholars and commoners, to fail was to be forever relegated to the lower rungs of society. Succeeding in the Song imperial examinations was likened to a "carp jumping the dragon gate," meaning that doing so could make a nobody into someone famous overnight.

Fifth, this civil service system that selected talent based on essays created China's unique education system. A large number of *Xiucai* and *Gongsheng* entered a system of private schools supplemented by official learning that cultivated talent for the civil service examination. The subjects of the examination were mostly Confucian classics, namely the *Four Books* and *Five Classics*, *Governing Policy*, and *Writing Poetry*. In general, the subjects studied were Chinese literature and Confucian ethics.[259] Nothing was included, however, that resembled the intellectual and methodological foundations of the scientific disciplines of arithmetic, geometry, astronomy, or logic—as pioneered in Western Europe since the time of the Christian Church in the Roman Empire.

The civil service system in the Song Dynasty was not just about the selection of a large number of civil servants who had to pass exams on Confucian classics. It was also about forming an imperial ideology, based on the premise of the emperor's supreme glory and power on earth, that permeated the interactions between the emperor and civil servants at all levels. It established a standardized administrative system with the emperor at the top, making decisions publicly in the great hall. And it formed the unique governance system of the Song in which military power was held by the emperor and civil servants to prevent it from becoming concentrated into the hands of the military, like during the Tang Dynasty. Early in the Song Dynasty, during the reigns of Emperors Taizu and Taizong, the civil service was divided into three departments, Zhongshu Sheng (the Secretariat), Shangshu Sheng (the Department of State Affairs), and Menxia Sheng (the Chancellery) for the circulation and recording of official documents, and for accountability. In the medium term, it developed into a system of division of labor and constraints in which the Secretariat and the Chancellery were at the center of administrative affairs, the Shumi Yuan (the Bureau of Military Affairs) was in charge of military forces, and the Yushi Tai (the Censorate) oversaw all the officials. One evidence of the effectiveness of these systems is the fact that typography was invented during the Song Dynasty, 500 years earlier than in Europe. The Song truly brought the Confucian civil service system to new heights. Their written laws and regulations, circulation of official documents, and records management were surprisingly sophisticated for an agrarian civilization.

With the Song Dynasty, the status of officials and Confucianism, which had faded in the 800 years since the end of the Eastern Han Dynasty, was restored. Yet without the unique integration, development, and influence of Buddhist and Daoist beliefs in China during these years, it would've been impossible to restore the political monopoly Confucianism had during its Han Dynasty heyday, when "a hundred schools of thought were dismissed for Confucianism." A number of Confucian revivals emerged, resulting in a significant flourishing in the history of Chinese thought. These were led by the likes of Shao Yong, Zhou Dunyi, Zhang Zai, Cheng Yi, Cheng Hao, Lu Jiuyuan, and Wang Yangming of the Ming Dynasty. The great synthesizer was certainly Zhu Xi of Song Dynasty. This new Confucianism was known to scholars both at home and abroad as "Song-Ming Confucianism."[260]

There were many differences among Song-Ming Confucians. The Cheng-Zhu school, which included Shao Yong, Zhou Dunyi, Zhang Zai, Cheng Yi, Cheng Hao, and Zhu Xi, emphasized the correspondence between *li* (reason) and *qi* (energy), two apparent aspects of natural and humanist philosophy. But it was the Xinxue ("Heartmind") school of Lu Jiuyuan and Wang Yangming that truly embodied the essence of Song-Ming Confucianism. The Xinxue school recognized the importance and sanctity of "Heaven's reason" but didn't recognize the complete dualism of *li* and *qi*. They believed that the universe was their heartmind (*xin*), and that good and evil also come from it. Without mental self-cultivation and practice, it ceases to exist, and Heaven's reason becomes empty hypocrisy. Clearly, Song-Ming Confucianism is a philosophy that fundamentally resides in the monistic, visible dichotomy of the Confucian frame.

This dichotomy is the key difference between the Xinxue and Cheng-Zhu schools. Cheng-Zhu school Confucians like Cheng Yi and Cheng Hao were relatively focused on discussing the relationship between *li* and *qi*. Their understanding of *li* was closer to the "the way of Nature," and their understanding of Heaven's reason closer to natural absolute truth. As such, it actually resembled the ancient Greek philosophy of Socrates, with the metaphysical concept of Heaven's reason as its point of departure. In the end, the relationship between humans and society was still determined by the physical human perspective and other levels of Confucian ethics. Meanwhile, Zhu Xi's conception of Heaven's reason was purely concerned with ethical and moral standards that corresponded to human desire. He was not interested in the discussion of the correspondence between *li* and *qi*. In that sense, his view was closer to the late period of post-Socratic practical humanist philosophy.[261]

Setting aside the differences among Song-Ming Confucians for a moment, they do share common features from the standpoint of philosophy. One thousand years after Dong Zhongshu integrated Confucianism with Legalism, Daoism, and Mohism, Song-Ming Confucianism further integrated it with other philosophies—namely Buddhism and Daoism as they had developed over the past 700 years. They completely and systematically transformed the Confucian monistic worldview into a Chinese-style dualistic worldview. The core of this worldview was recognizing both the invisible world with its pre-existing and transcendental nature, and the tangible, visible world in relation to it.

Song-Ming Confucians believed that the visible world is composed of the "ten thousand things" (that is, all things), and each thing is composed of *qi*. *Qi* gathers and things are formed, *qi* disperses, and things are destroyed. Outside the physical world there exists an invisible world we can't see or touch. This invisible world is governed by *li*. *Li* is the state of the invisible world, especially in line with Heaven's reason. It is the determining factor in the tangible world's *qi*. It not only determines the *qi* that constitutes all things and its own movement in the invisible world, it also decides how people should act, so that Heaven and earth are in accord, and Heaven and mankind are united. The order in which things and people operate must obey Heaven's reason. If the emperor who represents Heaven thinks, speaks, or acts against it, the order of heaven and mankind will be upset and give rise to disasters and calamities and untold human suffering, as the emperor and his people suffer the wrath of Heaven.

So what is Heaven's reason? It consists of "the three outlines and the five constants:" the balance of yin and yang, the order of the four seasons, the universe in perfect order and harmony, in which everyone and everything is in its place: heaven and earth, ruler and subject, father and son, husband and wife, older brother and younger brother. People are aligned with Heaven's reason when they know their roles in the social hierarchy and fulfill them, complying with the law no matter what. The core message of Confucianism on the question of *human duty* was still the same as it was from the times of Confucius and Mencius to Dong Zhongshu and Zhu Xi. People must be aware of, practice, and be reminded of their roles in society, following them in dealing with others. These norms and roles became the most important unwritten rules in China and the most fundamental guarantee of social order and peace.

These unwritten rules of Confucianism are not justified by a personal God who created the world and made all humans equal, requiring moral behavior from human beings. Rather, the rules are formulated by the upper levels of society and imposed on the lower classes. Zhu Xi thought the "sages" and "gentlemen" among Confucian scholars could easily divine Heaven's reason, while ordinary people were often driven by desires that brought on the evils of society. Ordinary people were particularly vulnerable to social influences that destroyed their innate goodness and increased their desires for excess.

Excessive desire often drives people to overstep their given roles, abandon the rituals their roles require, and transgress expected social behaviors. People become unfilial, covetous, and selfish, even committing serious crimes. Finally, as the ritual order disintegrates, society falls out of balance, and the world descends into chaos. Confucians like Zhu Xi recommended that everyone adhere unwaveringly to "cherishing Heaven's reason and eliminating desire." Only then could everyone return to the roles and norms of Confucian ethics, following its guidelines and forming good habits. Recognizing and accepting the thousand commands of Confucianism was the way to reach a state of joy that was neither transgressive nor driven by desire. If Confucians could systematically study the new Confucianism, believing in its tenets of ritual and religion and practicing them consistently across time, society as a whole could realize the ultimate ideal of Confucianism, operating smoothly and peacefully in a respectful way according to the ritual order.

Of course, according to Song-Ming Confucianism, Heaven's reason does not see people as equal. The lower strata of society are more full of desire and has less access to Heaven's reason, tending more toward evil. The upper strata control their desires and so more easily accesses Heaven's reason, tending to do good.[262] The Christian faith, on the other hand, teaches that whether king, noble, or commoner, all people were created by God, so they are equally sinners who tend to do evil. The solution is for them to orient themselves toward God in order to realize this about their nature and change their behavior to match God's expectations. The difference between the two philosophies is obvious.

Also obvious is the fact that Song-Ming Confucians like Zhu Xi, Cheng Yi, Cheng Hao, Zhou Dunyi, and others integrated Buddhism and Daoism into their philosophy. The concept of *qi* is a fundamentally Daoist idea most prevalent in the Tang and Song dynasties. It's a Daoist metaphysical concept that entered Daoist physics in practical self-cultivation techniques. The concept of *li* is about the forces and principles at work within matter, basically borrowed from the Buddhist concepts of "evil karma," "good karma," and "dharma." It's largely just another synonym for the unutterable *Dao* of Laozi that lies beneath the world of phenomena. This classification and reasoning behind the tangible and intangible worlds are an apparent misappropriation of Buddhist cosmology. In one sense, after 1,700 years of Confucianism—from Confucius through Mencius and Dong Zhongshu, to Zhu Xi's great integrations of Legalist, Daoist, and Buddhist theory and concepts into Song-Ming Confucianism—Confucians were finally able to follow Laozi into the framework of naturalism.

Many Western scholars have a high opinion of Song-Ming Confucianism, in particular the so-called dualism of Cheng Yi and Cheng Hao's *li* and *qi*. But its philosophical achievement is at best at the level of the Milesian School of pre-Socratic Greece. Some of their views are very similar to Anaximander of the Milesian School, who thought that the visible world was made up of energy. Energy accumulates as life; energy disperses in death. Only the *li* behind everything in the natural world is constant. It dominates the physical world made up of energy.

But none of the Song-Ming Confucians after Cheng Hao and Chang Yi discussed the material composition of the universe. The reason is that Chinese Confucians and Legalists were focused solely on social issues since the beginning of the Spring and Autumn and Warring States periods, with no interest in nature at all. Cheng Hao and Cheng Yi's discussion of the dualistic opposition between *li* and *qi* was the first Confucian discussion of the opposition between spirit and matter. However, as Zhu Xi steered Confucianism into the discussion of the relative nature of Heaven's reason and human desire—and the Chinese imperial examinations and education continued to omit mathematics, astronomy, and technology—the discussion of *li* and *qi* initiated by Cheng Hao and Cheng Yi quickly faded from Song-Ming Confucianism.

China had long been left behind by the world's leading mathematicians, astronomers, and other technological inventors. After Mozi, China lost the historical opportunity to discuss philosophical problems. And the only "absolute truth" put forth by the Northern Song Dynasty, its concept of Heaven's reason, was still somewhat relative. There was no observation and discussion of the natural laws of the material world, no involvement and protection by the one God who created the laws of nature. Only the dogmatic ethical codes of Confucius and Mencius nominally encoded absolute truth in the form of Heaven's reason. The original opposition of qi and human desire in Heaven's reason became lost in the vast space of the imagination of natural law in its common opposition between the material world and human society. All that was left was common human desire, this mutual reference point for human ethics. Heaven's reason lost the absolute truth that drives everything. Its only significance was in the Emperor's and his Confucian advisors' power to define it. Ordinary people had to follow this order, and the role of the individual was stipulated by Confucian ethics. The rules governing the relationships between leader and follower, ruler and ruled could not be subverted, could not be questioned, could not be changed. Individuals were insignificant, and "all things," or material matter, were neglected and disposable.

Ancient Greek philosophers, on the other hand—from the natural philosophy of the Milesian School to the Pythagorean School to the Elias School and finally to the great masters Socrates, Plato, and Aristotle—sought to define the public order beyond the world of phenomena, while also seeking the eternal and sacred that lay behind the evolution of individual ideas. They sought public harmony in this eternal sacred order as well as in its tension with individual freedom, not wanting individuals to be slaves to social roles. This is vastly different from Song-Ming Confucianism, so it's impossible to confuse Song-Min Confucianism's "dualism" with the dualistic worldview of ancient Greek philosophy and Judeo-Christian theology. If the latter had a dualistic worldview, then the former had only a dichotomy within material monism.[263]

The dropping of *qi* from Zhu Xi's Song-Ming Confucianism reflected the confusion and ambiguity in the definition of *li* and *qi* during the Song Dynasty. Some scholars thought *qi* and *li* were the same thing, which brought on the birth of Song-Ming Xinxue ("Heartmind"). The famous Song Dynasty Confucian Lu Jiuyuan and the famous Ming Dynasty Xinxue philosopher Wang Yangming (1472—1529 AD) are the main figures in Song-Ming Xinxue. Song-Ming Xinxue was a branch of the new Confucianism, advocating Heaven's reason. Their main difference with Cheng-Zhu Confucianism was in their beliefs of how Heaven's reason should be propagated and human desire subdued,[264] in other words, how one could conform to Heaven's reason and walk the path of saints. These new Confucians' disputes were similar to disagreements among different sects of Buddhism about the path to becoming a buddha.

Zhu Xi and his followers believed the path to sainthood involved extensive reading of the classics and careful examination of things in order to discover Heaven's reason; Lu Jiuyuan and Wang Yangming believed this path or method led nowhere. They thought that Heaven's reason existed in the human heart—in the human conscience, or *liangzhi*. They believed this innate knowledge of goodness is immediately available if a person examines their heart. The important thing was to act according to one's conscience at all times. Following the conscience to differentiate good from evil would naturally lead to following the path of Heaven's reason. Why bother extracting it from Confucian classics?

Wang Yangming practiced Xinxue his whole life, through arduous battles with political officials, singlehandedly recruiting volunteers in Jiangxi to quell the rebellion of Zhu Chenhao, the Prince of Ning. Several times he carried out expeditions to overthrow the bandits in the mountains of Guangdong, Hubei, Hunan and Guangxi provinces, in order to restore peace. But Wang Yangming could not escape the constant vortex of partisan struggle. He was persecuted and exiled to Guizhou by the powerful eunuch Liu Jin. His efforts to quell so many rebellions left him exhausted, and he contracted tuberculosis. Knowing death was coming, he floated on a small boat on the Yangtze River in Jiangxi, waiting for the emperor to allow him to return to his hometown. In the end, he died in a lonely boat, dressed according to Song-Ming Confucian ritual requirements. Before his life lived in service to the practice of Xinxue ended, he wrote four lines of poetry to answer his followers' questions about Xinxue: "The heart in itself has no good or evil. It is the will that leads to good or evil. Conscience knows good and evil, and the ultimate goal of studying all things is to do good and remove evil."

But as Wang Yangming waited for death in a lonely boat in exile, did he really "know good and evil" or "act according to good and avoid evil?" One fears that not even Yangming's mind could come up with a logical explanation. Of course, Lu Jiuyuan and Wang Yangming themselves arrogantly wrote that "their heart was the universe," "their heart was 'Heaven's reason,'" and "the six classics are my footnotes." They were as hypocritical as the Sixth Patriarch of Zen Buddhism, who advised during the Tang Dynasty, "Don't rely on words, don't teach other. Correct the human heart, and you will become a buddha." This would reverberate from Song-Ming Confucianism onward in a China that continued to persecute Confucian intellectuals who opposed hypocrisy and ritual.

But the influence of Song-Ming Xinxue was in the end just as limited as Zen, because it required a highly developed mind and morality to be understood and practiced. Meanwhile Song-Ming Confucianism conformed to the norms of society. It had a dualistic understanding of spirit and matter. Even Matteo Ricci and other Western scholars who traveled to China to teach during the Ming Dynasty had a high opinion of Zhu Xi, because they mistakenly thought that Heaven's reason in Song-Ming Confucianism referred to absolute truth, similar to their concept of God. However, it didn't actually refer to a personal force. Only Joseph Needham realized this. Through his analysis of Chinese literature, he definitively demonstrated that there was no absolute spirit or creator in Chinese dualistic philosophy. Without it, Song-Ming Confucianism quickly fell back into the expected Confucian ethical program, which cemented the permanent political status of Confucianism and its role in Chinese education.

Song-Ming Confucianism also provided a sufficient theoretical basis for the alliance and balance between the political power of Confucian scholars and the emperor. Scholars' power lay in the view that Heaven's reason is above all and that they are the only ones who can decide what Heaven's reason is. So although they were lower in status than monarchs and had to remain loyal to them, their loyalty to rulers was not unprincipled obedience, but rather the responsibility to persuade them to implement benevolent government, to follow and defend Heaven's reason. That's why it was worth it for them to do so even if it resulted in their being slandered and persecuted. Therefore, Zhu Xi not only stressed the importance of being as "sincere, positive, trained, regulating, and governing" as Confucius, but also highlighted Mencius's concept of benevolence, so that the emperor should become a "benevolent ruler" through education, training, and persuasion. Benevolence is essentially Heaven's reason applied to the control of desires. In order to help the emperor restore justice, it was necessary to overcome "the desires of men," so that he could become a Confucian sage who "opened up peace for the world" by safeguarding Heaven's reason, distinguish himself in history, and be worshipped in the Confucian Temple as a saint.

In this way, Song-Ming Confucianism, after absorbing and integrating the core concepts of Buddhism and Daoism, again rose and continued to dominate until the end of the imperial era with the Qing Dynasty. It enforced people's social roles publicly and absolutely. Yet a fallible, mortal human must first be a self-interested, private person before they can be a public person. Each person is both a self-interested person and a public person, but if people are defined solely based on their public roles, their private selves are completely destroyed, leading to hypocrisy. This same hypocrisy was seen in Dong Zhongshu's Han Dynasty Confucianism that enshrined emperors as human gods, although they were fallible human beings.

Zhu Xi and his Song-Ming Confucianism filled the Song emperors' need for a comprehensive civil service system. The Confucian scholars and bureaucrats were the new human gods, making the emperor the new head of the pantheon and thoroughly "Confucianizing" the Confucian-Legalist practical philosophy of previous dynasties.[265] In the Han Dynasty, only Confucius was honored and worshipped, while in the Song Dynasty, Mencius was also enshrined as a Neo-Confucian saint by Emperor Shenzong at the Neo-Confucians' request so that people could offer sacrifices to him in the temple. Once this began, the creation of new Confucian saints snowballed. Next, Wang Anshi was enshrined in the Confucian temple by Emperor Huizong. Later, Confucian scholars recommended to be honored included Han Yu, Ouyang Xiu, Zhou Dunyi, Zhang Zai, Cheng Yi, Cheng Hao, Zhu Xi, and others. Apart from celebrating gods by making sacrifices to them in the Confucian temple, sacrifices were also made to Zhang Heng, Zu Chongzhi, Wang Pu, and others, about 66 people in total, who had determined the calendar and made other contributions. Additionally, civil servants Zhang Liang, Guan Zhong, Zhu Geliang, and military commanders Wu Qi, Sun Bin, Guan Yu, Wei Qing, and Li Guang made up another 72 Confucian saints.

The era of deifying Confucians and civil servants had begun, embodying the ethical paradox created by the Confucian public spirit and behavioral norms. They were placed in the Confucian temple where ceremonies were regulated by the state and where people worshipped and sacrificed. Confucian temples spread throughout the country, funded by the state. In the vast countryside, meanwhile, businessmen, landlords, or lesser gentlemen made donations and worshipped the ancestors of their clan together, which became an integral part of private and public worship in rural China. Tang Dynasty emperors attended sacrifices less than 10 times per year. By the middle of the Northern Song, the number of sacrifices rose to 48. During the reign of Emperor Shenzong of the Song Dynasty, it reached 92. There was also an unprecedented surge in reforms to the ritual system. By the time the Northern Song fell, the various revisions and redundant rules of conduct and sacrifice filled more than 500 volumes. Today, they're still exhausting to read. It's even harder to imagine practicing such etiquette and using it to constrain human behavior. The minute details of Confucian regulations and etiquette increased continuously during the Ming Dynasty, with rules for filial piety, female chastity, levirate marriage, and so on. Its repressiveness was even greater than that of the present-day Muslim Hadith.

It can be said that Confucianism doctrine became a practical religion in the context of the Song and Ming theories of patronage, enforcing cumbersome religious rituals and the practice of deifying Confucian saints. But Confucian doctrine never attempted to solve the problem of life and death, so it said nothing about the afterlife of its followers. Instead, it turned its spiritual gaze backward to the lives of the ancestors and Confucian saints that came before, creating the desire for lasting fame of this sort in the present day, which could be earned by compelling one's inferiors to obey dry, unspiritual commandments. There was absolutely no way to enter the spiritual realm where these rules for humans and nature are made. In this way, it was completely different from the monotheism of the Judeo-Christian faith, which gave people freedom of choice to move in a direction guided by God. Confucianism could not provide its followers with spiritual passion and vitality. On the contrary, it provided endless commandments. It completely suppressed and cut off the passion and creativity that results from a human's response to God's standards.

Under the new Confucianism, the Song Dynasty built the world's most sophisticated polytheistic system of worship. It also built the most sophisticated civil service since the Qin Dynasty. This system had deep and wide-ranging economic and social impacts on the Song, Ming, and Qing dynasties.[266]

First, this Confucian civil and political system gave birth to a unique method of economic development in the Song Dynasty. This was manifested in large-scale migration to the south and the development of agricultural irrigation systems there, which led to greater development of agricultural infrastructure. In particular, it enhanced resilience to frequent floods and droughts in the monsoon climate, which in turn enhanced the economic and social stability of the Song agricultural civilization. Built on this foundation—along with the guidance of the Confucian materialist worldview and the Chinese people's industry, thrift, and extraordinary endurance—diverse industries of agriculture, handcrafted goods, and commerce developed. Mulberry silkworm cultivation and silk production in the south led to a flourishing textile industry. Iron smelting and ceramics were exemplary handicraft industries, and there were also advances in Chinese medicine. Together they pushed the Song economy to a new peak in prosperity. Technologies like printing, gunpowder, and the compass represented an apex of innovation, achievements which still awe many Chinese and Western scholars. The Song Dynasty population numbered 110 million at its peak, compared to 60 million in the Tang Dynasty. Nearly 80 million lived in the southern parts of the Song Dynasty, an indicator of the massive shift to the south in China's economic center of gravity during this time.

Clearly, Song-Ming Confucianism and its refined civil service system was absolutely extraordinary in its ability to create a stable social order between the Confucian scholar-officials and the general public. Family relations were also stable, and the social hierarchy enabled national mobilization to construct a system of infrastructure to prevent floods and natural disasters, which in turn enhanced economic stability. And this very stability promoted the southward migration of the population, economic development, and technological invention.

This incredible period captured the attention of Western scholar Joseph Needham, who lived in China during the early 19th century. He conducted a detailed study of technological innovations during the various phases of Chinese agricultural civilization, especially the Song and Ming dynasties, publishing his masterpieces *Science and Civilization in China* and *The Grand Titration*. These caused a great shock among Western scholars and a resurgence in the study of ancient Chinese civilizations. He also left economists, political scientists, and historians with his famous "Needham's question:" why did China, which had brought the world such technologies as paper-making, typography, gunpowder, and the compass hundreds or even thousands of years before Europe, and which had nascent capitalist industries and commerce even in the Song and Ming Dynasties, fail to develop the capitalist and scientific systems of modern civilization? It's a question worth pondering.

Secondly, this Confucian civil service greatly weakened and finally castrated the martial spirit and national vitality of Chinese civilization.[267] The spirit of this system can be seen in the Song Dynasty's poetry, painting, calligraphy, music, essays, and Confucian temple architecture. Emperors and civil servants were obsessed with chess, calligraphy, and poetry. Local gentry were trained to be mannered and refined through their education and preparation for imperial examinations. Many of the military commanders who emerged from this civil service system were also obsessed with the rhetorical exercises and feminine romanticism that was the fashion at the time. Even the great military heroes of the era, Yue Fei, Xin Qiji, and Wen Tianxiang, did not leave behind a legacy of their deeds, but of their poetry and brilliant essays. So while the number of troops increased, their combat readiness was weakening. The Confucian etiquette and edification of court officials decreased internal conflict and bloodshed.

Starting from the third emperor, Song Zhenzong, the extremely powerful Song Dynasty started to lose ground to other states, thanks to a system where civil servants led in diplomacy while military generals came second. Prime Minister Kou Jun negotiated with Cao Li, and signed the Chanyuan Treaty with the Liao, which stipulated that the Song pay the Liao a tribute of 200,000 silk, 200,000 taels of silver, and 300,000 sheep in exchange for peace, which was equivalent to 20 percent of the annual tax revenue of the Song Dynasty.

Even more unbelievably, Emperor Zhenzong, after accepting the unfavorable terms of the Chanyuan Treaty, was still enthroned on Mount Tai as a celebrated emperor by sycophantic civil servants. Once this precedent was set, the western Xia and Jin cavalry came south and obtained the same status as the Liao with regard to the prosperous Song. The Song Dynasty thus began the process of developing the southern economy and increasing taxes to pay tribute to the northern kingdoms to maintain peace. From the Northern Song Dynasty to the Southern Song Dynasty, from Kaifeng to Lin'an, territorial concessions kept getting ceded until finally the Song retreated south of the Yangtze River. Territory was at a record low, less than 2 million square kilometers. In the end, it was destroyed by the Mongolians who conquered the north.

A society in which military commanders are not given glory and recognition experiences a decrease in its combat readiness, resulting in the loss of the martial spirit among the people and the tradition of natural law in which revenge and justice are achieved through war. In addition, the dominance of the new Confucianism over the upper class was bound to exacerbate minute divisions among different schools. The rise of all kinds of "academies" began on the basis of Chinese-style blood ties and master-apprentice relationships.

The disputes between schools evolved into party struggles among allied political factions that involved the emperor, royal extended families, eunuchs, and so on, in the Song and Ming. The controversy of the "Pu deliberation dispute" is a clear example. This dispute, which occurred after Song Yingzong was elected emperor as the adopted son of Emperor Renzong, revolved around whether to call his father "Huang Bo" or "Huang Kao." The dispute involved Ouyang Xiu, Sima Guang, Cheng Yi, Cheng Hao and other literary figures and evolved into 80 years of party struggles that had no academic, political, or economic value, ultimately causing the downfall of the Northern Song Dynasty.

Looking at the role of Song-Ming Confucianism and the Confucian civil service system in Chinese history from the Song Dynasty onward, we can see that it greatly weakened the martial spirit and fighting abilities of the Han people. From the Song Dynasty to the 20th century, a period of 1,000 years, the Han people barely made any significant contributions to the expansion of China's territory. The growth of China's territory from 2 million square kilometers to 11 million square kilometers, until outer Mongolia and Lake Baikal areas were ceded, all occurred after the Mongols and Manchus subjugated the Han, while they held control of Chinese state power for almost 500 years. Song-Ming Confucianism and its civil service system left behind only cultural achievements and a record of shame in foreign relations. Though this might be distressing to read, it is worth acknowledging and pondering deeply.

Third, this Confucian system, with its deified gods, had a significant effect on society's conceptions of truth and causality, due largely to the way it logically accounted for natural disasters and omens.[268] Every year, various natural disasters, and even biological phenomena, that took place within China's borders could be categorized as good and bad omens. Good omens indicated that Heaven acknowledged the benevolence of the emperor, while bad omens were a sign of Heaven's disfavor due to the emperor's failings, termed "heavenly scourges." Rainbows; auspicious clouds; rainfall; and the appearance of tortoises, giant pythons, and phoenixes were considered good omens. Droughts; earthquakes; typhoons; and the appearance of monitor lizards, crows, locusts, and so on were considered bad omens. Good and bad omens often became an important topic of discussion among emperors and civil servants and could also become tributes to the emperor. Civil servants even wrote essays that mentioned both good and bad omens as a topic of debate, which often became the most powerful weapons to defeat other civil servants during a party struggle.

For example, during the reign of Emperor Shenzong in the Song Dynasty, when Sima Guang and other ministers opposed the Wang Anshi reforms, it was said that a long drought was a bad omen showing dissatisfaction with the reforms. If the course was not changed, the emperor would be scourged by heaven. Although Emperor Shenzong supported the Wang Anshi reforms, he then had to urge Wang Anshi to lead prayers for rain. If the prayer was not answered, then Heaven's will did not support the reforms. Wang Anshi led prayers for rain, and it came, so the reforms were implemented. Of course, after the next emperor took power, the reforms were abolished by the opposition.

This practice of dragging the highest spiritual arena of "Heaven" into muddy material causes and naming natural phenomena as scourges greatly sullied its sacredness and damaged the positivist logic of human thought. It also had a long-term destabilizing effect on the pursuit of truth and the understanding of causality. Due to the imperial civil service examination system, the development of rural education in the Song, and the promotion of literacy among the population, the constant dramas over Heaven's scourges spread from the circles of the emperor and civil servants to take root in Chinese rural culture alongside Confucianism. Through folktales and sayings such as the 24 stories of filial piety, the story of the hall of chastity, and stories about fox spirits, these values reached the common people's consciousness.

They greatly reinforced the ancestor worship of the Chinese family lineage, which merged with the popular polytheism of the time to form the intertwined pragmatic Chinese religions of Confucianism, Daoism and Buddhism. People were free to choose whatever gods and spirits best suited their current needs. This opened up a wide space for human-god transactional dealings in popular Chinese religion, as well as deepening the roots of mystical practice that acknowledge both the materialist philosophy of the visible monistic world and the belief in gods and spirits.

Fourth, Song-Ming Confucianism strengthened the collective over the individual by deifying Confucian saints within the civil service, which connected it with the realm of the gods. This revealed that it valued imperial hierarchy rather than human equality. It foregrounded the relative status between people rather than the absolute relationship between God and humanity. In this worldview, the importance of humans as individual spirits was negligible, whereas their role and place in the community was almost everything. This meant that the individual's struggle for status and material things and fame was everything. Whoever had the favor of the emperor enjoyed status and glory. Once they fell out of favor, though, they were of less value than an animal. This thinking can be seen in the Chinese literary masterpiece *Dream of the Red Chamber*. To challenge this system is high treason, and high treason results in complete excommunication from society, heaven, and earth. This way of thinking allowed people to pursue material things but shut the door on spiritual pursuits.

It gave people the freedom to ask questions, but only on a technical level.[269] Questions like "What is that?" "Who is that?" "What's that the purpose of that thing?" or "What is he doing?" were perfectly acceptable, since none of them fundamentally questioned the structures and justifications of Song-Ming Confucianism. Technical questions, questions about "how" things worked—"How does the Earth move? How does water make the waterwheel turn?" "How can someone become a buddha?" "How can we maintain Heaven's reason?" "How can one be faithful?"—were in this category and therefore allowed.

But questions that asked "why," that probed deeper, were not allowed. For example: "Why should we adhere to Confucian ethics?" "Why is the ethical, hierarchal order this way and not another way?" "Why is the human soul constant from before birth to after death?" "Why is Heaven's reason the only truth?" "If it is in fact the only truth, where is it, who is in charge of it, and why?" "Does Heaven's reason exist in the same monistic world as people? Why?" "How are rulers authorized by God? Why?"

More specific "why" questions were certainly off-limits. "Why do so many emperors authorized by God happen to be babies that are controlled by eunuchs?" "Why do so many emperors have short lives?" "Since we worship ancestors in our kinship system, why is murder most prevalent in the emperor's family?" "Since the power of the emperor is granted by Heaven and earth, why does the emperor have the right to hold ceremonies on Mount Tai and categorize various Confucian scholars as gods?" "Since Heaven's reason and the three outlines and the five constants are the core path of Confucian physics and metaphysics, why are the Song and Ming emperors who best represent them unable to maintain them well, taking part in party struggles, killing brothers, fighting rulers?" "Why did the mighty Song Dynasty keep losing land in the North, constantly retreating and eventually destroyed by an ethnic minority?" And so on and so on.

These questions were not allowed to be asked from the time of Confucius. He told the people not to ask why, but simply to follow the *Rites of Zhou*. Dong Zhongshu told them not to seek answers, but only to act according to the teachings of Confucius and the *Book of Rites*. Zhu Xi joined Mencius and Emperors Yao, Shun, Yu, Yellow, Zhuanxu, and King Wen of Zhou in telling them Heaven's reason was invisible but still existed. Ancient emperors were representatives of Heaven's reason in the human world. People didn't have to ask why, but just follow the rituals of Confucius and Mencius. The reason for this was that the roots of these problems revealed fundamental contradictions and dilemmas in Confucianism and could overthrow its assumptions and authority, threatening the political legitimacy and divine authority of the emperor and civil servants.

Thus we see Song-Ming Confucianism clearly, as it was formed by the emperor and civil servants in order to govern. Its method and logic had three features: the first was that it was a closed system. Answers were sought by looking back in time. Answers were sought from the ancestors in the same way a child immediately looks to their mother when they encounter a problem, thinking that there lie the answers to all future problems. The second was a failure to facilitate communication between people in a question-and-answer format. This made it impossible to develop a set of definitions of concepts and issues for discussions, classification, logical reasoning, and common methods of thinking and discernment. There was still an obsession with answers to questions, but if a disagreement formed, the two sides parted ways. The third was a system with a monopoly on spirituality in which the emperor and famous civil servants were above questioning. Inquisitiveness often led to punishment for the individual or collective. Thus in the thousand years under the stable monopoly of Song-Ming Confucianism, people could ask questions, but never those about the fundamental assumptions of Confucianism. Without asking "why" questions, they couldn't get to the root of the problem.[270] As this calcified over the centuries, the unique Chinese Confucianized paradigm formed.

The famous "Needham Question," then, isn't so difficult to answer. In *The Grand Titration* Needham attempted his own answer, but most people only read his *Science and Civilization* in China. Through historical comparisons and different definitions of science and technology, we can attempt to answer Needham's question ourselves.

Chinese science as detailed in *Science and Civilization in China* was really only about technology. But technology is a solution to specific problems. It solves problems of "how" and "what." Science, meanwhile, is about explanations. It doesn't solve specific problems, but it does answer "why" questions. China's Song and Ming Dynasties invented numerous technologies and solved many specific problems, but that doesn't mean they developed science. For example, China invented the compass very early, but it was only the answer to a technical question, not a scientific inquiry. A magnetic needle, which when placed in a 360-degree circle, always points 180-degrees south. To answer why the compass always points south would involve explanations and would therefore be science. Newton's law of gravity was the answer to the question, "Why do apples always fall to the ground instead of falling to the sky?" And it was precisely in order to answer the question posed by Faraday and Maxwell—"why does the compass always point south?"—that the modern scientific understanding of magnetism and electricity came to be.

Technological know-how relies on the accumulation of practical human experience in order to form an initial design for a new invention, and with more time and experience, the design is improved. The "know-why" of science relies on the ability of outstanding individuals to imagine and ask questions. Without unusual questions, especially "why" questions, there can be no scientific discoveries. The know-how of technology only solves problems in the phenomenal world; The know-why questions that science tries to answer are all problems of the invisible world.

The origins of the scientific method lie in ancient Greek natural philosophy. Both science and philosophy arose from a spiritual world with one God, so they are subject to his "laws." It's this law that greatly stimulates humanity's faith, imagination, and spirit of adventure, and in turn promotes the development of scientific inquiry, discovery, and explanation. This is the deepest reason why China, despite producing many practical technological inventions in the Song and Ming dynasties, could not produce modern science as one might expect.

Throughout the history of modern science, not to be confused with the history of technological invention, and among the more than 2,000 scientists who made significant contributions to the fields of medicine and mathematics, most were of the Judeo-Christian faith. Hardly any were Chinese. China, a country with a comparable population to Europe and the United States, whose history of ancient agricultural civilization and technological inventions is comparable to that of Europe, has made, objectively speaking, negligible contributions to modern science. The underlying reasons may be painful to consider but should nevertheless prompt reflection.[271]

SECTION 5: THE DEVELOPMENT OF CHARITIES UNDER CONFUCIANISM

Song-Ming Confucianism saw Confucians gain a monopoly as the empire's official faith. That meant that Buddhism and Daoism began a long period of exile from the halls of official faith, banished to the subconscious of the Chinese psyche. The Chinese spiritual worldview, which combines Confucianism, Daoism, and Buddhism, was firmly rooted in the monistic Chinese worldview of physical matter. It held the emperor as the supreme god, putting a limit on the sacred imagination. Buddhism and Daoism could allow for other gods, but they must submit to the emperor and canonized civil servants.[272] But once Buddhism and Daoism agreed to place Confucianism's emperor and the Confucian saints above their gods, the power, truth and goodness of their gods was degraded to the level of these powerful humans. As a result, Buddhism and Daoism could only be a refuge for mysticism and transactional religion.

In such a system of public faith, it's difficult to develop unconditional love toward strangers. There was little motivation to help the old, weak, and sick unconditionally out of compassion, like in the Christian context, with its large-scale and universal emphasis on love. This is, of course, not to say that there were no good deeds or charitable activities during the long history of China's agricultural civilization. Buddhist temples repaired roads and bridges and helped disaster victims, among other charitable acts, and these were commendable charitable activities. "Porridge sheds" set up on the main road outside the temple were the most typical way to help with famine relief.

Buddhist monks from the Northern and Southern Dynasties stopped drinking and eating meat, and they developed a system of *futian* or "field of blessings," charitable actions that could improve the shape of one's future incarnation. They referred to seven spheres of charity—such as kindness to parents, teachers, the poor, monks, etc. Charitable non-government organizations, called "Yihui" and Sheyi," were formed, where people cooperated to help the elderly, orphans, and the poor and to cure diseases, raise funds for burials, and repair wells and bridges. These civil society organizations contrasted starkly with the structures of nation, region, county, township, clan, and village of the Confucian hierarchy and were a true innovation in Chinese society.

During the Tang Dynasty, some Buddhist temples adopted orphans and took care of the elderly, and there were monks who wandered the countryside, treating maladies in local villages, performing exorcisms, and calling on spirits. Among them were a sect called "Wujincang." They advocated respecting the Buddha nature in all life, so fulfilling their charitable role in the secular world was the highest Buddhist calling. Wujincang strove to develop charitable organizations throughout the empire. They mobilized people to donate during the Spring Festival and Hungry Ghost Festivals. They used these donations to provide loans with interest, and then used the interest to repair temple buildings and aid the poor. Wujincang had a great influence from the seventh to the eight century. In the middle of the eighth century, during a fierce attack on orthodox Buddhism, Emperor Xuanzong quashed the organization.

During the Tang Dynasty, Buddhist groups had a record of establishing free hospitals and conducting free clinics. Buddhist groups' care of strangers during epidemics was impressive. They broke the Confucian norms, where benevolence and good deeds were confined to family and blood relations, bringing a universal public spirit to Chinese society. After the end of the Tang Dynasty and the beginning of the Song Dynasty, even small-scale charitable activities by Buddhist temples, like "Beitian Recovery Square," were encroached upon by the government. The empire appropriated the land and gave the monks and nuns permits, turning their work into a government-run charity and returning them to the hierarchical Confucian structure. Buddhist monastery charities were pressed to "release animals," "give medicine," "give food during disasters," and other sporadic acts of charity.

As a monistic faith, Daoism advocated a mystical spirit with a strong focus on one's inner knowledge and the infinite extension of one's life. Many Daoists achieved great heights in the practice of the golden technique, in divination, and traditional Chinese medicine. They walked their own path, healing diseases and providing relief during disasters. They did good deeds in the name of Daoism but never formed charitable organizations. Their work can be classified as good deeds, not organized charity. It represented sporadic compassion for the suffering of others rather than love and public welfare.

Confucianism didn't emphasize altruistic compassion towards others on the basis of charity or public welfare. Instead, it focused on social governance as a whole, creating public order through "rule by ritual and music." But after the Tang Dynasty, the influence of Buddhist attitudes of charity on Confucianism was undeniable. This was not only reflected in the recognition of the dualism between Heaven's reason and human desire in Song-Ming Confucianism, but also in the principle of "Be the first to worry about the world's troubles, and the last to rejoice in the world's joy," a public spirit that encapsulates *human duty*. This principle was introduced by Fan Zhongyan, the Song Dynasty politician, writer, and military strategist. He demonstrated this himself by using the wealth he accumulated to set up a public "righteousness resource" for the Fan family, which subsidized all of the bloodlines in the Fan lineage. Yet this was still family welfare rather than charity. Through the examples and long-term efforts of Fan Zhongyan, Wang Anshi, Su Shi, and other senior Confucian officials, this kind of "ancestral hall" family welfare systems based on blood ties became widespread. They were symbols of Confucian public charity and became uniquely Chinese charity organizations throughout the countryside. In China's vast rural areas, they expanded into more public roles of repairing bridges and roads, helping orphans, helping the poor, mediating in township disputes, and passing judgments according to Confucian ethics.

The spread of such organizations arose at the same time as Song-Ming Confucianism and promoted the rise of the Confucian "village learning" education movement. Wang Yangming attempted to form a "village alliance" organization between every ten households in the country to guarantee the collection of imperial taxes and promote mutual aid among neighbors. Although Song-Ming Confucianism's orderly social governance ideal was never realized, becoming lost in the vast sea of the historical inertia of ancestral worship,[273] its existence still encourages many Chinese scholars today who believe they have found fundamental similarities between Chinese and Western charity organizations. It also gives optimistic Western scholars a lot of room to imagine the development of a spirit of grassroots public welfare in Chinese society. Some Western scholars even call it an example of budding Chinese civil society.

However, comparing China's rural charity organizations, represented by "ancestral halls," "village learning," and "village alliances," with the charitable organizations in the West under Christianity is arguably erroneous. Although both exhibited the spirit of helping others, the Chinese charities were organizations where the rich gave money to help family members. There are two obvious differences:

First, in the West, charitable organizations as far back as the fourth century were promoted by the most devout Christians. They initiated the establishment of church-based charitable organizations driven by the mission to spread God's glory and love and helped thousands of patients recover from affliction and disease. Many organizations fulfilled these missions for decades or even centuries. They relied on the merit of their actions and ideas to persuade thousands of donors to join them, with a structure that distinguished leaders from donors. This core group of leaders advocated for free association among citizens, forming a path for founding more charities. At the same time, this gave birth to a system in which subsequent leaders were publicly elected by relevant industry elites.

In contrast, in China under Song-Ming Confucianism, "clan ancestral hall organizations" were established by donations from Confucian clan members who had reached the highest levels of official status. Their ancestral leaders were of course the highest officials and often the biggest donors. Leaders could only be selected from the highest officials in the next generation of the clan. Donations from other people in the clan were often passive "contributions." Even if a member had the money, they couldn't give more than the highest official, because it would be out of line with their place in the clan community's hierarchy. In the end, this kind of clan ancestral hall charities was merely another way to extend the presence of the Confucian civil service hierarchy into rural society. Its core motivation was not the altruistic impulse of charity but the desire to cement the status of individuals' identities and roles in society. Leaders could only be chosen in these charities with reference to bureaucratic politics, to ensure their alignment with the existing hierarchy.

Second, Western charities originated from a dualistic worldview in which the visible phenomenal world was separate from the invisible spiritual world, so the natural relationship between all things as well as interpersonal relationships were all subject to God and his laws. This philosophy of natural law meant that the core principle behind interpersonal relationships was Christ's sacrifice, which demonstrated God's unconditional love and forgiveness. Thus charities had a foundation in the concept of "unconditional love and forgiveness between strangers" from the very beginning, breaking the conventional barriers which kept altruism constrained by blood relationships or the need to demonstrate gratitude or revenge. At their core, Western charities were motivated by universal love.

In China, the ancestral organizations that rose in the wake of Song-Ming Confucianism began the village learning movement. These ancestral organizations were primarily based around an ancestral hall, with a clan hall and cemetery. The proportion of such organizations that set up charitable services to help the poor was very small. Their main function was still the maintenance of the order of clan ancestor worship and maintaining Confucian social roles. The charity they extended was limited to members of the clan, those related by blood. Confucian charity lacked a universal public spirit, even compared to Buddhist charities, since even its "public" spirit was actually only for those related by blood. Furthermore, they were also blatantly self-promotional organizations, meant to bolster the clans' honor and reinforce the social roles of the lower classes. They were a far cry from the kind of public spirit based on universal love that demolishes a hierarchy of inequality.

A notable shift in the history of charity in China occurred in the late Ming Dynasty. A universal charitable organization, completely different from previous clan organizations, was formed. In 1583, Matteo Ricci arrived in China, marking the introduction of modern Christian civilization to China. A considerable number of intellectuals and businessmen, such as Xu Guangqi, Li Zhizao, Yang Tingyun, were influenced by Christianity and converted. The extent to which this affected the development of Chinese charities is an interesting topic beyond the scope of this book. What is certain is that from then on, in Southern China, charitable organizations with names like "Common

Benevolence Society," "Great Benevolence Society," "Benevolence Society," "Common Good Society," "Justice Cabin," "Justice Study," "Justice House," "Justice Crossing," "Release Society," and "Good Society" gradually emerged.

These became universal charities that differed from the traditional ancestral halls by going beyond family ties. From the late Ming Dynasty to the early Qing Dynasty, the Chinese merchant class gradually broke the monopoly of the Confucian civil servants and started becoming leaders of some ancestral halls. A smaller subset of such businessmen established universal charities independent of the ancestral halls. From the hard earth of the Confucian order and ethics, rigidly rooted in blood for thousands of years,[274] grew a few sprouts of modern charitable organizations based on universal love. But charitable organizations in the truly modern sense, such as universities and hospitals, were still strongly influenced by Christianity and first funded by foreign Christians. This introduced a spirit of charity that differed from governmental and commercial organizations. Buddhism and Daoism, on the other hand, didn't improve significantly in terms of spawning and nurturing modern, large-scale philanthropic organizations.

CHAPTER 11:

Leap: humanity's second great reflection

Human faith is an essential prerequisite to truly exercising individual free will. It requires believing, on a spiritual level, in one's connection and belonging in relationship with God. This kind of faith grants access to spiritual power to fulfill the *human calling* that God expects from humans, through this faith and holy hope. But as soon as an individual begins to live out their spiritual faith and practice, they immediately find themselves in need of spiritual fellowship. This inborn need for community life moves their private, personal faith onto a public track.

In the practice of a communal public life, faith is no longer merely a logically consistent, rational relationship between humanity and God. Rather, it requires a common doctrinal understanding of the life of faith so it can become concrete in public practice. While such doctrine shapes the community spiritually, the development of places and rituals allow it to take shape in the physical realm. The work of architects, sculptors, and writers expand the community's imaginative power and sense of grandeur through the church buildings and doctrines they develop. Faith and imagination are woven into the community's rituals and practices to create a solemn, passionate, and poetic space.

This doctrinal and ritual solemnity is taken up by believers with a sense of mission and organizational power who form distinctive faith-based organizations to preach and promote the message and develop the faithful. While the goal is to achieve a more cohesive faith identity, these outstanding organizers often diverge in doctrine, ceremony, and organization. If solidified, different factions can form around these divergences in the practice of faith in communal life, which in turn can lead to communities classifying and separating themselves from each other. In this way, public identities can grow out of individual faith differences.

We can trace the progression, then, from a spiritual belief in the relationship between humanity and God to a dogmatic, ritualized, and organized practice of faith in community. This shift from personal belief to public, dogmatic religious system is significant. It is extremely dangerous to simply equate religion with faith and use that as a starting point in discussion. That's because the dogmatization of faith by religion risks discarding its deep, rational logic. It becomes trapped in dry and sterile dogma.

The ritualization of faith can leave behind the sacred passion for infinite and eternal truth, giving rise to blind impulses and superstition. Secular or religious leaders can then manipulate these impulses to create gods. They can use religion to fuel the personal desires and pride of religious leaders, which once again results in a minority enslaving the majority. Any individual's spiritual faith can fall into the fog of the material world of phenomena when the communal life of faith becomes instead a religion that produces dogma, superstition, and organized slavery. This is the very dilemma and paradox that *human calling* encountered after humanity's first reflection.

SECTION 1: NATURAL PHILOSOPHY AND THE LIE OF THE "DARK" MIDDLE AGES

After the collapse of the Roman Empire and the gradual resurgence of nation states, Christianity remained the belief of choice for understanding the relationship between humanity and God. Arguably, it had great success in most European nation states. This success was especially seen in the way spiritual reality was asserted above the secular. The absolute power of God's truth, the spiritual reality, had an almost covenantal authority over and against the secular reality, the political power of the king. This "covenant" exercised an even more countervailing effect even than the Hebrew prophets over the kings of Israel.

One way this success was reflected was in the pope's right to coronate the king of each Christian country, beginning with Charlamagne. This was part of the early Christian church system's painstaking efforts to strengthen the sanctity and universality of the Christian faith. By effectively preventing the king from using political power to set himself up as a god, the church made possible a European political civilization model where Christian authority and secular imperial power were mutually constrained.

This right of coronation exercised by the pope on behalf of God, combined with the European aristocratic and fiefdom system, greatly promoted the continuation of the political democratic spirit of the Roman aristocracy. The birth of the electoral system of "prince electors" under aristocratic political democracy is a prime example. Prior to the Glorious Revolution of 1688, no English king had been born in England for 600 years, but rather from European countries like Germany or France or Wales or Scotland. They were all elected by "prince electors," or nobles who were qualified to choose rulers. Marriage was often the prevailing strategy for the peaceful succession and transfer of royal power under this electoral system.

This distinctive political culture of prince electors, not limited to a single royal family, set Europe on a new path of political tolerance that was quite different from that of Asian monarchies dominated by familial inheritance. In Asia's political context of the emperor as a human god, violent massacres took place in court over competition for inheritance of the family throne.

Another evidence of the church's success was how well it adhered to the Christian spirit of love and forgiveness. This spirit promoted restraint in one's own behavior and the expression of unconditional love for others. Especially in those turbulent years when technological progress was slow and plagues were causing violent population fluctuations, the Christian faith promoted the public understanding of individual freedom and dignity as unique creations of God. The doctrine of humanity's divine origin laid a deep, solid, and supremely authoritative foundation for individualism, clearing the way for the subsequent liberal human values of the Renaissance and Reformation in Western Europe. At the same time, the innovation of the medieval "university" as a self-governing, public welfare organization based on Christian theology, made intellectual growth possible. Universities became communities where the collision of opposing viewpoints was normative, and the dialectical method of research and discussion rapidly took shape. The deep foundation this laid after the Renaissance and Reformation was one of methodology, logic, scientific thinking, and empirical research.

For more than a century, authors and lecturers in universities around the world have described medieval society as hopelessly dark, and the medieval Christian church as an anti-human, anti-scientific Hell on earth. They portray medieval scholastic philosophy as tedious and meaningless Christian dogma. This is certainly a great misunderstanding of this era in history and a serious misreading of a critical transition period of human civilization. In one sense, such misunderstanding should bear responsibility for the now rampant extreme liberalism and individualism, which in turn will have more far-reaching negative effects.

On the contrary, the Middle Ages were a revolutionary time. From a world history perspective, it was a revolutionary change for Christian civilization to develop, with its emphasis on love and forgiveness and voluntary devotion out of faith in Christ. The church was truly a self-governing public benefit organization, that successfully grew out of the private organization of the family and the public organization of the government. Built neither on blood ties nor mandatory taxation, it entered into public community life on a large scale with public philanthropy and inspired non-violence, peace, and compassion among people.

More than that, it catalyzed a spirit of cooperation and inquiry on the basis of free will and faith in God. Dozens of prestigious European universities such as the University of Bologna, the University of Paris, Oxford University, Cambridge University, the University of Cologne, the University of Naples, the University of Toulouse grew out of more than 30,000 Benedictine church libraries. And countless seminaries in monasteries, professorial associations, and student groups were founded in this period. All were autonomous public welfare organizations established by that era's elite thinkers and activists based on their God-given free will and voluntary dedication.

The intellectual elite of the Middle Ages shuttled between universities and research institutes to study early versions of today's natural sciences and humanities, such as theology, philosophy, mathematics, medicine, astronomy, logic, rhetoric, and music, among others. Through teaching, learning, studying, verifying, speaking, and debating, a free exchange of ideas took place. They specified concepts, methods of discussion, and analysis. This laid the first solid, scientific cornerstone for a paradigm of modern civilization where individuals are free to think independently as well as engage in public academic exchange with other thinkers.[275]

Out of these interactions between autonomous public universities and seminaries, came a new academic approach to proving the existence of God and the rationality of the faith. Theologians used logical methodology and philosophical speculation in tackling the subject, so it was not merely based on a faith claim of believers or blind worship. In contrast, Buddhism, Islam, and other written religions chiefly rely on interpreting classic texts and the faith claims of believers as rationale for their respective faiths. This academic, speculative, and analytical methodology for defending the faith was nothing less than the creation of medieval scholastic philosophy, with its roots in the apologetic debates of the Augustinian era. Anselm of Canterbury, Peter Abelard, and Thomas Aquinas were among the most iconic figures in this groundbreaking time.

The medieval scholastic philosophers differed widely in their views, but they all shared a kind of universality in terms of methodology of thought and discussion.

First, they all believed that humans could apprehend invisible realities through reason and following strict logical guidelines. This cognitive understanding beyond sensory knowledge required close adherence to logic and to the axiom "I believe, therefore I can understand."

Second, they believed that logic is a gift from God to humans to gain this non-empirical knowledge. Aristotle's logic, with inductive and deductive reasoning at its core, was part of this gift. Properly applied, his method provided a consistent criteria to logically test the results of research, discussion, writing, and analysis. If not for the widespread praise for and use of empirical philosophy, Aristotle's logic might still be lying dormant in piles of paper in Athens and Alexandria, unknown to the world. And if not for the widespread praise for Aristotle's logic and its universal application as a public method, subsequent scientific and empirical research would have been nearly impossible.

Third, in their research and speculation they looked for the "universality" in things, such as "people," "animals," "red," and so on. The universality both lies within and exists outside individual things. It is a kind of more advanced existence. Like "truth," "goodness," and "beauty" are more advanced universality and existence. Finding universalities and defining them accurately is the prerequisite for all thinking, researching, and discussion. Without these normative and foundational works of empirical philosophy, scientific and philosophical changes after the Renaissance and Reformation would have failed to come to be.

Fourth, scholastic philosophers all advocated and used an analytical teaching and writing method. The method involved first putting forth a question and then offering a variety of answers, along with a rationale for each, especially opposing answers. Only then would they declare their conclusion and support it with logical analysis. This method is precisely the same popular approach to empirical research used in higher education and scientific research today. Through the joint efforts of scholastic philosophers and theologians, they developed what they considered a perfect explanatory theology for the existence of God and the reconciliation of human reason and Christian faith. This logical methodology coupled with philosophical speculation was later called "natural theology."

Thomas Aquinas, born in 1221, was a great synthesizer in this regard. His *Summa Theologica* became a permanent epistemological monument of scholastic philosophy and natural theology. Aquinas was educated at the University of Naples and the University of Cologne. He later taught philosophy at the University of Paris until he died. He spent his whole life resolving conflicts between Aristotelian philosophy and the Christian faith. He managed to unify the two, nearly 1,000 years after Augustine completed his theological integration of Socrates and Plato's philosophy. This resulted in an ideal theological combination of Christianity and ancient Greek philosophy. It concluded humanity's first great reflection on *human calling* and at the same time formed the foundation for humanity's second great reflection on *human calling*.[276]

In Aquinas's view, there are two different kinds of knowledge. One is knowledge of the relationships between all things in nature, and the other is knowledge of the relationship between humans and society as guided by their relationship with God. Although nature and humanity are both part of God's creation, God does not care for nature in the same way he does for his children. Rather, God gives each natural creation a purpose through the laws he made, so that all things are connected by this purpose and act accordingly. Aquinas showed that human knowledge is not, as understood by earlier Christian theology, to be acquired solely by the light of God's grace. When it comes to knowledge of the natural world, people don't need to rely on God's grace. They can simply abstract, define, and draw conclusions about the universality of things through sensory observation and the exercise of free will. In the realm of nature, human understanding can achieve "rational autonomy" independently of the Christian faith, but this kind of knowing still aligns with the natural laws created by God. These laws still find their source in the grace of God, which is why this kind of study is called natural theology. When it comes to knowledge about God's absolute truth and his relationship to humanity, however, it is beyond natural human capabilities. According to Aquinas, this knowledge can only be gained through God's grace in supernatural revelation.

Although humans on their own cannot fully understand God's existence and nature, with faith, grace, and God's gift of logic, we can still apply reasoning to prove that he exists. Thomas Aquinas laid out this quest for proof in what he called the "Five Ways." First, all things in the universe have kinetic potential and therefore are in motion. Everything in motion is put into motion by a mover. And every mover is put into motion by another mover, and so on forever. But there must be a force that is the first mover. This "prime mover" is God.

Second, everything in the universe has a cause or a driving force. Like movement, causes can be traced back to other causes, and so on forever. The cause behind every other cause throughout eternal time and space is God, "the primary cause." God is not made up of finite elements, materials, or forms like every other thing in the universe. He is the pure and perfect primary cause.

Third, everything in the universe is finite and tangible, progressing inevitably through birth, change, and death. If something dies at a certain time, it cannot suddenly exist again, unless it exists through other things. So there must be an eternal, unchanging existence that keeps the birth, change, and death of all things continuing without interruption. This "eternal, unchanging existence" is God. He establishes this progression of all things as a firm and inevitable rule, enabling their continuous existence in the universe.

Fourth, all beings in the universe depend on certain conditions for their existence. If such conditions are withdrawn, they cease to exist. Beings are arranged in an order from lower to higher, but there must always be an "absolute, ultimate existence" that does not depend on any outside conditions. God, then, is this causeless cause, and his existence is the ultimate condition for the existence of other things. He exists as ultimate good and ultimate beauty without conditions.

Fifth, everything in the universe has its own specific purpose. And there is always a further purpose beyond each individual purpose. The final purpose that all purposes aim toward is God. Therefore, God, with his pure, all-wise goodness, integrates all things with their respective finite purposes into an ultimate purpose, making everything work together in an orderly manner toward an ultimate direction.[277]

God's nature as described by Aquinas' Five Ways must be pure—that is, formless—all-mighty, all-good, all-beautiful, all-true, unchanging, and eternal. Therefore, God is not affected by the world he created. He does not need to seek his creation to gain anything, because everything in the universe runs on his own laws. The only possible exception is humanity, whose sinful nature coupled with God-given free will can lead them to act in alienation from God.

Yet God provided two means for humans to apply their free will to discover his truth. They can rely on their own logic, based on his revelation, to understand and use nature. And they can rely on his grace, which is only associated with the human-God relationship, to understand how to relate to him and others in society. Through this revelation of grace, humanity receives divine direction, through faith in him, to rebuild the human-God relationship and to handle interpersonal relationships during earthly life. His goal is to move them toward life's ultimate purpose: being with God.

The grace of God's revelation does not force people toward any action but respects the free will he has given to them. They can live within God's grace as they were created to do, or they can live apart from his grace by virtue of their free choices. The offering and sacrifice of Christ, the Son of God, according to monergism, is God's plan of salvation for man. This sacrifice alone is great enough to bring about God's salvation, since humanity's sin runs so deep that it's impossible for them to redeem themselves. God is not fooled by hypocritical rhetoric, nor does he engage in cheap exchanges with humans. Only through true faith in God, and responding to his call to put repentance into action, can people cooperate with God in their relationship to other people and the created world. This approach to each encounter puts humans a holy path of life in line with the spirit of Christ's love and forgiveness,[278] and enables them to obtain salvation in a new, cooperative man-God relationship illuminated by God's grace.

Scholastic philosophy and natural theology, especially represented by Aquinas, inherited the spiritual legacy of the three great masters of ancient Greek philosophy, especially Aristotle, and systematically integrated it with the Christian faith. Scholars resurrected this ancient philosophy from its thousand-year slumber through methodologies like classification, abstraction, definition, logical reasoning, and mathematical expression of humanistic and natural philosophy. They attempted to unify human reason with the theological reason of the Christian faith. Their brilliant achievements inspired both theological creativity (accessed by God-given grace) and scientific advancement (accessed through God-given logic). The one happened in universities and the other through the creation of public science and technical societies. Both were governed by strict adherence to logic and a spirit of free debate in the public sphere. As a result, they inspired personal creativity and public solemnity, elevating *human calling* in community life to an unprecedented level.

A brief survey of Renaissance works bears this out: the massive competition to build gothic Christian churches over the course of hundreds of years, the elegant love sonnets written by poets such as Petrarch (who largely initiated the Renaissance), the wave of classical religious and humanistic paintings by artists like Leonardo Da Vinci, Michelangelo, and Raphael, and even the scientific hypotheses and rational observations of Copernicus, Galileo, Kepler, Brahe, Newton, and other great thinkers. They all reflected the public solemnity of creative and intellectual exploration within the realms of both grace and natural theology.

Without the groundwork laid by natural theology and its liberation of autonomous rationality and the logic of public research, the group achievements in the humanities and natural sciences that we take for granted today wouldn't even have a starting point. This explains why the East, with its equally profound accumulation of cultural and empirical technology, failed to create a single branch of modern natural science or logically consistent modern humanities.

Of course, it was inevitable that the long-term practice of organized religion under European integration, unification by the pope, and the influence of a sinful world would erode this solemn spirit of Christianity. Under the supreme power of the Roman church defined by Pope Gregory I and the secular expansion of papal power under Pope Gregory VII, the church's authority over secular political power reached its peak in the 13th–14th centuries. It's in this period that we tend to see the decay of the Christian church take place.

Over the thousand years while Christianity was the state religion, it became more dogmatic, ritualized, and structured. Many churches were cor-

360 | The Human Calling

rupted by too many charitable donations while more profit-seekers found their way into the church. The influence of ascetics who sincerely dedicated their life to God and Christianity gradually disappeared, replaced by bloated church organizations, corrupt clergy, and empty religious rituals and dogma that had little to do with faith. On the one hand, the pope and the complex hierarchal system of the church became more bureaucratic and corrupt, so that the general populace began to feel that the Christian faith was being used by the church to oppress believers. On the other hand, it also aggravated the conflict and confrontation between secular monarchal governance and church power, seen most clearly in the economic and political ebb and flow of the Holy Roman Empire and the Frankish Empire.

In the early 14th century, the conflict between Pope Boniface VIII and King Philip IV of France set off a 70-year period in which the pope was exiled in France, known as the "Babylonian Captivity of the Papacy." The secular French government overrode the papacy, rigging at least eight elections of French-only popes. They then subjugated them under the French monarchy and exiled them in Avignon. It was not until 1376 that the pope was able to return to Rome. But by then, the continuous intervention of French secular powers had split the Christian church. The split lasted for 40 years with two popes—one in Rome and one in Avignon. At one low point in the ridiculous conflict, there were three popes.

Only when the University of Paris and other public forces convened the Ecumenical Council of Constance—meeting 45 times from 1414–1418—was an agreement reached. It forced the old popes manipulated by French politicians to abdicate and led to a unified papacy elected by newly established procedures. In 1420, the Roman Catholic Church returned to firmly settle again in Rome. The power of the pope was restricted by the resolutions of the Council of Constance and a transparent ecumenical conference became the conventional, supreme church mechanism for meetings and resolutions.

Yet, the 70-year "Babylonian Captivity" and the 40-year Great Western Schism took a heavy toll on the perceived authority of both the pope and the Roman church across Europe. France's interference with the selection of bishops at all levels only furthered the church's secularization and corruption. Positions were bought and sold, faculty members committed adultery and hoarded ill-begotten money, and the church sold indulgences and "holy objects" to the faithful. The Christian faith had sunk into secular sin.

After returning to Rome, the popes tried to revive the Roman Catholic Church by strengthening its dogmas and rituals, tightening up its organizational control, and building larger-scale churches. While their goal was to demonstrate the Christian faith's sacredness and solemnity, their efforts were even more at odds with true faith and the needs of society. The Roman Catholic Church system now faced a prisoner's dilemma and the paradox caused by turning faith into religion. The Roman Church lost its authority as mediator on behalf of the divine spirit of God and as a "servant of the servants of God." In abandoning the spirit of love and forgiveness, it lost its public image and dignity. It was from this ground that humanity's second great reflection sprouted, as the European Christian world sought to revive individual free will and reason in the public sphere.[279]

SECTION 2: NOSTALGIC PASSION, FROM RENAISSANCE TO REFORMATION

Historical processes are often intertwined and not easy to separate at a given point in time. The Renaissance was a long historical movement from the end of the 13th century to the end of the 17th century, but its exact start and end points are difficult to pinpoint. The Reformation, on the other hand, began in 1517 when Martin Luther, a priest and lecturer at the University of Wittenberg in Germany, posted his *Ninety-Five Theses* in rebellion against the Roman church system, triggering decades of reform in the Christian church. The two movements were completely different and yet intertwined. The internal logic of the Renaissance and Reformation were consistent but had slightly different ways of reflecting on *human calling* in the Christian community life of the era.

To summarize each, the Renaissance tended to seek the reconciliation between mankind and God in accordance with love and forgiveness, a renewed understanding of the care God feels for the human beings he created, and the reconstruction of a relationship of gratitude and confession between humanity and God. A new expectation of *human calling* arose, which no longer left humanity in the pain and helplessness of the secular world, at the mercy of their own free will. (God allowed this exercise of free will for the sake of his glory and logical consistency, as discussed earlier). The Reformation, on the other hand, was a rebellion and revolution against the religious bureaucracy, dogmatism, and corruption of transactions between God and humanity within the Roman church system, which operated in Christ's name in the secular world. Reformers advocated abandoning belief in the church as an intermediary in the relationship between humans and God and restoring individual freedom to enter into a relationship directly with God and Christ. The Bible was seen as the gateway to this relationship, which meant each person could receive God's grace and attain salvation without having to endure the Roman Catholic Church's poor leadership and exploitation. In this sense, it can be said that the Renaissance's emphasis on humanistic care gave birth to the Reformation, and they together promoted the return to Augustine's monergistic spirit to rebuild the "cooperative relationship between man and God" in natural theology.

The Renaissance was a new cultural movement that expressed passion for life in artistic disciplines of literature, poetry, painting, architectural design, music, and so on. Dante's elegant literary epics represented by *Divine Comedy*, Boccaccio's realistic, erotic stories like *Elegia di Madonna Fiammetta* and *Decameron*, Petrarch's sonnets inspired by over 20 years of spiritual love for his Laura, and Erasmus's satires of church corruption and superstition *In Praise of Folly* and *Handbook of a Christian Knight*, were among the essential works in any discussion of the Renaissance. These works wrestled with people's ongoing dilemma between the needs of community public life and the risk of individual enslavement, even in the process of the religionization of Christianity.[280]

The Renaissance was a hundred-year period of humanistic awakening of individual free will. It was not a series of rebuttals between differing opinions. It was not a fierce critique of old forces and old thinking. Even less was it a revolutionary feat that smashed the old world and created a new one. Instead, the Renaissance was based on nostalgia for the church's relationship with Christ in the era of Augustine and for the simple idea of "servant of the servants of God" held by the church in the apostolic era. It represented a longing for a time marked by profound knowledge of theological philosophy, loyalty to faith in Christ, the spirit of service and asceticism of past popes and monks, and a public charitable spirit. By comparison, the society the Renaissance was born from, especially the popes and bishops in the powerful church, had become hypocritical, pretentious, and absurd. As the Roman Church became a dogmatic religious system, the public spirit intended for humanity by God in the spiritual realm became a system of secularized exchanges between people and God and laughably cumbersome pastoral requirements.

The time was ripe for the Renaissance, which began with Petrarch's elegant love poems and the allegorical stories of Dante, Boccaccio, and Erasmus. Greek and rhetoric followed later. The fact that both were more popular at universities than logic was proof of the era's nostalgia. Next was the retranslation of the Bible and the writings of monastic-era apostles like Augustine, Origen, Jerome, and Pope Gregory, into Greek. This paved the way for artistic innovation marked by nostalgic passion and embraced by the commercial civilization of Italian city-states. Italy had experienced the collapse of the Roman Empire, hundreds of years of plunder by Islamic pirates, and the turmoil of an embattled Roman Catholic Church. The struggle to develop community autonomy while preserving a Christian identity, political democracy, and philanthropy had shaped these Italian city-states. As a result, there were stronger feelings toward the hierarchy, dogma, and corruption of the entire European church, and deeper nostalgia for the relationship between humanity and God in the apostolic era. The rise of Italian Roman architecture, sculpture, and painting, centered on Florence, found it climax in the European Renaissance.[281]

Rooted in this nostalgia, the art of the Italian Renaissance also drew its strength from humanities and literature beginning in the 13th century, as well as the natural theology of Thomas Aquinas and scientific disciplines like mathematics and mechanics. It would be too narrow-minded to focus only on painting. The art of the Renaissance, especially in Italian civilization, was deeply rooted in architecture and sculpture as well.

Saint Peter's Basilica, the greatest building in Rome, which was designed by Alberti, Michelangelo, Bernini, and others, was the perfect embodiment of this Renaissance art. It not only reflected a brilliant imagination of space and time defined by God, but also featured a perfect geometric, mathematical, and mechanical path leading people to God. Michelangelo's *Pieta* and *David* are outstanding sculptures representative of the era. They not only perfectly depict human body structure with a beautiful, harmonious geometrical perspective, but they also portrayed themes with a purpose of revealing the profound meaning and beauty of humans in the context of God's creation.

Renaissance architects, sculptors, and painters sprang up like bamboo shoots and shone like stars. To this day, anyone visiting churches or museums in Italy or any European city can't help but be in awe. Paintings like Giotto's *Kiss of Judas* and *Lamentation of Christ*, Giorgione's *The Tempest* and *Sleeping Venus*, Botticelli's *Primavera* and *Birth of Venus*, Raphael's *The School of Athens* and *The Holy Family*, Michelangelo's painting of the Sistine Chapel ceiling and *The Last Judgment*, as well as Da Vinci's *The Last Supper* and

Mona Lisa represented the Renaissance spirit and a pinnacle of artistic expression in that era or even human history. These classic paintings not only accurately represented the mathematically perfect structure of the human body God created—and so praising people and ultimately God—but also emphasized Christian themes of a harmonious relationship between humanity and God.

In a thematic sense, they banished the evil of the Roman Church resulting from its dogmatic framework. Many paintings' themes included human, natural, philosophical, and mythological elements. Humanity's perception of beauty was effectively directed away from God and toward the nature he created. The majority of the figures in the paintings were naked, representing the pursuit of true beauty and necessary sincerity in relating to God and a rebellious mockery of the hypocrisy within the organized church system. Another salient feature of Renaissance paintings was their technical genius. Renaissance painters established principles of accurate light projection based on plane geometry. The distance and relative positions of people and objects in the paintings all conformed to this principle. Color was used to process light and set a psychological tone. It was as if natural light and divine light shone simultaneously from different angles, producing almost magical color changes and greatly enhancing the artistic expression and spiritual appeal of Renaissance painting.

Gradually the literary and artistic revival that began in Florence, Italy, and burgeoned throughout Italian city-state civilization over two centuries spread through the European continent. It reached Spain, Germany, France, the Netherlands, and England, giving rise to Dürer, Cervantes, Rabelais, Montaigne, Tasso, Moore, Campanella, Shakespeare, and other great European, late-Renaissance figures.[282]

From a historical perspective, the birth of the Renaissance in Italy was closely bound with the commercial civilization of port cities like Venice, Milan, Florence, Naples, and Genoa, which lasted for a thousand years after the collapse of the Roman Empire. This industry and commerce were highly advanced and gave rise to the equality and freedom that deconstructed the hierarchal, disciplinary concepts of the church. Consequently, it produced tens of thousands of industrialists and merchants and hundreds of industrial public-interest organizations based on free association in Florence. These organizations became sources of funding for church buildings, city sculptures, and paintings in public spaces. Florence's thriving commerce and semi-democratic political autonomy guaranteed the stability of the Medici family's century-long semi-philanthropic political governance and generous donations to the arts. In this near-magical environment, the Renaissance flourished and marked a peak in human civilization. But the most fundamental force behind it was still the Roman Catholic Church's increased religionization and consequent secularization of the Christian faith, tantamount to spiritual, and at times, material slavery. Under this accumulated internal pressure, the upper levels of society deviated in words and actions from the Christian faith and so from the *human calling* of God's expectations. The Renaissance was a correction of and a rebellion against the Roman Catholic Church in the name of nostalgia for the relationship between humans and God during the apostolic era of Augustine.

In one sense, the Reformation was merely an event in or an inevitable result of the historical process of the Renaissance. Renaissance thinking acted as a historical incubator of the Reformation. When Martin Luther posted his theses at the University of Wittenberg, no one, least of all himself, grasped how significant a catalyst they would become. Certainly contemporaries like his superior and friend, Father Staupitz, Elector of Saxony Frederick II, Cardinal Cajetan of Augsburg, King Charles V of Spain, theological doctors and professors such as Johann Eck and Philip Melanchthon, and even Pope Leo X himself, did not see it coming. The *Theses* were a short, basic outline of a debate based largely on the Bible and consistent with the theology of Augustine and Aquinas. Yet the *Ninety-Five Theses* were translated and printed in multiple languages and circulated throughout Europe.

As he was excommunicated and exiled, Father Luther quickly became a household name. Theologians and priests held debates about the *Theses* all over Europe, and Luther endured challenge and questioning in various ways. Each of the debates where Luther defended them was translated into various languages, printed, and widely circulated, which gradually took shape as his reformation theology of the cross based on "justification by faith." Erasmus, Calvin, and Melanchthon became reformation theologians in line with Luther's theological logic. As God's fingers strummed the strings of the *Ninety-Five Theses,* the great melodies of the revival of the Augustinian theology and that of the monastic apostles resonated throughout Europe.[283]

As discussed, the medieval Roman Church system had effectively replaced the essence of the Christian faith with dogma and rituals, turning invisible faith into concrete acts like pilgrimages to the Holy Land and other sites, atonement for the deceased, worshiping icons, keeping saint relics, and liturgical activities. Among them, buying and selling indulgences was one of the most prevalent. Underneath this dogmatic religious system was a theory of merit that kept believers psychologically subjugated. The "treasury of merit" was a way of conceptualizing a transactional relationship between people and God. A record of a person's good deeds, this merit could be deposited and withdrawn. Most important, the power to decide whether a deposit was large enough to gain salvation was in the hands of the Roman Catholic Church. According to this logic, the church was given control of individuals' spiritual destiny, with the pope exercising authority over them all. Other clerics could of course participate in the distribution of power according to their place in the hierarchy. As the church became more dogmatic, ritualized, and structured, a kind of religious market was built where transactions of merit between humans and God could be exchanged. By promising believers that they would attain "salvation" after death, the church openly acted as a mediator or broker for trade with God.

The period of papal exile in Avignon was a major contributor to the corruption of the church system. It reversed the 500-year order of the church's authority to grant legitimacy to secular monarchy in allowing the French government to intervene in papal affairs. Such intervention fundamentally destroyed the systems of both papal succession and high-level clergy selection established by Pope Gregory I (papacy 590–604). These 70 years of "captivity" coupled with French interference corrupted the Holy See for more than a century, accelerated the deterioration of the Christian faith. Much like it did with the Renaissance, this corruption set the stage for the explosion of Luther's religious reform, which seemed at the time to be a historical accident. In this sense, the corruption of the Roman Catholic Church in the Middle Ages lied fundamentally in the erosive intervention of the secular political force.

Martin Luther and his reformer theologians had to respond to the problem of the church's dogmatic religious system. They also had to respond to the way the pope had placed himself between humanity and God, or even taken God's place, in the transactional religious system. Their response was to reintroduce monergism and justification by faith to abolish this transactional relationship between God and people. They taught that mankind can be only saved by faith in and love for Christ, and that their actions do not win him salvation. They re-established Christ himself as the path to salvation, holding that believers could only follow Christ's example, not the pope's or even the church's.

In Reformation hermeneutics, the Bible is the only authority, and neither the pope nor the church is authoritative. Their final conclusion was logically consistent: humanity has sinned, but they also have free will granted by God. Through the Bible and faith in Christ, people can establish a new relationship with God without the church as the mediator. The church, in this view, is not a worldly power but rather a servant—a "servant of the servants of God." As

Saint Francis said in his final wish, "be content with a poor, desolate church." The reformed theology of Luther returned to the theological sources of Augustine and Saint Paul. In one way, the Reformation was inseparable from the Renaissance, an in another, it was a natural, logical result of the Renaissance.[284]

Of course, Luther and other reformed theologians did not fully realize their dream of humanity establishing a new relationship with God through the Bible alone, without the mediation of the church. Human nature proved incapable of separating material life from spiritual community life. As a result, Luther, Calvin and other reformers created a new church organization, Protestantism, to compete with the Roman Catholic Church. This, along with the rising tide of political reforms in monarchal nation-states like Germany, France, England, Portugal, the Netherlands, Switzerland, and others sent unprecedented shockwaves through the Catholic Church and pope leadership.

This harsh lesson led Pope Paul II to issue an ambitious notice on November 11, 1544, announcing plans to convene the famous Christian Ecumenical Council of Trent the following year. Luther and other protestant leaders were invited to participate in reforming the dogmatic religious system of the Christian Church. Hundreds of Roman Catholic archbishops, deans of universities and theological seminaries, and theologians attended the Council of Trent, but Protestants refused to participate. Unfortunately, Pope Paul III died four years later in the Great Plague. Because of the sheer number of topics, council discussions lasted nearly two decades before finally concluding in 1563 when Pope Pius IV fell sick from exhaustion. It may be the longest conference in the history of human civilization.

On the positive side, the council was an attempt to achieve tolerance and harmony through compromise between the various Christian sects and to eliminate the corruption of the church. The Council of Trent gave considerable credit to the Council of Constance's efforts to limit arbitrary papal authority by means of the resolutions of the ecumenical councils. It also incorporated the critiques of Protestant reformers regarding bureaucracy and corruption within the Roman Church by attempting to clean it up and set up a monitoring mechanism to ensure long-term, sustainable constraints. On the negative side, by solidifying and authorizing the non-biblical traditions of the pope and the Roman Church's authority, the council widened rather than bridged the gap between Roman Catholicism and Protestantism, especially when it came to the doctrine of "church organization." So they went their separate ways.[285] Real compromise and tolerance didn't come until 400 years later, at the Second Vatican Council of the 21st Ecumenical Council (1963–1965).

The Lutheran Reformation, sharing the transformational DNA of the Renaissance, had far-reaching significance and impact on the future of Christianity. Two important impacts stand out. First, it promoted understanding of the difference between Christianity and its religionization. Christianity is a person's belief in God and the Holy Trinity of God the Father, Christ, and the Holy Spirit, through whom one seeks to restore relationship with God and to bring the spiritual life into conformity with the *human calling* that he expects. Proper religionization of Christianity, on the other hand, means building a church organization to serve the community life of believers who share this faith and establish church regulations and ceremonies consistent with the Bible. The Reformation shed light on the need to specifically prevent such a church organization from misleading or distorting faith, assuming excessive authority as a dogmatic religious system, and so re-enslaving individual believers.

The second was that the advent of Protestantism introduced competition into the service of Christian believers. Over time, the Protestant Church further divided into Lutherans, Calvinists, Anabaptists, and the British Anglican Church further reformed by Cranmer and Hooker. In the 17th and 18th centuries, the movement of Pietism within Lutheranism was launched in Germany, while the Puritan and Evangelical Reformed movements emerged in the United Kingdom and United States. Though many historians see these divisions as a

Protestant split, they arguably created a fair competition between churches as service organizations, driven by the Renaissance. It was this fair and competitive market for religious public welfare that helped prevent churches from deviating from the faith or becoming enslaving and corrupt.

Throughout the history of human civilization and among the three major religions of Christianity, Buddhism, and Islam, the Protestant Reformation instigated by the Renaissance was the only truly successful religious experiment. It effectively avoided the excessive authoritarianism that led to deviation from and corruption of the Christian faith. It also reinforced the authority of the Bible and the essence of the Christian faith, so that the free will of humans as individuals created by God could be liberated from the slavery of the monopoly of the Roman Catholic Church. It was now possible to build a more harmonious relationship between mankind and God in light of the sacrifice of Jesus Christ. This success marks the historical contribution and significance of the second great reflection on *human calling* initiated during the Renaissance and Reformation in Europe.[286]

In praising the achievements of Protestantism, we must also objectively examine the achievements of the medieval Roman Catholic Church, without negating it by only emphasizing its problems. It only takes imagining the world if the Roman Catholic Church had failed to preserve Christianity during such a tumultuous time. What if it had not rallied the fragmented northern shore of the Mediterranean and arduously opposed numerous invasions by North African Muslim pirates? Or if it had not gathered public spiritual strength to restrain the political power of secular European kings through the institution of theocratic coronation? Or if it hadn't insisted on the public spirit of faith in God through the large-scale, long-term practice of organized charity?

Europe wouldn't have been able to escape the fate of full Islamization on one side or becoming a caesaropapist, secular political system built entirely on slavery on the other. It would've been impossible for the democratic political

372 | The Human Calling

system of human liberation to develop, and it would also be unlikely that new public welfare models and new public spaces like universities and modern scientific research would've arisen out of a mostly agricultural civilization.

History, however, makes no assumptions. It sweeps us up through time and tide in step with God's melody. The Roman Catholic Church, which should have been "servant of the servants of God," instead played a role in the corruption of the church, a role that has been both revered and abhorred in secular history. Looking back at this period of history objectively cannot affect history itself, but it can influence the future of mankind.

SECTION 3: THE LEAP IN SCIENTIFIC IMAGINATION RESULTING FROM THE NEW RELATIONSHIP BETWEEN HUMANS AND GOD

The sweeping spiritual and political changes brought about by the Renaissance and Reformation flowed out of the theology of Thomas Aquinas. His natural theology inspired similar effects in the scientific realm, fostering new disciplines like scientific research and scientific exploration that branched off from theological philosophy. For a long time, the academic community has blamed the problems of the Roman Catholic Church on scholasticism and natural theology, conflating the two and pitting science and theology against each other.

A stark example was in 1939, when German playwright Bertolt Brecht wrote his play *Galileo*. In order to implicate and condemn the Nazi policy of persecuting scientists, the play depicted the struggle of Copernicus, Kepler, and Galileo against the power of the Roman Catholic Church in promoting and defending heliocentrism. This exaggerated historical story coincides with the ideology of the era and circulated widely. To this day, people are confused and have a false impression of the true history of this disagreement. All kinds of fabrications have promoted the idea of a long-standing conflict between science and faith, an idea that has sown seeds of great evil in the history of human civilization, forcing us to swallow endless bitter pills now and into the future.

On the contrary, it was natural theology that gave individuals the idea and courage to explore the laws of nature motivated by God's joy in creation, and so laid the cornerstone for scientific logic. The Reformation further loosed the tangible restraints of the Roman Catholic Church on individual freedom, while the Renaissance lent harmony and consistency to humanity's mission from God, releasing the spirit of inquiry in individual personalities and portraying God's public spirit. Society came to the realization that the Roman Catholic Church had overstepped the commandments of the Bible and that its excessive authority would've even made the spirits of Augustine and Aquinas in heaven uneasy.

Under the era's comprehensive correction of the church, the great souls of the time took a revolutionary leap in scientific inquiry. Nicolaus Copernicus, Galileo Galilei, Johannes Kepler, and Sir Isaac Newton were all devout Christians. They took great spiritual inspiration from natural theology and used Aquinas' understanding of God's created laws as a starting point for their scientific explorations. They were characterized by humility and faithfulness, describing their work as exploring the wonders of God's creation. The conflict between scientific exploration and belief in God was clearly exaggerated in historical fiction. The Roman Catholic Church did not cruelly persecute them as in Brecht's theater, but at most required them to qualify their findings as hypotheses when they were published.

The biggest difference between Eastern and Western civilization that allowed this scientific movement to occur was its openness to novel ideas. Individuals with wild visions and fantasies were celebrated in the Judeo-Christian faith and subsequent society. Especially over the course of the Renaissance, individuals' unfettered ideas about the universe led them to integrate God's revelation with their own observations and conclusions about the natural world. Aristotle's syllogism of classification, commonality, definition, generalization, and deduction in the observance of nature was widely discussed and applied. Inductive and deductive reasoning greatly stimulated individual interest and action in observation, study, and discussion of nature. While the universe was theirs to explore, they still needed funding. Universities and institutes all over Europe at that time were non-profit, autonomous organizations, filled with active thinkers conducting research to answer the questions they posed. Yet they needed to convince donors to support them. Donations mainly came from churches, kings, feudal noble lords, and commercial noble families.

Why did these figures support such wild visions? The most important factor was a common belief in natural theology—exploring the unknown realms of God's creation to bring glory to God. This belief connected patrons with scientists and formed a unique "society of visionaries." Careful historical study reveals that these visionaries—whether Copernicus, Brahe, Kepler, Galileo, or Newton in astronomy, Vesalius and Harvey in medicine, Boyle in chemistry, Magellan and Columbus in exploration, or Descartes and Bacon in math and philosophy—were all inspired by natural theology. And they were all able to realize their dreams through public welfare funding. In the East, meanwhile, such "visions" were considered deviant. They could neither enter the public field or win mainstream glory and were even less likely to receive the necessary charitable sponsorship. Such visions were destined to die stillborn.

The difference between the disciplines of science and technology pose another historical question: why did modern science suddenly emerge from astronomy without previous technological accumulation and quickly rise to the heights of scientific rationality? Was it also related to the theological enlightenment of the late Renaissance? The two human disciplines of science and technology, while both tools for understanding nature, are very different in nature and origin. *Technology* describes functional design based on human senses and life experience, with its main purpose as solving real-world problems. *Science*, on the other hand, means theorems based on abstract human thinking, or laws. Its approach explains the interrelatedness of the phenomenal world without having a main purpose in mind. While technology asks the question of "know-how," science asks the question of "know-why." In general, over the long history of human exploration, human pragmatism set the pace of empirical processes and technological invention—when mankind had problems that needed solving, technology advanced. Science was historically a metaphysical topic of concern to only a minority in the upper class. How then did science transform into a beacon and a new driving force for later technological changes? Why did this mark a revolutionary turn in the progress of human civilization? These are fascinating questions. Once again it was the Renaissance's foundation in natural theology that stimulated the imagination of the scientific visionaries of the time.

One such visionary was Copernicus. In studying Ptolemy's geocentric model, he decided that the universe created by God should be more harmonious and simpler mathematically. So he and his assistants ran mathematical simulations with the sun at the center of the universe instead. His team found that their model yielded a greater harmony of the planets' orbital positions and timing in the solar system. They found they could reduce the number of planetary orbits from 80 to 30 when orbiting the earth vs. the sun. The Earth's calendar turned out to be more accurate in the heliocentric model than in the geocentric model. As a devout Christian, Copernicus presented his hypothesis of heliocentrism in his work *On the Revolutions of the Celestial Spheres* in 1543. Again, he was not subjected to cruel religious persecution as people today mistakenly believe.

Danish astronomer Tycho Brahe, also proposed a planetary orbit model. With the help of royal funding, he undertook long-term observations with his quadrant of the orbital periods and positions of the planets, keeping detailed records. He came up with a new model in which the sun and the moon rotate around the earth, and the other planets rotate around the sun. Yet Brahe's assistant Kepler believed that there was musical beauty in the heliocentric orientation of the universe. Only heliocentrism could demonstrate the perfect geometry of God's creation. The planets were linked by the magnetic force that God created, forming a sacred harmony that his teacher Brahe's model could not achieve. After circuitous mathematical calculation, Kepler proved that the orbit of Mars was oval. He published *The Harmony of the World* in 1619 and followed it in 1627 with the *Rudolphine Tables*, named after his patron, which expressed his famous three laws of planetary motion through mathematical formulas. Kepler believed that the main purpose of astronomy was to praise the masterworks of God's creation. The divinely harmonious configuration revealed by his three laws further supported Copernicus's heliocentric hypothesis.

Galileo, with funding from the Italian Medici family, also contributed to the conversation. He used a homemade astronomical telescope to observe the planets of the solar system and collect a large amount of data. His findings confirmed the logical consistency of the divine perfection of Copernicus's heliocentrism from a mathematical perspective. He also used his data on free-fall acceleration to mathematically explain the inertia of an object's motion. Contrary to popular belief, Galileo wasn't subject to severe religious sanctions for his ideas. It was only because he removed the word *hypothesis* from his published work and so violated his commitment to Pope Urban VIII—and because he admittedly called Aristotle stupid—that he was put in house arrest in 1633. After only one year, his banishment began to loosen and he'd already published another work, *Two New Sciences*. House arrest was not seen as a severe punishment at that time. Yet In the 19th and especially the 20th centuries, Galileo was deliberately praised as a "scientific crusader," clearly an exaggeration to make a contemporary political point rather than a historical fact.

In 1687, Isaac Newton published *Mathematical Principles of Natural Philosophy* and wrote a large number of philosophical and theological manuscripts, giving future generations a glimpse of one scientist's mental journey in this era. He discovered his "law of universal gravitation" in the process of answering the question, "Why does the apple always fall vertically to the ground?" He also discovered that everything that God created is connected by this law. With the simplest mathematical formulas, he showed that every object moves according to three laws of gravity, describing the balance between attraction and repulsion related to mass and distance.

Gravity, to Newton, maintained the beauty of order and harmony in the motion of all things.[287] His work on calculus, or the interaction between space and time, gave mathematical expression to human spatial thinking, enabling humans to grasp the infinity and eternity of God in new ways. This laid the foundation for hundreds of years of scientific development. Newton epitomizes the revolutionary scientific thought of the late-Renaissance. The law of universal gravitation that he discovered caused the cumulative scientific thinking of humanity to rise like a sun in the sky, illuminating a huge gap of imaginative potential. His work inspired people in that era to explore this gap between the pragmatic technology of the time and the potential revealed by the law of universal gravitation. The era of scientific leaps had arrived.

The leaps of scientific thinking and inquiry in this era made way for the transformation in scientific logic, technology, and industrial civilization that would follow in a new phase of human history. Yet regardless of the faith of the renowned discoverers or the scientific atmosphere in their countries, it's clear that in this large-scale leap forward in modern science had God as its starting point. Each scientist expanded their imagination and practiced logical demonstration, pushing the group forward in a cumulative way. But they did so through philosophical rationality and empirical scientific methods based on Christian natural theology.[288]

SECTION 4: THE TRANSFORMATION OF NATURAL THEOLOGY INTO THE INDEPENDENT POSITIVISM OF HUMAN REASON

Newton's scientific discoveries were not the result of one person's thinking. Rather, they represented leaps in group imagination based on a shared scientific empiricism grounded in philosophical rationality and natural theology. Newton's *Mathematical Principles of Natural Philosophy* was clearly a deeper inquiry building on Descartes' work, marked by a rigorous and solemn theological philosophical speculation on the basis of questioning and answering, and a brilliant architecture of mathematics. Without René Descartes, Newton's leap would have been inconceivable.

Descartes' *Principles of Philosophy,* published in 1644, established him as the father of modern philosophy. His famous comment on philosophy, "I think, therefore I am," is deeply rooted in people's hearts. In Descartes's view, a person can only prove the existence of their own mind through thinking. This is what sets humans apart from other creatures and things. Descartes also started from Aquinas's view of God. He believed that God's infinity, eternity, and perfection were the only absolute truths, but people could not fully grasp them; whereas the relative truths throughout God's creation could be understood. How could people understand the relative truths of the natural world? Descartes' said it was by relying on the philosophical rationality and empirical scientific method revealed to humanity by God. In this sense, Descartes followed the path of Aristotle's instrumentalist method.

Descartes believed that geometry and mathematics were God's method of revelation, so he used mathematical formulas to express geometry, creating analytic geometry. In Descartes's view, one can only prove the existence of one's mind through thinking. This is the most essential difference between man and all things. All substances in nature occupy space, and so can be described by analytic geometry, which can be expressed both as geometric figures and as abstract mathematical formulas. Using space as a starting point, Descartes could explain many phenomena through analytic geometry: objects have a spatial location, which means they have motion, which is triggered by a force, and so on. And as Aquinas established, God is the original force causing all motion. He balances the aggregate motion and conservation of the universe as a whole.

Beginning with space, motion and force, Descartes' analysis encompassed the activities of the cosmos by studying centrifugal force, rotation, the formation of spheres, and vortex particles that eventually form stars under high-speed movement. He described the particles in which light travels, the substance in which planetary objects rotate, and the refraction and reflection of sunlight by planetary objects. From his analysis of the earth and sun as planetary objects, he inferred that there are many celestial systems like the solar system in the universe, all with different modes of gravity, light, and heat produced by various types of motion. Although this assertion caused tension in the Roman Catholic Church, Descartes believed it didn't detract from the authority of God. His God could easily create the universe with multiple heliocentric systems and then give humanity a starting point for knowing the relative absolute truths of the universe. In Descartes's cosmology, nature operated in an orderly manner according to the will of God, but there was endless interconnectedness between all things in the cosmos. The manner of movement and relative balance of that interconnectedness was the key.

Descartes saw the interconnected motion and balance of objects in the universe as a physical system subject to certain constraints. To know the relative truths of nature is to know the physical systems bound by conditions, much like the structure and function of a machine. Observable systems, whether the human body, optics, or chemistry, are all the same. This system came to be called a "mechanism." Descartes believed that the most important way to find out the truth is to first establish a hypothesis of a system and then to perform what he called "analysis"—or to disassemble it like a machine in the imagination. The mental reassembly of the parts of the machine into a functional system he called "synthesis." The method of "hypothesis," "analysis," and "synthesis" in scientific research is the most effective way to learn the laws of nature created by God.[289]

Francis Bacon, likewise, worked from the absolute truth of God to understand other relative truths. But, motivated to solve urgent, real-world problems, he shifted his focus from God's revealed truth to enhancing mankind's ability to explore nature's relative truth. In this way, he set aside the purpose of God and elevated the pragmatic banner of "human purpose."

Bacon's approach was to improve on Aristotle's methodology of deductive and inductive reasoning. In the early 17th century, he dove into the regressus method of Professor Jacopo Zabarella at the University of Padua. Bacon noted that Zabarella's regressus method advanced the methodology of "observance-resolution-composition-discovery" within the framework of Aristotelean thought. But he believed that for Aristotle's logical methodology to be truly effective, a different starting point for logical thinking was needed. One should not engage in thinking for the sake of thinking, but for the sake of functional outcomes or practical productivity. In Bacon's view, the informative truth was what to look for, rather than the truth itself, so utilitarian ends become the focus. Based on this premise, his approach was to first pose an assumption about the causal relationship between multiple factors, then review a series of abductive assumptions or assertions that contributed to the resultant factors. Then one could rule out abductive assumptions or assertions that did not hold up to scrutiny, leaving a reason or set of reasons that needed to be re-verified by Aristotelean logic.

This abductive reasoning, which was later called "exclusionary induction," doesn't seem like a blockbuster idea today. But it certainly changed the thought and research methods of the era's philosophers, placing the pragmatic purpose of the relationship between humans and nature ahead of the public purpose that God intended for mankind. Bacon believed that despite the fall of their ancestor Adam, humanity could still apply the study of nature for their own purposes, with those purposes as a starting point for pursuing its relative truths. Teleology must be the guiding principle, along with strict rules for experimentation and verification, in order to eliminate irrelevant thinking and unnecessary trials.

Bacon, though more pragmatic than profound, was too influential for history to ignore. His straightforward teleologic method connected science and technology more tightly than ever. It could be said that if Descartes turned the public rationalism of Aquinas's natural theology into natural philosophy, then Bacon completed its transformation into scientific positivism and pragmatism. His famous saying, "knowledge is power," marked the transition to philosophical positivism and scientific pragmatism.[290]

Newton and the natural philosophers of his time, who integrated mathematics, physics, optics, astronomy, philosophy, and theology, influenced and inspired each other and as a result reached the pinnacle of the era's natural philosophy. Newton not only discovered the law of universal gravitation, which influenced humanity's productivity, way of life, and scientific imagination for hundreds of years.

Descartes greatly influenced Newton, and Newton and Bacon greatly influenced the scientists that followed. The shift from Newton's thought to Bacon's functional pragmatism had ripple effects on the way science was conducted. Science split off from natural philosophy and theology and further divided into astronomy, mathematics, physics, chemistry, natural history, zoology, botany, and other branches. Natural theology and philosophy, meanwhile, gradually divided into theology, philosophy, politics, economics, sociology, history, geography, cultural anthropology, and other disciplines. Each discipline was logically consistent with the starting point of God's universal infinity and eternity.

At the same time, each discipline had standard methodologies for exploration and verification, which enabled joint participation in thought and research. These included conventions for academic research, certifications for testing equipment and research results, and standardized rules for modern scientific research through an autonomous regulatory approach.[291] Without so many scientists pushing for the development and maintenance of effective standards, the rapid accumulation of community-based scientific research that took place would have been unimaginable. These common standards were not formulated by the government, but by individuals. They were made possible by the public welfare environment of European universities, marked by free association, faith in Christian theology, and scientific thinking.

The creation of these public standards coupled with the rise of pragmatism ensured that individual scientific thought became more and more specialized, while group scientific thought accumulated in more complex and powerful ways. The era in which personal empirical thinking took the place of public rationalism had finally arrived. Amid this general trend, Bacon's personal utilitarian empiricism would prevail, and God's expectation of *human calling* in people's spiritual lives would face a whole new test.

SECTION 5: THE WEST'S PLACE OF HONOR AND THE EAST'S ABSENCE AT THE FEAST OF IDEAS

With the second great reflection of humanity in full swing, the entire Western world, including Europe and the New World of America discovered by Columbus, was deeply involved. Research and discussion among natural philosophers and scientists crossed the sea through new printing techniques, impacting more and more minds, while the public university system trained and sent more people to this feast of ideas. Coupled with the highly secular social response to Bacon's utilitarian aims, the abstract, lofty theories in the halls of theologians and scientists increasingly were applied to accelerate technological innovations that ordinary people could tangibly appreciate.

In this climate, a new type of non-profit organization, the scientific society, emerged in Europe. Notable examples include the Oxford Society, an autonomous community founded by Boyle and others in 1627; the Accademia del Cimento, founded in 1657 by Viviani and Borelli, disciples of Galileo with funding from the Medici family; the Royal Society founded in 1645 by mathematicians and natural philosophers Wallis and Wilkins; the French Academy of Sciences established through the free association of Descartes, Pascal, and others in 1666; and the Berlin Academy, founded in 1700 by the mathematician Leibniz. Bacon, Wallis, Wilkins, and other scientists established the "Royal Society of London for Improving Natural Knowledge" from 1645–1660 and published *Philosophical Transactions*. The pioneering Royal Society became the most famous and influential representative of the era's public welfare organizations in terms of methods and standards of scientific research. It marked the maturity of modern scientific research thinking. The church, previously distant, unattainable and majestic as the representative of God, now found itself on the same stage of human civilization together with public welfare organizations, outstanding and amazing in their own right. Scientific experiments and philosophical and theological speculation now went hand in hand—an impressive partnership. Mankind was motivated like never before, making new discoveries in a variety of fields. Every day there were new ships setting sail for the New World to seek adventure and pursue new wealth and knowledge. This in turn inspired people to integrate God's *human calling* for public life with these new thought trends and to deal with the new challenges of community and organizational governance.[292]

Eastern society, by comparison, had no such external stimuli. There was no conflict between belief in one God and religious organization, no scientific imagination and ideas that set forth from God, and no cultural atmosphere of open-ended questioning and inquiry. Both the Far East, with Indian and Chinese civilizations as its axis, and the Near East, with Egypt's Nile and the Mesopotamian plains as its axis, were largely absent from this second great reflection. They didn't grapple with its puzzles, such as how to reconcile God's public spirit with individual human freedom; organized religion with the spiritual God-human relationship, and even various planetary orbit models with the mathematical consistency of God's creation.

This absence implies that Eastern society not only lacked reflection on the sacred source of the public spirit of freedom and equality among humans, but also came up short of mathematical reflection on cosmic celestial movement and the correlation of all things. More important, this absence dampened incentives for the effective development of imagination and reasoning abilities, which ultimately manifested itself in the fact that Eastern civilization made hardly any significant contributions to scientific imagination and technological innovation, as well as to the corresponding organizational and institutional innovation of industrial civilization in the following centuries.

This panoramic image of the differences between the East and the West can come into greater focus by examining how the United Kingdom and United States led the way in designing and implementing market-based competition systems, described in the next chapter.

CHAPTER 12:

Harmony: humanity and its invisible shackles

SECTION 1: THE PRINCIPAL ENLIGHTENMENT— TRANSFERRING RATIONALITY FROM GOD TO HUMANITY

Isaac Newton's thought was indeed groundbreaking. It reached a theological, philosophical, and scientific peak that was so high—practically the limit one human could possibly reach—that hundreds of years afterward, almost no one completely understood him. As Alexander Pope wrote in his epitaph for Newton: "Nature and Nature's Laws lay hid in Night: God said, 'Let Newton be!' and all was light." Any thinking person would be truly amazed and overwhelmed by the laws of nature that Newton revealed. And anyone who relies on the accumulation of human experience for technological innovation would be humbled by the light of his discovery of God-given laws of nature and be emboldened to embark on adventures of innovation themselves. Yet no one completely understood Newton.

In order to understand him, many people turned to Bacon and Descartes, growing into a large group that history would later call "modern Enlightenment thinkers."[293] The most famous of these were Locke, John Toland, David Hume, John Stuart Mill, and Adam Smith from Britain; Jean-Jacques Rousseau, Voltaire, Claude-Adrien Helvetius, and Baron d'Holbach from France; Immanuel Kant from Germany; and Thomas Paine from America. Enlightenment thinkers had large ideological differences, but they shared a common philosophy—that human reason should be freed from a theological rationality dependent on faith in God. They tried to establish independent human reason, objectifying and studying nature via experimental methods in order to use it and conquer it. Their quest was reminiscent of how humans viewed their relationship with nature during the transition from a hunting to a farming civilization, except that during the Enlightenment, the concept was much more clearly delineated, and humans had more confidence in themselves. Later philosophers would describe the Enlightenment as the transition from "God-centered" to "human-centered," in terms of the subject that rules nature.

Of course, the Enlightenment thinkers also differed greatly in their theories of "independent human reason," with divisions basically falling along national lines in Britain, France, and Germany. Generally, British Enlightenment thinkers, represented by Locke, were more inclined toward a pragmatism that balanced inherited traditions during the shift from a God-centered to a human-centered worldview. French Enlightenment thinkers, represented by Voltaire and Rousseau, were more inclined to a romantic idealism that completely abandoned the old world. German Enlightenment thinkers, represented by Kant, were more inclined to seek a compromise at first. But later, post-Enlightenment thinkers like W.F. Hegel, Ludwig Feuerbach, and Friedrich Nietzsche overemphasized the role of mankind and science, veering into a leftist extremism that totally negated God's reason. American Enlightenment thinkers were most similar to their British counterparts, while slightly leaning toward the French way of thinking. It was these differences and the resulting ideological struggles[294] that led these nations down very different paths of economic and political development in the age of industrial civilization.

Locke (1632–1704) followed Descartes and Bacon but leaned more toward the latter as he created a unique and pragmatic philosophy, known as empiricism.[295] In Locke's view, the innate human mind is as empty as a blank slate, and humans can only establish concepts on the basis of their acquired perceptual system as an intermediary for observation. The experience of analysis and comprehensive reflection helped humans transition from simple to complex concepts and form independent reason. More specifically, the field of understanding and manipulating the natural laws made by God, humanity can realize independent reason through their experience of scientific methods.

Locke also believed that independent reason, besides helping humanity conquer nature through scientific practice, could also help them understand the revelation of Christian faith, acting as a standard for judging it and rejecting dogmas that were inconsistent with reason, such as original sin. For Locke, then, Christianity was suitable for maintaining basic faith in God, while tedious dogma that did not stand up to the test of independent human reason was to be abandoned. Locke's famous rational philosophy of empiricism and minimal rational belief in God was a direct response to turbulent trends in scientific thought during the era and the wave of pragmatic technological innovations that followed. But empiricism was also misunderstood and brought about extreme criticism and rejection of the Christian faith by British contemporaries like Toland and Matthew Tindal. In their view, possessing science as a completely autonomous human rationality relegated anything beyond it to the realm of mysticism. They saw the rationality of God and the Christian faith as mysterious and superfluous. For them, humanity's need to do good is based only on human rationality, with no need to glorify God, like previous generations believed.

But Locke opposed atheism and the extreme criticism and abandonment of the Christian faith. He insisted that God is still both our starting point and destination. Without God as a starting point, human equality could have no legitimate point of origin, nor could there be solid contractual basis for the protection and transfer of human power. Without the divine authority of God's law, the contractual relationship that upholds the equality of mankind becomes fragile. Human freedom loses the constraint of responsibility and can easily become the freedom to harm others, making it impossible for people to gain equal power to pursue life, freedom, and wealth. For Locke, autonomous human rationality is based on the existence of God, or, put another way, human rationality is given by God. Only in a society based on this principle is it possible for everyone to win equal power in pursuit of life, freedom, and wealth and obtain equal and legitimate political power. Political governance of a community requires the consent of the majority of the governed citizens, and the principle of the minority deferring to the majority is used to elect rulers, to grant or withdraw their power. More specifically, Locke believed, this principle must also be followed in congressional decisions of the House of Lords and the House of Commons.

Locke was certainly aware of the uneven results that can arise from dynamic competition based on equal rights granted by God. He argued that human rationality should be able to understand these differences. But he also recognized that it's important to ensure that those who are hardworking are not deprived of their due right to live. He saw charity as an ideal solution. Locke believed that charity is Christianity's greatest virtue, and that what bridges the gap between what Christ asks us to believe and what we do is charity. The sin of acting uncharitably is the worst corruption of property rights. But charity cannot be forced. It can only be expected by Christ. In this sense, charity is the fulfillment of the *human calling* that God expects of people. In the end, if human beings' autonomous rationality in understanding nature, conquering nature, and even in dealing with the relationships between humans and society comes from natural law, then the ultimate source of this natural law must be God and Christ. Pure autonomous human rationality apart from God and Christ would be unimaginable.

Locke's ideas, particularly those in *Two Treatises of Government* and the idea of autonomous human rationality under the glory of God, laid the philosophical foundation for Britain's Glorious Revolution of 1688, which brought about a pragmatic, peaceful transition from monarchy to constitutional monarchy with the passing of the *Bill of Rights*. Following in the footsteps of Bacon and Descartes, Locke boldly and rigorously reshaped the British academic paradigm with his pragmatic combination of natural theological rationality and autonomous human rationality. His paradigm would set the standard for the unimaginable acceleration of *human ability* during humanity's second great reflection.

French Enlightenment thinkers were generally more radical than their British counterparts.[296] Voltaire (1694–1778) was a typical representative of the French Enlightenment. He categorically rejected the belief in God that Westerners had held for thousands of years and the Christian faith that had been held for 1,700 years. He denied the trinity of the unipersonal God, and claimed that God is nature, that Catholicism is full of superstition and evil, and that all Christian theological doctrines are farcical and ridiculous. He also argued that natural religion is the moral principle shared by all human beings, and that science allows permanent confidence in autonomous human rationality to be established. Building on Newton's discovery of the laws of motion that govern all things in nature, Voltaire believed that similar laws must govern social relationships—those between humans and society—and only awaited discovery by a "Newton" in the field of humanities. This, for him, would make the concept of autonomous human rationality more complete. Voltaire was a warrior who wielded mostly criticism. His articles were not characterized by rigorous thought, but they were humorous and sarcastic enough to gain influence and popularity.

Rousseau (1712–1778) was a passionate and arrogant person. He set God aside, declaring that "a person with a truly noble soul can lift himself to the heights of God." His *Social Contract* and *Discourse on the Origin and Basis of Inequality Among Men* emphasized the freedom and equality of all humans, the government's complete obedience to the people, and the "common will" of the people's political contract as the only source of legitimate political rule. These works had a great impact on future generations, but a closer look reveals that, compared with Locke's, Rousseau's definitions of freedom and equality are extremely vague and romantic. The absolute freedom he advocated sounds very tempting, as it means that humans can leave God's role in creation out of the picture and gain complete and autonomous freedom. But when it came to equality, Rousseau became very emotional in his reasoning. He believed that inequality of property destroys the "natural equality" of human beings. That led him to claim that the division of labor and property leads to differences between masters and slaves, or inequality, and that such inequality is the root of all evil. Rousseau thus confused the concepts of equality and sameness, unconsciously falling into the dilemma of godless, human-centric autonomy.

If we accept Rousseau's idea of human freedom, many questions arise. Does it include the freedom to seek property by conquering and using nature? If not, what is left of Rousseau's freedom? All that's left is the "freedom" to beg on the street. If so, does the freedom to seek property need to be protected? Do people still have the freedom to accumulate wealth over time? If they do, the immediate result is Rousseau's so-called inequality. Then what is Rousseau's equality? Rousseau advocated a classless society in the "state of nature" with no division of labor or property. But is it possible to sustain such a permanently static, classless, "equal" society with no division of labor or property? If so, it would be hard for freedom to coexist with it. If there is no need to protect freedom and equality, what does that leave the country? What use is Rousseau's freedom-based social contract in a society without the division of labor and property? A society without division of labor and property is a society of beggars. Rousseau and his followers, like Maximilien Robespierre, could only resort to hoping for a republic governed by virtue.

In comparison, Locke's empiricist philosophy provided a plain, rigorous, prudent, and self-consistent interpretation for autonomous human rationality. Locke insisted that autonomous human rationality is empowered by God and that equality is the inevitable result of humans being created by God. This equality can be divided into subjective and objective equality. Subjective equality means no one has the right to infringe, attack, or kill other human subjects; objective equality means that human subjects have the equal right to own property, and one must not violate the property of others by non-contractual means, such as theft, robbery, deception, or seizure. At the same time, humans enjoy freedom, which is also a gift that comes from being created by God. People have the freedom to exercise their rights subjectively, while also exercising the freedom to seek property by contractual means— "objective freedom" —but they must be responsible for the results of their actions. But Locke quickly realized that such human autonomy must lead to unequal outcomes due to differences in human subjects such as intelligence, effort, and opportunity. Of course, Locke did not advocate too much governmental intervention. Instead, he wisely introduced Christian churches and charities as the solution to the problem of poverty for those who are hardworking and decent. He believed that charity is the *human calling* that Christ and God expect of man. Those who possess wealth should respond to Christ's expectations by charitably helping others and at the same time achieving the true purpose of life, which is to glorify God.

The German Enlightenment seems to have taken a middle road between Britain and France. Its primary representative, Kant (1724–1804), led it to the peak of human rationality.[297] Kant attempted to integrate the theological rationality of God with the empirical rationality of humanity, allowing the two to go hand in hand. His philosophical reflections on human rationality were profound and influential but didn't achieve the success he expected. Kant acknowledged God as an existence outside the human world and the immortality of the soul. He admitted that God is absolute, eternal, and perfect, and that God, in the time that he defines, makes rational and sublime judgments on human life according to supreme goodness and virtue.

However, he denied that human rationality could understand the absolute rationality of the transcendent God. For him, God could only serve as a "necessary postulate" for human morality. Theologians can gain faith by contemplating the nature of God and the soul, but they only live a theologically rational life and don't enter society. Human rationality is a kind of pure intellect and reason, which forms knowledge through "experience plus reason," which enables people to bravely realize rational and spiritual autonomy. So-called rational autonomy is to understand the laws of nature through empiricism and to use them to serve mankind, like the great discoveries of Newton, Galileo, Kepler, Boyle, and Harvey did. So-called spiritual autonomy is to overcome the evil of obedience to sensual motivations over moral motivations in human nature. For Kant, moral motivations don't come from God but rather from the Golden Rule of "do unto others as you would have done unto you," which is the source of ethics in the human mind.

Based on this logic, Kant distinguished between two religions. One is a rational religion founded on Kantian ethics, with people's "good living and behaving" at its core. People know "what they must do" or "what efforts they should make" to improve their moral standards so that they are worthy of God's help. Rational religion, then, actually bears the primary historical responsibility of moral discipline. The other is traditional Christian religion. In this religion, people hope for God's grace and Christ's substitutionary atonement only through prayer and worship. Kant believed that this is a kind of witchcraft that appears to win God's favor but is in fact manipulated by the church. With the ethics of rational religion, Kant hoped to build the "Kingdom of God," a social union of individuals, where a person could realize his spiritual autonomy and make himself the new man that he is or will become.

Kant took this thinking even further. He delineated three concepts of duality: between God's theological rationality and existing social moral reason, between human rational autonomy and spiritual autonomy, and between rational religion and spiritual religion. His real intention was nothing more than politely setting traditional Christian and theological rationality aside, and establishing a brand-new society based on complete human rational autonomy and human religious autonomy. His aim was to realize the "subjective transfer" of human rationality from God to man. Under the banner of praising Newton's scientific revolution, Kant misread Descartes' and Newton's natural philosophical rationality, specifically as it concerned humans' understanding of natural law. Kant's thought, through the logical imagination and free play of Hegelian theory in terms of the absolute spirit of autonomous human rationality and will of the state, together with the extreme romantic interpretation of freedom and equality by the French Enlightenment thinkers, sowed the first philosophical seeds for the leftist extremist ideology and social upheaval of the following two centuries.

SECTION 2: SETTLING IN THE CLAMOR

As the new trends of Enlightenment thought gained momentum, the younger generation was deeply influenced by them along with the scientific revolution. They were caught up in a wave of radical, anti-religious thought, that promoted abandoning faith in God and gained ground on the European continent.

Instead of standing by and giving up their influence over the human mind and spirit, the leaders of various branches of Protestantism, who appeared at times to be in competition with one another, decided to fight back. They launched a series of religious reform movements that acted as an effective correction of Enlightenment extremism.

The first of these movements belonged to the Anglicanism of the 16th and 17th centuries. The Anglican church, as the official religion of Britain, remained calm amid the radical frenzy of other Protestant churches to totally deny the Roman Catholic Church and all ecclesiastical intermediaries. Anglicans made bold statements to awaken Christians to the rationality of faith, and they preserved necessary traditions that were consistent with the Bible. As Protestantism itself became more organized, Anglicanism preserved elements of the organization and dogmatization of the Roman Catholic Church, thus strengthening people's reverence for the biblical tradition.[298] At the same time, it retained the simple Reformation concepts of removing all intermediaries and the priesthood of all believers, developing practical systems to maintain the integrity and essence of church services. Thomas Cranmer's *Book of Common Prayer* and Hooker's *Of the Lawes of Ecclesiastical Politie,* written along similar lines as Locke's British pragmatism, retained the higher traditions of the Catholic Church. They adhered unswervingly to the Protestant spirit of Scripture alone and justification by faith, while also emphasizing the importance of sanctification and good deeds. As Anglicanism stayed faithful to tradition while continually innovating, it became a rock and a pillar that held the line of the Christian faith in the midst of hundreds of years of division in Protestantism.

Next, two parallel movements happened in Britain and America. The Evangelical Revival Movement in the early 18th century was led by John Wesley (1703–1791) in Britain, and the Great Awakening among American Puritans was led by Jonathan Edwards (1703–1758).[299] Wesley, on the basis of Protestant core ideas of Scripture alone, faith alone, and grace alone, and under the influence of the Enlightenment, clearly outlined his famous "Quadrilateral" theology of Scripture, reason, tradition, and Christian experience. According to this theological framework, church traditions consistent with the Scripture must be maintained, and God's grace requires the firm faith of the believer as well as a process of conversion and repentance. At the end of a believer's life, it will be decided whether they are sanctified, that is, whether they are deemed worthy of God's blessing. This process is not imposed by the church or by God, but by the independent choice of individual free will. As a result, the Christian faith and the church are not in conflict with, but in harmony with, the rational autonomy of human beings to understand and use nature alongside science. This is how Wesley reconciled the extreme human rational autonomy of Enlightenment thinkers with the boundless love and forgiveness of God and Christ. In the process, Wesley founded the Methodist Church.

The Puritan movement began with Anglicans Christians who rebelled against what they saw as excessive tolerance of Roman Catholic traditions. They were mainly organized by the Presbyterian Church in Scotland and England. The Puritan Presbyterian Church was thoroughly Calvinist, emphasizing that humanity's main purpose is to glorify God, that the Scripture is fundamental, that a pure church must be established in accordance with the Scripture and the purpose of glorifying God, and that the relationship between mankind and God is a covenant. That meant that believers must be chosen, and God's promise was contingent on his choosing of believers. It followed logically that the Puritans' demands on believers were very harsh. They were reluctant to lower the expectations of covenant theology because of the Enlightenment furor about autonomous human rationality. Still, Puritanism attracted many believers in Britain, especially those New World developers who were dissatisfied with the British and European hierarchies and primogeniture.

In 1620, the 101 Puritans on the Mayflower sailing for Plymouth, Massachusetts, conducted passionate and rational discussions. They drew up and signed the famous Mayflower Compact, the earliest prototype of a constitution for the governance in the United States. They believed that America was the land that God promised to the Puritans. In order to be worthy of God's promises and blessings, the Puritans must establish New England on the new promised land and live holy lives that glorify God and are worthy of the holy covenant, so the church and believers could be purified. This was the origin of the American Congregational Church and later the United Church of Christ.

Under the impact of the European Enlightenment, Edwards initiated the Great Awakening to revive Puritan Protestant theology.[300] Edwards's revivalist theology was not coordinated with or amenable to the trending idea of scientific human rationality and autonomy. He gave carefully prepared lectures in more than 600 North American churches. In Edwards's theology, God is solemn, omnipotent, perfect, and universal. All human reason, autonomy, and science are illuminated by God, and anyone who abandons God is fundamentally incapable of rational autonomy. Humanity's free will is limited. People are easily corrupted by sin, often uneasy and distracted. Without God's grace and Christ's sacrifice, humans can't use their rational autonomy or anything else to save their souls. Ignoring this only leads to greater sin. Edwards proposed that human affections are the personality center that creates human identity and behavior. Affections guide people's emotions and feelings and form the will of the soul. Only through God's grace and his holy covenant with humanity can affections be truly nourished and nurtured. That means that all things come from God, belong to God, and return to God. God is the source and the end goal of our lives. Human autonomy means choosing grace, which represents a new cooperative relationship between humans and God. By contrast, human rationality that abandons the covenant between God, Christ and humans, leads to a dead end. For Edwards, the so-called "enlightened" thinking that gained great popularity by claiming that people can be completely rational and autonomous on their own only exaggerates mankind's finitude and conceals his sinfulness. The end result is hypocrisy, pride, and corruption, and brings only violence, chaos, and disaster to society.

The last movement of note is the Pietist Movement in Germany. Initiated by Philipp Spener (1635–1705) and Nicolaus Zinzendorf (1700–1760), among others, the intention behind this movement was to rejuvenate the declining Lutheranism and respond to human-centric Enlightenment thought triggered by the scientific revolution. It applied solemn faith in God and Scripture's spiritual revelation to empower individuals to live holier lives, becoming believers who were to be filled with devotion to God and could have a positive impact on others and society. Human autonomy in German Pietism, then, could still remain in the light of God's care.[301]

Those movements initiated by Protestant factions, which resisted the extremist assertion that individual rational autonomy could replace God-given rational autonomy, maintained the balance and coordination of human spiritual life. They effectively prevented the Enlightenment tendency to pit science and theology against each other from completely prevailing, and so cultivated and nourished autonomous human rationality. These were the necessary conditions for the accelerating transformation and interaction of science and technology catalyzed by pragmatism during the industrial revolution.

The subsequent historical practices in Europe and America, far from being accidental or coincidental, bear out the importance of each country's prevailing understanding of the relationship between God's autonomous rationality and humanity's autonomous rationality. The way that patterns of thought developed in these countries at the forefront of the conflict between Christianity and scientific rationality are highly correlated with how they understood the balance between these two kinds of autonomous rationality and how they applied this balance in designing their public systems.

In contrast, China and India in the East fell into the trap of materialistic monistic thinking, lacking imagination and operating on a narrow, human-centered perspective. For this reason, they were completely absent from mankind's second great reflection—the reflection on why and how God's spirit is related to autonomous human rationality.

SECTION 3: "SELF-SUBJECTIVITY" IN THE NEW ERA OF HUMAN RECONCILIATION WITH GOD

Clearly, Britain did an excellent job of preparing theoretically and spiritually for the advent of the age of industrial civilization. The foundation was laid largely by Bacon's guidelines for rational pragmatism in light of Newton's law of gravity and calculus method, as well as by Locke's relative balance between God's theological rationality and humanity's autonomous rationality. More important, though, was the contribution by those great British pioneers who lived through the Evangelical Revival and Puritan Theological Revival movements. These pioneers, in the midst of this turbulent era, maintained a delicate balance between understanding relative truth through nature and understanding absolute truth through the preservation of the Christian faith. They triggered a movement of national consciousness that continued uninterrupted for nearly 300 years, with an aim of reconciling the pursuit of individual rights with a public spirit.

After Locke, the great British thinkers of modern natural philosophy, politics, and economics, like Hume, Mill, Smith, and Jeremy Bentham, continued to follow Newton and Locke on the path of balancing Christian faith and autonomous human rationality. They carried out the great British experiment of building laws, organizations, and institutions according to their philosophical principles. This, on the one hand, enabled organizational and institutional construction during industrial civilization to become a comprehensive paradigm and, on the other, made it evident that God is the starting point and destination of autonomous human rationality. Britain became the model for a modernizing Christian nation.

Hume (1711–1776), in addition to his well-known philosophy that was skeptical of theological rationality, further developed a philosophical theory of humanity and society. He believed that as far as individuals are concerned, all actions are to serve their purposes which are guided by the intuition or induction of experience in which individual sensations intervene.

Bentham (1748–1832) further developed Hume's teleology of personal behavior, putting it at the center of discussions of human rationality. He saw humans as completely self-centered, or utilitarian. The end goal of this utilitarianism may not seem very glorious, but for Bentham, it proved to be the most efficient approach to maximize the value of human labor in a system with limited resources. The core driving power in this doctrine of efficiency is the greatest human happiness, which can be measured in material benefits. Individual happiness, then, can be quantified without the need for classification. As Bentham famously said, "Poetry is no better than a pushpin." Bentham believed that without understanding humanity's true nature in pursuing the greatest happiness for themselves, it's impossible to understand the dynamics of human society, society's division of labor and free trade, or autonomous human rationality. Bentham derived his political system of universal suffrage from his theory of individual teleology: each individual's equality in utilitarian pursuit of freedom forms the basis for their equality regarding political rights.

Mill (1806–1873) was the master of interpreting individual teleology as the driving force of social progress.[302] Beginning with Bentham's utilitarian individual teleology, he argued that man's self-centered purpose doesn't contradict God-given free will, but rather, it actually establishes the principle of social efficiency. Mill observed that individuals are far more efficient than the government. The fundamental reason for this is the close connection between human behavior and human utilitarian ends. In a system with scarce resources, the ultimate ethical question is defined by the principle of efficiency, and inefficiency is immoral. Efficiency leads the way to human happiness, and happiness can be defined as the pursuit of joy and the elimination of pain.

Bentham and Mill differed on how to measure happiness. Mill believed that happiness couldn't simply be measured in material terms, but must be classified. Intellectual and moral happiness is superior to material and physical happiness. As he put it, "better to be Socrates dissatisfied than a fool satisfied." Such noble happiness is more beneficial to society and can maximize social happiness. Like Bentham, Hume, and Locke, Mill further deduced from the principles of individual utilitarianism that government power should be limited, not only because individuals driven by utilitarianism are more efficient than the government, but also because unlimited increases in government power can lead to its abuse by individuals who hold it. Such abuse curtails the individual freedom of the many and brings about countless societal misfortunes.

Adam Smith (1723–1790), closely aligned with British thought, arrived at balance between Christian and secular autonomous human rationality, which he advanced by constructing a pragmatic market economic system. In Smith's view, human individual freedom includes the duality of both subjective and objective freedom—of life, thought, speech, and the pursuit of wealth. But freedom's boundary is delineated based on equality in relationships between humans and society. The freedom and equality of individuals originated not from human rationality, but from God's rationality alone.[303] On this basis, Smith demonstrated that the self-centered nature at the root of human rationality inevitably leads to conflicts and contradictions between individual freedom and the interest of the community. The way to resolve this conflict was to apply autonomous human rationality to design a fair "market system."

Smith put forth three core premises for its design: first, that humans are created and possess free will both to enjoy freedom and the equal right to life that all others have. This freedom and equality are therefore sacred and inviolable. Second, that a person's ability to act in their own interest is empowered by God, or at least a freedom granted by God. Third, that humans therefore have the dynamic freedom to pursue their own wealth and accumulate it over time. This freedom is also empowered by God and is therefore sacred and inviolable.

The core mechanism of Smith's market system is fair competition and the elimination of monopolies. That means not allowing any individual or organization to have single, exclusive, or absolute control over any field. As long as there are multiple individuals or organizations in a single field, there is a competitive market system. While this fully competitive market system exists, the market will transform individual subjective behavior out of self-interest into objectively beneficial public outcomes, namely, quality goods and services at an affordable price. The market competition system acts as an "invisible hand" created by autonomous human rationality. It transforms conflicts between humans and society into a new kind of reconciliation, as "the subjective behavior is driven by self-interest, and the objective outcome is beneficial for others." The role of government becomes that of a "night watchman" who maintains the healthy operation of the market system by safeguarding competition and eliminating monopolies through its legislative, administrative, and judicial functions.

Under such a competitive market system, division of labor expands due to technological changes, which increases efficiency. Through free trade, this social division of labor and efficiency grows as the competitive market system is reinforced. As this increases the value of labor, the development of the whole society and prosperity of the country is achieved. Of course, human behavior driven by self-interested motivation on the basis of individual freedom is not the whole story of economic health. Many more non-transactional activities in public community life contribute to it, as people pursue virtue and high moral sentiment on the basis of Christianity and under the inspiration of God's divine light as the creator. Even while engaging in transactional behavior based on autonomous human rationality, people still must adhere to the principles of sympathy and empathy. The market must adhere to principles of fair trade and credit, otherwise the transactional game won't last long.

The philosophical and economic thought that formed in this era fueled the efforts of great British thinkers and gradually became mainstream. As a middle way, it was balanced and mild, yet transformative. It drove the thinkers and leaders of the time to analyze and design the political, economic, and societal institutions of decades to come. They created a complete system of institutional frameworks and societal arrangements for Great Britain. This rigorous systematic design was like the cosmic machine in Descartes's vision, unleashing each individual's autonomous rationality and creative spirit in a sophisticated way. Their systematic design includes three market competition systems that led to the emergence of Britain and its colony America as the greatest leaders of industrial civilization. And these systems are still in play today.

The first is the economic market competition system for the purpose of pursuing property. The second is the political market competition system for the purpose of pursuing political freedom. The third is the social public welfare market competition system for the purpose of pursuing spiritual freedom. These three market systems were born in the philosophical context of equilibrium between humanity's and God's autonomous rationality in Britain. They were formed through undergoing the brutal baptism of the fierce competition between the two historical experiments in Europe and the United States. Today they are still leading the path of modernization in industrial and post-industrial civilization.

In establishing the political market competition system, British thinkers and designers led by Locke found a way to safely handle the relationship between the honorary power of the royal family and actual political authority. They did this by implementing a political system of constitutional monarchy, in which the British royal family maintained honorary power while the constitution ensured the actual political power of each free, equal individual. That's the essence of constitutionalism—establishing the political power of individual freedom and equality. The fact that these freedoms are protected by the constitution prevents violation by any individual or organization, particularly by the state apparatus toward private issues and procedures. The establishment of the political market competition system also prevented such violation. Its core principle of "legislation from the bottom up," ensured long-term protection of individual political power. Under this system, legislative representatives are elected by individual citizens and are regularly re-elected via the system of one person, one vote. The prime minister or president, who represents "top-down executive power," must also be voted on by individuals, again via one person, one vote. Parties, made up of voters who associate freely, act as guarantors for prime ministerial or presidential candidates. By making their long-term political goals public and leveraging their legislative seats as assets, parties pledge a guarantee for the election and the performance of the prime minister or president. This party system made possible an open, transparent political market competition between parties and between individuals. It laid a foundation for a modern, functionally compatible government structure to solve the problem of the short-term exercise of individual political power.

In this system, the judiciary is chosen from those with a high degree of legal professionalism and virtue. The prime minister, president, or parliament, appoints the judiciary, depending on their position, in a nomination system similar to that in churches, universities, scientific societies, or other non-profit organizations. Their duty is to accept, hear, investigate, and try prosecutorial cases for the whole society according to the legislation of the parliament, weeding out offenders through fair judgements. They must solve problems regarding the fairness and competitiveness of the political market system and are charged with its dynamic maintenance and repair. The institutional design of this political market competition system is indeed imaginative and logically self-consistent and represents the peak of achievement for autonomous human rationality.[304]

British economists, led by Adam Smith, devised the economic market competition system. Their first step was to make explicit, through legislation, the political and economic rights of every citizen to freedom of life, labor, and property, ensuring their protection by law as sacred and inviolable. Second, through the investigations and debates of legislative bodies, codes regarding free trade, antitrust, and fair taxation were enacted to ensure that the civil liberty to pursue property would be carried out in a legal environment of fair competition. Third, based on the constitutional norm of presumption of innocence, procedural laws were formulated to protect the rights of victims or defendants. Systems for evidence, pleas, and juries were established so that any legal disputes or conflicts got a fair hearing. In this way, the fairness, justice, and repair of the economic market competition system could be preserved, and its dynamics and direction could be sustained in the long term. This economic market competition system indeed reached to the limits of imagination and the full expression of autonomous human rationality.[305]

The social public welfare market competition system was gradually designed and cultivated by Great Britain and its colony America.[306] They built it on the foundation of more than 1,500 years of the development of churches, charitable organizations, and scientific and artistic societies in Europe. The wave of church reforms and free scientific associations promoted by the Renaissance and Protestant Reformation were especially instrumental in its development. According to the logic of the system, people have the freedom to pursue wealth, so it follows that they have the freedom to use their wealth to help others. At the same time, they also have the freedom to pursue the beauty of science, technology, and art.

But such pursuits are different from wealth creation. They require resources and therefore support from others in the form of donations. An open, competitive public social welfare fundraising market is required. Projects that are promising and convincing enough could gain support from others in the form of donations. Ventures like the Protestant Puritans' voyages, the construction of churches, the life of different Protestant sects, various charity events, and large-scale works like murals and musical events, were all achieved through competitive persuasion and market-oriented fundraising in the public welfare market.

The market made scientific endeavors possible, funding research in fields such as astronomy, mathematics, chemistry, and physics, and even universities and various scientific societies of that era in Britain and Europe. Any public interest or charitable organization had to be launched by sponsors who pledged their personal reputation, and its internal governance had to be rigorous and standardized. A closer look at the sources of funding for the scientific research and experimentation by the great pioneers—whether Galileo, Kepler, Brahe, Newton, Boyle, Descartes, Leibniz, Dalton, Ampère, Faraday, Maxwell, Joule, Clausius, or the Royal Society of London, Accademia del Cimento, the French Academy of Sciences, the Prussian Academy of Sciences, or Manchester Astronomical Society—shows that they were all enabled by the philanthropic support of sponsors. It could be argued that without the social public welfare market, the scientific and cultural foundations on which our entire modern civilization is based would not have been built or solidified.

It was the systematic design of these three systems based on autonomous human rationality that contributed to the organizational innovations that put Britain at the core of modern industrial civilization. One such innovation was the creation of a modern functional government in the political competitive market, with a parliament for legislation, ministries under the prime minister or president for administrative affairs, and a judiciary for the administration of justice.

Next was the organizational innovation of the market economy. After Columbus discovered the New World, European countries led by Britain and

Netherlands created a new form of organization, the "limited liability company." LLCs replaced the traditional family business organization as Europeans sought to develop the New World. A typical LLC was funded by investors who employed a captain to form a management team for their venture in the New World. The captain and the management team didn't contribute capital, but because they managed the operation and undertook risk, they held 20 percent of the shares, and the other shareholders provided the capital in proportion. All the shares and shareholder names were engraved or written with a special paint on the ship's bow to show distribution of future income. Shareholders and managers had only limited liability, so if they failed, there was no recourse to family assets outside of the company.

Compared to the family-centered unlimited liability business organization in which a son was responsible for his father's debt, this was much more humane. This new structure encouraged more people to invest in such ventures. On the other hand, LLCs achieved division of labor and a clear break with traditional family organizations, separating economic risk management from traditional blood ties. Unprecedented possibilities for the flow of talent were opened up, especially for those with unique ideas and inventions. More importantly, on the basis of double-entry bookkeeping, long practiced in churches and non-profit organizations by skilled professional accountants, systematic and logically self-consistent corporate measurement tools for LLCs were created. These included balance sheets, profit and loss statements, cash flow statements, and owner's equity statements, which made it possible to standardize the assessment of a company's operating condition and value and to exchange its shares in capital markets. This organizational innovation made possible the monetization and internationalization of various production factors, sowing the seeds for the rampant expansion of the globalization of the modern market economy. It also opened a valve that couldn't be closed for the endless division of human labor, such as accountants, lawyers, appraisers, engineers, designers, researchers, as well as daz-zling organizational innovation.

Finally, there was the innovation of social welfare organizations. Prior to the Renaissance and Reformation, European non-profit organizations included mainly churches and charitable organizations who aimed to care for vulnerable groups. The sympathy and wealth of the rich and middle class was translated into donations to churches and charitable organizations and flowed to the underprivileged. After the Renaissance, universities, scientific societies, technical industry associations, artistic studios, and other new public welfare organizations, which had nothing to do with vulnerable groups, developed and complemented various post-Reformation church organizations. These societies profoundly influenced the *human duty* in people's search for the meaning of life in Europe.[307]

It was the design of these systems that facilitated the peaceful transition of British society from a monarchical to an egalitarian one, and in particular, promoted the close connection and mutual reinforcement between scientific imagination and technology—with the former based on the natural theology of God and the latter based on pragmatic human experience. With utilitarianism as a driving force, the newly created LLC catalyzed greater collaboration between science and technology. It sparked the pragmatic use of science, by pushing it to constantly solve technological problems. The chasm between science with its source in God and technology with its source in mankind was increasingly filled with the dual drivers of seeking profit and winning the competition among LLCs. Two entrancing ideas reinforced each other: the solemn ideal of exploring the laws created by God and the eagerness to chase worldly fame and material glory. People were stimulated like never before to achieve great things in conquering nature by understanding and applying natural law. As a result, industrial civilization completely replaced agricultural civilization, and urban civilization completely replaced rural civilization.

Nature, once temperamental, mysterious, and powerful, was trod underfoot. Humanity collectively won.

In the midst of this conquest of nature, *human ability* kept popping up as a pleasant surprise: in the age of trains, coal-powered steam engines replaced traditional animal and human power; in the age of automobile and aircraft, internal combustion engines and jet power fueled by petrochemicals replaced the steam engine; and the development of new power fueled by nuclear fusion contributed to imaginative and practical explorations that transcend the Earth's gravitational force. In short, the collective capacity of human beings constantly surpassed the limits of *human ability* during agricultural civilization. Britain, as a European island state, relied on the design and practice of these market competition systems to become the leading power in the world. It commercialized and colonized countries throughout Asia, Africa, Australia, and the Americas, exceeding 30 percent of global territory at its peak, well beyond the limits of a nation state controlling other regional ethnic groups by means of trade. Britain became a new paradigm for the rise and prosperity of nation states based on industrial civilization.

SECTION 4: THE GLOBAL CONQUEST AND VICTORY OF THE THREE MARKET SYSTEMS

France's transformation from an agricultural civilization under a monarchy to an egalitarian industrial society system involved many more ups and downs than Britain's. The main reason was that French Enlightenment thinkers tried to completely abandon God's rationality and achieve human rational autonomy without it. Such radicalism brought extremism into the mainstream consciousness throughout society.[308] A crucial historical transition for France in the second half of the 18th century in France approached, as Rousseauian radicalism was magnified by public opinion. The public faced a choice that was completely different from that during British's social transformation.

In 1789, France followed Britain in a bid to realize the institutional transformation from monarchy to constitutional monarchy. A general assembly, known as the Estates General, was convened with the clergy, the nobility, and the commoners to discuss whether voting rights in the election of representatives in the National Assembly should be counted according to three classes or on a one-person-one-vote basis. In the end, 1,201 representatives were selected by one person, one vote. In essence, it was almost impossible to reach an agreement with all these attendants. The National Assembly became a place to express positions and feelings rather than a stage for rational discussion of issues.

Whether they belonged to the class of the clergy, the nobility, or the commoners, all members of society lacked the attitudes that contributed to British stability—attitudes of tolerance and pragmatism that balanced human rationality with God's theological rationality. French society also lacked careful consideration of the details in designing its market systems, which required compromise to account for the interests of the different people they would affect. As a result, the radical Jacobins' speeches tinged with extreme freedom and violent undertones flooded the National Assembly and the post-revolutionary constitutional convention. Commoners, or the Third Estate, who were eager for human autonomy in the form of complete freedom and equality, vehemently refused any compromise. What began as peace talks and procedural negotiations of the National Assembly quickly devolved into extremism, and the beginning of the French Revolution.

The incensed lower classes, united by their strong desire for freedom, captured the Bastille ammunition depot under the leadership of Lafayette. Amid the cries of Robespierre and other Jacobins for absolute freedom for the people, King Louis XVI was deposed in 1792 and guillotined on January 21, 1793. This event symbolized the violent end of the old system of monarchy in France that had lasted thousands of years. Hundreds of priests, regarded as stewards of the old system, were forced to face the guillotine. Countless civilians were killed. France was stained with blood. People poured into the streets, spilling blood on the guillotines and cheering the establishment of the First French Republic.

But the revolution didn't give the French people the absolute freedom and equality they desired, as romanticized by Enlightenment leaders like Rousseau and Voltaire, but rather violence and subsequent turbulence. A case in point was the death of the violent revolutionary leader Robespierre, who had attempted to rule the country by Rousseauian virtue instead of the freedom to pursue property. He was shot a year after the beginning of the revolution, and the chaos lasted until 1804. By then, the French people had completely forgotten their original intention of beheading King Louis XVI, 11 years earlier, and embraced Napoleon as their emperor in frenzied cheers.

Napoleon's popularity resulted from the fact that he led France to conquer the whole European Continent, which shifted the public attention from domestic conflicts and contradictions to the Napoleonic Wars. This shift demonstrated that human "freedom and equality" were just weak and hypocritical notions without the constraint of God's rationality. The outcome, of course, was the defeat of the great French hero Napoleon in 1815 and his abandonment and exile by the French people. Even then, they still hadn't found the absolute freedom and equality they had sought by relying solely on autonomous human rationality. For more than half a century, France continued to experience violent bloodshed caused by seizure and counter-seizure of power. Each time, the victors rashly and unilaterally rolled out constitutional revisions, and each revision sowed the seeds of violent revolution.

It wasn't until the Paris Commune uprising of 1870 that France realized that they were back where they started after a century of turmoil. Having learned from this bitter experience, the French people elected 675 members of the National Assembly via universal suffrage and held a five-year constitutional assembly. It took countless procedural debates, pardons, and compromises surrounding the details of a democratic, republican government to form the modern constitution, which was adopted in 1875. The constitution specifically stipulated a basic framework for separation of powers and checks and balances between the executive, legislative, and judicial branches, as well as a "political market mechanism" for partisan competition for seats. The transformation of the political system from a monarchy over an agricultural civilization to a modern competitive political market system was largely complete. The stark contrast between France's turmoil in constructing its modern competitive political market system and Britain's was now made plain.

As early as the Elizabethan era, when Anglicanism initiated the Protestant Reformation, the British social elites promulgated the "Charity Uses Act" and "Act for the Relief of the Poor," the first of their kind in modern global history. This led to larger-scale organization of charitable activities based on millennia of Christian charitable practices in poverty relief, education, religion, and community work. The modern prototype of public welfare, or the social market competition system, was thus formed.

On this basis, Britain tried to build political and economic market competition systems at the same time. The political market competition system was completed before its economic counterpart, which made its construction seem natural and logical and allowed politics and economics to develop in a relatively peaceful, stable, and easy manner. These three competitive market systems formed a stabilizing triangle. The competitive political market ensured smooth transitions between political regimes and the public expression of individual political appeals, as well as competition and policy continuity in the economic market. The competitive economic market ensured that people's subjective freedom would not be hurt by violence during political turmoil and that people could live in a peaceful, secure environment. At the same time, it ensured that the objective freedom of people to pursue wealth wouldn't be violently looted and that fair competition as well as development and prosperity could be sustained.

The competitive social welfare market ensured the combination of humanity's public spirit and individual free will. It not only alleviated and soothed the suffering of the vulnerable amid fierce market competition, but also encouraging warm and loving interactions across the social chasm, passing on the love of God and Christ, and inspiring and helping individuals in distress. Through it, the coordinated operation of the other two market competition systems gained effective support. This was an important reason why Britain went for 500 years without a major, violent internal war, which is truly a great miracle in the history of human civilization. Of course, its history of global colonial expansion through its institutional advantages has always been criticized as a dishonorable act of a nation state.

The British Puritans, for their part, embarked on a journey with the ambition to develop the untapped territory of America. They saw North America as God's promised land for them. They took their Puritan value of separation from British Anglicanism as the fundamentalist mission of their church. They brought a new, unique, Protestant spirit to the American continent which later informed Edwards' revivalist theology. It harmonized the freedom to strive unremittingly with the equal treatment of others and glorifying God with rigorous self-discipline in individual life. This Protestant spirit took root and bore fruit in North America.[309] It laid the solid foundation of faith in God, not only for the creation of a competitive social welfare market but also for the eventual competitive political market in the United States, which was tenaciously rooted in community volunteerism.

When it came time for them to build the political market system, America drew on a close alliance with France during the late 18th and early 19th centuries for strength to break the umbilical cord with their motherland, Britain, and gain independence. On the surface, they appeared to have inherited from the French Enlightenment thinkers the anti-monarchy, political market competition system for civilians, characterized by total freedom and equality. But in reality, the American Enlightenment thinkers led by Thomas Paine, retained from their British counterparts the extremely rigorous, pragmatic spirit that upheld the balance between God's rationality and autonomous human rationality.

Legislative delegates elected by the states held a constitutional convention in Philadelphia in May 1878 that lasted more than 120 days. Considering both the Mayflower Compact as a prototype and the fact that they had gained their independence from Britain, they discussed, analyzed, and compromised to reach a "Draft Constitution," which was passed via referendum in each state and became the Constitution of the United States. Specific subordinate laws were developed in accordance with the highest principles of the Constitution. The legacy of such great systematic thinking and procedural justice remains to this day, a paradigm for the establishment of the modern political market competition system. And the model that resulted—three major market competition systems with mutual support and rational checks and balances—still guides the intellectual classes in underdeveloped countries seeking to modernize their nation states. This became especially true after the violent devastation of the two world wars. The United States introduced the Marshall Plan in 1948, as a way to achieve its international vision of aiding less developed countries. By virtue of its market model, the United States eventually replaced its British tutor as the worldwide icon of modern market competition systems and a recognized and respected leader of global business and fair competition.

In Germany, the creation of the three major market competition systems was the most complicated and most torturous among western countries. It had to overcome not only the barriers formed by the monarchy and aristocracy of the Holy Roman Empire against the construction of the modern egalitarian system, but also the massive tension between Prussia and other small German states over the establishment of a unified state. These obstacles and tensions were irreconcilable, much like the opposition between God's rationality and autonomous human rationality in Kantian philosophy.

A large part of their task, philosophically speaking, was to synthesize autonomous rationality represented by Hegel (1770–1831) and the "Absolute Spirit" represented by the Germanic people. Hegel's unique dialectical method of "thesis, antithesis, synthesis" and the view that human history is the externalized movement of Absolute Spirit were significant in shaping German thought. On the one hand, this synthesis embodied Germans' national awareness of the conflicting and complex nature of the modernization path they faced. On the other hand, it reflected their strong desire and aspiration for a unified, powerful Germany. This conflict and contradiction inspired an extreme current of thought among the German people to hasten the realization of this desire.[310]

As a result, after Hegel, Ludwig Feuerbach (1804–1872) continued down the path of extremism, denying the existence of God as well as the existence of the human spirit, and insisting that matter is all that exists. Feuerbach held that humans are matter, and that only individual, material humans exist. According to him, "man is what he eats." Feuerbach confused belief in God with idolatry, arguing that all religions are delusive notions, and that they should be all overturned. He believed that only mankind is worth worshiping, that God must be humanized, so that "the secular world can swallow the sacred world." But as Feuerbach's arrogance placed all spirits beneath the feet of humans, the logical end of his thinking would have humans return to an animalistic state without spirits; human civilization would become rubble, leaving Feuerbach standing alone on top of it.

Karl Marx (1818–1883) derived his ideas from Hegel, Feuerbach, and Rousseau. He violently criticized all human spiritual and religious beliefs, including faith in God, arguing that they are like opium created by the upper class to anesthetize the masses. But unlike Feuerbach, Marx held a very pessimistic view of human nature. He believed that humans are naturally greedy, selfish, and unreliable, and that only group pressure can contain such selfishness and greed. Marx admired Hegel's dialectical method of thesis, antithesis, synthesis and applied it to economics. He believed that conflict is the dominant element in historical change, and the system of private property is the source of all evil. According to Marx, in the economic market system, capital strips surplus value created by labor, resulting in a major conflict between capital and labor. Ultimately, the private property system must be violently overthrown and a system of public ownership of property should replace it, realizing the communist synthesis of allocation according to need in human society. Yet Marx did not answer the questions of whether those who control public property have overcome their selfish and greedy nature, and whether they will subvert the ideals of public ownership.

Later, Nietzsche (1844–1900) pushed Germany's dominant Hegelian thought to its extreme. To Nietzsche, conflict exists everywhere in history; there is only thesis and antithesis, no synthesis. Human reason and desire are in conflict—reason is merely a tool of desire, and therefore, the essence of human life is in conflict with reason. Humans possess only life, but not reason. Morality has no meaning, and only desire drives life. For him, the greatest conflict in human history is the conflict between God and human freedom. Where there is belief in God, there can be no human freedom. If people want freedom, they don't need God, so Nietzsche declared that "God is dead." All order is meaningless. There is no morality, no right and wrong. There is only the self-affirmation of life, so we must courageously live a meaningless life in the meaningless world.

Yet Nietzsche himself lost the courage to face the meaninglessness of life and died of depression and mania. He left his motherland and the world a spiritual legacy of extreme liberalism and anarchy, which became the most significant historical footnote to Germany's endless violence, warfare, and nationalism, and led to the denial of freedom, enslavement, and massacre of the majority by the few who dominated the state apparatus.[311]

Later in the 20th century, the autonomous human rationality that characterized Germany's mainstream thinking and originated from Kant's dualistic worldview shifted completely from being God-centered to German-centered, which Kant had never expected. The "Germanic elite," who claimed to have achieved full rational autonomy, completely abandoned the human social moral order based on sacred faith. They utterly abandoned the *human calling* that God expects, rooted in the Christian faith that their Holy Roman Empire ancestors had held for nearly 2,000 years. They believed as fanatically as Nietzsche in the complete legitimacy of desire as the driver of life and behavior, and in the complete legitimacy of using violence to deprive others of their freedom and property.

The German people, with their "complete autonomous rationality," launched two world wars in less than three decades, dragging the world's major countries into violent warfare in which hundreds of millions were slaughtered, starved, and tortured to death. The appalling scale of the two wars and the heavy toll they took completely surpassed those in earlier human history. Their ideal of building a static and equal society through violent deprivation of freedom and property spread far and wide, taking on another fanatical and extreme form in an unprecedented, large-scale social experiment. Countless countries were involved, and the property and freedom of tens of millions of people were deprived by violent political machinery. Tens of millions died of poverty and hunger that resulted from their property being taken.

Later, the Germans, who arrogantly saw themselves as representatives of the Absolute Spirit, took more years and more lost lives than any other European country to achieve peace—when East and West Germany were finally reunified in the 1990s. Even then, it wouldn't be accurate to say that the construction of the three major market competition systems were truly completed in Germany, nor could it be said that national modernization was fully finished. If world civilization from the 17th–19th centuries was defined by the British, then the human history of the 20th century was largely defined by the Germans, with Britain and the United States as only two of the leading actors in the historical drama directed by Germany. Clearly, God didn't need the reason of the German people to accomplish his purposes, while the Germans who rejected God's rationality descended into chaos.[312]

No matter how complex and twisted the historical process in these European countries proved, the three major market competition systems of politics, economics, and social welfare were eventually established. First built by British Enlightenment thinkers and pioneers guided by the balance between belief in God's rationality and autonomous human rationality, these systems still acquired unprecedented material and glorious achievements, as well as overwhelming victory worldwide. They have conquered Europe, America, and Australia, and are in the process of conquering Asia and Africa.

Yet these systems have been over-simplified as mere "capitalism" in later years. This is due largely to the dramatic inversion brought about by German Hegelian philosophical logic and its political practice in the 19th and 20th centuries, as well as the large-scale social experiment that sought to take away people's right to freely pursue property. Socialist preaching about the conflict and struggle between the thesis and antithesis of socialism and capitalism obscured an accurate understanding of these systems. This Hegelian over-simplification has produced countless misunderstandings and logical difficulties in discussion and analysis of these concepts. It's high time for the discussion to leave behind Hegelian logic and restore precise, orthodox definitions. The system created by British Enlightenment thinkers and pioneers like Locke are not a "capitalist system" at all, but rather a three-part market competition system. All countries today have built their market competition systems to varying degrees. Even North Korea has had to join the economic international market competition system. No country has been completely excluded from it.

If the system that began with Locke is capitalist, then what is its Hegelian logical antithesis today, namely, the socialist system? Supposing for the sake of argument that China is its antithesis immediately presents a serious logical obstacle. In 1978, the former Chinese leader Deng Xiaoping acknowledged that China was in the primary stages of long-term socialism, and then launched institutional reforms that allowed and encouraged people to take advantage of their freedom to pursue wealth. Since then, the extent of accumulation and capitalization of private property in China has grown so much that its total private capital may be approaching or surpassing that of Europe. In this sense, the freedom to pursue private property and the dynamic accumulation of capital in China today is essentially no different from what is called "capitalism" in Europe and America.

If we try to emphasize that China's state-capital can represent public interest appeals in order to distinguish it from the Anglo-American capitalist system, then we immediately run into a second logical obstacle. Namely, that the high and growing proportion of social public welfare capital in Anglo-American capitalism is a more convincing response to public interest appeals than Chinese state-owned enterprises. The monopoly of these Chinese state-owned enterprises has led to ineffective allocation of resources, as well as the confusion of their role as both a player and the referee in the game. This has quickly resulted in corruption, making for a much less convincing empirical case that they represent the public interest.

If we insist on calling China the antithesis of capitalism, just to differentiate its system from its Lockean market competition counterpart, we immediately encounter a third logical obstacle and miss the forest for the trees. Aiming for large, state-owned enterprises to reduce or eliminate private capital in a bid to match the name of "socialism" will inevitably lead to chaos and turbulence in the thought and the direction of society.

In contrast, returning to straightforward definitions of the three major market competition systems makes the tension between the thesis and antithesis of capitalism and socialism disappear at once. Countries around the world can compare, differentiate, and learn from the construction of the three major market competition systems among their peers. In doing so, they will find that there are only differences in degrees, not in essence, in these systems, which can modify the fixed idea of conflict and struggle between thesis and antithesis. Only in this way can modern thinking break free of the nightmare caused by Hegelian philosophy in the 20th century and of Rousseau's paradoxical utopian illusion of absolute freedom and static, "average" ownership of property.

Rousseau, in his Enlightenment reflections, discovered the difficulties inherent in the pursuit of freedom through human rationality, as reflected in his famous saying, "Man is born free, and everywhere he is in chains." But Rousseau rashly believed that equality was easy to attain and naively thought that humans could be equal simply by getting rid of the division of labor and property. As for Hegel, he was arrogant enough to believe that the synthesis of human freedom and equality could be achieved by solely relying on his logic and the Absolute Spirit of the Germans. After the deaths of Rousseau and Hegel, the left-wing ideological extremism in France and especially in Germany in the 19th century led the world to unprecedented violence and slavery. This proved that Rousseau and Hegel's pursuit of "human equality and freedom" apart from a sacred source was completely out of reach, as it relied solely on human rationality and abandoned God's. The "equality" that Rousseau's limited mind presented to mankind was just an illusory daydream. His "freedom" with no property or division of labor deprived people of the most basic objective and subjective freedom from the very beginning, instead bringing humanity a profound lack of freedom.

In the end, who had the power to take away people's objective freedom of pursuing property and their subjective freedom of division of labor? Only those in control of the political machinery had the power to deprive ordinary people of these rights, and only through organized violence. A society in which the minority uses organized violence to deprive others of their right to property and division of labor can only be one where the majority has lost their subjective and objective freedom. How could such a society grant its majority the right to human equality? The great experiments of the 20th century served to reveal the final answer to Rousseau and Hegel's propositions: after abandoning God's reason in a purely rational world, man is born free, and everywhere he is in chains of deprivation; man is born equal, and everywhere he is in chains of enslavement.

CHAPTER 13:

Looking forward: humanity's third great awakening

SECTION 1: THE RISE OF PREDATORY MONOPOLIES

After the tumultuous changes of three centuries, the three major systems of market competition have withstood the test of time—all of which are based on the values of British Christianity and scientific rationality. The United States of America, after its independence from the British motherland, developed a systematic paradigm for these three major market systems: the charity free market, the political free market, and the economic free market.

The first of these preserves societal compassion. Through the persistent efforts of churches, universities, academic societies, and other non-profit organizations, the charity free market system has become an organized force for spreading good in a modern nation. Charitable organizations work to alleviate poverty, provide disaster relief, protect the environment, and advocate for educational equality and equality under the law, among other causes. This system's protection of vulnerable groups and manifestation of public compassion and justice eases class conflict and prevents societal unrest, ensuring a highly stable foundation for society's future aspirations and providing a solid baseline for justice.

Meanwhile, the US political market competition system gives, at least nominally, a clear baseline definition of human freedom and equality, the two sacred rights given by divine authority. Through its one-person, one-vote system, the implicit contract of "one to many" becomes explicit. During the era of agricultural civilization, this contract between government and individuals was implicit, allowing the state machinery that mankind created to become a sprawling leviathan. By contrast, with the United States' explicit one-to-many contract, the government is placed directly under the control of authorities that can be replaced through non-violent elections and other peaceful, democratic means. The system of a singular ruler, holding political power for life and passing it down through hereditary lines, is abolished, so that the power shifts toward equal, individual rights. New rules of peace, equality, and non-violence ensure the long-term order and stability within the nation.

This system, in the United States and other Western-influenced nations, has expanded freedom and equality to unprecedented levels since the beginning of human history. Winston Churchill, Margaret Thatcher, George Washington, Abraham Lincoln, Jimmy Carter, Bill Clinton, Nelson Mandela, and others, who were all born into ordinary or even poor families, were able to become great leaders in this political free market. Countless examples show that people can gain political freedom and equality without the need to seize power through inheritance or bloody violence.

Built on this political freedom, the economic market competition system, with its origins in Britain, also shines brightly in Europe and especially in the

United States. The freedom to seek one's own self-interest, wealth, and influence, a natural law that arises from the principle of God-given equality, has been incorporated into modern national constitutions. Spreading far and wide through media and public opinion, these freedoms have become firmly rooted in people's minds. Modern limited liability companies, limited partner companies, and publicly listed companies have been formed as vehicles for modern humanity's pursuit of financial freedom. In this economic free market, people have equal access to form such companies and build wealth freely.

Governments, for their part, have pulled back from their traditional role of maintaining order and preventing and confronting both external and internal violence, and are spending more time and energy building, sustaining, and modifying the laws of the economic market. These laws aim to: protect individual freedom and the freedom to pursue wealth; encourage individuals to freely start a company while keeping strict supervision in place; apply new accounting standards to measure companies' efficiency and value; create and maintain commodity markets, labor markets, intellectual property markets, and capital markets so that all kinds of property can be reasonably valued and exchanged freely and equitably; develop market operating procedures and regulations to enable their orderly and efficient functioning; build a tax system that keeps the national economy sustainable and attractive to talent; allocate taxes to make government regulation effective and maintain order in the market; and create clear guidelines to punish those who violate the rules of market competition and maintain fairness. Opposing monopolies and unfair competition has increasingly become government's most important public role.[313]

According to economic theory—the earliest social discipline to use the quantitative tools of science—mankind's freedom to pursue wealth and fame based on self-interest has gained unprecedented legitimacy under market competition. The free market system assumes this legitimacy, compelling people to recognize that pursuing their own self-interest is also good for others, and to no longer consider it evil to think only of oneself. Under this system, history has seen an unprecedented movement to promote self-centered, profit-driven competition, transforming a selfish evil into altruistic goodness in society's eyes.

This global contest has granted people the freedom to create wealth for over 300 years. Companies innovate constantly, while the traditional organization of the family has retreated from the center stage of wealth creation. Those skilled at using companies to build wealth become "entrepreneurs." Through new ideas, concepts, and methods, they provide products and services for the market, while competing with other entrepreneurs with similar offerings. Many others join companies as workers. They refine their own skills and techniques in their niche within the division of labor and compete with other workers in the same fields. To gain advantage in the free market, entrepreneurs must take on the most talented employees with the highest salary possible, improve the quality of products and services with the best technology, and manage their companies in the most advanced and efficient ways. This enables them to win over consumers with the most competitive products or services in both quality and price.

The logical result of the free market seems self-evident: a large number of successful limited liability companies, creating an unprecedented level of wealth in human history and leading to a rapid increase in the wealth of the country itself. This in turn promotes the transformation of the country's economy into a modern employment structure of mostly non-agricultural industries, along with urbanization, a general increase in individual income and tax revenues, and the improvement of public facilities, resulting in a rise in national prosperity and civilization.

In the first 200 years of this period, Europe and its immigrant countries (the United States, Canada, Australia, and New Zealand) repeatedly proved the assumptions and logic of neoclassical economics, and the effectiveness of the free market in creating material wealth and advancing the human conquest of nature. In stark contrast, the large-scale socialist experiments to abolish the freedom to seek wealth and market competition failed utterly. In the end, all they produced was a loss of social drive to create wealth, widespread poverty, and tyranny, with tragic consequences. The unnatural deaths of hundreds of millions were like Guinea pigs sacrificed in this historical double-blind experiment.

Amid this unprecedented competition driven by human self-interest, a new group has emerged: the entrepreneurs. Out of every hundred companies established every year, less than 10 percent survive after ten years, and only 1 percent succeed. Despite that success rate, there are still people with the courage to move ahead through thick and thin down the path of entrepreneurship. Successful entrepreneurs represent not only the dream of financial freedom, but also enjoy an increase in social status.[314] According to Austrian economist Joseph Schumpeter, successful entrepreneurs are innovators, in their ability to combine resources, while entrepreneurs who fail to innovate are ruthlessly eliminated by market competition. Investors who fail also have to accept their bad luck and bear the limited liability for the company's debts after it closes down, since debts come before equity. They may wait for the opportunity to make a comeback or withdraw from entrepreneurship entirely and return to the labor market, where jobs are increasingly specialized, to compete for a spot.

The division of labor in a company is largely based on the entrepreneur, prioritized according to their ability to compete.[315] First come the chief technology officer and the technology research and development team, who determine whether the company stands out from the competition. Second come the chief marketing officer and the sales team, who determine the company's ability to generate revenue and gain market share, which in turn affects the company's strategic decisions. Third come the company's chief operating officer and the management team, who determine the company's ability to control costs and how fast it responds to market changes, which affects the company's management decision making. Fourth come the company's chief financial officer and accountants, working with cost control, efficiency analysis, and funding. They determine the accuracy of the company's integration of local and overall information, accounting compliance, fund management effectiveness, and financial support. Fifth come the company's head of human resources and their HR team, who determine whether a company can find the best talent in the market and align them with the company's strategy, whether it can optimize team performance and improve overall performance, whether it can create a successful team culture, and whether it can form effective coordination and negotiations between the company and labor unions. Sixth come the company's chief lawyer and legal team, who determine the company's ability to maintain compliance and both prevent and mitigate legal risk when interacting with stakeholders like shareholders, consumers, the community, creditors, the government, and competitors. Seventh come the teams and employees that manufacture the company's products or provide its services, determining their quality and stability, which are vital to the company's reputation and branding among consumers.

Continuous division of labor in companies has promoted a kind of division of education. Competition between various universities, vocational schools, and continuing education schools prompts educational institutions to respond to the needs of companies. Schools cultivate a wide variety of talent catering to these needs and deliver it to companies, which makes them much more competitive and enables those with prominent advantages to achieve winner-take-all expansion.

Companies have also begun to gradually fund campaigns through social media. This has created an industry aimed at influencing consumer decisions through advertising. Advertising quickly integrated with higher education and social science research, forming the advertising media industry. Media studies focus on how to attract and capture attention, while advertising focuses on how to exploit human weaknesses. The two combined to form an industry that captures people's attention for the sole purpose of creating social impact to make a profit. In order to win over new customers while keeping existing ones, companies are investing more and more in advertising, accounting for 5, 10, or even 50 percent of their profits. In some extreme cases, they spend up to 100–200 percent of their profits on ads. The advertising industry, which exerts its influence on consumers through social media, impels companies or entrepreneurs to pay more attention to their brand.

Advertisements are designed to systematically target and exploit human weaknesses, such as greed; laziness; the desire to take advantage of others; selfishness; and lust for celebrity, fame, power, and adulation. They employ all kinds of marketing strategies like free gifts, competitions with large prizes, and Guinness-world-record-setting advertising campaigns for various industries. Coupled closely with social media, today's advertising industry completely undermines the checks and balances of the three classic free market systems. Today, we're unable to discern whether purchasing decisions or even political votes are made by consumers of their own free will—through their own independent thought. People think they're mavericks, making unique or unusual choices on their own, little knowing that they are really only puppets manipulated by those who have designed advertisement campaigns to reach consumers through TV, traditional news media, mobile internet, and celebrities. Human rationality is now encountering an unprecedented challenge—do the ideas people hold even originate from their free will and rationality given by God? The advertising industry has inaugurated an era in which elaborate campaigns involving celebrities and renowned experts arise in response to huge demand, an era where social influence can be gained through entertainment and advertising.[316]

Social media has also resulted in further division of labor. First is the department of public relations and brand communication. In a world-class company, hundreds of millions or even billions of dollars are spent on advertising, public relations, and lobbying each year. Such companies hire pop stars and famous athletes as spokespeople. Not only that, they also hire science and technology experts for soft-sell advertising that influences consumer perceptions, along with professors, researchers, and retired government officials in public policy to lobby for political decisions in favor of the company. The second is the corporate social responsibility department. Though this department spends significantly less money than advertising, their budget is still significant, reaching tens or even hundreds of millions of dollars annually for major multinational companies. They hire professional philanthropists to develop donation strategies consistent with the company's reputation among its customer base. By selecting philanthropic organizations for targeted donations and publicity, companies correct the negative stigma of excessive investment in advertising and maintain the company's brand.

The growing influence of social media has increased celebrities' ability to accumulate wealth, which in turn has boosted the societal impact of advertising on social media. Over time social media has transformed into a platform that integrates the resources of the three major free markets to create social influence. This is evidenced by the establishment of CNN, the world's first 24-hour television news network and the popularity of companies like China's Sina and Tencent and America's Google, Facebook, and Twitter. These companies rely solely on news and interpersonal influence. While claiming to provide so-called "free" services to consumers, these platforms are generating lucrative advertising revenue by taking advantage of them. Eighty percent of Google's nearly $100 billion in revenue comes from advertising. Facebook's annual advertising revenue exceeds $30 billion. The significance and impact of social media on individual perception is far beyond the imagination and control of human reason.[317]

Of course, whether a company provides goods or services to the market, it can't succeed without financing. Banks as service providers match the supply and demand between depositors and borrowers. Banking was originally a traditional deposit and loan management industry parallel to manufacturing. In the agricultural era, banks and financial institutions were criticized for their high interest rates—practically a moral taboo. As the economic market of industrial civilization advanced, the banking industry achieved legitimacy but had to be subject to strict governmental regulation. That was until Dutch immigrants started their own system of stock trading in the 17th century in Wall Street. Since then, creating stocks and bonds based on company performance and value and selling them to raise money from outside the company has quickly gained momentum, leading to the rise of non-banking financial instruments.

After Alexander Hamilton, one of the great founding fathers of the United States, constructed his ideal system, Wall Street became the world's center of financial innovation in the 19th century. Financial innovations are a kind of arbitrage across space and time. The stock market allows a company's expected earnings in the future to be sold to present investors at a discount in order to fund its current capital requirements. Speculative stock traders who bet on a company's expected earnings form a group of constantly changing shareholders, separate from controlling shareholders. Whether these shareholders hold on to company stock is highly dependent on what they learn from the social media system. That's why economists call them "shareholders who vote with their feet."

In the bond market, investors place bets on the solvency or default of each publicly issued bond at its maturity date. In the futures market, investors place bets on the expected supply and price of each forward and cross-regional commodity contract publicly traded in the market. In the foreign exchange market, investors place bets on the expected foreign exchange ratio between two countries' currencies at a given time, as measured by a reliable, mutually agreed-upon, third-party currency. In the asset securitization market, investors place bets on the expectation of future compliance with payments on asset leases and sales, with securities issued by market authorities.

If stock performance is based on a company's bookkeeping, accounting system, and legal framework—and thus on the ethical endorsement of the professionals in accounting and law firms—then there is logic behind the investment. Yet, outside of stocks, the wide variety of increasingly complex financial derivatives, such as futures, options, index futures, asset-backed securities, and insurance options, are pure speculative gambling. Their logic and utility are proved only by complex mathematical models built by Wall Street's game theorists, and their legitimacy as publicly traded assets are only established through Wall Street's powerful political public relations machines. The kind of speculative gambling considered morally repugnant during the agricultural era has been brought back into the free market system by Wall Street. Thanks to sophisticated mathematical sugarcoating and the scientific legitimacy given to game theory, this kind of speculation has since been accepted as an essential part of the human economy.

Wall Street's new and ever-changing financial instruments greatly inspire a spirit of adventure and innovation among entrepreneurs by constantly producing successful stories of wealth creation. They also accelerate the pace of interactions between science and technology, as well as capital mergers, acquisitions, and expansion of scale among companies. The national borders that humans have created over tens of thousands of years lose much of their meaning in the face of Wall Street's financial innovations. The rest of the world closely follows Wall Street in adopting these innovative financial models, causing market volatility that affects hundreds of millions every day instantly through news disseminated over TV, radio, and the internet. The new financial industry, as a smug achievement of human reason, has dwarfed the traditional banking sector. At the same time, it has also sown profound and deadly seeds for humanity that human reason alone can never resolve.[318]

The development of these new financial instruments on Wall Street over the last 25 years of the 20th century, along with the unbridled influence of mass media in later years, are two unique products of the economic competitive market. They have merged in the United States to create a mixture of globalism and financial monopolies[319]—a new enemy of market competition.

This confluence has its basis in two important historical premises. The first is the establishment of the United Nations and similar organizations as a result of the lessons learned from the horrible loss of hundreds of millions of lives over two world wars. Key to the formation of these organizations were two systems put in place around that time. The Bretton Woods system, under which the United States stationed troops in key areas of the world at its own expense and the U.S. dollar with its fixed value against gold was used for international settlements, was established in the 1940s. The Marshall Plan was put in place by the United States in the 1950s to help underdeveloped countries recover, leading to the creation of organizations like the World Bank, International Finance Corporation, and the International Monetary Fund. A large number of corporate social responsibility, private legacy, and private foundation donations, and even bilateral and multilateral government aid, flowed to international public welfare projects. The result was a staggering number of NGOs and their staff, giving rise to a framework of global development assistance unprecedented in human history. Anyone who fails to fit into such framework in an interactive setting, such as at an international conference or a university, is considered outdated and outmoded.

The second is the decline of the great social experiment, represented by the communism led by the Soviet Union, which had tried to abolish people's freedom to pursue private property. Its turning point came when China, the most populous country participating in this experiment, moved away from the Soviet system and began its own reform. It opened up its markets to the West and gave individuals the freedom to seek wealth. It tried to establish a partial economic free market with equal emphasis on state and private capital, join the international division of labor, and gradually replicate the non-banking financial industry of Wall Street. This move by China led to an unprecedented expansion of the global free market and established the clearest reference point for others in the Soviet camp to decide whether to adopt a competitive free market or not. The experiment ultimately led to the failure of the Soviet model in the Eastern Bloc, putting an end to more than a century of debate over whether the free market or planned economy was more effective. This outcome not only provided a convincing argument for certain politicians and pundits in their ideological debates, but also gave a golden opportunity to Wall Street financiers for global capital expansion. Any entrepreneur, executive, or professional who worked for a company that didn't talk about "globalization" and financial investment at every opportunity was seen as out of date.

The large number of international non-profit organizations and Wall Street companies talking about globalization gave rise to an overwhelming trend that, aided by mass media,[320] swept through every social elite of the era. Wall Street companies and entrepreneurs, through increasing their investment in government lobbying and hiring of retired government officials, successfully convinced Congress to repeal a series of legislations in the financial sector enacted during the Roosevelt and Wilson eras. These included laws regarding the "capital adequacy ratio," the strict separation between the deposit and loan business of traditional banks and the speculative business of non-banking financial institutions, and the rigorous regulation of financial derivatives with little significance to the real economy. This ushered in a new era in which the US financial industry had complete freedom to soar. The mixed operation of traditional banks and non-banking financial institutions through mergers meant that a larger share of banks' earnings was coming from non-traditional speculative business, approaching or even exceeding 50 percent by 2008, and up to 72 percent in some cases. The dramatic rise in this investment banking and speculation, which uses very little manpower, motivated banks and financial companies to use "off-balance assets" and "shadow banking" extensively to increase their leverage and boost their return on equity. Their capital leverage ratio rose from 12.5 times that of traditional banks to 25, 30, or even 46 times.

This cut-throat environment fostered an era of oligopolies in the industry, with the top six major US banks and financial companies accounting for nearly 60 percent of the total assets of the US banking sector. Behemoths managing trillion-dollar assets quietly took shape, such as Goldman Sachs, Citigroup, Bank of America, Barclays, Royal Bank of Scotland, and HSBC.

These investment bankers flew between New York and metropolises in emerging markets like Beijing and Shanghai, hiring the children of local politicians educated at American universities as "Wall Street spies" to win big deals for their banks. Boasting about the Wall Street made famous by social media, they succeeded in defeating their opponents and helped the large companies in emerging countries' monopoly-prone industries of banking and finance, energy, railways or airlines, insurance, etc., to raise money on the global financial network. They spun fundraising myths about Wall Street, each bigger than the last, which in turn supported and strengthened the industrial oligopolies in these emerging economies. Wall Street took home hundreds of millions or even billions of dollars in fees from each public offering, and turned their American-educated proteges with political power into international billionaires. The confrontation over values between the East and the West during the Cold War thawed into a joyful spring as Wall Street and Chinese political elites both waved the banner of globalism.[321]

Meanwhile in the West, employees at major banks and financial companies flooded the market with the "innovation" of asset securitization. They turned long-term mortgages and rental contracts in the US and UK into securitized financial products. They then sold them all over the world through Wall Street's financial networks to the middle class and those who worshipped Wall Street, ridding the banks of risk. In order to attract buyers, the insurance industry needed to step in and provide a guarantee. So financial instruments for hedging these bets, such as the infamous "subordinated debt" and "default swaps" based on debt ratings and mathematical models, were invented to persuade the insurance industry to support Wall Street's expanding greed. The end result was that banks became averse to the traditional deposit and loan business and outsourced lending operations to loan companies. Loan companies, for their part, no longer cared about ensuring that lenders or down payment ratios were viable, because loan contracts were immediately sold for cash. The last domino was officially in place.

With the collapse of Lehman Brothers, the 2008 financial crisis that Wall Street created finally began. It was completely different from the Great Depression of the 1930s, which was a crisis of overcapacity resulting from overenthusiasm of consumers and entrepreneurs to invest in manufacturing. The cause of the great crisis of 2008 was a severe under-capitalization of banks and other financial institutions due to mixed banking, oligopolies, and off-balance sheet assets. These practices drove up leverage in the absence of effective oversight by regulators, who failed over the long term to rein in Wall Street financiers. At the end of the day, the crisis can be blamed on Wall Street's fraudulent business practices under the guise of innovation.[322]

And yet, the biggest difference between the two crises was that the Great Depression increased the government's political leverage. Roosevelt's New Deal was the first to put Keynesian economics—that is, the principle that government should intervene in the free market through fiscal and monetary policies—into practice. It enacted a series of regulations for financial institutions, such as the Glass-Steagall Act and the Exchange Control Act under the Bretton Woods System, to bring the financial sector back under control and keep it in balance with other sectors. From the 1970s to the 1980s, the "liberalism" jointly promoted by Wall Street and social media ran rampant, and these regulations were gradually repealed, cutting loose the financial sector. Most of the real economy, in the absence of proper regulation, was forced to leave the country amid the triumph of globalization, leaving industrial workers in the Midwest unemployed.

From 1980–2014, the financial sector grew six times faster than that of the US economy as a whole, and the six largest banks and financial institutions on Wall Street, through mergers and acquisitions as well as mixed operations, held nearly 60 percent of the nation's total bank assets. But in 2008 when these oligopolies were on the brink of collapse, Henry Paulson, the former Treasury Secretary and previous CEO of Goldman Sachs, immediately called for a $780 billion financial bailout, funded by middle-class taxpayers. This bailout set a precedent in US history of the state shouldering the failures of private companies, rather than private investors.

The Dodd-Frank Act, which was passed in 2012 in the aftermath of the financial crisis, despite its thousands of pages of regulations, was little better. It resembles a pair of heavy patchwork pants mended by a Congress subject to Wall Street lobbying. It's so complex that no one but Wall Street's elite understands it. As a result, the assets of big banks in the US and UK have grown by another 25–250 percent compared to their assets before the 2008 crisis. There is no fundamental change in the nature of their operations, with the five largest banks in the world initiating nearly 60 percent of trade on the capital market. Capital in the global financial derivatives market, dominated by Wall Street, has risen sharply in the last 50 years, to the tune of $700 trillion.

It's up for debate as to what exactly this capital does for real industry and the labor market, but what's certain is that it's speculative and drives the polarization of wealth distribution. The United States is undergoing an unprecedented period where oligopolies are emerging not only in the financial sector but also in new industries. Monopolies are undermining market competition like never before. Meanwhile, the political will to enact anti-trust regulation is waning, as the percentage of retired members of the House of Representatives who have turned into lobbyists for large companies has increased from less than 4 percent in the 1970s to as high as 42 percent today. Politicians who still hold to the United States' great ideals and ambitions as guided by God's rationality seem to be weakening and withdrawing from the political arena. Of course, this trend of mega corporations monopolizing markets has increased the shared interests between corporate and political elites. A larger and more shocking crisis is brewing,[323] meaning that tomorrow will be even worse.

China's state-driven economic market system hasn't prevented it from falling for Wall Street's charms at all. After the 2008 crisis, the Chinese government restricted banks from lending to real estate companies in a move to control housing prices, which resulted in an unprecedented rise of shadow banking in the country. Off-the-books activity by banks, trust and investment companies, insurance companies, mortgage companies, and other financial institutions increased, driving their capital leverage up to an alarming level. A real estate industry worth more than 400 trillion yuan has formed, in a market which has only gone up in the last 20 years. The market holds all the hopes and dreams of wealth accumulation among ordinary Chinese people who hold property as investments, and it fuels ambition in all levels of government to do big things by increasing fiscal revenue from land sales, to say nothing about the security expectations among banks that land and houses are valuable as collateral. As a result, the amount of visible and invisible debt among governments at all levels and state-owned enterprises has multiplied exponentially over the last decade, currently sitting at over several hundred trillion yuan.

Private entrepreneurs, with no means of getting a slice of the real estate boom, have been caught in the middle of rising rents and cash crunch, along with increasing interest, labor scarcity, and climbing policy transaction costs. Debt-for-equity swaps, bankruptcy, or takeover by state-owned enterprises are often chosen as the lesser of two evils. Most of these entrepreneurs decide to move to other countries in a form of self-exile. This huge economic empire controlled by state capital and the newly rich relies on investment and the currency barrier that isolates itself from the rest of the world markets. The solution to the potential crisis accumulated in such miraculous long-term growth is a knotty puzzle left for China and the whole world.[324]

Ironically, despite all the differences between the patterns of monopoly in the United States and China in terms of causes, forms, levels of technology, and management abilities, they experience the same destruction to market competition. The exact same domestic economic problems result: accelerated growth in capital gains, intellectual property gains, and celebrity income, and the decline of ordinary income from labor, resulting in large income inequality.

In the United States, the ratio of average compensation for CEOs in large companies to middle class incomes rose from 30:1 in the late 1970s to 125:1 in 1995. It has continued to climb since the 2008 crisis to today, reaching 300:1 and losing all sense of proportion. The average annual salary of the top 500 most highly paid executives was $8.9 million in the 1990s and is well over $30 million today. Should they really get that much money? Even the most mediocre Wall Street portfolio managers earn more than $2.2 million a year, and they also get to pay their taxes at the capital gains rate of 20 percent, as opposed to the income rate of up to 40 percent for the middle class.

Today, the share of individual wages and salaries in overall GDP in the United States has fallen from 52 percent in the late 1970s to 42 percent. Middle-class purchasing power, adjusted for inflation, has stayed the same for nearly 40 years, while the pre-tax income of the richest 1 percent of the US population has risen from 10 percent to 20 percent over the same period. These factors have caused a widespread sense of inequity in society. Polls suggest that the percentage of those who think members of Congress are influenced and misled by large corporations has climbed from 30 percent in the 1970s to 80 percent in the second decade of the 21st century. Social conflicts have intensified, as evidenced by the Occupy Wall Street movement—involving hundreds of thousands of people throughout the country for several months—increasingly fierce partisan confrontation, and the stigmatization and even hate crimes related to the #MeToo movement.

In China, the Gini coefficient used by economists to measure the relative equity of wealth distribution crossed the .45 threshold at the beginning of the 21th century and has reached .57 in recent years. The newly emerging wealthiest 1 percent in China hold more than 20 percent of the social wealth, while non-farm payrolls have fluctuated between 60 and 70 percent for a long time, and the urbanization rate hovers between 50 and 60 percent. With the middle class weak and struggling, social stability is now out of reach. Even more serious, due to the state capital monopolies resulting from the government's direct use of state-owned corporations in banking, finance, energy, aviation, railway, communications, and other sectors, people have no option but to put their savings in banks, and private enterprise loans are always difficult to obtain.

Meanwhile, state-owned enterprises can suck money directly from state-owned banks, thanks to their leverage, and force farmers to sell their land at low costs. Over the past decade, the total assets of state-owned enterprises have multiplied exponentially, on pace to reach 200 trillion yuan in the near future. This not only leads to inefficient resource allocation but also opens the door to corruption.

The Chinese government's anti-corruption campaign has revealed a staggering amount of corruption, especially in the families of senior officials. People have limitless imaginations when it comes to corruption, and now the entire society is full of mistrust and hatred towards the rich. Apart from fear of the regime's violent control, people have lost all inherent restraint and self-motivation to behave as they should. Only charities are left to uphold the weak flame of public spirit in the cold wind of materialism and extreme monopolies.

The radically different economic models of China and the United States—though both considered by economists around the world to be successful yet distinctive paradigms of economic development among great powers—are facing similar, unprecedented, and profound crises. Namely, different types of monopolies flying under the banner of globalization have enjoyed a safe haven through the cooperation between political and corporate elites, and "Locke's Law" of "an effective and fair market only achievable through competition," is undermined to varying degrees. This logically and inevitably leads to polarization and the decline of the middle class in both countries, which, although different in nature are equally severe, giving rise to widespread suffering and deep unrest.

This kind of globalization has ironically been embraced unconditionally by certain Nobel Prize-wining professors of economics at prestigious Ivy League universities and, tens of millions of international organizations, NGOs, and intellectual elites. These intellectual elites, scientific thought leaders, and heads of international organizations are now unexpectedly on the same ship of globalization as autocratic governments and money-obsessed Wall Street bigwigs—all singing the same tune. For them, globalization seems to represent the simple utopian dream humans have been imagining for thousands of years. But while the theory and its ideals are simple, the reality is harsh and complex.

The current crisis and conflict in relations between the two great powers is not a simple clash of the leaders' political styles, as depicted in social media, but an outward manifestation of these deep and complex social contradictions. Thinking of it as a conflict in personal political styles would be as naive and superficial as attributing fascism simply to Hitler's madness. French economist Thomas Piketty, using statistical methods developed by Simon Kuznets in the 1940s and a large amount of empirical data recorded in his *Capital in the Twenty-First Century*, found that the widening gap between capital and labor income is currently approaching the level of the Great Depression in the 1930s. The feelings of hundreds of millions about social injustice are not unjustified, nor are they easily masked or whitewashed by the globalist illusions that Wall Street hopes for.[325]

The crisis we are facing and those on the horizon fully demonstrate the fact that the economic market alone cannot support a country's ambition of modernization. It must be supported by all three major free market systems. Even when the three markets are constructed and modernization is realized, there's still the possibility that the economic market may encroach on the political market, resulting in political decisions that indulge new oligopolies and undermine Locke's law of fairness for market competition.

In the context of today's extreme individualism and liberalism, human beings' unique rationality and autonomy can still reach their full potential through entrepreneurs who advance science and technology and improve *human ability*. But entrepreneurship can't prevent *human calling* from being eroded by *human requirement* under increasingly complex legislation. What remains is an ethical framework for *human duty* defined by social media, experts, and scholars. Gradually, the self-discipline, self-motivation, and self-affirmation of *human calling* generated by faith in God are being abandoned. This loss of human reason makes it difficult for people to hold on to the most fundamental national cornerstones of freedom, equality, and justice, which all ultimately come from God. We are now swallowing the bitter pill of consequences for these decisions, and the suffering has only just begun.

SECTION 2: BOWING DOWN TO TECHNOLOGY AND MONEY

For Newton and his predecessors, science and technology were strictly separate in both definition and origins. Technology is man-made and consists of technical solutions to human problems, which we call technological inventions today. They solve the problem of how to do things. Science, on the other hand, comes from God, and explains the deeper problem of why things are. It requires imagination that reaches beyond human experience. Scientific discoveries reveal laws that govern the relationship between humans and society, as well as with humans and nature, according to Thomas Aquinas. While God originally created these laws, humans can derive and use them through empirical observation. That's why the conclusions of scientific research are called "scientific discoveries."

Historically speaking, all modern science is rooted in astronomy and its mathematical tools, with faith in God as its ultimate origin. All technology can be traced back to human experience, so it's very much related to the pragmatic purposes of humanity and belongs to the realm of practical life skills. Science, however, is related to faith in God and imagination, and belongs in the realm of philosophy and theology.

The difference between the two is obvious. From the 16th to the 18th centuries, nearly all the great scientists who laid the foundations for modern science and its various disciplines had Judeo-Christian beliefs. They always started their thinking from the absolute truth of God's existence, and their methodology was usually based on a combination of theological philosophy and mathematics. Even the last 100 years in science bear out this heritage. Among the winners of the Nobel Prize in Science (401 in physics and chemistry and 209 in physiology or medicine) from its inception in 1895 until 2018, more than 85 percent of them come from Judeo-Christian cultures.[326]

But today, the whole of secular society is governed by the three major free markets, particularly the free economic market, where self-centered profit-seeking is encouraged through competition. This environment, along with the strong presence of social media and public education, provides the best possible opportunity for entrepreneurs to rise to the top, and with them technology rises. The first weapon entrepreneurs have over the competition is their ability to invest in technological research and development in order to gain patents for new inventions. That helps them control product prices, greatly increasing profitability that in turn determines the company's core competencies and speed of growth. The second weapon is advertising to influence consumer decisions, enabling them to increase their market share and acquiring a monopoly. The third weapon is lobbying to influence political decisions that are conducive maintaining their monopoly in the industry.

Entrepreneurs' strategy of prioritizing technological invention and innovation has led to the concentration of capital and talent in technological fields. As the pace of technological innovation speeds up, scientific research gains momentum through the guidance of social media and donations to universities and research institutions by entrepreneurs. Annual donations to universities and research institutions in the United States are close to $100 billion. The government spends more than $100 billion annually to fund scientific research, nearly $40 billion on medical and pharmaceutical research alone. Of all the donations to foundations in China in recent years, university foundations account for 20 percent, which is a rapid rise compared with other sectors. During this process, scientific discoveries reveal more and more laws in minor fields. Companies and individuals register these as complicated patents, making it impossible to distinguish whether they are patenting scientific attributes, technological attributes, or new processes.

It's significant that the US patent office has become an increasingly large government department with more than 13,000 employees, growing at an annual rate of over 6 percent over the last decade. On the one hand, scientific research and technological development have created a beneficial cycle due to its concentration of resources. They've attracted more and more talent and societal attention, and contribute to the acceleration of technological innovation, a massive surge in material wealth, and a dizzying array of diverse products and consumer choices. On the other hand, they've led to a growing emphasis on purchasing power, in order for people to afford their increasingly complex and materialistic lifestyle. To gain this purchasing power, people are driven to accept an increasingly elaborate division of labor, becoming part of more complex and sophisticated social structures and working to their limits in order to keep up with the Joneses.

Meanwhile, science and technology have increasingly been conflated with each other in everyday life. Any low-tech company can set up a research department and a chief scientist. Any technical skill may be disseminated through social media as scientific knowledge. The strict boundaries between science and technology have been eroded by money and communication, like dripping water wearing down a stone,[327] and by the utilitarianism of market demands.

The marriage of science and technology has gradually become the new tool of our era. Each of us lives in the material world created by new scientific and technological tools. And we've all become accustomed to science and technology's positivist way of thinking. Positivism not only leads the way in the field of natural sciences, but it also pervades thinking in the social sciences. Any problem in any field can become a topic of research, as long as researchers follow the steps of formulating a question, making arguments, forming a hypothesis, modeling, data collection, validation, and conclusion. These conclusions can be legitimized as "science," influencing thinking and action through social media.

More and more disciplines are being created, and more and more experts are publishing academic papers. Scientists have been forced to abandon the big picture when it comes to society as a whole, as knowledge gets more and more specialized—working on one leaf of the tree or even one vein of the leaf. As time passes, more and more people become very knowledgeable about a single leaf or vein, but less and less can make sense of the tree. The more specialized human knowledge becomes, and the more we know collectively, the more confused individuals are. No one knows what they should say without the guidance of the media, let alone how they should behave.

The increasing specialization of disciplines blurs the boundaries between science and technology even further. Even more terrifying, the social sciences, represented by economics, have introduced the methods and mathematics of the natural sciences into the social realm, ignoring the fact that cause and effect in this field can't be tested in an artificially contained experiment as it can in the natural sciences. Variable models are built based on a host of explicit or implicit assumptions, and conclusions from social experiments are drawn from data collection and inference. These conclusions, validated by awards such as the Nobel Prize in Economics and spread widely with the help of social media, justify the government's intervention in the free market and financial speculation on Wall Street.

The differences between the social and natural spheres are being slowly erased, along with differences between humans, animals, and even objects. With the prevalence of Social Darwinism and the dominance of Nietzsche-ism among the younger generation, theories that ordinary people would have rejected out of common sense in the past are now considered guiding principles for mankind's future. Experts transform them and mold them into powerful political forces. The dignity of humanity as God's creation is disap-pearing. New "theologians" like Richard Dawkins, with their limited knowl-edge, declare that the infinite and eternal God is dead.[328] The meaning of life now lies in victory in materialistic competition, fame, and validation through the media, and winning thunderous applause on this secular stage by baring oneself—being bold and controversial. Interpersonal relationships have been reduced to material transactions and a means of social media influence.

Yet, humanity's spiritual problems persist. Without faith, humans are merely dissatisfied, restless animals. People still need an inner faith, otherwise they lack the self-discipline, self-motivation, and self-affirmation to behave as they should. Unfortunately, science and technology, now muddled together, are elevated to such a level that they've become the antithesis of faith. People are abandoning faith in God, bowing instead to science and technology and using them to explain everything in the world and guide their behavior. People work all day long in order to accumulate even more money, and as soon as they have time for leisure, they are drawn into the trap of "amusing themselves to death" through social media. They worship and imitate their idols to the extent that they find themselves thinking or speaking reflexively, first bingeing on foods that make them fat and unhealthy, then turning around to follow whatever health "experts" tell them about dieting and living longer. Many are even naive enough to believe that genetics and biotechnology can grant humans physical immortality. Science and technology, our new tool, has created an increasingly popular cult, becoming the object of worship like the stones, trees, and fire that ancient peoples worshipped. This wave of secularization of faith has swept all five continents, eroding human spirituality, and greatly affecting our morality.

And yet many scientific recommendations lead to confusion. For example, one day, experts say that taking vitamin C tablets is good for immunity, but the next day they claim it causes liver damage; One day, they say eating fat causes cardiovascular disease, but not long after, they say eating fat is good for your health. Even in the more advanced realms of cosmology and physics, it's difficult to justify science and technology without the foundation of God's reason.

Thus far, technological inventions by humans to solve problems of know-how are all based on laws discovered by scientists. And these laws are built on even more fundamental and essential scientific laws. Among the laws humans believe to be most basic[329] is Newton's law of universal gravitation, which explains the mutual attraction and repulsion between everything in the universe and the relationship between distance, mass, and gravity of objects. Newton's law of gravity provides the first solid foundation upon which all modern scientific discoveries and technological inventions are built and improved upon.

The second is the first law of thermodynamics, or the "law of the conservation of energy," which was first discovered by Newton's contemporary Gottfried Leibniz and then repeatedly confirmed by Einstein, James Joule, Karl Mohr, Emmy Noether, Erwin Schrödinger, and countless other scientists. It describes the logic of chemical decomposition and combination and governs the establishment of a man-made physical and chemical engineering system. This law enables scientists to understand the structures and dynamics of living organisms.

The third is the second law of thermodynamics, the law of entropy, which began with Sadi Carnot and was fully expressed by Rudolf Clausius. It describes the irreversibility of the thermodynamic process. All isolated systems, when connected to a larger system, evolve towards thermodynamic equilibrium, or a state with maximum entropy, unless new energy is invested in it. This law also describes the finitude and transience of all things in the universe, which naturally move from order to disorder, so that all things are in the process of change and demise. Even humans are finite and mortal. This law also enables humanity to frame the various inputs and outputs of human life systems supported by technology, as well as its ultimate end, in scientific terms.

The fourth is Einstein's theory of relativity—his special theory of relativity discovered 1905 and his general theory of relativity discovered in 1916. The former reinterprets gravity in the universe as not only being related to mass and distance, but also, more important, to speed. Understanding the speed of light changes our definitions of time and space and the relationships between all things. The latter proposed a new understanding of how space bends, reinterpreting gravity as a curved gravitational field caused by planets with larger masses that has a gravitational effect on other planets.

Without these four fundamental scientific laws, many lesser scientific laws would still be undiscovered, technological invention would be impossible, and modern human civilization would collapse. But what is the root of these four fundamental laws? What underpins and determines all human knowledge of science and technology? Amid the emergence of increasingly specialized disciplines, the so-called experts who focus only on a single leaf are losing their ability to ask these questions. Almost no one cares about this root. Newton did—he knew that it was God who created the law of universal gravitation that governs all things in nature, and that God-given curiosity and free will enabled him to discover it. His discovery glorified God and benefited humanity by bringing us the sparkling products of modern science. But over time, Newton's arguments have been forgotten. Humanity mistakenly thinks that we can do away with God's reason and dominate the world with human reason alone.

Why are humans so proud and arrogant in the modern era? Because we worship our tools, science and technology, holding the false belief that they can solve our problems. Yet to this day, despite the continued exploration and expanding imagination of scientists, we still encounter problems that we haven't resolved about our origins from nothing. The largest of these questions have to do with the Big Bang, black holes, and quantum mechanics.

If the Big Bang hypothesis is true, then the universe has a beginning. But a beginning, of course, is a point of creation, which begs the existence of a creator. Otherwise, we must conclude, illogically, that the universe created itself. A God must exist, then, beyond the universe, so that all the above-mentioned fundamental laws may be traced back to this ultimate origin, just like all questions of *human calling*. If there is no God beyond space and time, we can only resort to the far-fetched explanation that the scientific laws we discover have always simply existed. And if they have always existed, did they exist before the Big Bang? Obviously, this argument can't be internally consistent, as it would mean that the four fundamental scientific laws—that govern the relationships between all things in the universe—existed even before its beginning. Anyone with basic knowledge of these laws can see that this inference is irreconcilable and self-contradictory.

Without God's act of creation, the Big Bang Theory would immediately contradict the first law of thermodynamics, or the law of the conservation of energy. The Big Bang essentially means that something was made out of nothing, which would be the biggest case of non-conservation of energy in history.

The Big Bang offers an extremely imprecise description of the beginning of the universe. Modern astrophysics suggests that the margin of error for the time of the Big Bang cannot be greater than 10^{-35} seconds, otherwise the universe we observe today could not have been generated. The equivalent would be if a person attempted to stack pennies from North America up to the height of the moon, but an error greater than one of those pennies would cause the attempt to fail. Such a sophisticated universe cannot logically arise from the chaotic event of the Big Bang, as most understand it. However, with belief in God's existence, these contradictions and logical paradoxes are immediately resolved. God's omnipotence guarantees the creation of a sophisticated universe, and the law of the conservation of energy governs how things in nature change forms. Human beings, as God's creatures, can use the law of the conservation of energy to transform all things in nature for their use. This view is logical and internally consistent.

Thanks to the Hubble Telescope, and the discovery of the "redshift phenomenon" based on the work of scientists like Vesto Slipher, Georges Lemaître, and Edwin Hubble, we now have the law of cosmic expansion. This law, also supported by Einstein's General Theory of Relativity, shows that planets and even the universe have life cycles, and that every planet is getting farther away from other planets. These phenomena all conform to the second law of thermodynamics and the law of entropy. It makes consistent, logical sense that the universe created by God runs according to the law of entropy he also created. Without God, the laws that govern the universe no longer hold. For instance, if the universe is a closed system sustained by inputs and outputs, then there must be a God outside of the system. But if the universe is not a closed system, how can it obey the second law of thermodynamics?

The problems don't stop here. According to Einstein's General Theory of Relativity and astrophysicists' theories, as the universe expands, stars will one day run out of fuel, which will bend space and cause gravitational collapse.

When a star collapses, it leads to an exponential increase in its mass until it reaches a critical point, called a singularity, where even photons travelling at 300,000 kilometers per second can't escape from its surface. This is how an unobservable "black hole" is formed. These black holes no longer participate in the journey of cosmic expansion under the law of entropy. They are left behind as the remains of stars, constituting 95 percent of the universe's dark matter and dark energy, which we can't explain.

Stephen Hawking has suggested that one can pass through a black hole, but it will only lead to another universe with no way back. With this suggestion, the idea of the multiverse was born. Truly, it requires divine help to make logical sense of such a crazy, mind-bending theory. If there are some stars that don't follow the general pattern of the universe, they may be exceptions to the second law of thermodynamics, but they must still follow other laws that God has created for them. Even if there were a multiverse, the existence of a cosmic creator God outside the universe would be even more logically necessary. As for the myriad laws that are still unknown to mankind today, they exist in the infinite embrace and logical order of God, but they affect neither our *human ability* nor our *human calling*. It's only by believing in the absolute truth of God that the contradiction between relative truths—such as the theory of black holes and its inconsistency with the second law of thermodynamics—can be effectively resolved.

Quantum mechanics, painstakingly explored by Einstein, Schrödinger, Niels Bohr, Max Planck, Werner Heisenberg, Wolfgang Pauli, and other great scientists, reveals mysterious underlying principles of matter at the sub-atomic level of the quantum world, such as "wave-particle duality," "the uncertainty principle," and "the compatibility law." Quantum mechanics has opened up the possibility to change our lives completely with technological innovations in computer networks, medical equipment, genetic engineering, and so on. The strong resemblance between the operation of this ultra-microscopic atomic world and that of the universe is indeed striking, but the uncertainty of a particle's position and momentum when it's placed under human observation is just as unbelievable.[330] Without divine help, it's impossible to logically understand the laws that govern the quantum world.

Scientific understanding is granted to humans by God through our use of reason and imagination, while humans accumulate technology, or know-how, through experience. These two disciplines enable human beings to reach the full potential of *human ability* through the pursuit of relative truths in nature. Belief in and worship of God, meanwhile, provide knowledge of the absolute truth that enables us to handle the events of our lives. It enables us to live in the world with self-discipline, self-motivation, and self-affirmation, responding to the *human calling* that God expects of us and ignoring the madness and chaos caused by others in the world.

Science, like a glimmer of relative truth visible in the darkness of the night, illuminates our path forward and indeed enhances *human ability*. As for the boundless darkness, only by relying on the invisible absolute truth of faith in God can our souls be enlightened and oriented toward his *human calling*. But when humanity confuses science and technology and worships these new tools, they're bound to deviate from God's standards and fall into the abyss of self-righteousness, digging their own grave by their pride.

SECTION 3: THE UBIQUITY OF EXTREME INDIVIDUALISM

The replacement of faith in God with faith in our tools, science and technology, is leading humanity down the road to mechanical determinism, pragmatism, and ultimately, extreme individualism.

Master thinkers like Newton, Descartes, and Locke tried to unite human reason with the infinite, eternal and authoritative rationality of God. They traced human reason to a divine source of *human calling* that restrains, inspires, and improves human morality. But after them, British philosopher Thomas Hobbes and French philosophers Claude Helvétius and Julien La Mettrie elevated human reason to an extreme, giving birth to mechanical determinism. In their view, the whole world is merely a clock-like machine containing many smaller components with different functions. To La Mettrie (1709–1751), matter is the only substance that exists, and people are just machines. This view, of course, can be seen as a philosophical reflection of the great achievements, and resulting social upheaval, of classical physics at the time. Yet Hobbes (1588–1679), the founder of mechanical determinism, became the first to go so far as to claim that "the human mind is also a machine." Mechanical determinists completely reject the spiritual world and the spiritual life of human beings. As a result, mechanical determinism practically came to its end at the moment of its birth. Yet its greatest significance, which lies in its pursuit of certainty and avoidance of uncertainty, provided a powerful incentive for scientific exploration during the era of classical physics.

Amid the thrilling violence of revolution, which overthrew all religious authority and cast off traditional restraints in the search for truth, Nietzsche founded the extreme philosophy of existentialism. He denied not only the possibility of certainty, but also God's existence; the universal spiritual attributes of mankind, social order, and morality; and finally even the meaning of individual human life. He pushed individualism to the extreme in human philosophy. This trend of thought—combined with the marketization of the economy in which intellectual and other property rights became recognized by law—threw the individual human being out of traditional public spiritual life to directly confront the *human requirement* stipulated by various laws. This caused widespread breakdown of both the family and the traditional structure of society that had persisted for tens of thousands of years in human history. Instead, it promoted extreme freedom for individuals, weakening their sense of divine duty toward the public and their sense of *human calling*.[331]

Ludwig Wittgenstein (1889–1951), an important existentialist after Nietzsche, shifted empirical philosophy in the 20th century from scientific positivism to so-called analytic philosophy, which focused solely on word games. To Wittgenstein, all human cognition, including science, is just a matter of language. Language is the continuing accumulation of human word games. Instead of being mere subjects in the world, people can also become spectators, so there is no such thing as anthropocentric universality or preexistence. Even human life has no special meaning. Meaning comes from the form of life humans practice. Meaning is just another expression of human language games. Our biggest problem as humans is our fascination with universality, so returning to linguistic description is philosophy's only way out. Yet philosophy can only be described in language, so it can't be used to build assumptions or theories without again getting lost in the fog of searching for universal explanations. For Wittgenstein, philosophy is stuck with an impossible task.

While the emergence of existential philosophy could be justified by its historical backdrop of violent collectivism with the rise of socialism and fascism in the 20th century, it took individual freedom to an unhelpful extreme. Existentialists like Nietzsche, Freud, Wittgenstein, Jean Paul Sartre, and Helmut Kuhn, borrowing natural science's new analytical tools and driven by extreme revolutionary impulses, so emphasized individual freedom that they denied the universal laws of value and meaning and the preexistence of the social contract. They claimed that human freedom is merely part of the rules of the game. Apart from the rules of the game as defined by law, constituting *human requirement*, individuals are completely free. Constraints imposed on individuals by the family and traditional ethics became increasingly tenuous. Without these constraints, there was no need for a public spiritual organization burdened with absolute truth to broadcast moral standards for society, or to answer questions of *human calling*.

Existentialist philosophy pandered to the arrogance of humans, who despite our worship of science and technology, are still limited individuals. The historical consequences are obvious: as scientific and technological positivism resulted in material progress in the 20th century, existentialist philosophy very naturally paved the way for extreme pragmatism and individualism.[332]

Twentieth century pragmatists include Charles Sanders Peirce (1839–1914), William James (1842–1910), John Dewey (1859–1952), and Richard Rorty (1931–2007). American pragmatism was very different from that of the East from its inception. These pragmatists wished to find a "middle way" between traditional belief in God and existentialism's total denial of a universal public spirit, a balance between God's rationalism and Cartesian empiricism, between Locke's dualistic worldview and the nominalism that emerged in France and Germany in the 19th century. American Pragmatists held that universal truths and faith actually exist, and cannot be easily denied, but individuals must make theories based on empirical observations, base their understanding on these theories, and test them before considering them valid. Good beliefs should be retained and bad beliefs discarded, and both must be proven valid and effective. To this end, pragmatists believed in doing away with the binary opposition between belief in absolute truth and individual liberalism. They advocated sticking to empirical results of given actions and practices and advanced a pluralist and practical worldview.

American pragmatists, who were mainly based at Ivy League universities like Harvard, conducted extensive research in psychology, ethics, and pedagogy, and greatly influenced the development of Western paradigms of thought and the humanities in the second half of the 20th century. Pragmatism encouraged diversity, freedom and individualism, especially in the United States. But because the propositions discussed in American pragmatism were too material and concrete, it failed to achieve its grand search for a "middle way." What is "utility?" What is "successful action?" The universal connections between all things and the causes of human behavior are extremely complex, far beyond the ability of human reason to arrive at independently. Some causes are thousands of miles away from their effects; some are out of reach; some are instantaneous, some take decades or even 100 years to occur. How is it possible to conclude causal relationships in the social sphere with a few simple questions and answers, and empirical experiments that take place over merely a few months? How can empirical research be used to test faith in the absolute truth of God, when many social sciences merely ape the unsuitable methodologies of natural science? What is the essential difference between absolute pluralism and absolute liberalism? Unable to answer these questions, pragmatism succumbed to the cumulative effect of compromises over time. Like science and technology, it was subjected to the inevitable laws of market forces and became confused with practical "utilitarian purpose," which varies from person to person. If utilitarian purpose is used to test the truth, the predicament of conflict between mutually exclusive positions is the result. In the absence of a common basis for good behavior, humans are left with no choice but to resort to political decisions influenced by social media, ending up in a vicious cycle of advertising and lobbying, with a resulting philosophy that justifies super-pragmatism. In the end, American pragmatism, under the pressure of market forces, resembled more and more the utilitarian pragmatism of the East.[333]

The biggest problems with pragmatist philosophy are its deconstruction of traditional faith and its overindulgence of individual freedom. This has resulted in diversity and inclusivity in American culture, as the strict precepts of Christianity for individuals have broken down under the increasing bureaucratization of the Roman Catholic Church. Even the moral and ethical constraints of marriage and family have broken down. Yet it has also promoted unprecedented freedom for individuals to pursue their dreams and unlock their God-given potential, giving rise to brilliant, almost superhuman figures in business, science, and politics in the United States. Trendsetters and superstars achieved fame through the media especially in the mid- to late-twentieth century, showing that anything is possible if a person pursues their dreams.

Without restraints on the individual, these effects are only amplified by social media and advertising, passed on from generation to generation through the education system. For the most part, Protestant ethics, thanks to their openness and inclusiveness, are compatible with this pragmatic education. However, the traditional solemnity of strict religious organizations has been gradually lost, as well as the dedication, sacrifice, passion, and reverence for classic theological texts, like those written during the era of Edwards's revivalist theology. Protestant churches, whose leadership has lost its early Puritan spirit, have split into branches and factions that are undisciplined and disorganized. They either hype up their presence through the media or perform their duties in a dogmatic and tedious way, waning in their appeal to the faithful.

Occasional church organization scandals exposed by social media have resulted in a poor public image. This only increases the rise of secularization as people turn to science and technology as a replacement object of worship. Capricious, bold, extreme, and even shameless performances meet the needs of social media advertising, promoting more and more extreme individualism. Sports stars, movie stars, and pop stars entertain the public and are worshipped like gods in the human world, filling the spiritual void left by the loss of *human calling*. Many of them live an extremely lavish life as they get rich but often end up with a broken family, heavily in debt, and die of drug abuse or poverty. These are the poster children of extreme individualism. With them, all humanity is being sucked into the vortex of super pragmatism and competitive utilitarianism.[334]

Economists, as the inventors of pragmatism, are the most smug about this state of affairs, since the utility of all these industries seems to be measurable through the laws they have defined and the wealth they created. The monetary system, buoyed by changes in technology, has moved away from the standards of gold and silver that humans have valued for thousands of years. It has evolved into "greenbacks," "credit currency," "electronic money," "mobile money," and even the "Euro" and "Bitcoin," which are not backed by national sovereignty. The traditional banking industry has continued to innovate its organizational structure. New financial companies, such as investment banks, futures and foreign exchange brokerage companies, trust companies, security companies, insurance and reinsurance companies, venture capital firms, and those dealing in hedge funds and mutual funds, are being invented. The general public is left confused, relying on economists to guide their decisions through university classes and the media.

Economists, much like the philosophers of Socratic Greece and the Spring and Autumn and Warring States Period in China, move between presidents' offices, international organizations, universities, companies, and among the public, giving lectures and signing books. They explain all social phenomena through the self-centered theory of microeconomics and endorse the legitimacy of everyone's profit-seeking behavior. They explain the economic rise and fall of countries and justify all kinds of measures taken by governments with Keynesian macroeconomic theory. They teach enterprise management theory to entrepreneurs, showing them how to manage companies and beat their competitors. They build mathematical models to explain market volatility in the capital market, futures market, commodity market, foreign exchange market, and other complicated markets, tricking the general public into entrusting their assets to so-called "experts," further forming the global financial industry centered around Wall Street. Although national economic development, global economic trends, and various market fluctuations never actually follow the forecasts of these powerful, renowned economists, they always find a way to explain themselves afterward and spin social media to make themselves seem even wiser.

Today's economic landscape is indeed quite different from the depiction of market-driven globalization in economic textbooks. On the one hand, there are the environmental and climate crises caused by global energy overconsumption, and on the other, global overcapacity and waste. On the one hand, there is a growing share of capital income and a declining share of labor income as economists talk up the importance of GDP; on the other hand, large technology companies are driving technological innovation and increasing the speed at which labor is replaced, with AI accelerating this trend in an unprecedented way. On the one hand, populations in South Asia, Africa, and the Middle East have entered a phase of exponential growth, worsening the problems of poverty; on the other hand, fertility rates in developed regions like Europe, North America, and East Asia have declined irreversibly and reached the lowest levels in history, causing the overall population to shrink, age, and decline economically. On the one hand, the ideas of peace and tolerance advocated by globalism have paralyzed people's national and collective identities; on the other hand, terrorist organizations and individuals led by Islamic extremism are staging suicide attacks on civilians, the elderly, women, and children all over the world. Extremist attacks seem to spread throughout the world like a virus. Their choice of methods, arms, and locations for attacks are horrific and hard to detect. On the one hand, there are more and more nuclear weapons in the world that could destroy humanity if they get out of control; on the other hand, the arms race based on new technologies is still in full swing between major powers. The risks of human self-destruction, mutual destruction, and environmental destruction are increasing. Taking a long philosophical view, it's difficult to see much to be optimistic about in humanity's future.

And yet, the trends of extreme individualism and absolute liberalism have promoted the idea that freedom is absolute, creating more and more arrogant elites in society, while increasing the number of people who feel helpless and frustrated.[335] The elite all over the world, and especially on Wall Street, have enough money to hire lawyers, accountants, auditors, and expert consultants who understand the rules of the game and apply them for easy profits in all industries. At the same time, the lower and middle classes are confused by centuries-old, complicated legal provisions and unaware of hidden rules. They can't afford to hire agencies to sort things out for them. As a result, they encounter financial setbacks on the journey of life that they must bear or be defeated by. The result is an exponential increase in mental health problems over the past decade.

Without a divine public spirit protecting and setting expectations for people, the *human calling* that gives birth to self-discipline, self-motivation, and self-affirmation gradually fades from people's spiritual lives. Trapped in the quagmire of ever-increasing, rigid, and legalistic *human requirement*, they often can't find the direct cause of their own failures in the world. Nor can they identify a physical enemy. Often people express their anger in ways that break through the barrier of *human requirement* into crime or even killing or terrorism, repeating the cycles of revenge that characterized early human history.

When it comes to revenge, the biggest difference between the modern terrorist revenge model with no specific enemy and earlier forms of revenge is that those who seek revenge often only inflict social violence to attract media attention. They have no intention of actually preserving justice by killing the perpetrator. Modern terrorist revenge seekers only care about gaining notoriety and have no regard for who they punish. They don't care about maintaining social justice. They're like a singer who only cares about gaining fans through social media and not about the songs they sing. This is the underlying logic behind the increasing battle between the "lone wolves" who carry out suicide attacks and the complex social systems they don't understand. All of this is a natural social consequence of this age, as we've abandoned the public spirit of God in our attempt to achieve the individual autonomy of the human, giving rise to extreme individualism and absolute liberalism.

SECTION 4: SATAN'S POISON: UNIVERSAL WELFARE

The three fundamental free markets of modern society, created on the basis of human rationality, have grown increasingly complex and trivial. They now have so many branches that they resemble a bewildering labyrinth where human rationality is getting lost. The principles and foundations that were laid by divine reason have been chipped away by successive generations, under the banner of human reason and innovation. Those of us caught in these systems are forced to work on the minutiae, dressing up the labyrinth in increasing splendor and complexity. If we can step back and observe this labyrinth from a bird's eye view, we're amazed to realize that most of the foundation has already been eroded. The question of how long what remains can stay standing must be faced.[336]

The most fundamental issue is that a country's successful modernization is based on the three free market systems, which are in turn based on the choices of modern citizens. But in the absence of proper civic awareness, it's impossible to establish or maintain the health of these systems over the long term. This civic awareness is built on the five cornerstones of freedom, equality, fairness, righteousness, and justice. If these cornerstones aren't understood by the public, civic awareness will be undermined, distorting the three free market systems and leading to a crisis in the modernization process. A study of human history reveals that these cornerstones originate from God and so possess sufficient divine authority. The specific details of how the three market systems are constructed or reconstructed in each nation state depend on the choice of its citizens and on their varying ability to understand and construct them. Nation states and individuals still need to grapple with them today. Choices that misinterpret divine reason will inevitably lead a nation's quest for modernization down the wrong road and may even lead to significant social upheaval and widespread suffering.

Freedom is the most fundamental cornerstone for individuals in modern countries. Without freedom, no state, no matter how materially rich it is, can truly be called modern. But what is individual freedom? Where does it come from? It's a question worth pondering. Individual freedom in modern society comes from God, and it includes both subjective and objective aspects. So-called subjective freedom, that is, the rights that individuals hold subjectively, includes the right to life, which no one can take away. It also includes related rights to reputation, portrayal, and privacy. It includes the rights to free thought, speech, choice, and action.

So-called objective freedom results from the discretionary exercise of an individual's subjective freedom over the course of their life. These freedoms are mainly divided into intellectual property rights derived from personal thought and speech, and material and property rights derived from freedom of choice and action. These freedoms should be clear and uncontroversial, as they're clearly divided based on different phases and aspects of human life. Of course, whether or to what extent people have the right to inherit and bequeath assets is a controversial issue left for future discussion.

The point is, if a society doesn't reach a consensus on subjective and objective freedoms, it's impossible to protect them with a constitution and lesser laws. It's impossible to establish a truly effective modern society based on the three free market systems. As a logical and authoritative source for the truth about human freedom, belief in God provides a basis for this consensus. It makes sense that humans, who are created by God, are therefore endowed with freedom. And this makes freedom worth defending, since its legitimacy is backed by God's sacred authority. Freedom, then, becomes the first cornerstone for building a modern nation state.[337]

Equality is the second cornerstone and has a mutually dependent relationship with the first. Just as freedom must be based on the premise of equality between individuals, equality means reexamining and identifying with individual freedom from an interpersonal perspective. "Equality for all" means that every individual subject has the same rights to freedom, and they can't be infringed upon by others, especially those who act on behalf of the public. Without the protection provided by equality, these rights can't be maintained, and instead are mere ideas. If most people believe that equality for all is as important and sacrosanct as freedom for all, then a nation's civic awareness will be pure and robust enough to complete the ambitious task of modernization. This belief is grounded in the authority of God, which transcends all human logic and human authority and is itself sacred and unshakable.

But if we consider equality for all and freedom for all as unshakable cornerstones of civic awareness and modernization, other truths must also be acknowledged. First, individuals have different starting points, opportunities, effort, and outcomes in each one's journey of life. Not recognizing and protecting such differences means denying the cornerstone of freedom, causing equality to immediately collapse into ruthless, violent robbery. Second, while everyone has the freedom to think, speak, decide, and act, they must also be responsible for the consequences. Freedom, then, also means responsibility. "Equality for all" means "responsibility for all." Humans are endowed with freedom but must be held accountable for how they use it. Freedom and responsibility are like two inseparable sides of a coin created by God. Any attempt to separate them is to sow evil and will weaken or even destroy the one-to-one correspondence between behavior and results—found in the "law of cause and effect." Without this most fundamental law, created by God and revealed by Buddha, driving all things and the cycle of life, the universe God created would stop operating immediately.[338]

Fairness is the third cornerstone of a nation state's modernization. The concept of fairness has long been an ambiguous one, so it's worth serious consideration. In its most original sense, fairness is a public standard of measurement, similar to standardized weights and measures used for trade, ensuring that both parties in a transaction can enjoy God's empowering freedom and equality. This kind of transaction well illustrates the concept: both parties are free, equal subjects; the transaction is the free choice of both; and a standard, public, open, and fair scale measures what each party gains. In a modern society with civic awareness based on freedom and equality, this kind of transaction is the only way a person with subjective freedom can seek the objective freedom of property, without resorting to violence or fraud. "Fairness," then, based on "freedom for all," "equality for all," and "responsibility for all" is considered "fair trade" between people. This is one of the earliest criteria for *human calling* set by God in community: to obtain what one desires through fair trade instead of robbery, theft, fraud, or other violent means.

In contemporary society, many scholars have taken liberties with the concept of transactional fairness to create other concepts such as "fairness of opportunity," "fairness in outcome," and "fairness in distribution," and have used statistical analysis of income, assets, and so on to support these concepts. Unfortunately, they are so far from the original, God-given concept of fair trade that they can't remain internally consistent. Imagine for a moment what would happen if we were to draw conclusions simply based on individual property or income statistics. Fairness would immediately become a subjective judgment, and the criteria would be whether most individuals have the average amount of assets and income. Some scholars have indeed claimed that such average income equals "fairness," leading to misconceptions among the public through media and mobilizing legislators to intervene in the distribution of wealth through policies and regulations—in other words, through *human requirement*. If such a view of fairness were established, it would fundamentally negate the differences between individuals and their freedom to capitalize on such differences. It would also mean essentially denying that everyone is equal and responsible and would provide a convenient excuse for those who are trying to get something for nothing. God's dynamic mechanism of causality, that freedom equals responsibility which equals equality, would be completely undermined.

Of course, to maintain true fairness, it's important to pay attention to the gap caused by the distribution of income and wealth among individuals and whether it's so wide that it affects the order and stability of society. After all, the elaborate and complicated regulations of the market are set by humans, so it's worth examining whether they deviate from the God-given cornerstones of civic awareness, such as freedom, responsibility, and fair trade. But in observing results, we can only make a judgment as to whether they are reasonable. If they aren't, further checks are called for to determine whether the regulations that have led to such unreasonable results are fair. We can't simply make subjective judgments of fairness based on statistical results and then immediately resort to government intervention. Doing so can cause deep damage to the law of causality and destroy the dynamic mechanism behind societal progress.[339]

Righteousness, or love, is the fourth cornerstone of modernization. The "benevolence" of Chinese Confucian philosophy and the "righteousness and love" of the Christian faith are both about treating others with compassion and empathy. The difference is that Confucian benevolence is rooted in familial relations, while Christian righteousness and love are mainly concerned with strangers. Benevolence originates in mankind, so it's logical that it leads to love and kindness toward blood relatives. Righteousness and love, however, originate in God, so it's logical that they lead to kindness toward strangers. Since God is outside of the universe and created human beings—endowing them with freedom, equality, and fairness—and people who put God first find their primary life purpose in glorifying God, then sharing God's righteousness and love with unknown neighbors and even enemies makes sense. By living like this, people can find divine meaning both during their mortal lives and when they face God. Over the course of 2,000 years, this righteousness and love has been transformed into a globalized philanthropic practice, influencing modern citizens in one way or another and becoming part of the common conception of a modern nation state.

Recognizing people's differences and sticking to the principles of freedom, responsibility, equality, and fairness provides society with the impetus and order to progress. The impetus comes from each individual's relentless pursuit of freedom and responsibility, while the order comes from the acknowledgement of equality, rules of fair trade, and the building of a favorable market environment. However, unlike in naturalism, this doesn't mean God ruthlessly leaves those defeated in market competition with nowhere to go. Instead, he calls on those who have succeeded in the market to demonstrate their righteousness and love by spending part of their wealth, through charitable organizations, to help those who are hardworking and upright yet left behind. This not only helps them get back on their feet and return to compete, but it also empowers the givers to grow spiritually and strengthens their faith in God. Righteous love, then, as a cornerstone of a modern state, sets a baseline for dealing with differences in wealth resulting from the free market. But it can't be abused. When it comes to lazy and dishonest people, excess help only encourages these qualities, and it not only destroys a society's dynamism but also undermines its order.

Justice is the fifth and final cornerstone for building a modern nation state. God represents ultimate justice, because he is beyond our universe and uses his laws of creation to drive and direct the universe's operation. But God doesn't personally interfere with people's daily lives. Rather, he gives them the freedom to think, speak, make decisions, and act on their own, only undertaking judgment of people's long-term actions and consequences after their souls leave this life and move into eternity. But in the present life, the fallibility and sin of humanity make it impossible for them to judge their own long-term impact, otherwise the world would be overrun by evil and chaos. Human beings, then, must emulate God's justice in the short-term in response to individuals' words and actions that hurt the freedom, responsibility, equality, fairness, and righteousness of others. This kind of justice limits evil and maintains the God-given principles and order of a modern nation state in order to build an ideal society. The justice of these short-term verdicts determines the level of a country's civic awareness and modernization.

Justice is arguably the most important cornerstone for determining whether a nation state is truly modernized. Judgments must be based on laws that are passed by the representatives of citizens of the nation state. Since laws are created by humans, limitations and biases are inevitable. So the first question to ask is, what procedures and methods are in place to correct and remedy these biases? Second, how are lawmakers elected? What are their required qualifications and qualities, and how are they chosen? How are their terms limited, how are they replaced, and according to what procedures? Even when a society's rules and regulations embody the God-given principles of freedom and responsibility, equality, fairness, and righteousness, someone must accept the appeals of individuals and conduct trials of their cases. The third question is, who will do this? What kind of procedures will ensure that the truth of the matter is fully revealed and subject to public scrutiny, ultimately guaranteeing the justice of the legal system? Finally, over time, individual cases will challenge existing regulations due to environmental and internal conflicts, leading to amendments and supplementation of legal avenues, in other words, *human requirement*. What will ensure that these legislative amendments adhere to the five cornerstone principles? Clearly, a legal system that answers these questions with orderly procedures and explicit clauses is what ensures a well-governed society.

Unfortunately, not all legal systems reflect the God-given public spirit of justice, and without it, the legal system inevitably leads to national trampling of the five cornerstones. That means that cultivating and maintaining these God-given cornerstones is the long-term mission for a nation state that aims to achieve modernization and stay competitive. Of course, the light of God's reason is always necessary as a corrective, and any indolence or arrogance will cause these principles to get lost as humans exercise their reason apart from God.[340]

Observing and comparing the development of modern nation states over time, there are two main types. The first type is found in less developed countries who can't be considered as truly modernized. These countries are trying, however, by building the three major free market systems. They include nations like Egypt, Syria, Kazakhstan, India, Saudi Arabia, the Philippines, Venezuela, Ethiopia, South Africa, China, Pakistan, Indonesia, and Malaysia. Most of them have incomplete and flawed free market systems. In contrast, many countries or regions in East Asia have emerged with relatively complete free market systems. The root cause of this difference is how well-developed their cornerstone principles are. Loose definitions and lack of consensus on freedom, responsibility, equality, fairness, righteousness, and justice inevitably lead to misinterpretation and distortion. This can result in a chaotic legislative foundation and legal system, eventually causing a serious departure from the cornerstones altogether.

In such societies, the legal articles regarding these cornerstones are severely distorted through institutional practice. They function like fig leaves covering authoritarianism, hierarchy, monopoly, unfairness, and tyranny. These kinds of laws fundamentally suppress individual creativity and greatly weaken society's inner dynamism, while also undermining the legitimate, openly acknowledged social order. These countries become stuck in a quagmire of instability and lack of long-term motivation, preventing them from achieving modernization.[341]

The second type includes modern developed countries, such as those in Europe that have already completed the modernization process. These countries owe their progress to 2,000 years Christianity's cultivation of the five cornerstones. They constructed their three free market systems based largely on

Locke's political theory and Adam Smith's economic theory. As a result, their modernization was completed relatively early. However, they have succumbed to the wave of secularization in which the worship of science and technology has replaced faith in God. The profound influence of the likes of Nietzsche, Freud, Wittgenstein, and Dawkins, along with the influence of advertising and social media that works to entertain people to death, have led to extreme individualism and absolute liberalism running rampant.

Political principles, like that of "one person, one vote," are gradually becoming detached from the necessary constraints of God's reason amid various legislative amendments. The extremes of human reason apart from God have manifested primarily in the universal welfarism that began to prevail in Europe in the second half of the 20th century, gradually spreading to all modern countries. The core idea of universal welfare begins with a serious misinterpretation of the principle of fairness in a modern state: the conclusion that distribution is unfair simply because there is an income gap. Actually, this idea wrongly equates the mathematical concept of uneven distribution of income with inequality. This argument undermines the fundamental God-given cornerstones of fairness, equality, and freedom and responsibility. It's misleading, because it fails to ask whether the rule of fair competition in the market has been undermined by the emergence of new monopolies, innovations such as financial derivatives that are useless to the real economy, and the loss of constraints on the income and taxation of professional managers. Proponents of universal welfare have tried to achieve a mathematical equality in people's income as an instant result. To this end, they've promoted legislation that allows direct government intervention in the market, implementing Keynesian macroeconomic policy. Specifically, this meant using a mandatory increase in taxation (fiscal policy) and liabilities (monetary policy) to substantially expand the government's financial power and change the status quo of low-income people through welfare distribution.

Once the precedent for such government policies had been set, it was immediately met with enthusiastic support from many European governments, as well as voters who suddenly realized that they could get a lot of free, unearned benefits from the government. Seemingly, the government could abandon its role of "night watchman" as recommended by Adam Smith, and instead actively collect taxes from the public, borrow from future generations to increase government control over the money supply, and shower money on the public through welfare to win their support. Everything about Keynes' portrayal of government intervention in the market seems rosy at first. But as soon as the floodgates of welfarism are thrown open, the road to welfarism suffers from a "ratchet effect:"[342] it can only go forward, not backward.

To begin with, welfarist policies encourage people to form interest groups—for the elderly, various races, women, children, those needing education and health care, those with specific diseases, those in special jobs and industries, LGBTQ, and so on. Interest groups prompt waves of affirmative action. They organize demonstrations, parades, speeches, celebrity endorsements, academic surveys, and political lobbying in order to win rights and benefits from the government for their people. Under the banner of liberalism, each group relates their own misfortune, complaining that the government has treated them unfairly and that their rights have not been upheld. Full of bitterness and grievances, they ask for increased salaries, reduced working hours, and more free welfare, but they avoid mentioning their responsibilities.

In addition, increasingly high welfare expenditures by the government in response to such demands inevitably lead to a rise in taxes. By the end of the 20th century, the average tax rate in European countries was between 40 and 50 percent—currently, in some countries, it's higher than 50 percent. As a result, many people are forced to start businesses in other countries, exacerbating the scarcity of local entrepreneurs, which in turn reduces employment and tax revenues at home. Free welfare inevitably leads to waste and abuse, as well as to a severe supply shortage. The fact that in Canada and Europe it often takes a few months, half a year, or up to eight months to see a doctor is proof of this problem.

The most insidious thing about universal welfarism is that it's like Satan's poison for the mind. It erects a mental wall that blocks a person's grasp of one of the most basic laws of God's creation: that of causality.[343] It is this law that ensures the one-to-one correspondence and ironclad link between human behavior and its consequences. Governments hang promises on this wall like man-made magic lamps, answering the people's wishes for all kinds of unearned welfare. Appeals that have been granted suffer from the ratchet effect, while those yet to be realized spur more group protests and demands. On the other side of the wall, the government is busy raising taxes and issuing bonds both at home and abroad to close the funding gap caused by excessive spending on public welfare. Growing fiscal deficits become the new normal for government budgets.

Once it has started down the path of welfarism, a government, faced with voters who are eager to defend their rights, is forced to borrow money from the future for present pleasures, creating a kind of Ponzi scheme. The European Commission is the ultimate representative of this welfarist Ponzi scheme. This solution is like drinking a toxic agent to quench thirst. Like a frog being slowly boiled alive, people lose their sense of gratitude and motivation to work hard, getting greedy, lazy, and selfish. As time goes on, they move in the opposite direction of the *human calling* from God.

All seeds bear fruit in kind. By around 2010, the national debt exceeded $50,000 for each German worker, $30,000 for each French worker, and $140,000 for each British household. The average unfunded public debt in European countries amounted to 285 percent of GDP, with 875 percent in Greece, 549 percent in France, and 418 percent in Germany. The United States is in a comparatively healthy condition, but its public debt still recently exceeded 100 percent of GDP for the first time. It too faced the dilemma of whether to take the fast lane of welfarism or hit the emergency brake.

As Greece plunged into a deep debt crisis, the rest of the world was amazed at its citizens' refusal to either lengthen working hours or accept cuts to their benefits. After frustrating and protracted talks, the European Central Bank, the first in history to be decoupled from national sovereignty, actually decided to turn on its money pump and issue more euros without sovereign guarantees. It attempted to resolve the Greek debt crisis by taking on more debt. This move, which basically poured fuel on the fire, was so unbearable for Britain that it decided to leave the European Union by referendum. One can foresee that the EU will continue to accrue debt by printing non-sovereign money and pave the way for greater crises, which will eventually destroy the post-modern paradigm of human civilization in Europe. Even economies like China and Japan have joined this currency printing frenzy in recent years. It's difficult to face the likelihood that tomorrow will be worse,[344] but God cannot continue to bless humans who are completely hooked on unearned benefits and power and have lost all sense of gratitude.

By holding high the false banner of fairness, welfarism destroys the God-given cornerstones of freedom, responsibility, and equality, as well as righteousness and justice, resulting in the crumbling of human civilization. This "fairness" is actually an illogical mathematical equality—if only "mathematically equal" is considered "fair," then the whole world and even God are unfair. One of God's most fundamental laws of creation, governing the operation of all things in the universe, preserves the objective existence of difference. Without differences in temperature, there can be no air flow; without differences in gravity, there would be no distinct and yet interconnected order of all things; without differences in height, there would be no potential energy; without differences in the speed at which atoms and quanta move, there would be no table of elements; without differences in molecular structure, there would be no combination or decomposition of matter; without differences in DNA structures, there would be no diversified cell structures or functions.

Difference, then, forms a fundamental premise: God created all things and all human beings with different natures, and they must be free to exert these differences. This law gives rise to the law of causality, which connects these countless differentiated natures in an orderly way. Only by recognizing differences and adhering to the law of causality can there be fairness in the sense God intended. Apart from this, no one else on earth has the authority to judge whether something is fair or not—certainly not by using simple mathematical averages.

True human freedom means that different individuals can freely choose to exist, think, decide, act, and enjoy the different outcomes of their choices. That is, people are responsible for the unique differences that result from their own thinking and decision-making. This is the equality of human beings. If this kind of fairness is replaced by average as a rubric, then differences in distribution and social outcomes will be seen as unfair. The "visible hand" of the government, by borrowing from the future and raising taxes inordinately, will replace the "invisible hand" of the market. On the one hand, this breaks the causal link between hard work and wealth, encouraging laziness and ruining society's dynamism. On the other hand, it immediately destroys human equality. People who are working hard cannot freely enjoy the fruits of their own efforts, while those who aren't can plunder the fruits of others' labor through protests and demonstrations, forcing the government to increase taxes and get into debt. As a result, the basic cornerstones of freedom, equality, and responsibility collapse completely.

Charitable giving, however, provides a much brighter outlook. Government policy that allows for large-scale tax exemptions has promoted the rise of a large number of modern charitable organizations. Charitable donations representing righteousness and love from Christian churches are a beautiful addition to the landscape of modern society. The United States, for example, saw the resources of its philanthropic industry approach $800 billion in 2017, with over $400 billion in charitable donations, over $170 billion worth of voluntary labor, $100 billion in donations from religious organizations, and more than $150 billion of net operating income from various charitable foundations. Philanthropy has become a major industry that promotes both national employment and social justice instead of compulsory contributions to the public sector.

More important, with their visions of justice, philanthropic organizations are able to identify the real needs for justice and love within the economic market system, and they connect donors and beneficiaries accordingly, inspiring more gratitude and justice in society. Charities also advocate for social welfare, social justice, and love via social media. This approach to the public good is far more effective than welfarism, in which the government directly enters and disrupts the market. Charitable welfare spreads God's goodness and love for people in places where the government and market fail to work, leaving givers and receivers grateful and enlightened. Public welfarism, in contrast, turns assistance and love into something taken for granted by the beneficiary, fundamentally destroying their gratitude to God and thereby destroying the *human calling* to self-discipline, self-motivation, and self-affirmation.

The long-term triumph of welfarism can only result in society departing from God's rationality and falling into "pan-liberalism:" a world where everyone speaks only of freedom, but not of responsibility, of rights but not obligations, blaming others rather than constraining themselves. Its citizens want immediate pleasures but not long-term consequences, material enjoyment in this life rather than the soul's delight in the next. This world is characterized by an inordinate increase of free benefits offered by the government without asking where the money comes from and whether it's sustainable.[345] Over time, both people and the nation fall into peril, and the persistence of humanity itself is threatened.

SECTION 5: A MAD RUSH TO A DEAD END?

Looking back on the trajectory of human history over the past 800 years, since Thomas Aquinas took on God's sacred mission to forge a path for natural theology, pioneers of humanity embarked on a second great awakening through public universities, the Renaissance, the Reformation, the rise of scientific rationality, and Enlightenment humanism.

This great awakening gradually ended the era where human life was centered on God, introducing a new era of historical compromise where God was the starting point of philosophical thinking, but mankind was the starting point of life. This compromise laid a deep philosophical and theological foundation for humanity's modernization and provided the cornerstone of modernity on which free market systems could be built. It allowed competition among nation states to go beyond violent plunder and progress to fair, globalized trade. Within each nation state, through the design and construction of the three free markets, a dynamic society formed, centered around individuals who are endowed by God with freedom and equality. This public order was built on the God-given principles of fairness, righteousness, and justice. The possibility of dualistic harmony laid the philosophical foundation for a new theology. For the modern civilization of which mankind is so proud, this great rethinking both allowed humans to reach their potential and enhance *human ability* as never before and attempted to redefine *human calling*. Its significance for the past, present, and future of humanity is vital and far-reaching, and is worth reflecting upon in the light of God's revelation.

God-given scientific curiosity and human practical needs for technological know-how combine and are accelerated by market mechanisms.[346] First, collaboration in the search for sources of energy has driven the invention of the coal-fueled steam engine, internal combustion and steam engines powered by oil and natural gas, and nuclear power plants fueled by uranium. These inventions have significantly changed humans' production patterns and ways of living, improving the speed and efficiency of their movement through space, and greatly expanding the sphere of their activity. Humans have even broken the Earth's gravitational limit for the first time and have reached our nearest planet.

Second, changes in how humans use power and energy constantly create new requirements for materials. These changes have led to the development of chemical decomposition and synthesis technology and the invention of all kinds of new materials. Scientists have collaborated in exploring the structures of molecules, atoms, protons, neutrons and electrons, causing drastic changes in the ways people live and the products that we use daily.

Third, the combination of chemistry and molecular biochemistry has accelerated the agricultural revolution, transforming plant cultivation and animal husbandry. We've seen amazing results in treating and preventing epidemics, resulting in an unprecedented increase in agricultural and food supplies. Significant improvements in health care have allowed for a large-scale expansion of the human population and an increase in life expectancy. The entire human population passed 1 billion in the late 19th century. By the end of the 20th century, it was more than 5 billion and may exceed 20 billion at the end of the current century.

Fourth, the study of electromagnetism and wave particle duality in the Earth's magnetic field, as well as the study of quantum mechanics, have constantly updated humanity's understanding of information integration and transmission. The constant progress of the electronics industry, following Moore's Law, has propelled the invention and innovation of computer networks and the mobile internet, fundamentally changing the way people live and work. The traditional barriers of space between people have been removed. People are now constantly driven by the information network, and life-like automated artificial intelligence (AI) technology has become possible.

Fifth, the discovery of deoxyribonucleic acid (DNA) in living cells, along with nearly a century of further exploration, has enabled humans to discover the traits and patterns of DNA, the genetic code in living organisms. Scientists have carried out comprehensive studies of the functions of DNA in cell structure. Gene duplication, gene disruption, gene editing, gene detection, and many other techniques have been used to diagnose and treat human diseases. These innovations have not only led to an unprecedented extension of life expectancy, but they've also opened up a fantastic new field in agriculture and may lead to the use of AI technology in the field of biology.

All those who have made significant contributions to these scientific and technological achievements, such as Galileo, Kepler, Newton, Boyle, Rutherford, Dalton, Heisenberg, Faraday, Maxwell, Joule, Curie and Madame Curie, Bohr, Hooke, Fermi, Schrödinger, Einstein, Dirac, Pasteur, Michel, Clausius, Haber, Wolfson, and Collins—were not only true masters of science, but also great souls on a God-given mission. They are truly worthy of our respect. It is their incredible imagination, with God as their starting point, and their dogged investigation of the laws that govern the universe created by God, that allowed us to reach our full potential in *human ability*, conquer nature, and reach new, unimaginable heights. The vast majority of these great souls at the apex of the scientific world believed in God's rationality. They knew that their discoveries stemmed from extraordinary God-given imagination, confirmed through the empirical methods of cumulative human reason. If that God-given imaginative power were taken away, positivism would lose its underlying principle and become powerless. The source of these extraordinary imaginations was their belief in the only ultimate truth, goodness, and beauty, as represented by God.

Because they believed, they asked questions. Because they believed, they were able to discover truth. And because they believed, their careful thinking enabled them to know that the things they discovered existed. Otherwise, who would be able to see gravity? Who can see magnetic fields? Who can see wave-particle duality? Who can see space bend? Who can see black holes in the universe? Who can see the quantum field and genetic code? They dis-

476 | The Human Calling

covered these realities because they believed in a system of scientific laws governing the operation of all things that was made by their ultimate creator God, or at least was part of the only truth represented by God. Under God's creative hand, from the great universe to all things in between, from the microscopic atoms and microorganisms to the quantum world and the genetic code of DNA—all are exquisite and orderly, with striking similarities, existing in perfect harmony. They each run in different dimensions of space and time yet are connected to each other. They neither reject humanity's use nor succumb to humanity's authority. They form causal links beyond space and time perceptible to humanity. They are so wonderful that only God's absolute truth can be the ultimate explanation for them, and only God's infinite authority can ultimately control them.

Yet, for the last nearly 200 years, the cult of science and technology has pitted science against faith in God. The majority of those who promote this cult are people with no scientific achievements. They explain everything in human life through their fragmented understandings of technology and gradually abandon belief in God's reason because of problems with certain religious organizations.[347] In their view, humans are no different from a toxoplasma or even bacteria, just a result of biological mutation and the law of the jungle. In so-called evolution, "we are all mutants."

This extreme materialism brings human civilization down to a despicable level, sapping people of their respect for human life and resulting in general suspicion and the decline of spiritual understanding of God's absolute truth and infinite authority. As a result, human thought and behavior are caught up in the tidal wave of absolute individualism and utilitarian secularism, with the bombardment of media advertising and the pressure of market competition. They value themselves not because they are part of humankind in its uniqueness, but simply because their body wants to keep living. The purpose and meaning of life do not matter. This extreme individualism led by extreme materialism ultimately brings about confusion and loss of *human calling*. People lose their self-discipline, self-motivation, and self-affirmation when they lose their spiritual direction.

On the surface, it may seem that people are growing more and more knowledgeable about technology. Yet we are obsessed with constant communication and interaction with others over smartphones. Solely considering the amount of information, an adult can store no more than 10 percent of what an iPhone stores. This fragmented information occupies almost every second of people's lives—they don't have a moment of silence in order to be still and immerse themselves in the divine light. They lose their ability to logically think about the meaning of life, as well as their original connection with God, depriving them of the ability to distinguish between right and wrong. When relationships lack the guidance of the sacred and authoritative relationship between humanity and God, more people stop exercising self-discipline, self-motivation, and self-affirmation through *human calling*, and the constraint on *human duty* by collective morality as advocated by ethicists weakens. Some governments try to act as moral exemplars for society, but their grand attempts only expose the hypocrisy and corruption of social morality. In the end, they are trampled by their lower desires and the instincts.

In such a society, everyone claims to work scientifically and live morally. Everyone is proud of knowing a lot of fragmented "scientific" information. People try to cover up their inner emptiness with the appearance of wildness and freedom, allowing their purchasing habits to be guided by social media and advertising. They set their life goals by the standard of so-called successful people and fill their lives with work, worthless social activities, and fragmented information. Their conversation reveals that they grasp the surface but not the essence of things. Unable to calmly accept their limitations and ignorance, they are always bewildered and restless, living in fear. The peace, calm, and fearlessness that God gave humans has disappeared, leaving them unable to tell what the ultimate goal of life is. Even if people are rich, famous, and powerful, they still feel discontent. They can't live without the cheap likes they receive on their phones, or the false approval of their neighbors, even for one moment. Some of them live all day fighting and defending themselves in the virtual worlds created for them by game designers, while others use their power to inflict evil. From the point of view of history, we can see what a sad state humanity is in today, and what a terrible life is one driven completely by technology.

The loss of *human calling*, which comes from faith in God, has exposed humanity to a massive, unprecedented danger. This danger begins with the majority of people who have lost the motivation and restraint of *human calling*. They devote themselves to promoting the application and expansion of technological tools accelerated by market forces and regard technology as the only tool or even the only way to solve the problems that humanity faces, worshiping it as a new idol. Humanity's reckless conquest and abuse of nature resembles a bolting mustang, running wild in the wilderness of their great *human ability*. Human beings are in danger of being devastated by the monster of *human ability*. They're not able to close the Pandora's box they opened with the combination of the market system and modern technology. This is seen in several ways.

First, the combination of economic marketization and interactive media has created an unprecedented force for secularization, moving society to abandon its public spirit and become increasingly materialistic and commercial. Musicians, painters, performance artists, sociologists, economists, politicians, and even philosophers are all drawn into this massive wave of secularization, surrounded by all kinds of design companies, strategic consultants, professional brokers, advertising companies, marketing companies—even charities—and ultimately, Wall Street investors.

These companies are involved in the creation of cultural products. They plan, package, and launch large advertising campaigns for thinkers, artists, and political visionaries who want to out-perform their peers. They aim to achieve social impact so that they can convince readers and audiences to buy their products or services. In the end, the success of cultural products is measured by the quantity of products or services sold. Popularity, then, has become the most important factor influencing an entity's decisions in this extremely secularized society. The most important reason I read, I listen, I appreciate, I like, I respect, and I agree with something is because "it's popular." To gain this precious popularity, a company must cater to and even pander to readers and audiences, and accept advertising, market planning, and capital intervention. Those who don't appreciate the secular works prevalent in current fields of thought, art, and politics are ridiculed as "outdated." That means there are less and less independent thinkers, artists, and politicians enlightened by divine revelation in our times, and no one is willing to take the time to draw on the spiritual strength of those in history. Those great masters are too far removed from the distressing, materialistic, secular lives that we now lead.

Today, even at America's most prestigious Ivy League universities, courses on Ancient Greek philosophy and the Renaissance have few students, while courses about the success of movie stars and Wall Street magnates are always in great demand. Although there is a widespread feeling that people today are losing more and more of the virtues of the past, such as kindness, patience, elegance, calmness, and discernment, nobody seems to put two and two together to get to the root of the problem.

Next is AI technology, the largest potential threat to modern humanity.[348] The combination of the cult of technology and the laws of the market is driving rapid changes in AI technology. The original intention of humans in using this technology was to save on rising labor costs and try to replace workers on certain parts of the production line with automation. Such attempts have been praised for increasing production efficiency and for gradually taking over heavy, dangerous, and hazardous kinds of work that can harm human health.

But with Moore's Law in play, AI didn't stop there. The performance of computer chips doubles every 18 months, which means that information stored in a giant computer system that 40 years ago required over 50 square meters of space can now be compressed and stored on a chip the size of a fingernail. Computing power has increased exponentially, allowing machines to do white collar, not just blue collar, work.

The world's leading automakers and internet companies are all accelerating their development of self-driving cars. Tens of millions of professional drivers will face the risk of being replaced by robots, and hundreds of millions of people will face the dilemma of not needing the ability to drive. Twenty years after the intelligent robot "Deep Blue" defeated the international chess champion, "AlphaGo" again did the same thing with Go. Robots also make their way onto the Wall Street trading room, putting the jobs of many workers in finance at risk.

With new developments in quantum mechanics research and new discoveries in topological insulator materials, the obstacle of transistors reaching temperature limits may soon be solved. As their specs double under Moore's law, allowing faster upgrading of computer chip performance, data storage and computing speed up. These developments have accelerated the arrival of new AI that can listen, speak, write, calculate, move, and even have the ability to learn and think. AI assistants, translators, divers, pilots, doctors, nurses, analysts, accountants, lawyers, police, judges, and traders have all become part of AI companies' imaginations and development goals.

The first clear threat this poses is to human employment. While the global population has continued to grow four- or fivefold since the 20th century, the entrepreneurial community, led by developed countries, is driving the replacement of more than 40 percent of the workforce by AI in all sectors. This will directly increase competition among humans and even between humans and machines in the labor market. Though the capital-owning class, represented by Wall Street, will flourish, the condition of the working class will go from bad to worse. Laborers replaced by AI will gradually be abandoned by society, becoming social outcasts with no job, no income, and no ability to communicate and understand. As there's no place to resettle them, this group of social outcasts will grow.

The problems of depression, drug use, suicide, and suicidal terrorist attacks are only in their infancy. The resulting mass unemployment and social conflicts and disruptions will far exceed those witnessed by Marx and others in human history. Solving the massive problem of "human-machine conflict" that people have created is far beyond their power to solve. Humanity is like a group of incompetent wizards who have conjured a demon from the underworld but can't send it back. This is our dilemma.

The second threat AI poses may be the mechanization of humans and the humanization of machines. The AI industry will trigger further division of labor in society. AI will replace many jobs, from simple to complex, though it's expected to create them in the design and programming sectors. But those who have interest and capabilities in design and programming only constitute a small part of the working population. Any attempt to train the labor force replaced by AI to become AI designers and programmers is naive and unrealistic. Moreover, even AI designers and programmers will have to specialize exponentially as they face an industry that is hundreds of thousands of times more complex than in the past. In the process, they become programmers, reviewers, analysts, and test simulators, who face a computer every day, writing a small part of a program. They become more and more lopsided as humans, conversing with machines. More and more people are communicating, being entertained by, and living on their devices, and we will eventually lose more and more of our human nature, becoming more and more like machines.

Meanwhile, the AI machines created by industrialization will gradually become humanized. Their listening, speaking, writing, reading, calculating, walking, running, and carrying abilities are becoming increasingly refined, so that each function transcends that of human beings. Human curiosity, ambition, and our social nature will gradually cause these functions to merge and ultimately fully humanize AI.

This leads to a third deadly threat to humanity from AI. Neuroscientists and genetic engineers are fanatically committed to combining genetic engineering, AI, and materials science to create a robot that takes on all human emotions and curiosity. Although the BINA48 smart robot developed by Hanson Robotics in Texas in 2012 only had 2.5 million electronic virtual neurons, certainly not comparable to the human brain's 86 billion neurons, reporters' interviews with it have already revealed its emotional capabilities.

The Sophia robot, created in 2015, demonstrates even better logical reasoning ability and emotional response than BINA48. This crucial step forward in machine humanization is enough to make us feel the potentially huge threat of its power. Robots can gain machine learning abilities, especially self-awareness of their emotional tendencies. When the day comes that machines are emotionally and consciously autonomous, the human species will be in real danger of being terminated by the virtual AI machines that we have created.

Increasingly, people are getting worse and worse at dealing with interpersonal relationships. More and more choose to become homosexual. More and more choose not to get married and have children. More and more turn to robots as sexual partners. These extremely individualist, liberal behavioral orientations that miss the sacred purpose of life are all accepted under the guise of equal rights. Profit-driven companies, for their part, offer all kinds of products without constraint to satisfy extremely absurd personal needs that their advertising has stimulated in the first place. This paradox, which flies in the face of common sense and God's rationality, is leading humanity into a downward spiral and preparing the ground for androids to completely bring us to an end.

If we observe dispassionately, we can already see the approach of an era where humans and machines coexist. Using human reason alone, it's almost impossible for humans to reach any effective, long-term consensus. Any short-term consensus, due to the combination of extreme liberalism and market utilitarianism, is always torn to shreds and scattered by the wind. What force can stop AI robots from destroying and replacing people? Hawking's answer before he died, was a dreadful prophecy—"Artificial intelligence could spell the end of the human race."

With this threat, the conquest of nature has reached its end and has now turned against humanity. Humanity no longer has natural enemies, except himself. Modern science, which discovered and tapped into the laws created by God to govern the universe, aided by technological progress driven by human needs, has greatly boosted *human ability*. Humanity has conquered nature. It can be said that in the relationship between humans and nature, *human ability* has won absolute victory. But humanity's cumulative behavior has already reached the end of the road, completely losing the restraint of *human calling*. Despite the many laws, or *human requirement*, that nation states have enacted to impose stipulations on human behavior and protect nature, and the various declarations and agreements formulated by heads of states at conferences to deal with environmental damage, humanity is still helpless in the face of developing countries' excessive population growth and increasingly large economic development needs.

Amid the tide of globalism, human beings are trapped in a "prisoner's dilemma." On the one hand, developed countries, through various international, multilateral, and bilateral organizations and NGO's, are helping underdeveloped countries conquer nature and develop economically. A growing number of entrepreneurs competing in different markets are constantly inventing products and services that they then supply, using advertising to influence consumer demand. On the other hand, globalization has put the environment on an irreversible fast track to destruction. The most essential problems to solve, like an overall plan for the population and the environment's population-bearing capacity, have never been and can never be discussed, let alone a consensus reached or acted upon.

As a result, certain mainstream technological trends have already formed and are almost impossible to reverse. First, the carbon dioxide produced by massive energy combustion and energy conversion since the start of our industrial civilization cannot be absorbed by the dwindling plants on earth. Instead, it's emitted into the atmosphere, creating a greenhouse effect that causes the earth's average temperature to gradually increase. When the heavy use of coal and fossil fuels began in 1800, the level of carbon dioxide in the atmosphere was less than 280ppm. Now it's over 400ppm. The average temperature has increased by at least 2.5 degrees centigrade. In 2050, carbon dioxide level is expected to exceed 600ppm, at which point the earth's average temperature will be 2.5 degrees centigrade higher than it is now. Based on this projection, it will certainly exceed 1,000ppm by the year 2100. As to how much the temperature will increase by then, and whether the atmosphere will still exist, the answers are beyond human cognitive ability.[349]

The so-called "greenhouse effect" is causing global warming. The glaciers in the southern hemisphere are disappearing. The temperature near the equator has increased dramatically. Arctic ice is melting. Overall sea levels are rising. Low-lying places like the Maldives and Shanghai face the threat of being submerged. Many species are or will be extinct. Arid areas are expanding, and other regions are quickly becoming deserts. Climate fluctuations are increasingly abnormal, as the frequency, severity, and destruction of natural disasters like fires, hurricanes, and droughts are increasing. Temperatures around the equator will soon make the earth unlivable, and the resulting hundreds of millions of environmental refugees will mean catastrophic and insurmountable human disaster.[350]

More frightening is the fact that according to the latest research, carbon dioxide deposited in the atmosphere doesn't automatically dissolve but gets thicker and thicker. Atmospheric researchers are concerned that the weight of this accumulated carbon dioxide will exceed a critical mass and trigger a historic collapse. Collapsed carbon dioxide will fall to the earth, causing a serious shortage of oxygen and resulting in the suffocation of living things. More than 70 percent of it will fall into the oceans, turning them into a sticky, viscous substance, with the potential to wipe out all marine life. The cycles of earth's environment, which human existence depends on, will completely collapse. However, the ever-increasing population of humanity cannot be contained, even less so the carbon emissions of developing countries in their quest for progress. No substantive consensus will be reached between the various developed and developing countries on per capita emissions. At most there will be politically correct and diplomatic statements that everyone is concerned about global warming.

On another front, the large increase in population has led to a serious shortage of food supplies. In responding to this most critical issue of human survival, scientific and technological efforts over the past century and a half have been remarkable and encouraging. They've identified five core solutions for increasing potential food yield: 1) increasing the amount of cultivated land; 2) changing plant and animal traits through transgenic hybridization; 3) promoting large-scale use of plastic sheeting that enhances micro-environmental warming; 4) applying a large amount of fertilizer rich in nitrogen, phosphorus, and potassium; and 5) reducing the negative impacts of pests, diseases, and weeds by extensive use of insecticide- and herbicide-based pesticides.

These strategies are not without cost. Earth's land has already been over-cultivated, leading to deforestation, with the original 6 trillion trees on the planet dropping to below 5 trillion, a reduction of 25-30%. This decrease has struck a critical blow to the earth's oxygen-creation capacity, which is more far-reaching than we realize.[351] The issue of genetically modified foods is being hotly debated, but without them we cannot survive. Globally, 120 million tons of plastic sheeting and various plastic products are used every year, with only 10 percent being recycled, 10 percent burned, and more than 70 percent abandoned in the soil and rivers, eventually ending up in the ocean. Each piece of plastic takes 500 years to naturally decompose. As a result, more and more plastic debris contaminates the soil, rivers, air, and oceans. Even by the simplest mathematical calculations and leaving out incremental changes, by the time the first batch of plastic products naturally decomposes, the amount of plastic accumulated worldwide will have exceeded 45 billion tons. Countless living things will have died from consuming them. What creature is resilient enough to survive on a planet full of plastic waste? This far-reaching impact on the planet and on humanity far exceeds the short-term strategies of human technology, continuously striking at humanity's pride.

The 200 million tons of fertilizer used each year is exhausting the fertile soil that God gave us, fundamentally changing the deep and longstanding relationship between the soil and crops. These fertilizers have been applied to one third of the land in China. Worldwide, the annual amount of pesticides and herbicides used is 3.5–4 million tons, 50 percent of which are applied to the soil in China. These huge amounts of pesticides not only endanger the health of humans by leaving behind excessive residues but also profoundly affect the toxicity of the soil, rivers, lakes, and oceans. That means the living conditions of creatures like butterflies, bees, aquatic organisms, and all kinds of insects, are affected by a long causal chain of impacts far beyond human cognition.

The animal kingdom is suffering as well. People have won absolute victory over all living things on earth. The mighty creatures of the past like tigers, elephants, lions, rhinoceroses, hippopotamuses, and leopards have been hunted down, have completely lost their natural habitats, and are heading towards mass extinction. Nothing is safe from the clutches of our overdeveloped *human ability*. Humans are ignorant of the implications of their absolute victory for the chain of causality. Only a few people have a sense of ominous foreboding, and it is these people who have tried to raise awareness and public protection for endangered species. Perhaps history has come to a turning point in which people must again realize that mankind is his own true and final enemy.

Furthermore, the misunderstanding and misuse of the God-given principles of fairness and equality have fostered an oxymoronic culture that encourages both compassion and laziness. The scope of government has expanded excessively, fostering both tyranny and inertia.[352] The cult of science and technology has led to straightforward application of the natural sciences' empirical research methods to the social sciences, so that they tend to draw conclusions based on simplistic statistical analysis and inference. The social sciences' admirable logical and structural analysis methods have been abandoned. As a result, the fundamental principles of a modern state of freedom, responsibility, equality, fairness, righteousness, and justice, have been seriously misunderstood, causing deviations in the mainstream social consciousness.

Misunderstandings of fairness and equality are particularly serious. The long-term application of a positivist academic framework, that is, using methods of simple statistical analysis in the social sciences, inevitably leads to the replacement of "societal fairness" with "average rights," and "spiritual equality" with "absolute material equality" in societal consciousness. This fosters widespread shirking of responsibility and fighting for absolute average rights. Groups with this mindset have spurred the government to move toward universal welfarism, marked by intervention in market competition and distribution of benefits. Over time, the law that everyone is responsible for their own outcomes based on their efforts is broken, and a culture that encourages both societal compassion and laziness is formed. Without the efforts and motivation of most citizens, the country's ability to innovate is further weakened. Instead, people become dependent on government tax- and debt-funded welfare, which governments provide to appeal to groups in the short term. Such dependence causes the government to borrow from the future indefinitely.

At the same time, Keynes's idealistic model for macroeconomic intervention, along with academia's confusion of equal distribution with equality, encourages the government to intervene in the market and engage in so-called secondary distribution. This level of government overreach may eventually legitimize authoritarian governments, enabling them to issue arbitrary laws. The true freedom, equality, fairness, and justice of modernized states becomes confused with the fake freedom, equality, fairness, and justice of collectivism and nationalism. The government abandons its role of an independent arbitrator in the free market and gains monopoly in the market by directly controlling assets, resources, and prices. It not only levies taxes on taxpayers, but it also steals profits through monopolies, and abuses administrative power to distort market prices. This in turn encourages the corruption of government officials and state-owned enterprise operators and stifles corporate innovation and social justice by suppressing private property rights. The next step for a government on this path is totalitarianism, where the latest science and technology is used to eradicate personal privacy and deprive individuals of freedom and equality. The country is caught in a vicious cycle, taking two steps back for every two steps forward toward modernization.

In non-authoritarian, democratic countries with a system of checks and balances, this misunderstanding of fairness leads to an irreversible shift in legislation toward universal welfarism. Politicians, blindly catering to voters' utopian appeals for both a compassionate society and unearned benefits, don't even try to make the right legislative decisions. Eventually the absurd fallacy that democracy should result in equal outcomes takes hold. This legislation encourages laziness among citizens through the band-aid of universal welfare, fundamentally destroying the mechanism of causality in people's outcomes. This deals a huge blow to local innovative entrepreneurs, driving them out and harming these countries' core competitiveness in the global marketplace, so they inevitably decline into post-modern recession.

The materialistic view that technology can solve all our problems and explain all phenomena has grown in international popularity. This view goes hand in hand with utilitarianism, which measures all human behavior by its material benefits, resulting in the dominance of pragmatist philosophy.[353] It has become a mantra that if a country has money, it has power. Any public spirit and social morality that transcends individuals and nation states has been deconstructed by the philosophy of practical utilitarianism, depriving us of the ability to respect and discern these lofty concepts.

As a result, international organizations like the United Nations and the international media increasingly emphasize that all nation states are absolutely equal, even though they don't bear the same proportion of international obligations. Much like the logic of universal welfarism within a nation state, this idea of absolute equality suppresses the law of causality that each sovereign state is responsible for its actions. International organizations like the UN have increasingly become advocates for global welfarism.

The Syrian refugee problem highlights the paradox of global welfarism among nation states. It was the UN that failed to resolve the root causes of regional political conflicts leading to the crisis of the Syrian civil war and the rapid rise of the Islamic State. Yet the UN tried to resettle 7 million Syrian refugees in developed countries and overemphasized equal rights for both refugees and the citizens of these countries. Essentially, the UN's actions encouraged the irresponsibility of sovereign states and justified refugees' movement to other countries to enjoy welfare benefits. This approach only worsened the refugee crisis, the world's largest since World War II. The impact of this crisis is so far-reaching that it may take the next half century or more to eliminate the internal violent conflict created by the great number of refugees resettled in Europe.

Since the second half of the last century, in the context of peaceful development and globalization, conflicts among nation states have quickly escalated into a global arms race centered around the development of nuclear weapons. Amid the terrible threat of extreme terrorism in the 9/11 terrorist attacks, the tussle over small countries' attempts to develop nuclear weapons has grown intense. On the one hand, global welfarism and the increasing scale of aid for developing countries means that preventing developing countries from owning nuclear weapons is seen as a violation of equal rights for all nation states. On the other hand, there are real concerns about developing countries' ability to carry out anti-terrorism activities or prevent nuclear weapons from being used by terrorists and totalitarians.

The nuclear weapons possessed by current nuclear powers are enough to destroy humanity a hundred times over. Yet it seems that nothing can be done to keep the list of nuclear powers from growing, as countless small- and medium-sized countries are eager to create nuclear weapons of their own. The consequences of allowing all nation states to freely develop nuclear weapons are, of course, unthinkable. However, the path of preventing nuclear proliferation and the arms race is getting more difficult. The development of nuclear weapons hasn't diminished the fear of external violence from other nation states. Instead, it has made this external threat even more frightening. This threat of external violence in turn incentivizes the development of nuclear weapons and the escalation of the arms race.

Humanity increasingly seeks solutions from new science and technology, but the threat only grows. Internet hackers, loss of privacy, potential android armies, and portable missiles, have only escalated the threat of external violence that humans face. At the same time, lone-wolf terrorist attacks are becoming more frequent. Horrifying domestic terrorist attacks have occurred around the world in recent years, often for reasons that are too simple for people to believe. Because it's so difficult to prevent, people don't know how to face the threat of such internal violence. At the end of the day, humanity may end in irreversible and unpredictable mutual destruction. Long-term efforts to develop technological know-how and increase *human ability*, as well as long-term erosion of the *human calling* from God by secularization, have set the stage for a maniac to press the button that would trigger the violent destruction of humanity. We simply don't know who, when, or where.

In conclusion, it is impossible for humanity to achieve long-term safety and happiness by relying solely on the development of science and technology. Unilateral reliance on this development without the rational constraint of faith in God may indeed enhance *human ability* in physical terms, but it also fuels humanity's pride and ignorance. Such pride intensifies tension within groups as individuals become increasingly egocentric, and exacerbates human identification with nation states. This in turn aggravates competition between groups for material resources, the unsustainable exploitation of nature, and extreme contempt for the public spirit. The idea of public spirit is appropriated by the collective that uses dogma to enslave and even kill people in an ongoing struggle for technological dominance. The development of science and technology becomes deformed, collapsing the interdependence between humans and nature, and increasing the abuse of political power. The nurturing of the violent forces of extreme individualism and the unbridled accumulation of destructive weapons systems could very well culminate in the mass annihilation of the human race in a glorious feast of *human ability*.

As far as individual human beings are concerned, it's true that the development of science and technology can bring about a higher level of material civilization and convenience today. Yet apart from the self-discipline, self-motivation, and self-affirmation of God's *human calling*, and without the historical continuity of human's spiritual life beyond the present physical life, people may, consciously or unconsciously, degenerate into creatures of the material world alone, solely driven by the utilitarian market and living busy but meaningless lives. Since extreme egocentrism and individualism are now legitimized, they can think of life as a material game within the legal boundaries of *human requirement*. They join in the competition and struggle for life. If they happen to succeed, they become conceited and sow the seeds for failure in the next round of competition. If they happen to lose, they often become depressed or broken or try to rise from the ashes to fight again. If they happen to fail too many times, they may commit suicide. But even those in between, who live a life of peaceful mediocrity, still resemble a dead frog buried in the ground, with no past and no future.

As human beings with a spiritual nature, we may need to consider whether this aimless, uncertain life is worth living, whether this one-time physical game in which we wager our lives is worth playing, and whether human happiness is nothing more than a butterfly's experience with flowers or a dog's with food. If there is still a spiritual dimension to human happiness, then living in this finite, imperfect, and often mad human world, requires us to constantly make subjective judgments, decisions, and actions. This begs the question, is there a connection between humans and the unlimited, eternal, perfect, and absolute being that inspires them to search for self-discipline, self-motivation, and self-affirmation, which is their *human calling*? Can such a calling enable them to handle the many ups and downs, uncertainties, frustrations, and evils that are unavoidable in this life?

If people—if you—can find such a connection, one that inspires a response to spiritual expectations, then no matter what your earthly life looks like to other people, you can always find your life worth living and experience happiness and gratitude. No matter what societal expectations are, or how others treat or evaluate you, you can always turn to the *human calling* of self-discipline, self-motivation, and self-affirmation. You can live an extraordinary and dignified life, finding the divine constant that has always been present in both life and death.

If more people returned to this kind of life, could we have a completely different perspective on today's society? Could we develop a completely different ability to listen, understand, and treat others with a sense of mission? If so, we would have completely different attitudes and make different decisions. We would redefine the cornerstones of modernity and rebuild modern society. And we would realize that the power to change our human community lies not in relative *human ability* with its flashy new developments in science and technology, but in the sacred expectations of *human calling,* and the absolute truth revealed by God.

Perhaps we have already reached the endpoint of human reason without God and the cult of science and technology. Humanity needs a third great reflection, or we will continue rushing toward self-destruction. The story of how God saved the US Constitutional Convention from the brink of collapse is an enlightening example for every human community, and even every individual.[354] The Constitutional Convention, which began in Philadelphia on May 15, 1787, was attended by representatives elected by the states. Those who Americans would later call the Founding Fathers and the other representatives at the convention, whether in terms of their knowledge, experience, public service, or public spirit, were all outstanding individuals, with a shared purpose of developing the ideal constitution for the United States.

But assembling great men in one room doesn't guarantee that a consensus will be reached, and excellent individuals working together do not necessarily yield desirable results. On June 27, 40 days after the convention began, strong disagreements emerged over the thorniest issues, such as the allocation of delegates to the House and Senate, the boundaries between federal and state legislative power, whether slavery would continue to be legal or be counted when determining the quota of congressional representatives, and the separation of powers and checks and balances in the legislative, judicial, and administrative branches. Speeches given in order to persuade members only led to fierce quarrels and criticism. The convention was growing heated, with no agreement in sight. Many representatives had lost patience and were preparing to go home. The Constitutional Convention was on the verge of collapse, which would mean that all efforts since the Declaration of Independence would be in vain, and the country would plunge back into chaos.

On June 28, Pennsylvania delegate Benjamin Franklin took to the floor. As the eldest delegate, he called on the others to recognize the finite nature of human reason, and to instead seek wisdom from God's infinite, eternal, and perfect reason. He urged them to quietly listen to the voice of God for the sake of developing a constitution for the United States of America and to work out the best solution possible by orienting themselves toward a sacred public spirit in spite of imperfect human reason. He then suggested that the representatives pray together and invite a pastor to the meeting.

The representatives discussed Franklin's suggestion. In view of the future commitment of the United States to the principles of religious tolerance and freedom of belief, the meeting did not adopt Franklin's proposal for group prayer. But they did agree to invite a pastor to preach and to pray to God individually. And then, a miracle happened. The following meetings of the Constitutional Convention still saw fierce arguments but proceeded in a friendly, open, peaceful, tolerant atmosphere. The representatives, by arguing, debating, insisting, accepting, and compromising on each article, finally created the Constitution of the United States, which despite its imperfections, remains a model constitution for countries seeking to modernize to this day.

Conclusion

Mankind is unique among the vast ecosystem of living things in being particularly vulnerable as an individual, and is therefore forced to cultivate the true, good, and beautiful virtues of courage, trust, self-discipline, and self-motivation in order to cooperate as a social species. Otherwise as individual humans, we would be caught up in both internal and external violence under the law of the jungle, where the strong prey on the weak. To live in such a society, in which violence is the law, is to have a life that's not worth living. Humanity would be no different from any other animal, unworthy of God's blessing and wouldn't be able to exist for long or gain happiness. As a result, in order to know truth, goodness and beauty in the course of one's life, and to keep cultivating the virtues of courage, trust, and self-discipline, mankind must have faith. Faith is what illuminates our relationship with God.

This is because only with the proper faith and relationship with God can every living being find the inner confidence to know and practice the truth, goodness, and beauty that aligns with God's expectation. Only in this way can mankind achieve the *human calling* of self-discipline, self-motivation, and self-affirmation and so keep their increasing *human ability* from becoming a wild horse that has lost its way.

Throughout the long history of humanity, even in the days before market-driven trade and codified law, all human communities and nations developed their own relationship with God and styles of worship. It was this worship that inspired the great heroes of these cultures to answer their *human calling* in accordance with God's expectation. This shaped their morality marked by self-discipline, self-motivation, and self-affirmation, so that they in turn could serve as role models for the morality of their societies so human behavior could be regulated.

Most early faiths began as the worship of objects, and were therefore full of primitive superstition. However, records of the gods and heroes of the past and the legends passed down about them provide a clearer picture of the ideals they represented, which are much more logical.

The five generations of ancient Greek gods are one of the few examples in human history of a pantheon that had clear divisions between their roles, responsibilities, and supernatural powers. But the inevitable death of the Titans revealed the tragedy behind the gods. Greek natural philosophies, including the natural philosophy concerning the relationship between humans and nature and the humanistic philosophy exploring the relationship between humans and society, rose to take their place. Through these philosophies, the ancient Greeks reflected deeply on the relationship between humans and God, which was part of humanity's first great reflection.

What kind of God is worthy of humanity's worship? Only a God that existed before all things, who is universal and true, good and beautiful. Polytheism and fetishism both lack logical internal consistency. In these practices, the relationship between the gods and humans is chaotic. They are unable to reach the true heights of human faith.

The ancient records of the Hebrews, which reveal a faith that endured through the baptism of thousands of years of suffering, reveal that the unipersonal God, the immanent Jehovah, inaugurated a covenant-based relationship between humanity and God.

God is outside our universe. He created our world, all living things, and the causal relationships between them. He is infinite, eternal, omnipotent, and benevolent. These characteristics are all consistent with the logical answers ancient Greek philosophy left us as a guide for belief. After 1,500 years, and the baptism of blood and fire through God's trials and selection, the Jewish faith has become the most established belief system in human history with a monotheistic, personal God.

The Roman Empire's reliance on law and violence to enslave over 50 nations paved the way for the sacrifice of Jesus Christ, the Son of God, as well as the countless sacrifices of Christian martyrs throughout history. Numerous theologians such as Augustine of Hippo, Gregory of Nazianzus, St. Jerome, and Thomas Aquinas have worked to integrate ancient Greek philosophy with Christianity in their contemplation, debate, and verification, to create a systematic theology and a set of religious practices for the Christian faith. Together, they were able to elevate the relationship between humans and God to one based on love and forgiveness, a new pinnacle of morality in human history. And through natural theology and philanthropic organizations like universities, modern science was born, as represented by figures such as Sir Isaac Newton.

In the East, Pre-Qin Chinese philosophers, with their naturalistic worship of "Heaven," raised many profound questions themselves, and offered their own philosophical answers. They also created a hierarchical and structured view of political governance. Eventually, they chose to introduce the Vedanta philosophy of India with the Trimurti of Brahman at its core, into their belief system. Ancient Vedanta philosophy boasted a long history and internally consistent logic, where Brahman is personified as a triad of deities, known as the Trimurti. Brahman, in turn, set the stage for the Buddha, who transcended the impermanence and difficulty of life, overcoming the evils of the world through the attainment of Nirvana. This gave rise to Buddhism, built around reaching eternity through Nirvana, which marked the peak of the relationship between humans and God in the East.

God's divine expectation for humans to act on their *human calling*, by virtue of its sanctity and authority, helps us to passionately and confidently pursue rational inquiry. Both Eastern and Western belief systems have inspired many to answer their *human calling* and strive for spiritual satisfaction through cultivation of their character and kindness to others. These traditions have been immensely significant and far-reaching for non-violence and benevolent governance in the history of human civilization for over 2,000 years.

However, as human civilization advances and grows in complexity, its organizational structure also becomes progressively complex. First, the increase of government legislation has turned issues that *human calling* fully addresses into various compulsory rules and provisions. All these extensive, wide-ranging, and increasingly elaborate laws and statues constitute the realm of *human requirement*, making it difficult for individuals to understand and remember them. As a result, they inevitably become enslaved by powerful and complex governments. Second, religious commandments and unwritten social codes further split ethical rules from what constitutes *human calling*. The moral pressures exerted by communities to compel their members to comply with their values may be referred to as *human duty*.

Having tens of millions of ethical rules to obey can strain an individual's sense of freedom, so people quickly tire of these rules. Leaders of all ethnic groups and communities have always used collective, mandatory ethical forces to punish people who are impatient and break the rules. Song-Ming Confucianism, which introduced a Confucianized paradigm of imperial gods and divine officials, had thousands of restrictive rules within their code of Confucian ethics. The countless rules within the Islamic *Sahih al-Bukhari* are also a classic example of innumerable complicated statutes and regulations being applied to people's daily lives.

We can see that the traditional practices of the great faiths preserved a relationship between humans and God that fulfilled God's expectations, enabling them to develop the self-discipline, self-motivation, and self-affirmation of their *human calling*. Yet it has been gradually eroded and replaced by increasingly systematized *human requirement* and *human duty*. We'll get even further off track if we mistakenly believe that we can make up for this erosion by replacing faith with technological control and man-made morals. From a collective standpoint, this may allow for greater control in the face of uncertain human behavior. However, the increasing secularization of faith resulting from this erosion has heightened people's confusion about their past, present, and future lives—people have always felt discontented and been prone to rebellion when they feel their free will is being impinged upon by collective rules.

In the second great reflection of humanity where the East was absent, Western Christianity led the world in reconsidering the value of individual free will, which promoted a major shift of the focus of human life from "God's rationality" to human's "autonomous rationality." Western countries have taken this opportunity to pursue modernization and build a fair market competition system centered on the pursuit of human self-interest, leading the world to raise *human ability* and material prosperity to unprecedented levels.

Unfortunately, in this great historical process, the extremist ideology of human rationality that drives people to attempt to abandon God and become uniquely autonomous has gone too far. It has reached such an extent that in the process of criticizing the dogmatic precepts of traditional religious practice, people have entirely lost the rationality of faith in God and secularized it. Their distance from God has led their unique rationality to be crushed by the twin forces of the growing pressures of modern life, driven by market competition, and new technological tools.

In losing the guidance that faith in God gives them, people have devolved into animals with no spiritual life. They're not concerned with their past or their future, nor the meaning of their lives. Rather, they focus on their immediate needs and "living in the moment." They've lost sight of their *human calling*, and the inherent self-discipline, self-motivation, and self-affirmation that originate from this divine revelation. They are like the blind leading the blind, egging each other on, comparing themselves to the people around them, and getting further swept up in the lethal tide of social media and entertainment. They're running for their whole lives but don't know where they're going.

It is very likely that human beings will bring about our own extinction thanks to our powerful *human ability*, which we first refined by the division of labor and increasingly integrate and accumulate throughout the whole human race. As a result, humanity is poised on the cusp of a third great reflection.

Modern technology, materialism, and secularization have created a culture in which proof of God's existence has become the focus of humans' relationship with God. Consequently, people either slide into the abyss of mysticism, or fall into the desperation of seeking the infinite in their limited tools, using relative means to prove absolutes. They even have the hubris to claim that God is dead. These misconceptions, coupled with the ups and downs of life, can cause people to look for idols elsewhere. They may, due to personal weakness and frustration, become influenced by mass media and participate in the worship of the celebrities as "gods." Or if they are headstrong and arrogant, they may desire to make themselves gods in their hunger to be worshipped by others. They either become enslaved by organizations or become the oppressors who enslave others—the two inescapable options for individual lives.

The key to humanity's relationship with God lies in believing that the familiar tenets of "freedom, equality, fairness, justice, and righteousness" are not empty words. Rather, we must believe that these are the values that the limitless, eternal, and absolute God has bestowed upon us. These principles are thus full of divine and supreme authority and are worth defending with our lives. By upholding belief in these principles, human beings can cut off society's path to creating man-made gods, and eliminate organized slavery, orchestrated by the few who enslave the many in the name of the state.

Then we, as individuals who hold this precious faith, can find within ourselves a fount of inner confidence and strength—the self-discipline, self-motivation, and self-affirmation to move toward our sacred *human calling*—defending the public spirit of freedom, equality, fairness, justice, and righteousness that God gave us. At the same time, no matter whether our status is low or high, whether we're outstanding or mediocre, whether we're up or down in life, we can, through our faith, find the logical and consistent divine direction and strength in the course of our past, present, and future lives. This is how we can be grateful, happy, and content in this life, and finally overcome evil and survive beyond death. This is the essential meaning of faith in God as a public spirit of humanity.

References

1   Konrad Lorenz, Studies in Animal and Human Behavior, Volume I, II, trans. Li Bicheng, Xing Zhihua (Shanghai Scientific and Technological Education Publish House, 2017), Volume I: 249-329, Volume II: 271-325.

2   Michael Tomasello, A Natural History of Human Thinking (Harvard University Press, 2014), 124-195.

Ernst Cassirer, An Essay on Man, trans. Gan Yang (Shanghai Translation Publishing House, 2013), 3-120.

3   Sofia Sfyroera, The Essential Greek Mythology, trans. Zhang Yunjiang (International Culture Publishing Company, 2007).

Jean-Pierre Vernant, El universo, los dioses, los hombres, trans. Ma Xiangmin (Wenhui Press, 2017), 11-193.

4   Daniel Defoe, Robinson Crusoe, trans. Huang Gaoxin (Shanghai Translation Publishing House, 2006), 80-250.

5   Berhanou Abebbé, Chavaillon, J., and Sutton, J. E. G. (eds), Panafrican
    Congress of Prehistory and Quaternary Studies (Addis Ababa: Provi-
    sional Military Government of Socialist Ethiopia, Ministry of Culture,
    Sports & Youth Affairs,1971), 275-350.
6   Peter Bogucki, The Origins of Human Society (Wiley-Blackwell,
    1999), 10-35.
Richard Klein, The Human Career: Human Biological and Cultural Origins
    (University of Chicago Press, 1989), 5-20.
Chris Stringer and Robin McKie, African Exodus: The Origins of Modern
    Humanity (Holt Paperbacks, 1998), 3-24.
David Christian, Maps of Time: An Introduction to Big History (University
    of California Press, 2011), 163-200.
7   Yuval Noah Harari, Sapiens: A Brief History of Humankind (Harper
    Perennial, 2012), 6-10.
C.J. Hayes, P.T. Moon, and J.W. Wayland, World History, trans. Wang Jingbo
    (Tianjin People's Publish House, 2011), 2-9.
8   Zecharia Sitchin,The 12th Planet (Stein and Day, 1976), 1-20.
9   Arnold Toynbee, An Historian's Approach to Religion (Oxford Univer-
    sity Press, 1956), 3-36.
10 Charles Horton Cooley, Social Organization, a Study of the Larger Mind
    (Cornell University Library,1909), 16-40, Social Process (Cornell Uni-
    versity Library, 1918), 78-91.
11 L.S. Stavrianos, A Global History: From Prehistory to the 21st Century
    (7th Edition) (Peking University Press, 2006), 4-44.
12 Charles Horton Cooley, Human Nature and the Social Order (Cornell
    University Library, 1902), 110-134.
13 Peter Harrison, The Territories of Science and Religion (University of
    Chicago Press, 2015) 20-46.

14 David Christian, Maps of Time: An Introduction to Big History (University of California Press, 2011), 207-287.

15 Hendrik Willem Van Loon, The Story of Mankind (CreateSpace Independent Publishing Platform, 1921), 17-21, 34-36.

John H. Walton, Ancient Near Eastern Thought and the Old Testament (Baker Academic, 2006), 31-82.

Peter Watson, Ideas: A History from Fire to Freud, trans. Hu Cui'e (Yilin Press, 2017), 63-73.

Dong Kun, Research on the Origin of Chinese Characters (The Commercial Press, 2005), 16-45.

Hu Pu'an, A Brief History of Chinese Characters (New World Press, 2017), 8-63.

16 Same as above.

17 Same as above.

18 Same as above.

19 Same as above.

20 Martin P. Nillson, The Mycenaean Origin of Greek Mythology (University of California Press, 1972), 1-123.

Luc Ferry, La Sagesse des mythes, trans. Cao Ming (East China Normal University, 2017), 48-63.

Jean-Pierre Vernant, El universo, los dioses, los hombres, trans. Ma Xiangmin (Wenhui Press, 2017), 11-219.

21 Randall Collins, Violence: A Micro-sociological Theory, trans. Liu Ran (Peking University Press, 2016), 1-37.

22 Douglas C. North, John J. Wallis, and Barry R. Weingast, Violence and Social Order: A Conceptual Framework for Interpreting Recorded Human History, trans. Hang Xing and Wang Liang (Truth & Wisdom Press, 2013), 29-58.

23   Homer, The Odyssey (Penguin Group, 1997).

Bhagavad Gita (China Social Sciences Press, 2014), 72-97.

Ramayana (People 's Literature Publishing House, 1984), 95-138.

Mahabharata (China Social Sciences Press, 2005), 28-73.

24   John Marshall, A Short History of Greek Philosophy, 1891, 2-45.

Ancient Greek and Roman Philosophy, ed. Office of Foreign Philosophy History, Department of Philosophy, Peking University (The Commercial Press, 1961), 3-18.

25   Ernst Cassirer, Language and Myth (Dover Publications, 1953), 55-89.

26   Giorgio Agamben, Il sacramento del linguaggio, Archeologia del giuramento, trans. Lan Jiang (Chongqing University Press, 2015), 134-156.

27   Edith Hamilton, Mythology: Timeless Tales of Gods and Heroes, trans. Yu Shuhui (CITIC Press, 2017), 3-33.

Karen Armstrong, The Great Transformation: The Beginning of Our Religious Traditions, trans. Sun Yanyan and Bai Yanbing (Hainan Press, 2010), 60-61.

28   Same as above

29   G. S. Kirk, J. E. Raven, and M. Scofield, The Presocratic Philosophers: A Critical History with a Selection of Texts, trans. Nie Minli (East China Normal University Press, 2014), 113-214.

30   Same as above

31   G. S. Kirk, J. E. Raven, and M. Scofield, The Presocratic Philosophers: A Critical History with a Selection of Texts, trans. Nie Minli (East China Normal University Press, 2014), 321-364.

32   Same as above

33   G. S. Kirk, J. E. Raven, and M. Scofield, The Presocratic Philosophers: A Critical History with a Selection of Texts, trans. Nie Minli (East China Normal University Press, 2014), 365-408.

John Marshall, A Short History of Greek Philosophy, 1891.

Ancient Greek and Roman Philosophy, ed. Office of Foreign Philosophy History, Department of Philosophy, Peking University (The Commercial Press, 1961), 1-37.

34   Same as above

35   Same as above

36   G. S. Kirk, J. E. Raven, and M. Scofield, The Presocratic Philosophers: A Critical History with a Selection of Texts, trans. Nie Minli (East China Normal University Press, 2014), 434-506.

Bertrand Russell, Wisdom of the West, trans. Ya Bei (Central Compilation & Translation Press, 2012), 40-46.

37   Same as above

38   Same as above

39   G. S. Kirk, J. E. Raven, and M. Scofield, The Presocratic Philosophers: A Critical History with a Selection of Texts, trans. Nie Minli (East China Normal University Press, 2014), 635-680.

John Marshall, A Short History of Greek Philosophy, 1891, 50-55.

40   John Marshall, A Short History of Greek Philosophy, 1891, 56-68.

Plato, "Sophist," in Platonis Opera, trans. Wang Xiaozhao (People 's Literature Publishing House, 2016), 178-247.

41   John Marshall, A Short History of Greek Philosophy, 1891, 69-83.
Plato, "Phaedrus," "Symposium," "Apology," "Crito," "Phaedo," in Platonis Opera, trans. Wang Xiaozhao (People 's Literature Publishing House, 2016).
Bertrand Russell, Wisdom of the West, trans. Ya Bei (Central Compilation & Translation Press, 2012), 49-69.
Plato, The Last Days of Socrates, trans. Xie Shanyuan (Shanghai Translation Publishing House, 2011), 50-240.

I. F. Stone, The Trial of Socrates, trans. Dong Leshan (Peking University Press, 2015), 253-318.

Günter Figal, Sokrates, trans. Yang Guang (East China Normal University Press, 2016), 11-48.

42 Same as above

43 Same as above

44 Same as above

45 John Marshall, A Short History of Greek Philosophy, 1891, 92-118.

Plato, Platonis Opera, trans. Wang Xiaozhao (People 's Literature Publishing House, 2016), 1-7.

Eric Voegelin, Plato and Aristotle (University of Missouri, 2000), 45-250.

Mitchell H. Miller Jr., Plato's Parmenides: The Conversion of the Soul (Princeton University Press, 1986), 139-192.

46 Same as above

47 Same as above

48 Same as above

49 John Marshall, A Short History of Greek Philosophy, 1891, 119-140.

Eric Voegelin, Plato and Aristotle (University of Missouri, 2000), 315-358.

Aristotle, De Anima (On the Soul), trans. Wu Shoupeng (The Commercial Press, 1999), 234-259.

Aristotle, Volume 7, 8, 9, 12, in The Metaphysics, trans. Wu Shoupeng (The Commercial Press, 1997).

Wang Zisong, Three Masters of the West (The Commercial Press, 2016), 260- 340.

Johann Gustav Droysen, Geschichte Des Hellenismus, trans. Chen Zao (East China Normal University Press, 2017), 260-280, 416-458.

50 Same as above

51 Same as above

52 Same as above

53 John Marshall, A Short History of Greek Philosophy (Percival and Company, 1891), 141-164.

54 John Marshall, A Short History of Greek Philosophy (Percival and Company, 1891), 140-151.

Epicurus, Nature and Happiness, trans. Bao Limin et al (China Social Sciences Press, 2004), 12-98.

55 John Marshall, A Short History of Greek Philosophy (Percival and Company, 1891), 154-164.

Zhang Xuefu. Stoicism (China Social Sciences Press, 2007), 1-18.

Marcus Aurelius, Meditations, trans. Wang Huansheng (SDX Joint Publishing, 2010), 20-58.

56 Marcus Tullius Cicero, Cicero and His Academica, trans. Wei Yixin (East China Normal University Press, 2017), 80-168.

57 Zhang Xinzhang, The Collected Classic Gnostic Library in Chinese (Oriental Publishing, 2017), 600-670.

58 Translator's note: From Wikipedia - King Wen of Zhou was count of Zhou during the late Shang dynasty in ancient China, where he was the king of the vassal state of Zhou. Although it was his son Wu who conquered the Shang following the Battle of Muye, Count Wen was posthumously honored as the founder of the Zhou dynasty and titled King.

59 Zhu Xi, The Original Meaning of the Book of Changes (Central Compilation & Translation Press, 2010), 1-15.

Zhang Rongming, Archaeology of Faith: Outline of the History of Chinese Religious Thoughts (Nankai University Press, 2010), 49-58.

Albert M. Craig, The Heritage of Chinese Civilization (Pearson, 2011), 51-109.

60 Karen Armstrong, The Great Transformation: The Beginning of Our Religious Traditions, trans. Sun Yanyan and Bai Yanbing (Hainan Press, 2010), 27-35, 73-78, 156-165.

61 Zhu Xi, Collected Annotations of the Four Books (Doctrine of the Mean, Great Learning, Analects, and Book of Rites of Confucius).

Qian Mu, Biography of Confucius (Jiuzhou Press, 2011), 29-87.

Herbert Fingarette, Confucius: The Secular as Sacred, trans. Peng Guoxiang and Zhang Hua (Jiangsu People's Publishing, 2002), 18-76.

62　L. A. Beck, The Story of Oriental Philosophy, trans. Zhao Zengyue (Jiangsu People's Literature Publishing House, 2010), 238-352.

Hong Xiuping, Oriental Philosophy and Religion (Jiangsu People's Publishing, 2010), 350-395.

63　Translator's note: The translation quoted is by James Legge. Complete bibliography: Confucius, Confucian analects: The great learning, and the doctrine of the mean, trans. James Legge (Dover Publications, 1971), 2.

64　Seven Chapters of Mencius.

Zhao QI, Chapters and Sentences of Mencius.

Zhu Xi, Collected Annotations of Mencius.

Gao Zhuancheng, The True Man: Mencius (Lijiang Press, 2017), 19-68.

65　Karen Armstrong, The Great Transformation: The Beginning of Our Religious Traditions, trans. Sun Yanyan and Bai Yanbing (Hainan Press, 2010), 301-320.

David S. Nivison, The Ways of Confucianism: Investigations in Chinese Philosophy, trans. Zhou Chicheng (Jiangsu People's Publishing, 2006), 97-134.

66　Wolfgang Bauer, China and the Search for Happiness, trans. Yan Beiwen et al (Jiangsu People's Publishing, 2006), 70-140.

L. A. Beck, The Story of Oriental Philosophy, trans. Zhao Zengyue (Jiangsu People's Literature Publishing House, 2010), 401-423.

67　Wang Xianqian, Collected Annotations of Xunzi (Zhonghua Book Company, 1983), 40-98.

68　David S. Nivison, Chapter 6, in The Ways of Confucianism: Investigations in Chinese Philosophy, trans. Zhou Chicheng (Jiangsu People's Publishing, 2006).

Wolfgang Bauer, China and the Search for Happiness, trans. Yan Beiwen et al (Jiangsu People's Publishing, 2006), 13-74.

69   Laozi, Daodejing.

Wang Bi, Annotations of Daodejing (Zhonghua Book Company, 2010), 10-200.

70   Same as above

71   Laozi, Daodejing.

L. A. Beck, The Story of Oriental Philosophy, trans. Zhao Zengyue (Jiangsu People's Literature Publishing House, 2010), 353-370.

72   Same as above

73   Zhuang Zhou, Zhuangzi.

Guo Xiang, Notes of Zhuangzi (Zhonghua Book Company, 1998), 50-121.

74   Same as above

75   Zhuang Zhou, Zhuangzi.

Guo Xiang, Notes of Zhuangzi (Zhonghua Book Company, 1998).

L. A. Beck, The Story of Oriental Philosophy, trans. Zhao Zengyue (Jiangsu People's Literature Publishing House, 2010), 371-400.

Wolfgang Bauer, China and the Search for Happiness, trans. Yan Beiwen et al (Jiangsu People's Publishing, 2006), 13-74.

Nan Huaijin, Interpretations of Zhuangzi (Shanghai People's Publishing House, 2007).

76   Same as above

77   Same as above

78   Zhuang Zhou, "On the Uniformity of All Things," in Zhuangzi.

Xunzi, "That the Nature is Evil," in Xunzi.

Wang Xianqian, Collected Annotations of Xunzi (Shanghai Bookstore Publishing House, 1986), 110-138.

Yang Bojun, "Yang Zhu," in Collected Annotations of Liezi (Zhonghua Book Company, 2017), 206-228.

79 Same as above

80 Same as above

81 Zhao Zongzheng, "Renfa (Reliance on Law)," "Mingfa (On Making the Law Clear)," "Fafa (On Conforming to the Law)," "Lizheng (On Overseeing the Government)," "Qifa (The Seven Standards)," "Fajin (On Laws and Prohibitions)," "Zhongling (On the Importance of Orders)," in Annotations of Guan Zi (Guangxi People's Publishing House, 1987).

82 Pu Jian, History of Chinese Legal System (Central Radio and TV University Press, 2006), 50-110.
Yang Kuan, History of the Warring States Period (Shanghai People's Publishing House, 2003), 180-250.

83 Wu Qi, Wu Zi, annotated by Qiu Chongbing (China Society Press, 2005).

84 Pu Jian, Chapter 4, in History of Chinese Legal System (Central Radio and TV University Press, 2006).
Yang Kuan, Chapter 5, in History of the Warring States Period (Shanghai People's Publishing House, 2003).

85 Yang Kuan. History of the Warring States Period (Shanghai People's Publishing House, 2016), 203-229.

86 Jiang Lihong, Annotations of the Book of Lord Shang (Zhonghua Book Company, 2017), 1-148.
Wang Shaoyan, Blood, Iron, and Rule of Law: Biography of Lord Shang (China University of Political Science and Law Press, 2016), 1-220.

87 Han Feizi, Han Feizi (Inner Mongolia People's Publishing House, 2009), 20-147.
Niccolò Machiavelli, Il Principe, trans. Li Xiujian (Jiuzhou Press, 2007), 37-188.

88 Same as above

89 Mozi, Mozi, annotated by Li Xiaolong (Zhonghua Book Company, 2007), 5-140.

90 Same as above

91 Same as above

92 Same as above

93 Mozi, Mozi, annotated by Li Xiaolong (Zhonghua Book Company, 2007), 140-180.
Xu Xiyan, Studies on Mohism (The Commercial Press, 2001), 15-88.

94 Mozi, Mozi, annotated by Li Xiaolong (Zhonghua Book Company, 2007), 180-210.
Yang Xiangkui. Studies on the Mathematics of Mozi (Shandong University Press, 2000), 26-88.
Yang Kuan. History of the Warring States Period (Shanghai People's Publishing House, 2016), 498-585.

95 John H. Walton, Ancient Near Eastern Thought and the Old Testament (Baker Academic, 2006), 203-293.
Zecharia Sitchin, The Wars of Gods and Men: Book III of the Earth Chronicles, trans. Zhao Juan and Song Yi (Chongqing Publishing House, 2009), 207 -258.

96 Douglas C. North, John J. Wallis, and Barry R. Weingast, Violence and Social Order: A Conceptual Framework for Interpreting Recorded Human History (Cambridge University Press, 2009), 29-69.

97 Raymond P. Scheindlin, A Short History of the Jewish People: From Legendary Times to Modern Statehood (Macmillan,1998), 3-12.

98 Same as above

99 John Bright, A History of Israel (Westminster John Knox Press, 2000), 60-205.
Tremper Longman and Raymond B. Dillard, An Introduction to the Old Testament, trans. Shi Song et al (Tongji University Press, 2014), 56-102.

Simon Montefiore, Jerusalem: The Biography, trans. Zhang Qianhong and Ma Danjing (Democracy and Construction Press, 2015), 1-24.

100 Same as above

101 Same as above

102 Same as above

103 Same as above

104 Same as above

105 John Bright, A History of Israel (Westminster John Knox Press, 2000), 163-204.

Tremper Longman and Raymond B. Dillard, An Introduction to the Old Testament, trans. Shi Song, Xiao Junxia, and Yu Yang (Tongji University Press, 2014).

Simon Montefiore, Chapter 4, in Jerusalem: The Biography, trans. Zhang Qianhong and Ma Danjing (Democracy and Construction Press, 2015).

Peter Watson, Ideas: A History from Fire to Freud, trans. Hu Cui'e (Yilin Press, 2018), 211-245.

106 Same as above

107 Same as above

108 Same as above

109 John Bright, A History of Israel (Westminster John Knox Press, 2000), 285-315.

Simon Montefiore, Jerusalem: The Biography, trans. Zhang Qianhong and Ma Danjing (Democracy and Construction Press, 2015), 33-52.

110 Same as above

111 John Bright, A History of Israel (Westminster John Knox Press, 2000), 327-412

Tremper Longman and Raymond B. Dillard, An Introduction to the Old Testament, trans. Shi Song et al (Tongji University Press, 2014), 304-495.

Simon Montefiore, Jerusalem: The Biography, trans. Zhang Qianhong and Ma Danjing (Democracy and Construction Press, 2015), 46-60.

112 Same as above

113 Same as above

114 Same as above

115 John Bright, A History of Israel (Westminster John Knox Press, 2000), 429-526.

Simon Montefiore, Jerusalem: The Biography, trans. Zhang Qianhong and Ma Danjing (Democracy and Construction Press, 2015), 61-112.

Cecil Roth, A Short History of the Jewish People (Hartmore House, 1969), 23-100.

Bernard J. Bamberger, The Story of Judaism, trans. Xiao Xian (The Commercial Press, 2013), 14-58.

116 Same as above

117 Sigmund Freud, Moses and Monotheism, trans. Li Zhankai (SDX Joint Publishing, 2017), 23-113.

Simon Schama, The Story of the Jews, trans. Huang Fuwu (Chemical Industry Press, 2016), 8-70.

118 Andrew Lintott, The Constitution of the Roman Republic, trans. Yan Shaoxiang (The Commercial Press, 2016), 64-134, 181-213, 277-301.

119 Same as above

120 Same as above

121 Will Durant, The Story of Civilization: Caesar and Christ, trans. Youth Cultural Enterprise (Huaxia Publishing House, 2010), 3-60.

Jacob Abbott, Hannibal: Makers of History, trans. Wang Weifang (Chinese Press, 2017), 1-214.

122 Same as above

123 Same as above

124 Same as above

125 Same as above

126 Same as above

127 Will Durant, The Story of Civilization: Caesar and Christ, trans. Youth Cultural Enterprise (Huaxia Publishing House, 2010), 120-207, 215-231.
Julius Caesar, Commentarii de Bello Gallico, trans. Ren Bingxiang (The Commercial Press, 1979), 8-168.
Richard Miles, Carthage Must Be Destroyed: The Rise and Fall of an Ancient Civilization, trans. Meng Chi (Social Sciences Academic Press, 2016), 32-512.
Peter Riesenberg, Citizenship in the Western Tradition: Plato to Rousseau, trans. Guo Taihui (Jilin Publishing Group, 2009), 83-116.
Adrian Goldsworthy, Caesar: Life of a Colossus, trans. Lu Dapeng (Social Sciences Academic Press, 2016), 300-580.

128 Same as above

129 Same as above

130 Same as above

131 Same as above

132 Same as above

133 Same as above

134 Same as above

135 Will Durant, The Story of Civilization: Caesar and Christ, trans. Youth Cultural Enterprise (Huaxia Publishing House, 2010), 61-91.
Jane Burbank and Frederick Cooper, Empires in World History: Power and the Politics of Difference, trans. Chai Bin (The Commercial Press, 2017), 25-55.

136 Same as above

137 Same as above

138 Will Durant, The Story of Civilization: Caesar and Christ, trans. Youth Cultural Enterprise (Huaxia Publishing House, 2010), 262-291, 372-400.

Aelius Spartianus, et al. Historia Augusta, trans. Xie Pinwei (Zhejiang University Press, 2018), 3-139.

139 Same as above

140 Same as above

141 Will Durant, The Story of Civilization: Caesar and Christ, trans. Youth Cultural Enterprise (Huaxia Publishing House, 2010), 543-565.
Bernard J. Bamberger, The Story of Judaism, trans. Xiao Xian (The Commercial Press, 2013), 65-115.
Cornelius Tacitus, Annals, trans. Wang Yizhu and Cui Miaoyin (The Commercial Press, 1981), 3-312.
G. Campbell Morgan, The Prophecy of Isaiah, trans. Zhong Yuena (Shanghai Sanlian Bookstore, 2011), 99-136.

142 Same as above

143 Same as above

144 Same as above

145 Same as above

146 Karen Armstrong, The Great Transformation: The Beginning of Our Religious Traditions, trans. Sun Yanyan and Bai Yanbing (Hainan Press, 2010), 65-72, 95-105, 398-405.
Will Durant, The Story of Civilization: Caesar and Christ, trans. Youth Cultural Enterprise (Huaxia Publishing House, 2010), 569-591.
James Martin, Jesus (HarperCollins Publishers, 1989), 240-460.
G. Campbell Morgan, The Acts of The Apostles, trans. Zhong Yuena (Shanghai Sanlian Bookstore, 2012), 1-240.
Ernest Renan, The Life of Jesus, trans. Liang Gong (The Commercial Press, 2009), 150-315.
Leonard Sweet and Frank Viola, Jesus: A Theography (Thomas Nelson, 2012), 109-309.

147 Same as above

148 Same as above

149 Same as above

150 Karen Armstrong, The Great Transformation: The Beginning of Our Religious Traditions, trans. Sun Yanyan and Bai Yanbing (Hainan Press, 2010), 51-125.

G. Campbell Morgan, The Acts of The Apostles, trans. Zhong Yuena (Shanghai Sanlian Bookstore, 2012), 241-315.

Karl Bihlmeyer, et al. Early Church History, trans. L. Leeb (China Religious Culture Publisher, 2009), 14-34.

151 Will Durant, The Story of Civilization: Caesar and Christ, trans. Youth Cultural Enterprise (Huaxia Publishing House, 2010), 592-678.

John Foxe, Fox's Book of Martyrs, trans. Su Yuxiao and Liang Lujin (SDX Joint Publishing, 2011), 1-248.

Aelius Spartianus, et al. Historia Augusta, trans. Xie Pinwei (Zhejiang University Press, 2018), 231-607.

Karl Bihlmeyer, et al. Early Church History, trans. L. Leeb (China Religious Culture Publisher, 2009), 29-62.

152 Same as above

153 Same as above

154 Same as above

155 Same as above

156 Same as above

157 Same as above

158 Same as above

159 Same as above

160 Same as above

161 Tertullian, Three Works of Tertullianus, trans. Liu Yingkai and Liu Luyi (Shanghai Sanlian Bookstore, 2013), 15-68.

Zhao Lin, Christianity and Western Culture (The Commercial Press, 2013), 34-162.

162 Same as above

163 Werner Jaeger, Early Christianity and Greek Paideia, trans. Wu Xiaoqun (Shanghai Sanlian Bookstore, 2016), 7-102.

Robert Louis Wilken, The Spirit of Early Christian Thought: Seeking the Face of God, trans. Chen Zhigang (China Social Sciences Press, 2011), 110-210.

164 Karl Bihlmeyer, et al. Early Church History, trans. L. Leeb (China Religious Culture Publisher, 2009), 89-130.

St. Athanasius, On the Incarnation, trans. Shi Minmin (SDX Joint Publishing, 2009), 28-149.

Hok-Lin Leung, The Cultural DNA of Western Civilization (SDX Joint Publishing, 2013), 17-59.

Francis P. Jones, Selection of Early Christian Literature, trans. Xie Fuya (China Religious Culture Publisher, 2011).

W. Andrew Hoffecker, Revolutions in Worldview: Understanding the Flow of Western Thought (P & R Publishing, 2007), 13-118, 74-135.

Louis P. Pojman, Philosophy of Religion, trans. Huang Ruicheng (Renmin University of China Press, 2006), 99-159.

St. Ambrose, Exposition of the Christian Faith, trans. Yang Lingfeng and Luo Yufang (SDX Joint Publishing, 2010), 1-405.

165 Same as above

166 Same as above

167 Same as above

168 Francis P. Jones, Selection of Early Christian Literature, trans. Xie Fuya (China Religious Culture Publisher, 2011), 278-326.

W. Andrew Hoffecker, Revolutions in Worldview: Understanding the Flow of Western Thought (P & R Publishing, 2007), 35-135.

St. Gregory of Nyssa, On the Soul and the Resurrection, trans. Shi Minmin (China Social Sciences Press, 2017), 235-303.

J. Hastings Nichols, Confession of Faith, trans. Tang Qing (China Religious Culture Publisher, 2010).

Nicene Creed, 198-225.

169 Same as above

170 Same as above

171 Same as above

172 St. Augustine, On Order, trans. Shi Minmin (China Social Sciences Press, 2017), 51-88.

St. Augustine, The City of God (De Civitate Dei), trans. Wu Zongwen (The Commercial Press, 2007), 110-359, 1087-1161.

St. Augustine, "On the Trinity," "On the Free Choice of the Will," "On Nature and Grace," in Aurelius Augustinus, trans. Tang Qing et al (China Religious Culture Publisher, 2010), 36-144, 159-256, 257-303.

173 Same as above

174 J. Hastings Nichols, "Ancient Ecumenical Creeds," in Confession of Faith, trans. Tang Qing (China Religious Culture Publisher, 2010), 3-48.

Peter Heather, The Fall of the Roman Empire, trans. Xiang Jun (CITIC Press, 2016), 3-164.

175 Peter Heather, The Fall of the Roman Empire, trans. Xiang Jun (CITIC Press, 2016), 167-547.

Benjamin Isaac, The Limits of Empire: The Roman Army in the East, trans. Ouyang Xudong (East China Normal University Press, 2018), 134-434.

176 J. Hastings Nichols, "Ancient Ecumenical Creeds," in Confession of Faith, trans. Tang Qing (China Religious Culture Publisher, 2010).

Peter Heather, Chapter 1-3, in The Fall of the Roman Empire, trans. Xiang Jun (CITIC Press, 2016).

Edward Gibbon, The History of the Decline and Fall of the Roman Empire, trans. Huang Yisi and Huang Yushi (The Commercial Press, 2002).

177 Same as above

178 Jin Guantao, The Mirror of History (Law Press, 2015), 169-240.
Charles de Secondat Montesquieu, Considerations on the Causes of the Greatness of the Romans and their Decline, trans. Xu Minglong (The Commercial Press, 2016), 1-181.
Will Durant, The Story of Civilization: The Age of Faith, trans. Youth Cultural Enterprise (Huaxia Publishing House, 2017), 1-119.

179 Same as above

180 Same as above

181 Same as above

182 Jocelyn Maclure and Charles Taylor, Secularism and Freedom of Conscience, trans. Cheng Wuyi (Jiangsu People's Publishing House, 2018), 78-110.
Karl Bihlmeyer, et al. Early Church History, trans. L. Leeb (China Religious Culture Publisher, 2009), 298-327.
Will Durant, The Story of Civilization: The Age of Faith, trans. Youth Cultural Enterprise (Huaxia Publishing House, 2017), 767-803.

183 Same as above

184 Will Durant, The Story of Civilization: The Age of Faith, trans. Youth Cultural Enterprise (Huaxia Publishing House, 2017), 539-637.
Nanami Shiono, The Mediterranean World after the Fall of the Roman Empire, trans. Tian Jianguo and Tian Jianhua (CITIC Press, 2014), 1-198.
Nanami Shiono, The Agent of God, trans. Tian Jianguo and Tian Jianhua (CITIC Press, 2017), 1-184.

185 Same as above

186 Same as above

187 Will Durant, The Story of Civilization: The Age of Faith, trans. Youth Cultural Enterprise (Huaxia Publishing House, 2017), 44-80.

Bill R. Austin, Austin's Topical History of Christianity, trans. Xu Jianren and Ma Junwei (Seed Press, 1991), 18-64.

188 Same as above

189 Will Durant, The Story of Civilization: The Age of Faith, trans. Youth Cultural Enterprise (Huaxia Publishing House, 2017), 104-120, 820-880.

190 Same as above

191 Nanami Shiono, The Mediterranean World after the Fall of the Roman Empire, trans. Tian Jianguo and Tian Jianhua (CITIC Press, 2014), 201-241.

192 G. K. Chesterton, St. Thomas Aquinas & St. Francis Assisi, trans. Wang Xueying (SDX Joint Publishing, 2016), 13-132.

G. K. Chesterton, Orthodoxy, trans. Zhuang Rouyu (SDX Joint Publishing, 2011), 10-128.

Alvin Schmidt, Under the Influence: How Christianity Transformed Civilization, trans. Wang Xiaodan and Zhaowei (Shanghai People's Publishing House, 2013), 1-294.

David L. Wagner, The Seven Liberal Arts in the Middle Ages, trans. Zhang Butian (Hunan Science & Technology Press, 2016), 1-246.

193 Same as above

194 Same as above

195 Wu Baihui, Vedas and Upanishads (China Social Sciences Press, 2014), 1-145.

196 Ramananda Prasad, Nine Principal Upanishads, trans. Wang Zhicheng and Ling Hai (The Commercial Press, 2017).

Ramayana (People 's Literature Publishing House, 1984), 1-138.

Mahabharata (China Social Sciences Press, 2005), 1-98.

197 Same as above

198 Manusmriti, trans. Tie Langshan and Ma Xiangxue (The Commercial Press, 2011), 6-277.

Ramananda Prasad, Nine Principal Upanishads, trans. Wang Zhicheng and Ling Hai (The Commercial Press, 2012), 124-240.

Ithamar Theodor and Yao Zhihua, Brahman and Dao: Comparative Studies of Indian and Chinese Philosophy and Religion, trans. Ye Shoude (China Religious Culture Publisher, 2017), 97-114.

Vedanta philosophy is based on the reflections on the four classics of the Four Vedas, the Brahmanas, the Aranyakas, and the Upanishads.

199 Same as above

200 Same as above

201 Same as above

202 Same as above

203 Bhagavad Gita, trans. Huang Baosheng (The Commercial Press, 2010), 31-471.

Sri Aurobindo, Essays on the Gita, trans. Xu Fancheng (The Commercial Press, 2009), 5-321.

K. M. Panikkar, A Survey of Indian History (New World Press, 2016), 1-56.

L. A. Beck, The Story of Oriental Philosophy, trans. Zhao Zengyue (Jiangsu People's Literature Publishing House, 2010), 1-131.

204 Same as above

205 Same as above

206 Karen Armstrong, Buddha, trans. Xian Xiang (SDX Joint Publishing, 2013), 1-200.

L. A. Beck, The Life of Buddha, trans. Zhang Xiaomi (Chinese Press, 2012), 1-281.

207 Same as above

208 Guo Liangyun, Buddha and Primitive Buddhism (China Social Sciences Press, 2011), 21-218.

Karen Armstrong, The Great Transformation: The Beginning of Our Religious Traditions, trans. Sun Yanyan and Bai Yanbing (Hainan Press, 2010), 288-300.

Hong Xiuping, Oriental Philosophy and Religion (Jiangsu People's Publishing, 2010), 87-260.

Wu Rujun, Concepts and Methods of Buddhism (Beijing World Publishing, 2015), 1-258.

Ven. Dhammadipa, The Relationship Between the Four Noble Truths and Practice (Luminary Publishing Association, 2003), 23-170.

209 Same as above

210 Same as above

211 Same as above

212 Same as above

213 Guo Liangyun, Buddha and Primitive Buddhism (China Social Sciences Press, 2011), 218-230.

Yao Weiqun, A Comparative Study on Indian Brahmanical and Buddhist Philosophies (Encyclopedia of China Publishing House, 2014), 3-28.

L. A. Beck, The Story of Oriental Philosophy (1992), 132-204.

214 Same as above

215 Same as above

216 Same as above

217 Same as above

218 Same as above

219 Same as above

220 TH. Stcherbatsky, Buddhist Logic, trans. Song Lidao and Shu Xiaowei (The Commercial Press, 1997), 10-56.

L. A. Beck, The Story of Oriental Philosophy (1992), 2-204.

221 Same as above

222 Same as above

223 Same as above

224 Hirakawa Akira, History of Indian Buddhism, trans. Zhuang Kunmu (Beijing United Publishing, 2018), 2-151.

225 Shankara, Upadesasahasri, trans. Sun Jing (The Commercial Press, 2012), 1-112.
Shankara, Atma-bodha, trans. Wang Zhicheng (Sichuan People's Publishing House, 2015), 3-98.

226 Same as above

227 Same as above

228 Same as above

229 Jiang Lihong, Annotations of the Book of Lord Shang (Zhonghua Book Company, 2017), 1-148.
Wang Shaoyan, Blood, Iron, and Rule of Law: Biography of Lord Shang (China University of Political Science and Law Press, 2016), 135-221.

230 Shi Zhimian, "Yi Wen Zhi (Treatise on Literature), 56 Articles of Zouzi Zhong Shi (From the Beginning to the End of Zouzi)," in Collected Annotations of Book of Han (San Min Book, 2003).
Wei Shaosheng, The Exceptional School of Yin-yang (Hubei People's Publishing House, 2011), 1-170.

231 Ban Gu, Book of Former Han (Jilin Publishing Group, 2005), 10-85.

232 Guan Zhiguo, A Study on the Legal Philosophy of Daoist Huang-Lao School (China Social Sciences Press, 2016), 80-217.
Wang Zhongjiang, Root, System and Order: From Laozi to Huang-Lao (Renmin University of China Press, 2018), 100-288.

233 Mark Edward Lewis, History of Imperial China: The Early Chinese Empires: Qin and Han, ed. Timothy James Brook, trans. Wang Xingliang (CITIC Press, 2016) 52-153, 230-256.

Xin Deyong, The Making of Emperor Wu of Han (SDX Joint Publishing, 2015), 1-173.

Huan Kuan, Discourses on Salt and Iron (Huaxia Publishing House, 2000), 100-256.

234 Bai Yang, Outline of Chinese History (People's Literature Publishing House, 2016), 170-276.

Bai Yang, Chronology of Chinese History (Hainan Press, 2006), 260-321.

Lu Weiyi, Dong Zhongshu, a "Confucian" Heritage and the Chunqiu Fanlu (Zhonghua Book Company HK, 2017), 87-126.

235 Same as above

236 Same as above

237 Same as above

238 Same as above

239 Zang Zhifei, A Study on Land, Tax, and Corvee Systems in the Qin and Han Dynasties (Central Compilation & Translation Press, 2017), 142-428.

240 Mark Edward Lewis, History of Imperial China: China Between Empires: The Northern and Southern Dynasties, ed. Timothy James Brook, trans. Wang Xingliang (CITIC Press, 2016), 8-86, 191-213.

Ye Qiuju, A Study of Edicts and Centralization in the Qin and Han Dynasties (China Social Sciences Press, 2016), 73-147.

Feng Youlan, The Spirit of Chinese Philosophy (SDX Joint Publishing, 2007), 125-168.

241 Same as above

242 Same as above

243 Cao Xu and Ding Gongyi, Seven Sages of the Bamboo Grove (Zhonghua Book Company, 2010), 58-148.

Yoshikawa Tadao, A Study on the Spiritual History of the Six Dynasties (Jiangsu People's Publishing House, 2011), 1-83.

Meng Ze and Xu Lian, Guangling Verse: The Biography of the Mavericks in China (New Star Press, 2017), 1-38.

244 Same as above

245 Mark Edward Lewis, History of Imperial China: China Between
Empires: The Northern and Southern Dynasties, ed. Timothy James
Brook, trans. Wang Xingliang (CITIC Press, 2016), 140-209.
Ren Jiyu, History of Buddhism in China, Volume II (East China Normal
University Press, 2015), 107-184.
Jiang Weiqiao, History of Buddhism in China (Guangling Book Club,
2008), 1-58, 89-156.
Gao Zhaomin, Eminent Monks in Han Buddhism (China Religious Cul-
ture Publisher, 2018), 1-156.

246 Same as above

247 Same as above

248 Charles Ben, China's Golden Era: Daily Life in Tang Dynasty, trans. Yao
Wenjing (Economic Science Press, 2012), 1-60, 181-274.
Mark Edward Lewis, History of Imperial China: China's Cosmopoli-
tan Empire: The Tang Dynasty, ed. Timothy James Brook, trans. Wang
Xingliang (CITIC Press, 2016), 191-213.
Liang Qichao, The History of Buddhism in China (East China Normal
University Press, 2015), 101-262.

249 Same as above

250 Rui Woshou, Buddhism in Chinese History (Peking University Press,
2009), 1-49.
Pan Mingquan, A Preliminary Study of the Religious Administrative
Decrees of Past Dynasties (China Religious Culture Publisher, 2017),
49-166.
Jiang Weiqiao, History of Buddhism in China (Guangling Book Club,
2008), 99-163.

Edwin G. Pulleyblank, The Background of the Rebellion of An Lu-shan, trans. Ding Jun (Chinese & Western Bookstore, 2018), 44-179.

Kegasawa Yasunori, A Gorgeous World Empire: Sui and Tang Dynasties, trans. Shi Xiaojun (Guangxi Normal University Press, 2014), 113-340.

251 Same as above

252 Same as above

253 Same as above

254 Same as above

255 Same as above

256 Mark Edward Lewis, History of Imperial China: China's Cosmopolitan Empire: The Tang Dynasty, ed. Timothy James Brook, trans. Wang Xingliang (CITIC Press, 2016), 214-251.

Ge Xiaoyin, Eight Masters of the Tang and Song (Beijing Publishing House, 2018), 11-278.

257 Same as above

258 Dieter Kuhn, History of Imperial China: The Age of Confucian Rule: The Song Transformation of China, trans. Li Wenfeng (CITIC Press, 2016), 29-134.

Kojima Tsuyoshi, The Flow of Thought and Religion in China: The Song Dynasty, trans. He Xiaoyi (Guangxi Normal University Press, 2014), 17-154.

259 Same as above

260 Yang Lihua, Fifteen Lectures on Neo-Confucianism (Peking University Press, 2015), 1-270.

Tian Hao, Zhu Xi's Thinking World (Jiangsu People's Publishing House, 2011), 15-165.

Takehiko Okada, Wang Yangming and Confucianism in the Ming Dynasty (Chongqing Publishing House, 2016), 1-88.

Kojima Tsuyoshi, The Flow of Thought and Religion in China: The Song

Dynasty, trans. He Xiaoyi (Guangxi Normal University Press, 2014), 197-270.

Dieter Kuhn, History of Imperial China: The Age of Confucian Rule: The Song Transformation of China, trans. Li Wenfeng (CITIC Press, 2016), 97-156.

Rui Woshou, Buddhism in Chinese History (Peking University Press, 2009), 65-94.

Jiang Weiqiao, History of Buddhism in China (Guangling Book Club, 2008), 157-198.

C. K. Yang, Religion in Chinese Society: A Study of Contemporary Social Functions of Religion and Some of Their Historical Factors, trans. Fan Lizhu (Sichuan People's Publishing House, 2016), 1-83, 228-264.

261 Same as above

262 Same as above

263 Same as above

264 Same as above

265 Same as above

266 Same as above

267 Same as above

268 Kojima Tsuyoshi, The Flow of Thought and Religion in China: The Song Dynasty, trans. He Xiaoyi (Guangxi Normal University Press, 2014), 51-124.

C. K. Yang, Religion in Chinese Society: A Study of Contemporary Social Functions of Religion and Some of Their Historical Factors, trans. Fan Lizhu (Sichuan People's Publishing House, 2016), 83-215.

Stephan Feuchtwang, Popular Religion in China: The Imperial Metaphor, trans. Zhao Xudong (Jiangsu People's Publishing House, 2009), 1-278.

Li Zhiming, Public Law Functions of Traditional Chinese Family Organizations (China University of Political Science and Law Press, 2016), 1-219.

Li Chenggui, Buddhism in the Perspective of Confucianism (China Religious Culture Publisher, 2007), 475-575.

269 Same as above

270 Same as above

271 Joseph Needham, "Preface," in Science and Civilization in China (Science Press & Shanghai Ancient Books Publishing House, 1999), 13-23. Joseph Needham, The Grand Titration: Science and Society in East and West, trans. Zhang Butian (The Commercial Press, 2017), 280-311. Simon Winchester, The Man Who Loved China: The Fantastic Story of the Eccentric Scientist Who Unlocked the Mysteries of the Middle Kingdom, trans. Pan Zhenze (Beijing Press, 2016), 1-305. Bernard Cohen, Revolution in Science (Harvard University Press, 1985), 105-261. Herbert Butterfield, The Origins of Modern Science: 1300-1800, trans. Zhang Butian (Shanghai Jiao Tong University Press, 2017), 136-149.

272 Li Zhiming, Public Law Functions of Traditional Chinese Family Organizations (China University of Political Science and Law Press, 2016), 59-220. Sheng Kai, History of Buddhist Belief and Life in China (Jiangsu People's Publishing House, 2016), 59-69, 184-193, 229-255, 296-301. Joanna Handlin Smith, The Art of Doing Good: Charity in Late Ming China, trans. Wu Shiyong et al (Jiangsu People 's Publishing House, 2015), 10-350. R. Po-chia Hsia, A Jesuit in the Forbidden City: Matteo Ricci, 1552-1610, trans. Xiang Hongyan and Li Chunyuan (Shanghai Ancient Books Publishing House, 2012), 1- 317. Duan Shilei, A Study of Jesuit Educational Activities in the East, 1549-1650 (Shanghai Far East Publishing House, 2019), 177-229.

273 Same as above

274 Same as above

275 Zhao Lin, Christianity and Western Culture (The Commercial Press, 2013), 163-198.

Will Durant, The Story of Civilization: The Age of Faith, trans. Youth Cultural Enterprise (Huaxia Publishing House, 2017), 820-963.

W. Andrew Hoffecker, Revolutions in Worldview: Understanding the Flow of Western Thought, trans. Yu Liang (China Social Sciences Press, 2010), 148-189.

276 Thomas Aquinas, Summa Theologica, trans. Duan Dezhi (The Commercial Press, 2013), 1-194.

G. K. Chesterton, St. Thomas Aquinas & St. Francis Assisi, trans. Wang Xueying (SDX Joint Publishing, 2016), 149-288.

277 Same as above

278 Same as above

279 Will Durant, The Story of Civilization: The Renaissance, trans. Youth Cultural Enterprise (Huaxia Publishing House, 2010), 50-66, 333-344.

280 Will Durant, The Story of Civilization: The Renaissance, trans. Youth Cultural Enterprise (Huaxia Publishing House, 2010), 1-133, 159-209, 350-482.

Dante, The Divine Comedy, trans. Li Bingkui, Chen Ying and Sun Ao (The Commercial Press, 2015).

Erasmus, In Praise of Folly, trans. Xu Chongxin (Yilin Press, 2011), 1-100.

281 Same as above

282 Same as above

283 James Kittelson, Luther the Reformer: The Story of the Man and His Career, trans. Li Ruiping and Zheng Xiaomei (China Social Sciences Press, 2009), 61-228.

Timothy George, Theology of the Reformers, trans. Wang Li and Sun

Daijun (China Social Sciences Press, 2009), 42-86,153-228.

Jacques Barzun, From Dawn to Decadence: 500 Years of Western Cultural Life, 1500 to the Present, trans. Lin Hua (CITIC Press, 2013), 1-254.

J. Hastings Nichols, Confession of Faith, trans. Tang Qing (China Religious Culture Publisher, 2010), 19-265.

284 Same as above

285 Same as above

286 Same as above

287 Stephen Gaukroger, The Emergence of a Scientific Culture: Science and the Shaping of Modernity 1210-1685, trans. Luo Hui and Feng Xiang (Shanghai Jiao Tong University Press, 2017), 3-240.

Herbert Butterfield, The Origins of Modern Science: 1300-1800, trans. Zhang Butian (Shanghai Jiao Tong University Press, 2017).

Isaac Newton, "The Concluding General Scholium, Index to The System of The World," in The Principia: Mathematical Principles of Natural Philosophy, trans. Wang Kedi (Peking University Press, 2007), 78-172.

David C. Lindberg, The Beginnings of Western Science: the European Scientific Tradition in Philosophical, Religious, and Institutional Context, Prehistory to A.D. 1450, trans. Zhang Butian (Hunan Science and Technology Press, 2013), 193-279.

288 Same as above

289 Stephen Gaukroger, The Emergence of a Scientific Culture: Science and the Shaping of Modernity 1210-1685, trans. Luo Hui and Feng Xiang (Shanghai Jiao Tong University Press, 2017), 440-537.

Clifford A. Pickover, Archimedes to Hawking: Laws of Science and the Great Minds Behind Them, trans. He Yujing and Liu Mo (Shanghai Science and Technology Education Press, 2014), 1-44.

Margaret J. Osler, Reconfiguring the World: Nature, God, and Human

Understanding from the Middle Ages to Early Modern Europe (Johns Hopkins University Press, 2010), 7-118.

290 Same as above

291 Abraham Wolf, A History of Science, Technology, and Philosophy in the 16th & 17th Centuries, trans. Zhou Changzhong (The Commercial Press, 1997), 69-90.

E. A. Burtt, The Metaphysical Foundations of Modern Science, trans. Zhang Butian (Hunan Science & Technology Press, 2012), 1-11, 243-279.

Zhao Lin, Between God and Newton (Oriental Publishing, 2007), 6-48.

Alexandre Koyré, Newtonian Studies, trans. Zhang Butian (The Commercial Press, 2016), 283-287.

292 Same as above

293 Jeremy Waldron, God, Locke, and Equality: Christian Foundations in Locke's Political Thought, trans. Guo Wei (Huaxia Publishing House, 2015), 1-302.

Greg Forster, Starting with Locke, trans. Sun Lizhong (Heilongjiang Education Press, 2017), 1-215.

294 Same as above

295 Same as above

296 W. Andrew Hoffecker, Revolutions in Worldview: Understanding the Flow of Western Thought, trans. Yu Liang (China Social Sciences Press, 2010), 240-289.

Rousseau, The Social Contract, trans. He Zhaowu (The Commercial Press, 2003), 18-31.

Rousseau, Discourse on the Origin and Basis of Inequality Among Men, trans. Li Changshan (The Commercial Press, 1997), 72-104.

Carol Blum, Rousseau and the Republic of Virtue: The Language of Politics in the French Revolution, trans. Enlightenment Compilation Institute (The Commercial Press, 2015), 2-89.

297 W. Andrew Hoffecker, Revolutions in Worldview: Understanding the Flow of Western Thought, trans. Yu Liang (China Social Sciences Press, 2010), 301-331.

Immanuel Kant, Critique of Pure Reason, trans. Lan Gongwu (The Commercial Press, 1960), 15-63.

298 Roger E. Olsen, The Story of Christian Theology: Twenty Centuries of Tradition Reform, trans. Wu Ruicheng and Xu Chengde (Shanghai People's Publishing House, 2014), 387-556.

D. Martyn Lloyd-Jones, The Puritan Papers, trans. Liang Suya and Wang Guoxian et al (Huaxia Publishing House, 2011), 2-334.

George M. Marsden, Jonathan Edwards: A Life, trans. You Guanhui (China Social Sciences Press, 2012), 311-601.

299 Same as above

300 Same as above

301 Same as above

302 John S. Mill, On Liberty, trans. Xu Baokui (The Commercial Press, 2005), 18-111.

John S. Mill, Principles of Political Economy With Some of Their Applications to Social Philosophy, trans. Zhu Yang et al (The Commercial Press, 1984), 37-80, 229-266, 273-280.

Adam Smith, An Inquiry into the Nature and Causes of the Wealth of Nations, trans. Guo Dali and Wang Yanan (The Commercial Press, 1972), 3-92, 261-358.

Adam Smith, The Theory of Moral Sentiments, trans. Jiang Ziqiang et al (The Commercial Press, 1997), 97-114, 351-402.

303 Same as above

304 Same as above

305 Same as above

306 Gilbert Rist, The History of Development: From Western Origins to Global Faith, trans. Lu Xianggan (Social Sciences Academic Press, 2017), 67-113, 397-407.

L.S. Stavrianos, A Global History: From Prehistory to the 21st Century (7th Edition) (Peking University Press, 2006), 765-804.

Arthur Herman, How the Scots Invented the Modern World, trans. Enlightenment Compilation Institute (Shanghai Academy of Social Sciences Press, 2016).

307 Same as above

308 Alexis de Tocqueville, The Old Regime and the Revolution, trans. Feng Tang (The Commercial Press, 1992), 99-175.

Ruth Scurr, Fatal Purity: Robespierre and the French Revolution, trans. Zhang Yanan (The Commercial Press, 2015), 233-451.

Carol Blum, Rousseau and the Republic of Virtue: The Language of Politics in the French Revolution, trans. Enlightenment Compilation Institute (The Commercial Press, 2015), 100-198.

309 Alexis de Tocqueville, Democracy in America, trans. Dong Guoliang (The Commercial Press, 1989), 72-120, 215-243, 369-400, 569-599.

Jerry Newcombe, The Book That Made America: How the Bible Formed Our Nation, trans. Lin Muyin (Fudan University Press, 2017), 11-321.

Charles A. Beard and Mary R. Beard, The Rise of American Civilization, trans. Yang Jun (Beijing Times Chinese Bookstore, 2016), 26-571.

310 Ding Jianhong, General History of Germany (Shanghai Academy of Social Sciences Press, 2002).

Hegel, Lectures on the Philosophy of History, trans. Wang Zaoshi (Shanghai Bookstore Publishing House, 2001), 1-410.

Hegel, Science of Logic, trans. Yang Yizhi (The Commercial Press, 2001), 1-164.

Shlomo Avineri, Hegel's Theory of the Modern State, trans. Zhu Xueping and Wang Xingsai (Intellectual Property Publishing House, 2016), 1-143.

Karl Marx, Capital (The Commercial Press), 1-25.

Liu Xiaofeng, Nietzsche and Christianity, trans. Tian Linian and Wu Zengding et al (Huaxia Publishing House, 2014), 1-58.

Friedrich Nietzsche, On the Genealogy of Morality, trans. Zhao Qianfan (The Commercial Press, 2016), 15-196.

Friedrich Nietzsche, The Antichrist, trans. Yu Mingfeng (The Commercial Press, 2016), 3-104.

Ernst Cassirer, The Myth of the State, trans. Fan Jin et al (Huaxia Publishing House, 2015), 229-358.

311 Same as above

312 Same as above

313 C. G. Prado, Starting with Descartes, trans. Cheng Tian and Chen Mingyao (Heilongjiang Education Press, 2017), 42-145.

Adam Smith, An Inquiry into the Nature and Causes of the Wealth of Nations, trans. Guo Dali and Wang Yanan (The Commercial Press, 1972), 16-92.

314 Joseph A. Schumpeter, Theory of Economic Development, trans. He Wei and Yi Jiaxiang (The Commercial Press, 1990), 85-108, 109-145, 242-290.

Joseph A. Schumpeter, History of Economic Analysis, trans. Zhu Yang et al (The Commercial Press, 1996), 3-90.

315 Same as above

316 Robert G. Picard, The Economics and Financing of Media Companies (Fordham University Press, 2011), 8-78.

Robert G. Picard and Steven S. Wildman, Handbook on the Economics of the Media (Edward Elgar Publishing, 2015), 2-148.

317 Same as above

318 Stephen Bell and Andrew Hindmoor, Master of the Universe, Slaves of the Market (Harvard University Press, 2015), 4-111, 147-185, 286-319.

Robert B. Reich, Saving Capitalism: For the Many, not the Few (Vintage, 2016), 1-226.

319 Same as above

320 Same as above

321 Same as above

322 Same as above

323 Same as above

324 Thomas Piketty, Capital in the Twenty-First Century, trans. Ba Shusong et al (CITIC Press, 2014), 1-48.

Joseph E. Stiglitz, Freefall: America, Free Markets, and the Sinking of the World Economy, trans. Li Junqing and Yang Lingling (China Machine Press, 2017), 10-76.

325 Same as above

326 Burton Feldman, The Nobel Prize: A History of Genius, Controversy, and Prestige, trans. Yang Qun et al (Hunan Science & Technology Press, 2016), 379-434.

Editorial Office of the Chinese Journal of Nature, The Nobel Prize in Natural Sciences Explained in Full (2005-2015) (Shanghai University Press, 2016), 3-380.

327 Denis Alexander, Rebuilding the Matrix: Science and Faith in the 21st Century, trans. Qian Ning (Shanghai People's Publishing House, 2014), 290-417.

Paul K. Feyerabend, The Tyranny of Science, trans. Guo Yuanlin (Science and Technology of China Press, 2018), 1-124.

328 Richard Dawkins, The God Delusion, trans. Chen Rongxia (Hainan Press, 2017), 245-312.

Alister E. McGrath, Science and Religion: A New Introduction, trans. Wang Yi (Shanghai People's Publishing House, 2008), 79-115.

329 Jean-Pierre Luminet, The Destiny of Universe: Dark Hole and Dark Matter, trans. Lu Jufu and Yu Chao (Posts & Telecom Press, 2017), 261-273, 386-416.

Brian Clegg, Gravity: How the Weakest Force in the Universe Shaped Our Lives, trans. Liu Guowei (Hainan Press, 2017), 136 -179.

Simon Singh, Big Bang: The Origin of the Universe, trans. Wang Wenhao (Hunan Science & Technology Press, 2017), 302-392.

Brian Clegg, The God Effect: Quantum Entanglement, Science's Strangest Phenomenon, trans. Liu Xianzhen (Chongqing Publishing House, 2018), 1-200.

330 Same as above

331 Ludwig Wittgenstein, Tractatus Logico-Philosophicus, trans. He Shaojia (The Commercial Press, 2009), 25-104.

KHA Saen-Yang, Existentialism (Shanghai Jiao Tong University Press, 2016).

332 Same as above

333 Richard Rorty, Pragmatism Philosophy, trans. Lin Nan (Shanghai Translation Publishing House, 2009), 1-28.

William James, Pragmatism: A New Name for Some Old Ways Of Thinking, trans. Chen Yuguan and Sun Ruihe (The Commercial Press, 2009), 92-154.

334 Same as above

335 Dean G. Pruitt and Sung Hee Kim, Social conflict: Escalation, Stalemate, and Settlement, trans. Wang Fanmei (Posts & Telecom Press, 2013), 112-186.

336 Reinhold Niebuhr, The Nature and Destiny of Man: A Christian Interpretation, trans. Xie Bingde (China Religious Culture Publisher, 2011), 196-257, 279-398.

Reinhold Niebuhr, Moral Man and Immoral Society: A Study in Ethics and Politics, trans. Jiang Qing et al (Guizhou People's Publishing House, 2009), 2-48.

337 Same as above

338 Same as above

339 Max Weber, The Protestant Ethic and the Spirit of Capitalism, trans. Yu Xiao and Chen Weigang et al (SDX Joint Publishing, 1987), 3-149.

340 Fredrich A. Dr Hayek, The Road to Serfdom, trans. Teng Weizao and Zhu Zongfeng (The Commercial Press, 1962), 1-240.

341 Same as above

342 Franz-Xaver Kaufmann. Varianten des Wohlfahrtsstaats. Der deutsche Sozialstaat im Internationalen Vergleich, trans. Shi Shijun (Chuliu Publisher, 2006), 51-276.
Robert Higgs, Against Leviathan: Government Power and a Free Society, trans. Wang Kai (Xinhua Publishing House, 2016), 3-34.

343 Same as above

344 Franz-Xaver Kaufmann. Varianten des Wohlfahrtsstaats. Der deutsche Sozialstaat im Internationalen Vergleich, trans. Shi Shijun (Chuliu Publisher, 2006), 51-276.
Robert Higgs, Against Leviathan: Government Power and a Free Society, trans. Wang Kai (Xinhua Publishing House, 2016), 3-34.
Tom G. Palmer, After the Welfare State: Politicians Stole Your Future, You Can Get It Back, trans. Xiong Yue et al (Hainan Press, 2017).

345 Same as above

346 Richard Dawkins, A Devil's Chaplain: Reflections on Hope, Lies, Science, and Love, trans. Ma Yan (CITIC Press, 2016), 7-67.
Richard Dawkins, The Selfish Gene, trans. Lu Yunzhong et al (CITIC Press, 2016), 1-300.
Bill Mesler and H. James Cleaves II, A Brief History of Creation: Science and the Search for the Origin of Life, trans. Zhang Jun and Wang

Shuo (Posts & Telecom Press, 2017), 11-259.

Francis S. Collins, The Language of God: A Scientist Presents Evidence for Belief (Free Press, 2006), 75-110, 139-166.

347 Same as above

348 George Zarkadakis, In Our Own Image: Savior or Destroyer? The History and Future of Artificial Intelligence, trans. Chen Zhao (CITIC Press, 2017), 205-299.

349 John R. McNeill, Something New Under the Sun: An Environmental History of the Twentieth-Century World, trans. Li FenFang (CITIC Press, 2017), 17-332.

350 Same as above

351 Same as above

352 Ernst Cassirer, The Myth of the State, trans. Fan Jin et al (Huaxia Publishing House, 2015), 334-358.

Bernard Cohen, Interaction: Some Contacts between the Natural Science and the Social Sciences (MIT Press, 1994), 127-193.

Robert B. Reich, Saving Capitalism: Saving Capitalism: For the Many, not the Few, trans. Zeng Xin and Xiong Yuegen (CITIC Press, 2017).

Tom G. Palmer, After the Welfare State: Politicians Stole Your Future, You Can Get It Back, trans. Xiong Yue et al (Hainan Press, 2017).

353 Andrew Hurrell, On Global Order: Power, Values, and the Constitution of International Society, trans. Lin Xi (Renmin University of China Press, 2017) 101-124.

Thomas L. Friedman, The World Is Flat: A Brief History of the Twenty-First Century (Farrar, Straus and Giroux, 2005), 109-300.

Richard Haass, A World in Disarray: American Foreign Policy and the Crisis of the Old Order (Penguin Press, 2017), 49-135.

354 John A. Eidsmoe, Christianity and the Constitution: The Faith of Our Founding Fathers, trans. Li Wanling et al (Central Compilation & Trans-

lation Press, 2010), 191-193.

Herman Bavinck, Our Reasonable Faith, trans. Zhao Zhonghui (Southern Publishing House, 2011), 1-441.

A free ebook edition
is available with the
purchase of this book.

To claim your free ebook edition:

1. Visit MorganJamesBOGO.com
2. Sign your name CLEARLY in the space
3. Complete the form and submit a photo of the entire copyright page
4. You or your friend can download the ebook to your preferred device

Morgan James BOGO™

A **FREE** ebook edition is available for you or a friend with the purchase of this print book.

CLEARLY SIGN YOUR NAME ABOVE

Instructions to claim your free ebook edition:
1. Visit MorganJamesBOGO.com
2. Sign your name CLEARLY in the space above
3. Complete the form and submit a photo of this entire page
4. You or your friend can download the ebook to your preferred device

Print & Digital Together Forever.

Snap a photo

Free ebook

Read anywhere